Social Justice

Social Justice

Distributive Principles and Beyond

Editor

M.P. Dube

RAWAT PUBLICATIONS

Jaipur • New Delhi • Bangalore • Guwahati • Kolkata

ISBN 978-81-316-0680-3

Published by
Prem Rawat for **Rawat Publications**
Satyam Apts, Sector 3, Jawahar Nagar, Jaipur 302 004 (India)
Phone: 0141 265 1748 / 7006 Fax: 0141 265 1748
E-mail: info@rawatbooks.com
Website: www.rawatbooks.com

New Delhi Office
4858/24, Ansari Road, Daryaganj, New Delhi 110 002
Phone: 011 2326 3290

Also at *Bangalore, Guwahati* and *Kolkata*

Typeset by Rawat Computers, Jaipur
Printed at Chaman Enterprises, New Delhi

Contents

Part II: Social Justice and Marginalized Sections in India

Part III: Gender Perspectives of Social Justice

Contributors

Mohit Bhattacharya, Former Vice-Chancellor, Burdwan University, West Bengal.

P.K. Chaubey, Professor of Economics, Indian Institute of Public Administration, New Delhi.

Naresh Dadhich, Professor of Political Science, University of Rajasthan, Jaipur, former Vice-Chancellor, MV Open University, Kota.

M.P. Dube, Dean, Faculty of Arts, University of Allahabad, and Professor and Former Head, Department of Political Science, University of Allahabad, Allahabad.

Debashis Guha, Professor of Philosophy, University of Allahabad, Allahabad.

Sanjay Gupta, Professor of Political Science, Lucknow University, Lucknow.

M. Kistaiah, Former Professor of Public Administration, Kakatiya University, Warangal.

Bhaskar Majumdar, Professor of Economics, G.B. Pant Institute of Social Science, Allahabad.

Anand P. Mavalankar, Professor of Political Science, University of Baroda, Gujarat.

Asok Mukhopadhyay, Netaji Subhash Chandra Bose Chair Professor of Political Science, University of Calcutta, West Bengal.

Chandrakala Padia, Dean, School of Social Sciences, Banaras Hindu University, Varanasi.

S.V. Pande, Ex-Director Institute of Social Sciences, Dr B.R. Ambedkar University, Agra.

Sumita Parmar, Director, Centre of Women's Studies, University of Allahabad, Allahabad.

Ramashray Roy, Fellow (Retd.), Indian Council of Social Science Research (ICSSR), New Delhi.

Ashish Saxena, Professor of Sociology, University of Allahabad, Allahabad.

Papia Sengupta, Associate Professor, Kirori Mal College, University of Delhi, New Delhi.

K.L. Sharma, Former Vice-Chancellor, University of Rajasthan, Jaipur.

T.R. Sharma, Former Professor and Head, Department of Political Science, Panjab University, Chandigarh.

Mahendra Prasad Singh, Former Professor of Political Science, University of Delhi, New Delhi.

Archana Srivastava, Associate Professor of Sociology, Kumaun University, Nainital.

D.K. Verma, Head, SC/ST and OBC Development, Dr Babasaheb Ambedkar National Institute of Social Science, Mhow, Madhya Pradesh.

Introduction

Justice is one of the primary qualities of a good political order. Political theorists have proclaimed that justice is the first virtue of any political community. There is no doubt that all human societies have had standard of justice. The questions of justice have exercised human ingenuity since ancient times. Philosophers in ancient times speculated and argued about justice. The earliest record of sophisticated philosophical concern with justice is found in the Greek tradition.

All over the world, racial, ethnic, caste, regional, linguistic groups speak in the language of justice in demanding what is due to them. In the same way various political, economic, social and environmental movements, local, regional or global, talk in terms of justice. Feminists invoke justice to counter their subordination and exploitation. Similarly some men's groups and gay rights organizations demand justice. Thus, justice can be a concern of any one for one's rightful due, what one deserves. The basic question is about the specific standard to be employed in assessing what one deserves. The focus of all justice talk is what people ought to receive as their due. What principles should we use to decide that a person deserves in any given situation.

Disparities of income, wealth and access to opportunity are growing sharply in most of the liberal societies. Persistent and rising inequalities threaten the ideals of equal citizenship and responsive government. Voices are raised and heard unequally. Privileged people have better access to and response from government. Scarcity of resources implies some competitions between individuals which needs to be regulated. As each one wants and expects one's fair share when wealth, income, political power, social recognition, education, and other resources and opportunities are distributed. It calls us to address what principles and procedures should be used to achieve more fair distributions; how to equalize citizen voice across lines of income, race, caste and gender.

There have been two major conceptions of justice – formal and material (or substantive). Former requires distributions which are in accordance with agreed criteria or rules. This involves standards of procedural justice, and formal equality. Material or substantive justice relates to the identification of the appropriate distributive criteria on the basis of which benefits or burdens are distributed. It is generally identified with social justice, that is, people should end up with whatever it is they deserve or need.

Utilitarian theorists avoid to give fundamental place to either merit and desert or need. To them all questions of distribution are to be resolved by reference to overall consequences. A socially just allocation is ultimately an allocation that produces the greatest sum of happiness. The most ambitious attempt to answer these questions was provided by John Rawls. Rawls argues that 'a well ordered society is effectively regulated by a public conception of justice. Rawls's view is that justice demands 'maximum equal liberty' and a distribution of economic benefits which makes the least favoured person as well off as possible – the so called 'maximin' conception of justice, which concentrates on maximizing the minimum benefit. Rawls recommends an activist and interventionist role for government, not only to promote liberties, but to bring about greater social and economic equality. Hayek and Nozick challenge the arguments of John Rawls. They argue that distributive principles are incompatible with individual liberty. On the other hand Rawls argues that commitment to liberty and greater social equality are compatible.

The traditional distributional approach has been challenged by various theorists during the 1990s and onwards; the sole emphasis on distribution without an examination of the underlying causes of the mal-distributions was not acceptable to several contemporary political theorists. Iris Young, Nancy Frazer, Axel Honneth and Charles Taylor argue that while justice must be concerned with classic issues of distribution, it must also address the process that constructs mal-distribution. To them individual and social recognition, rather than simply fair process for the distribution of goods and benefits, are the key elements of attaining justice. In fact, they are influenced by the real world of political injustice. Their central concern is recognition and participation in the decision-making.

Amartya Sen and Martha Nussbaum expand the conception of justice beyond John Rawls (distributive justice) by advancing capability approach. They have developed a theory of justice that focuses on the capacities necessary for individuals and groups to function and flourish. Along with distribution of goods, focus is on how those goods are transformed into functioning and flourishing of individuals and communities; focus is to judge how those distributions affect our well-being and how we 'function'.

Traditionally, questions of justice have been central to political life. But in recent years issues of environment have become an integral part of the discourse of justice. Today environmental and ecological justice have become very important themes of discussion for social and political theorists and movements. Central to the environmental justice is distribution of goods and bads, but at the same time it is tied with some discussion of recognition, political participation and capabilities at both the individual and community level.

The idea of social justice has wide ramifications and is an evolving one as new vistas can be added to this idea. It implies more than only granting political and legal equality by the state. The best of the country may be from among the poorest or socially suppressed. Democracy gains authenticity only if the minorities and other weaker sections have a just opportunity to play their creative, uninhibited part in the shape of fair opportunity for dynamic actions, development and cultural advance. Those handicapped in terms of their numbers or social disability, have the right to special concern. Social, economic and political justice considerations must govern the policies to uplift the weaker and poorer within the minorities and other handicapped sectors.

The book has been divided into three broad themes – viz. Theorizing Social Justice, Social Justice and Marginalized Sections in India, and Gender Perspectives on Social Justice. The different dimensions of the theory of social justice have been analysed in the first part of the book. During the 1960s serious questions were raised about the future of political theory especially in the United States in the context of the ongoing debate over the Vietnam War, the raising racial inequality, large scale unemployment and rising inequality.

The need to search principles for realizing a just social order and political system became the main thrust of social theorists. In Chapter I, Debashis Guha presents a philosophical analysis of the term 'Justice'. The paper tries to show what philosophers in particular are apt at when they consider terms such as 'just', 'unjust', 'justice', and 'injustice', 'distributive justice', 'legal justice' and many more. The use of inverted commas is special for it focuses our concern here with particular concepts and conceptual expressions rather than events or facts or percept. The specialty goes well with philosophers than the fact oriented positivists because philosophers are expected to take up the task of meaning clarification of some such terms and expressions which are used in abundance in positivistic and non-positivistic literature. It is important to note that the philosopher does not propose definitions here; he attempts at cure of language use. Moreover, the philosopher is interested in critique of definitions, explanations and methods or models. He tries to find out the outfalls of justice as well as likely pitfalls when the logical and ethical scanners are available to him.

Justice theorizing became the dominant theme in moral theory and political philosophy during 1970s and onwards. During this period John Rawls's theory of 'justice as fairness' established the terrain upon which subsequent theorists have fought with one another for supremacy. Today one can agree or disagree but cannot be indifferent to John Rawls's theory of justice. Nozick has hailed a theory of justice as 'a powerful, deep, subtle, wide-ranging, systematic work in political and moral philosophy which has not seen its like since the writings of J.S. Mill'. In Chapters II and III, Naresh Dadhich and Asok Mukhopadhyay respectively discuss the idea of justice as developed and presented by John Rawls. Rawls's idea, justice as fairness proposes that the most reasonable principle of justice are those, which can be agreed upon by mutual consent of individuals under fair conditions. Both of them try to show how Rawls unites the libertarian ideal of liberalism with economic egalitarianism of democratic socialism into a single theoretical frame, and thereby bring back liberalism to the centre of political debates and discussions. Both the contributors discuss how the traditional ideas of liberty, equality and fraternity are incorporated in the two principles of Rawlsian justice.

Chapter IV presents a review of social justice theorizing beyond distributive principles. Several theorists have challenged the distributive principles of justice during 1990s and onwards. They argue that the sole emphasis should not be on distributive principles only, rather the underlying cause of mal-distribution must also be examined. To them individual and social recognition are the key elements of attaining justice. The notions of justice based on distribution, recognition, democratic participation as well as capability approach have been analysed in this chapter. The author argues that Gandhian views on just social order are much more comprehensive. It can enable man and nature to live in peace and harmony with mutual respect and recognition. In Chapter V, Ramashray Roy discusses three different approaches to tackle the problem of social justice in a situation of unequal distribution of talents and assets – state welfarism, trusteeship principle of Rawls and trusteeship principle of Gandhi. He argues that only Mahatma Gandhi's principle of trusteeship has any hope of tackling the problem of social justice in a situation of unequal distribution of talents and assets. To arrive at this conclusion, he takes a close look at the Indian experience in the area of social justice, examines the theoretical status of group right, and discusses the proper way of securing social justice in a situation of inequality. T.R. Sharma, in the VI Chapter, tries to conceptualize the notion of social justice and marginality in the specific context of Hindu *varna* order which has become a pan-Indian phenomenon as other faiths have also, willy-nilly, adopted some of its discriminatory practices. Sharma's main contention is that for societies which are organized on the principle of social hierarchies, like the *varna*-based Hindu society or any other society which practices social apartheid or racial segregation in day-to-day interactions among people belonging to different ascriptive social stratums, social justice ought to have a much wider connotation. He makes an attempt to spell out the contours of a decent society in which lies the essence of social justice.

Chapter VII presents a multicultural critique of Rawls's theory of justice. Liberals recognize individuals and not groups, as holders of rights, whereas multiculturalists, feminists and communitarians believe that individuals are not abstract and are deeply embedded in their culture, community and group identity. Hence principles of justice should deal not only with liberties and material resources but also with cultural rights and opportunities. Justice in multiculturalism demands that not only let cultures survive and recognize them as equals but also greater concern, is to acknowledge their worth.

In Chapter VIII, Anand Mavalankar argues that in the contemporary global order, the question of justice needs to be addressed at the analytical level of the global order itself. Some of the guiding considerations that should shape our exploration into this question include 'justice' in the hierarchy of values, absence of global sovereign authority vis-à-vis the idea of fundamental human equality, political economy context of international society and distinction between 'international justice' and 'global justice'. The question of justice in the contemporary global order is indeed multi-dimensional, but this essay contends that the idea of global justice is the most credible way of inquiring and acting upon the sources and nature of injustice within the contemporary global order.

Distinguishing economic development from social development, S.V. Pande and Archana Srivastava, in Chapter IX, illustrates how social development can be achieved through social justice. In this analysis, an attempt has been made to formulate a more adequate construct of social development by including in it the normative dimension of social justice as its supreme indicator: the more we achieve it, the higher is the level of social development achieved in any specific society. He concludes that the process of social development consists the rise or evolution of a society from less just to more just or less human to more human stage. That is where the crux of the truly social dimension of social development lies.

K.L. Sharma, in Chapter X, discusses the relevance of 'caste' in present-day Indian scenario. Touching different genres of evolution of caste system in India, he first describes the historical nitty-gritty. He describes the importance of caste in society and polity. He maintains, caste retains its dominance in electoral politics and marriage. However, caste is quite elusive and slippery a phenomenon and it has an episodic expression and articulation rather than a systemic institution.

D.K. Verma, in Chapter XI, discusses how politics of social backwardness plays important role in policy formulations. On the basis of empirical data collected by the author himself, Verma discusses status characteristics of socio-educational backwardness and the implementation status of the welfare measures for empowerment of OBCs. He maintains that the Directive Principles of State Policy in India lay foundations for a 'Welfare State' which needs to work for weaker sections of society. So there is a need to identify specific groups among OBCs and EBCs for whom specific welfare measures could be designed and ensured. He suggests for policy-making and programme implementation, there is need for a separate ministry for OBCs and EBCs.

P.K. Chaubey, in Chapter XII, argues that modern State of India has tried, particularly through its constitutional provisions, to preserve diversity while mitigating disparities. It tries to foster harmony without imposing homogenization and promote unity without imposing uniformity. The goal has been to reduce disparities in various spheres of secular domain. It is considered a goal worth pursuing though difficult to achieve. Several schemes for inclusion of 'excluded' and marginalized or vulnerable sections and disadvantaged regions through differential treatment have been devised and partial success has also been achieved.

M. Kistaiah, in Chapter XIII, elaborates public policies initiated by the Indian state to ameliorate the socio-economic problems of the people living at the margin. Kistaiah has chosen the 'suicide belt' as area of study, consisting of Maharashtra, Andhra Pradesh, Karnataka, Madhya Pradesh and Chattisgarh. He examines the adverse effects of Indian public policy regarding national resources, permitting unbridled exploitation by the private sector. He suggests that we should seriously evaluate the public policies and examine to what extent do they serve public interest, failing which we may have to confront Hobbesian state of nature which is of not very far as things stand today.

Chapter XIV evaluates efforts towards social inclusion and justice for the marginalized section of Scheduled Castes of Jammu and Kashmir State. After detailing prevailing *varna* composition in Jammu and Kashmir, Saxena describes trends leading to changes among the Scheduled Castes of 'Jammu region' and touches different issues like socio-religious reform movement; land reform initiatives; role of various social organizations; and governmental efforts in enhancing the status of Scheduled Castes. He comments that the changing position and the attainment of social justice among the Scheduled Castes in J&K are better as compared to other counterparts in the rest of the Indian states.

Chapter XV deals with the question of social justice in India in the context of apparent economic compulsions to compete in the global economy by industrialization. Bhaskar Majumdar illustrates how late industrialization rests on state-led acquisition of agricultural land displacing people in exchange of compensation. Based on some recent evidences on acquisition of agricultural land for industrialization in India, the paper addresses the question of social justice in praxis.

While unravelling the role of the Supreme Court in institutionalizing legal aid in India and the various policies and programmes enacted as a result of judicial activism, Sanjay Gupta in Chapter XVI notes that though significant progress has been made, a lot still remains to be done as the legal aid movement has not yet benefitted the teeming millions owing to a host of reasons, such as the tardy implementation of government policies by public authorities, the pathetic ignorance of people about their legal entitlements and the inexperienced and junior legal practitioners being drawn into the system who owe little commitment and empathy for the poor. He suggests suitable measures for reviving and revitalizing this democratic instrument failing which glorious notions like legal equality and equal access to law would remain a sheer dream for the numerous under-privileged and deprived masses that still live in sub-human conditions and heavily depend on State succour for alleviation from their miseries.

In Chapter XVII, Mohit Bhattacharya analyses the discourses on the gender development for better understanding of the gender-related development issues and to properly integrate gender interests and needs into policies and programmes. After depicting the main theoretical feminist perspectives in international development policies – Ester Boserup's perspective of Women's role in Economic Development (WID); Women and Development (WAD), and Gender and Development (GAD) – the author at last discusses DAWN (Development Alternatives with Women for a New Era) as the groundbreaking network of feminists from the global South. To illustrate the contemporary situation of worldwide women development, Bhattacharya later discusses components and criticisms of Women, Environment, and Sustainable Development (WED), which was sparked by grassroot women's experiences in 'Third World' social movements such as the Chipko, Narmada Valley, and Greenbelt movements. Bhattacharya puts utmost importance on awareness generation of women, by which he thinks women can become a participant in the process of social change.

Mahendra Prasad Singh, in Chapter XVIII discusses how women got sidelined in the sphere of human rights. Singh says, in view of all-pervasive patriarchy and the diversity theorem of postmodern feminism, the full realization of women's human rights would not be a cakewalk. It will require a concerted strategy of action by the State, civil society, market, and national and international organizations to actualize the goals of gender equality and justice advocated in the feminist thought and national and international declarations of human rights. Singh suggests that constitutional entrenchment of these rights, conforming laws and public policies, including affirmative action by way of special rights such as reservations on the part of nation-states, hold the key to the achievement of women's rights as human rights in India and the world at large.

In Chapter XIX, Chandrakala Padia discusses how 'attitudinal fundamentalism' attributes to increasing violence and discrimination towards women. However, the sphere of the paper is limited to the analysis of fundamentalism at the philosophical level. It tries to project how, since the dawn of civilization, most of the philosophers have adopted a viewpoint which totally overlooks the experiences of women and often supports such ideas which put them in a position of subordination and servility. In conclusion, Padia agreed with Catharine MacKinnon claims that 'gender here is a matter of dominance, not difference ... Feminists have noticed that women and men are equally different but not equally powerful'.

Sumita Parmar, in Chapter XX, depicts the concepts, contents and contribution of selective Indian women's fiction. Parmar says it has been frequently said about great novels that they are more accurate in their depiction and rendering of the social realities of their times than historical, economic, or sociological books/archives. Thus, novels have become socio-cultural documents fulfilling more roles than just literary. Moreover, Parmar comments, what is found today when we look at the fiction written by women in India is not just a wide variety of thematic concerns and narrative styles, but a confidence of tone and the presence of feminist concerns clearly stated. Agency, articulation, autonomy, explorations and acknowledgements of the needs of the body, sexuality, and strategies of survival and of surviving whole are the features that mark contemporary Indian women's fiction and short stories.

The book, *Social Justice – Distributive Principles and Beyond,* pursues this line of inquiry by providing students, scholars and policy makers with an extensive review of research on social justice. The book is written for a wide audience that includes academics, policy-makers, social activists and students concerned with social justice issues. I hope that the book contributes to public understanding of the most important social justice problems, issues, and policies that society now faces and with which it must deal.

I am grateful to all the contributors for their cooperation. I am thankful to Rawat Publications, Jaipur, to consider this book for publication. The views expressed in the papers are those of the contributors and not of the editor.

M.P. Dube

Part I

Theorizing Social Justice

1

The Concept of 'Justice'

Debashis Guha

Philosophers are not the best people to propound models for social, political and economic justice. They are not apt at the nitty-gritty of any kind of justice. Nevertheless, they are well placed in analysing the *meaning* of justice to let us know what we mean by 'justice' when the concept is used. Equally important is to note that philosophers are well placed to indulge into *critique of models* of justice because they are apt at finding out the incongruencies involved in the essential *logical structure* inherent in the models of justice as well as to discuss the *ethical desirability* of the models of justice. The flow of justifications and thus arguments in favour and disfavour of methods of justice or the ways to be just socially, politically, distributive and so on, can and should be properly analysed by someone. Philosophers should take this task for them. They should find out the end and means of justice and inquire into the good, right and desirable of the same. Philosopher's involvement with the concept 'justice' is in some way *corrective* because they tell us where our understanding of the meaning and significance of the concept has gone astray and how to cure it. Much misconception concerning justice is due to an ill-understanding of the meaning of the concept itself. Therefore, our ill-understanding needs cure. In this paper, we try to find out the nature and meaning of the concept 'justice' in accordance with the various interesting use it has.

It is an unfounded sweeping statement that 'justice is fairness or lawfulness'. It is not difficult to find such cryptic definitions of the term, which tells us almost nothing about the meaning of the 'umbrella notion' that 'justice' is. An 'umbrella notion' such as 'justice' is so-called because it has divergent use and meaning though by virtue of their family resemblance, we can find out covering import of the notion. It will be an intellectual injustice to assert that 'justice' necessarily and sufficiently *means* 'fairness or lawfulness' or that which is in accordance with law, whether such justice is in the main, 'distributive' and retributive. Truly, 'justice' is used to mean 'fairness' in many contexts, but it is not equivalent to 'fairness'. In many contexts, the word 'justice' or 'just' is used to signify a 'formal attribute' as in case of 'fairness', but the terms are not interchangeable. The reason is that 'justice' is used at many places as a 'non-formal attribute' meaning thereby 'beautiful', 'unblemished', 'pleasant' and so on. In this sense, 'just family' and 'a justly played game' is not the same as 'fairness' bearing a legal sense as case of distribution of fairness in prize and punishment. Clearly, 'justice' cannot be over simplistically used in the sense of 'being fair'. We need to keep in mind its *non-formal use and meaning*. On the same ground we can say that if legal and fiscal justice is one way to understand what is 'justice' then to understand the concept properly, we should consider 'justice' used in the contexts of games, sports, family, social life and so on. It is important to note at the outset that for a proper understanding of the meaning of the term 'justice', we should not merely enrich ourselves with various use of the term emerging in various contexts, we should in the words of Ludwig Wittgenstein try to understand the 'family resemblance' (*Cf. Philosophical Investigations,* 1953), among different use of the term to depict what meaning is evidently clear to us. Hence, 'justice' is an 'umbrella concept'; meaning clarification of it needs some care on the part of those who are careful of proper use of the term. J.R. Lucas writes in his work *On Justice* (1980): while we go through a range of use of 'justice', it may be too scrappy, better we should look into the 'family resemblances' among the use of the term to find out the broad range of the meaning of the term conveyed to us. Only then can we know why 'justice' conveys the sense of 'good', 'commendable', 'beautiful' as well.[1] If we go through a number of uses of the term 'justice', such as, 'killing is just in a war', 'it is just to earn a living', we find a clear 'evaluative meaning' of the term because it has clear 'evaluative use'. It is much like *supporting or advocating* some decisions or acts on whatever grounds are available to us. It is exactly in this sense that while evaluating two people for their deeds, we use the words 'just' and 'unjust'. We, thus, commend and advocate Buddha-hood vis-à-vis Angulimal's ways when the words 'just' and 'unjust' are used in evaluative sense. However, when we relate two people and find them interacting or behaving, we normally think that 'to be just', is 'to be friendly'. We also have ideas of 'benevolence', 'sympathy' and 'empathy' when we relate two people and evaluate one of them to be just. This does not mean that 'to be just' in such a situation is necessarily 'to be friendly', 'benevolent' and so on because when someone gives property to his criminal son by virtue of a legal deed, such an act of benevolence mixed with sympathy *should* not be called 'just'. Hence, evaluation of 'just' by simply 'seeing' an act results into a loose evaluative use; such acts are unjust nevertheless, when grounds for evaluation are scrutinized. Yet, no one prevents us to use the word 'just' in this loose evaluative sense. The evaluative use of the term 'just' and 'justice' is thus 'context dependent' and might turn out to be *unfounded evaluative* use on scrutiny of the 'grounds' of evaluation itself.

In some contexts, 'justice' is used to mean 'political ideal or ideals', which is again unfounded if the use turns out to be essentialist or covering some kind of 'equivalence' of the terms. In fact, 'justice' is not to be equated for its meaning with terms like 'freedom', 'liberty', 'equality', 'unity' and so on. The reason is that 'justice' is used as a *non-emotive* term in relation to the terms which are used to signify political ideals. Hence, 'freedom is justice done to a population' is an instance of 'non-emotive' use of the term 'justice' (along with the term 'freedom'), wherein the speaker is not clarifying his emotion or attitudes or beliefs but states as a 'matter of fact' that the said ideal is valuable and not a disvalue because there are *political justifications* and/or *ethical justifications* available for such valuation. In this sense, 'justice' is used to mean a *non-emotive virtue or value*. In Aristotle's *Nicomachean Ethics*, justice emerges as some 'value' when we ponder *negatively,* that is when we find, for instance, that political bondage of population is politically and ethically extremely unjust or bad.[2] It is only when we ponder on the negative aspects such as political injustice that 'justice' emerges to be a positive good for us. This is not a testimony to what we *'feel'* or what our emotions are. For Aquinas and Lucas, 'justice' has, thus, a *derivative use* and *derivative meaning*. The evaluation of say, a political ideal as 'just', is to use the word 'derivatively' on grounds available to us. We 'put a value' to the said ideal 'matter-of-factly', before we actually use the word.

Nevertheless, it will be unwise to think that the word 'justice' is in essence non-emotive because in other contexts it has clear *emotive use* and *emotive meaning*. Precisely, 'justice' has both non-emotive and emotive meaning. The 'emotive force' in the word 'justice' is due to the latent force of 'retribution'. In this sense, 'justice' bears the forces of 'complain' and 'revenge'. For this we express our emotions of complain and retribution as: 'Let justice be done to me' (or else I have serious complain to file and that I will teach him or her lesson). If non-emotively, 'justice' is used to mean a *positive virtue* or simply a 'value' matter-of-factly, *negative virtue* expressed in the emotional demand for retribution bears a negative force ('or else I shall drag you to some teachings'). In some contexts, the use of the term 'justice' signifies both following *laws* and facing *consequences*. In the ordinary parlance, the evaluation of 'just' than 'unjust', as well as 'justice done' than 'injustice', refers to some such 'laws' which are both pragmatic and desirable, to follow these laws or to abide by them being mandatory. Hence, 'rule following' or 'law abiding' is referred to as 'justice'. In this 'justice is lawfulness'. Most of the time we conceive of intrinsic goodness of these rules or laws, much like the laws in judicial system.

Hence, the concepts of prize and punishment that goes with either abiding intrinsically good legal rules or violating them is basic for fair justice on the part of judge. In fair justice, therefore, 'justice' refers to 'lawfulness', provided laws are intrinsically sacrosanct. Similarly, in following the intrinsically good laws established in a society, one cannot outrightly reject the idea of *good consequences*. In that case goodness of laws and rules are not intrinsic in nature rather, *extrinsic* in nature because abiding by such and such established laws turn out to be 'good' as it has 'good consequences'. Hence, to follow a law is good, consequentially. Most of the time we evaluate an action to be lawful just because that is most congenial to social harmony or social well-being. Truly, 'justice', if that is 'lawfulness', goes well with the idea of 'good consequences'. Justice is thus 'teleological good'. The 'teleos' might refer to 'usefulness' (utility), 'benefit', 'wellness' and thus 'effectiveness'. The concept of 'effectiveness' that goes with the concept of 'justice' is basic to judicial justice. If 'justice' as lawfulness goes well with the idea of 'effectiveness' or the teleological good, it is basically different from 'friendship', 'sympathy' and 'empathy'. It is odd to think that following a socially good rule or a law that is conducive to social good is to refer to a bond of friendship in society among the population or a kind of harmony or showing sympathy or to have empathetic relationship. Because 'social wellness' does not necessarily demand friendship, sympathy and empathy, when wellness is anchored to the idea of lawfulness, it demands us to overlook a number of personal relationships if 'teleos' is basic to that relationship. At the level of personal relationships (teleos being the focal point), we cannot necessarily say that such relationships are legally just. One can be a party to a goose club, Robinhood or even an empathetic charity worker, but that does not go on to justify the lawfulness of such acts. Lawfulness, on the other hand, might demand going beyond personal relations for greater social good. In that way two friendly thieves or Robinhoods or self-proclaimed benevolent saints cannot be seen as 'just in the eyes of law' when we refer to greater social teleos.

It may be noted that 'justice' bears a sense of 'down', that is, the several uses of the concept 'justice' in legal, social, economic and distributive contexts neither refers to 'that what is up', rather refers to 'that what is down'. In this sense, 'justice' does not refer to an equilibrium state, rather refers to *disequilibria state* or a state of neither neutral nor up, rather 'down'. According to Plato, for ethical justice or to be ethically just, one has to conceive movements from down to middle and middle to up (*The Republic:* 'Comparison of Just and Unjust Lives').[3] Whenever we conceive of even non-ethical or positivistic justice as mentioned above, if it is ethically grounded, no doubt we should look to the mid-level and to the up. There is clear indication that the movement itself must be from a 'state of the fallen' (*down*) to 'up'. The parity of reasoning allows us to justify that justice (positive) makes any sense when we conceive of a 'fallen state' of injustice, or a state of disequilibrium. Otherwise why should a state of economic equilibrium need any justice! This must have played in the mind of John Rawls (*A Theory of Good,* 1980), when he thought that distributive justice is to reach an equilibrium state for which it will be ethically (and practically) unjust to bring 'down' the well placed people to a state of the deprived.[4] Then 'down' must be basic to an understanding of 'justice', that is, the concept is used to refer to some conditions in our society that demands positive social mechanisms for uplift or to equilibrium. In cases of legal justice, we are just to those who are deprived by others. Even distributive and political justice refers to some injustice and deprivation that needs correction. Closely related to this analysis is the reflection that 'justice' is often used to signify 'fairness', where 'fairness' is as simple as 'not taking sides' in distribution of rights, entitlements and so on. This Aristotelian legacy of *dichaste,* that is, proportionately just distribution, is basic to an understanding of *dikaiosyne* or 'justice', particularly in cases of distributive and legal justice. For Aristotle, 'distributive justice' is thus *proportionate* or *arithmetic justice* (two or more people being exactly in a similar state, needs proportionate distribution of entitlements and for that matter injustice should be proportionately corrected). But this is true only of quantitative justice. In case of qualitative justice, where two or more persons are not in similar states, that is given essential relativism among the population in terms of different states and capacities, the conception of *geometric justice* or *justice in relation to us vis-à-vis justice in relation to things* are different. Aristotle's careful analysis of 'justice' as 'proportionate' and 'relative to us' enable us to rethink about 'justice as fairness', where 'fairness' is 'not taking sides'. This appears to be over simplistic, so much so that it treats the Rawlsian idea of not bringing down the handful fortunate people for greater social justice, and for that matter to deliberately 'take sides' by virtue of delicate and well deliberated social engineering, as in, affirmative actions. Therefore, 'justice' does not necessarily and sufficiently signify 'fairness' by not taking particular side when social engineering is a means towards an ethically and practically desirable end, namely, human and ecological well-being. In this sense, justice is not being necessarily and sufficiently understood as perfect harmony among people or classes or groups in society wherein, a social engineer does not intervene. It has to be seen that in the complex social fabric we can perceive entropies as well as equilibrium. In this climate of equilibrium and disequilibrium are placed the social engineers to decide and act in just ways or to do justice. We cannot by our mere whims snatch the *authoritative* powers bestowed on the engineers, the power that are not arbitrary or self-proclaimed, rather, obtained as part of one's duty and obligation in an 'official' way or that which provides some lawful powers on the person by social and political institution or organization. The engineers having authority face the music of desires and aspirations, claims and wants, demands and their fulfillment. It is a queer conflict situation in the social milieu wherein authorities face conflicts among people and have to do justice. The fortunate few have aspirations to remain fortunate and even grow in fortune; the unfortunate masses aspire to be fortunate. What does it *mean* in this entropic situation to be 'just' or to do 'justice' on the part of the 'authority' holding some power? It cannot be holding a middle path between the positive and the negative powers the authority has been bestowed upon. There is really no middle path with regard to the aspirations of the fortunate and the unfortunate. However, in that relative situation, the authority is said to be just when he or she has not taken recourse to either *minimal advantage* or *optimal advantage*. In this sense, 'justice' refers to *not* to do the *minimal* at least. It is impropriety in decision-making and action. Justice as 'propriety in decisions and actions' on the part of the social engineer does imply 'taking some side' based on the rightful powers for giving advantages and benefits rightfully to those who have claims for that. The reason is that he or she cannot be docile, minimal in giving advantages because to maximize advantages of some people may be both ethical and pragmatic. Justice as taking some side at some point of time with regard to some classes or groups, is propriety in decision and action, which, however, *does not logically entail* being harsh on or to ruin the future of the fortunate because we do *not logically necessarily* conceive dictatorship of the proletariat. Neither do we *logically necessarily* conceive of oligarchic or bourgeois chauvinism to grow in fortune by systematically ruining the already deprived masses. What is demanded of us is not a mid-way either, much like the half-way house of democracy. The propriety of engineers in the maximization of social well-being on the whole is relative only to the actual social demands and the broader reflection of ethical desirability of meeting these demands. This takes the engineer along with authorities and powers, the office and its duties, the laws and rules of the office to a *corroborative ethical exercise* with the public on the desirability of methods of bestowing more advantages on some while withdrawing dangerous optimization of benefits to the already fortunate. A half-way house of touted welfare state often misconceives social engineering of affirmative action and stands fooled at the tension of fortunate and unfortunate masses just because propriety of taking sides needs ethical judgments in and with the public before the engineering itself. Often the methodological part of social justice goes on a moral holiday to stick to positivism, and thus cause social disaster. To put methodological intricacies first, powers second and activism third, is to put the horse before the cart because the just, right and good of methods, powers and action were put in the oblivion.

This might be the ground for understanding why all well deliberated decisions and actions of people cannot be called 'just' though they were in no case whimsical or arrogant. More often than not our governments and other social institutions take so-called 'well deliberated' or 'rational decisions', but far from being just, they are in fact unjust. This may be the basis to realize why our so-called just social engineering though thought to be highly 'rational' was irrational and unjust. Justice is not a logical entailment of rationality. As said before, rationality can be foolhardy if it goes on a 'moral holiday'. The 'how' and 'what' of decisions and actions bereft of 'why' or 'why should' tells us why some rational decisions of authorities are *not* just. Justice cannot be thus handmaiden of so-called 'sound reasons'. The essentialism of 'soundness of reasons' is detrimental to justice at many times. It is exactly in this context, we shall now find out the meaning of 'justice' given the concept of 'freedom' and *egoistic backward-looking vis-à-vis altruistic forward looking* aspects inherent in the freedom for justice. Yes, we 'are' and we 'should' be free in doing social, political distributive and legal justice. We 'are' free because that is often a stark truth needing no repeated proving exercise. However, our institutional decisions and actions which are touted to be free from all deterministic factors are contested by the determinists. For them, we are really *not* free to intend, decide and act such as to be just at the social realm because we are essentially determined by several factors that surround us in the social maze of politics, economics and legal bindings. Even cultural snags or fixity of dogmas, fear of traditions, cultures and values are deterministic factors that does not leave us free for just intentions, decisions and actions. It is exactly here that we come up with the idea of 'ought' or 'should' that goes with 'freedom for justice'. We are equally capable of 'moral critique', that is, to reflect on 'ought' of justice based on moral arguments either in isolation or in communion. If we are capable of being free to intend, choose, decide and act, we better 'ought' to or 'should' apply our capability to do, and that 'freedom' is in the true sense our moral criticisms of factors that threaten all actions to be determined in one way or the other. We are really 'free' to come in unison in social milieu to consider the moral criticisms of our social, cultural, political and legal dogmas. We are 'free' to come out of the determinism imposed by 'authorities' of many types. Humans are 'vectors' of dogmas and easy prey to authoritarian determinism. But humans are bestowed upon with an uncanny ability to be self-critics and become critics of social dogmas and authoritarian peer pressures. For that reason, in the climate of determinism, we 'are' and we 'ought' to free ourselves through the powers of common rationality and common ethicality that we possess. Freedom for justice is our power to be just based on criticisms of several deterministic and authoritarian snags, for this the said 'common' rationality need *not* be 'necessarily and sufficiently' 'theoretic'. Our freedom for criticisms of the derogatory factors involved in prevention of the just are not necessarily and sufficiently intellectual freedom to apply one or more standard theories of morality or moral justice.

Having ethical theories does not imply having 'common rationality' and critical ethical ability to dispel dogmas and determinism. Being member of teeming ecological community we swap common *moral experience* of right, just, good and desirable, and thus have *moral knowledge.* This is vital in the emergence of critical ethical acumen that has the 'backward looking freedom' to evaluate the right and the just for 'me' and the 'forward looking freedom' to evaluate the right and the just for 'them' or for 'us'. I 'should' be free to enforce myself to be just to other-selves. 'Justice' has then forward and backward looking features in the context of moral agents' freedom and the avoidable determinism that clouds freedom. In this sense, the concept 'justice' cannot, without a logical contradiction be taken to imply the sense of 'other-centredness because defeating 'ego-centredness' or 'care for individuals' by virtue of encouraging cynic and ascetic whims does not withstand moral criticisms of reasonable nature. Hence, while we are just in being 'other-centred', we are still 'looking back' for moral reasons to be 'ego-centred', and while are just in being 'ego-centred', we are looking 'forward' for moral reasons to be 'other-centred'. Understood in this sense, 'justice' refers to a 'limit put to us', that is, it refers to an 'internal limit' (imposed freely on us), to restrict us to be either purely egoistic or purely altruistic when we are considering any just decision and action by individuals or groups or institutions whether that is economic or legal or socio-political. A just professional is thus an agent who voluntarily applies limit on himself to look back. There is no doubt that the word 'just' and 'justice' can be analysed for meaning by considering the complex concepts such as 'distributive justice', 'legal justice', 'social and political justice' and even 'ethical justice'. However, we were concentrating on the simple notion of 'justice' for its meaning and to synthesize from that exercise what the concept most clearly convey to us.

Notes

1. Readers may refer to detailed meaning analysis of the terms 'justice,' 'social justice', 'political justice' and 'economic justice', to find out what meaning the term and expressions conveys to us by virtue of 'family resemblance' among the various use of the terms and expressions in J.R. Lucas' work: *On Justice,* Oxford: Clarendon Press, 1980.
2. A good account of 'justice', 'distributive justice' and 'legal and ethical justice' is provided by Aristotle in the *Nicomachean Ethics* (Trans) W.D. Ross, London: Methuen & Company,1949. It is helpful in analysing the 'positive' and the 'negative' significance of the term 'justice'. In case of distributive justice, the word 'justice' signifies a 'positive' sense of 'proportionate' or what Aristotle calls, 'arithmetical' (quantitative) justice, wherein fairness in distribution is to move along positive scale of *equality* in distribution. This is not the corrective sense in which the term is used. Nevertheless, in 'legal justice', the term 'justice' has altogether different 'negative' sense in which proportionate justice still being 'equal' in the eyes of law, is not quantitative in nature.

   For Aristotle, legal justice is negative as: 'an eye for an eye' or to *take* (not to give), *life for a life taken.*
3. In *The Republic,* (Trans) A.I. Melden, *Ethical Theories. A Book of Readings,* Englewood Cliffs, New Jersey: Prentice–Hall, 1960, Plato discusses 'just life' as the one that moves from the lower strata of *doxa* (mere belief) to highest strata of *episteme* (knowledge) through the neutral (partial knowledge). Qualitatively (ethically) speaking, it is better that just life moves from down to neutral and up than unjust life that moves from up to neutral and even down.
4. John Rawls in his milestone work: *A Theory of Justice,* Cambridge,Mass.:Belknap Press of Harvard University, 1973, is at pains to justify that for distributive justice, the social engineer should be under a 'veil of ignorance'. However, he or she cannot and should not forcibly take away advantages of the 'fortunate few' because that would not amount to help unfortunate people in any way. For social harmony and ethical good, the uplift of the unfortunate must be desirable good through just social engineering. But how that would help harmony when there is always a persisting gulf, is at the centre of controversy.

2

The Idea of 'Justice as Fairness'

Naresh Dadhich

Justice as Fairness is the idea that was fully developed and presented in book form in 1971 by John Rawls. The idea simply proposes that the most reasonable principles of justice are those, which can be agreed upon by mutual consent of individuals under fair conditions. The mutual consent of individuals is a form of social contract. Rawls says that the conception of justice which he wants to articulate is but an attempt to generalize and create higher level of abstraction the familiar theory of the social contract as found, say, in Locke, Rousseau, and Kant.[1] The contract takes place in Rawls in an initial situation called, Original Position[2] (a different situation, dissimilar to state of nature used by most of the social contractualists). The procedure to arrive at the principles of justice is also fair and individuals choose them rationally after rejecting all other options possible in those conditions. The principles of justice that are chosen in original position are liberal in content, which gives primacy to right to liberty over distribution of primary goods. The distribution of primary goods should be equal among individuals until and unless unequal distribution of goods is beneficial to the least advantageous person of society. Primary goods here mean those things, which every rational individual is presumed to want. After the contract a constitution be framed on the basic principles of justice as fairness and a government is elected to rule under this constitution. The political system that emerges from this is known as Constitutional Democracy.

To clarify his idea of justice, Rawls thought it befitted to criticize utilitarianism and intuitionism, two formidable philosophical alternatives, which dominated philosophical tradition for a long time.

John Rawls started working on the idea of 'justice as fairness' in 1957 when he published his nine-page article in *Journal of Philosophy* on justice as fairness. The idea was ultimately expressed in full philosophical rigour in *A Theory of Justice*, a 600-page compact book in 1971. The book attracted wide publicity because of the novelty of idea and lucid presentation and was generally accepted to have revived normative political theory after a gap of almost 100 years. Rawls did not stop, in 1971, he went on adding, improving and spreading his idea of justice as fairness till his death in 2002. But the main idea remained intact.

Why the idea of justice was dear to Rawls? Rawls as we will see was a pucca liberal. He time and again stressed that he is using social contract theory to explain his concept of justice. He even claimed that he is taking the social contract theory to a higher level of abstraction. John Locke, the most popular user of social contract theory, advocated natural rights and specially right to property. Rousseau, on the other hand, gave primacy to liberty. Justice was inherent in the thought of Locke and Rousseau but they were not primarily concerned with the question of justice. Rawls is the first liberal thinker who gave importance to justice. Rawls explained reasons for his infatuation with justice.

He says:

> Justice is the first virtue of social institutions, as truth is of systems of thought. A theory however elegant and economical must be rejected or revised if it is untrue; likewise laws and institutions no matter how efficient and well-arranged must be reformed or abolished if they are unjust.[3]

We can very well recall Plato's obsession with justice. Justice for Plato was the supreme virtue, which defines goodness in human beings. Aristotle summed up Greek political understanding about the nature of human beings when he says, 'man, when perfected, is the best of the animals; but if he be isolated from 'Nomos' and 'Dike' he is worst of all.'[4] Aristotle further explained that 'Dike belongs to the polis; for Dike, which is the determination of what is just (to dikaion) is an ordering of the political association.'[5] Justice was the favourite concept for Greeks. After almost 23 centuries; Rawls made it a desirable word of vocabulary of political theory. For him truth and justice are uncompromising. People can tolerate injustice only when it is necessary to avoid an even greater injustice.

Rawls's search for justice begins with certain assumptions. We assume that a society is almost self-sufficient in the wider sense of the term 'sufficient' and is composed of reasonable persons who recognize rules of social behaviour and generally accept them in social behaviour. Further we assume that these rules help in advancing the interests of those persons who follow them. In this situation (which reminds us of John Locke's state of nature) also, there are possibilities of identities of interest resulting into conflict. Social cooperation makes life better for all and each wants to take advantage of it and wants more shares as per his efforts or needs. Thus requires a set of principles for distribution of goods, which everybody accepts, as these may prove satisfactory to each. On the basis of these principles, state assigns rights and duties to persons and distributes goods and benefits to them.

Rawls further argues that this society is a well-ordered society, which is committed to welfare of its members and is regulated by a public sense of justice. It also means that persons know that state normally functions while accepting the fact that there is a public sense of justice and each member is abides by this justice and knows that everybody else will also abides by it in the normal circumstances. In the existing societies, public sense of justice is in dispute. It is difficult to distinguish between just and unjust in law and its implementation, particular actions of many kinds and the functioning of institutions. The primary subject of justice is basic structure of society, which in Rawlsian sense includes constitution and principal economic and social arrangements like family, market, private property and constitutional safeguards of liberty, equality and justice. While formulating his theory of justice, Rawls declares that he is interested in formulating a reasonable conception of justice suitable only for a well-ordered society existing as a closed system isolated from other societies. The principles of justice conceived in this way may not be suitable for any other kind of organization, say a private firm or an international institution.[6]

In order to arrive at the principles of justice, Rawls uses traditional theory of social contract as found in Locke, Rousseau and Kant.[7] The idea here is not to explain the origin of society or government through social contract but to point out that the principles of justice are chosen by mutual agreement of free and rational individuals in an initial position under free and fair condition. These principles are to regulate all further agreements. The contract that takes place in the initial situation, known as original position, is not a historical fact and cannot be taken as the primitive stage of culture. It is purely a hypothetical situation.

The essential feature of this situation is that no one knows his place in society, his class position or social status, nor does anyone know his fortune in the distribution of natural assets and abilities, his intelligence, strength and like.[8] Rawls further assumed that the individuals do not even know their conception of good and the principles of justice are chosen behind a veil of ignorance, which ensure that the principles are chosen in a fair condition. Justice as fairness requires that the initial conditions in which these principles be chosen must be fair. The conditions are fair only when all the logical requirements are made to ensure that no one can possibly take advantage of the principles chosen. One more feature of this initial situation is that the individuals are not only rational but are mutually disinterested. Individualists are not altruistic. It does not mean that they are self-centred or egoistic in a negative sense. They are simply interested in themselves and not interfering in the affairs of others. Rationality here is defined narrowly, as in most economic theories, of taking the most effective means to achieve given means. In this initial situation, principles of justice as enunciated by Rawls were not the only one available to the individuals. They arrived at this decision to agree to these principles after careful consideration of other options. In arriving at this decision, individuals use 'contract' as a form of means. The use of contract theory suggests that rational persons choose the principles of justice in a rational manner and making this exercise a part of rational choice theory.

For a rational and correct decision to choose principles of justice, it is necessary that the initial situation should provide such objective conditions, which help in executing the necessary decision. Rawls argues that 'thus it seems reasonable and generally acceptable that no one should be advantaged or disadvantaged by natural fortune or social circumstances in the choice of principles.'[9] If someone knows that he is wealthy he would like to oppose taxes as unjust principle. For maintaining objectivity, person should be deprived of such information about himself and thus veil of ignorance is a natural characteristic of original position. Veil of ignorance means that everyone in the original position forgets about one's past, status, class, position and honour. It helps in making choice more rational and objective. Original position is that of such a state of affairs in which we can enter anytime by following a particular procedure. The individuals here are also equal in choosing the principles. They are equal in the sense that they have equal right to be heard, make proposals and suggest amendments during discussion for choosing principles of justice. These individuals[10] are also moral beings who know the distinction between right and wrong and have a sense of justice. Rawls concludes by saying:

> Together with the veil of ignorance, these conditions define the principles of justice as those which rational persons concerned to advance their interests would consent to as equals when none are known to be advantaged or disadvantaged by social and natural contingencies.[11]

The original position, thus, seems to provide fair objective conditions for search for principles of justice. It is this situation, which expresses both reasonable conditions and actually produce principles of justice that is called reflective equilibrium by Rawls. It is equilibrium because in it principles and rational judgments coincide, and it is reflective because we know the basis of derivation of these principles.

In this original position, individuals have many choices before them. Rawls reduced these choices to three major strands namely utilitarianism, intuitionism and justice as fairness. While asserting that justice as fairness is the right choice, Rawls brings out limitations of the other two alternatives.

Criticism of Utilitarianism

Rawls is concerned with classical utilitarianism formulated by Bentham and Edgeworth and which is present in clear and concise form in Henry Sidgwick's work.[12] In its classical sense utilitarianism stands for a society in which sum of satisfaction of maximum number of individuals is maximized and thus makes that society just. This idea of utility is attractive to common sense.

1. It believes that the principle, which is applied to individual can very well be applied to society. An individual balances his losses and gains and try to maximize the gains in his life (whatever he thinks as rational being as what are the gains). In

similar fashion, society can also try to maximize its gains by calculating gains and losses of individuals who are part of it.

2. Utilitarianism is a teleological theory. In a teleological theory, good is defined independently of right and then the right is defined as something which maximizes the good. It means that the judgment of deciding which things are good is separate from its rightness. So right is simply a means to achieve good which is defined separately and not necessarily (generally by intuition) by reason. Morality is separated by rationality and this becomes attractive for average man to follow as it is less complex and easily practical. For instance, if Michael wants to become senator of his state, he does not have to rationalize his wish and as a rational man he can chart out a plan for achieving this. The notion of good is defined differently in teleological theories and they are named accordingly. For instance, in perfectionism (Aristotle, Nietzsche) it is defined as realization of human excellence; in hedonism good is defined as pleasure. In its classical sense good is defined as satisfaction of rational desire. Utilitarianism is not concerned about the distribution of sum of satisfaction among individuals. The only criterion it has is of maximum fulfillment. In normal circumstances, it means equal distribution of goods by assuming no distinction among individuals and their specific demands or needs.

John Rawls compares his theory of justice as fairness with utilitarianism and tries to prove that his theory is better than utilitarianism in providing basis for ideal society.

1. Justice as fairness is a contract theory, which accepts priority of justice as necessary for an ideal society. The natural right tradition of social contract theory gives priority to rights over good and this is accepted by Rawls in his principles of justice. Utilitarianism on the other hand gives priority to utility and considers doctrine of justice as a useful social illusion.
2. While utilitarianism extends the principles chosen for an individual to the society as a whole, justice as fairness being a contract theory makes principles of justice a part of the original agreement in which all individuals participate.
3. While utilitarianism is a teleological theory, justice as fairness is a deontological theory. In Rawlsian theory, thus, good is not defined independently of right and right is not defined as maximizing the good. Here priority of rights is maintained and individuals accept a principle of equal liberty.

Justice as fairness and utilitarianism have different notions of ideal society. One thinks of a well ordered society in which principles to provide basis of such society are chosen in the initial situation while the other thinks that the efficient administration is required to exploit resources and maximize the satisfaction of maximum number persons.

Criticism of Intuitionism

Rawls believes that there is a plurality of intuitionist theories and these sometime differ in their approaches. He includes G.E. Moore, H.A. Prichard, W.D. Ross, Richard Price and others in representing intuitionism.[13] Intuitionists believe that there is no objective criterion to judge suitability of first principles to choose. Intuitionism also consists of a plurality of first principles which may not give unified directives in particular cases and secondly, there is no priority principle which may help in choosing first principle. Ultimately, we have to choose on the basis of intuition. In Rawlsian justice the role of intuition is limited in many ways.

1. The principles of justice are chosen in the original position. Persons being rational decide their priority on the basis of some ethical norms and they cannot rely only on intuition for choosing their priorities.
2. The principles, thus, chosen may be put in lexical order.[14] This is an order in which first principle is to be satisfied before we go to second principle, the second before we consider third and so on. Rawls proposes:

   > An ordering of this kind by ranking the principle of equal liberty prior to the principle regulating economic and social inequalities. This means, in effect, that the basic structure of society is to arrange the inequalities of wealth and authority in ways consistent with the equal liberties required by the preceding principle.[15]

3. The role of intuition can be minimized by given preference to prudential judgment on moral judgment.

Rawls does not want to eliminate role of intuition in judgment making which is not even possible, what he wants is to minimize its role so that a common conception of justice can be emerged. Rawls here introduced a novel concept of lexical order in moral theory. Traditionally moral theory was either a single principled theory or intuitionist theory.

Two Principles of Justice

John Rawls begins by describing his principles in a general way and gradually deduct his final version. The primary version of his two principles is as follows:[16]

> *First:* each person is to have an equal right to the most extensive basic liberty compatible with a similar liberty for others.
>
> *Second:* social and economic inequalities are to be arranged so that they are both (a) reasonably expected to be to everyone's advantage, and (b) attached to positions and offices open to all.

These principles are to be applied to the social structure of society. Here basic liberties of the citizens are:[17] political liberty (the right to vote and to be eligible for public office) together with freedom of speech and assembly; liberty of conscience and freedom of thought; freedom of the person along with the right to hold (personal) property; and freedom from arbitrary arrest and seizure as defined by the concept of the rule of law. These liberties are all required to be equal by the first principle, since citizens of a just society are to have the same basic rights.

The second principle says that the distribution of wealth may not be equal but must be to everyone's advantage and position and offices must be accessible to all.

These two principles are arranged in a lexical order so that in the name of arranging social and economical inequalities, right to liberty may not be disturbed. Rawls considers these principles as specific in nature and formulate a more general conception of justice, which is expressed as follows:[18]

All social values – liberty and opportunity, income and wealth, and the bases of self-respect – are to be distributed equally unless an unequal distribution of any, or all, of these values is to everyone's advantage.

In explaining the priority of first principle over the second principle, Rawls argues that the social structure distributes primary social goods[19] and sometimes it looks that by sacrificing right to liberty one can get more wealth but priority of first principle prevents it and no one is allowed to sacrifice right to liberty for the sake of wealth. It is quintessential liberal value. Rawls further says that he will concentrate on the principles of justice, which are special case of justice rather on the general theory of justice. It will help in analysing priority principle, which is essential in determining the character of state. Rawls then goes on to clarify the second principle. Phrases, 'everyone's advantage' and 'equally open to all' used in second principle are ambiguous. This principle thus has four interpretations as indicated in the table given below:[20]

	'Everyone's Advantage'	
'Equally open' to all	Principle of efficiency	Difference principle
Equality as careers open to talents	System of natural liberty	Natural aristocracy
Equality as equality of fair opportunity	Liberal equality	Democratic aquality

Rawls prefers democratic equality and accepts equality as equality of fair opportunity and difference principle instead of principle of efficiency. The reasons he gave for this preference are highly vague but he certainly takes a particular position from which social and economic inequalities are to be judged in the society. By opting for this preference he avoids the indeterminateness of the principle of efficiency. Difference principle is an egalitarian principle, which believes that equal distribution of goods is to be preferred until and unless unequal distribution benefits both the parties in which distribution is done. Rawls explains his difference principle by using a graph (Graph 1).[21]

In Graph 1, x1 represents the most well off person of the society, while x2 represents the least advantageous. The curve OP represents the contribution to x2's expectation aroused by the greater expectation of x1. The point O represents the imaginary state of affairs when primary goods are distributed equally. The OP curve is always below the 45° because x1 is always better off than x2. The difference principle is satisfied when OP curve is tangent to the highest indifference curve that it touches. In the graph it is at the point a.

There are three methods in which the uneven distribution can take place. First, the expectations of the least advantageous are increased without increasing the expectations of the well off. This is the socialist method and requires abandoning liberal state. Second, the expectations of the least advantageous and of the well off persons both are increased but the gap between them also increased. This is free market strategy. Third, the expectations of both least advantageous and well off persons increase in such a way so that the difference between them gradually decreases. This is difference principle of unequal distribution of goods. Difference principle

Graph 1

Difference Principle

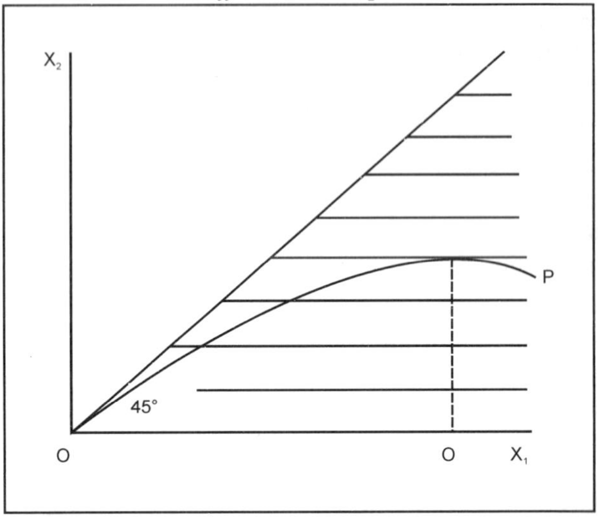

believes in social cooperation. It is also consistent with efficiency principle because no one gets worse off in this. It believes that good of all is inherent in good of one and vice versa. But justice is prior to efficiency. So for implementing justice if efficiency is not maintained it is acceptable. Difference principle maintains that each one gets benefitted through it and it does not matter what was the initial position of someone. The important thing here is the maximization of expectations of the least advantageous. By applying difference principle, everyone improves his position in society.

Rawls gives one more argument to prove that difference principle is better than other choices in dealing with inequalities in society. He says that expectations in society are connected with each other in a chain. It means that if any benefit raises expectations of the least advantageous then it will automatically raise expectations of all those who are holding positions between the lowest position and the highest position. For instance, if any decision or policy benefits the worker of a company it should also benefit all those who are working under the president of the company. Rawls's insistence on social cooperation and overall beneficial scheme makes him idealistic or worse romantic. This abstract notion of difference principle is difficult to implement and is one of the most controversial concept of Rawlsian justice. A general principle of distribution can be found on this which first maximizes the benefits to the worst off then maximizes the benefits to the second worst off and so on and so forth till we reach at the best off person for maximizing his welfare. This may be viewed as lexical difference principle. But Rawls preferred a simpler form and reformulated his second principle as follows:[22]

> Social and economic inequalities are to be arranged so that they are both (a) to the greatest benefit of the least advantaged and (b) attached to offices and positions open to all under conditions of fair equality of opportunity.

Rawls believes that the difference principle is the basis of general conception of justice and one which can be applied to all primary goods, including liberty and opportunity. Rawls is criticized for not giving adequate reasons why rational individuals will choose difference principle in original position where they will accept that social and economic inequalities be arranged in such a manner so that it benefits the least advantageous.[23]

The second part of the second principle is the liberal principle of fair equality of opportunity. It is possible that by not opening position to all and by restricting positions to meritorious persons only it is possible that least advantageous may get that position on account of his merit. It is also possible that those meritorious persons who are holding such positions may take such decisions, which help the least advantageous, but this will not amount to fair equality of opportunity. It can be assumed that the group of least advantageous persons may not get position because of some problems and may get benefit from the policies made by persons holding positions but will feel that the group has been left out of positions and this may be treated by the group members as an example of injustice. For instance if Afro-Americans or women don't get representations in decision-making bodies of US government, they may be devoid of a sense of self which comes out of discharging responsibilities in a social set-up.

This fair equality of opportunity is possible only when distribution of primary goods take place in a fair manner. It is the basic structure of a society, which does the work of distribution. This is imaginable only when we believe that society is interpreted as a cooperative venture for mutual advantage. If such is the case then justice is primarily a procedural justice.

In defining justice as fairness as a prime example of procedural justice, Rawls distinguishes between perfect and imperfect procedural justice. For illustrating perfect justice he gives an example of fair division.[24] A number of men are to divide a cake. Assuming that fair division means equal division in this case, the just procedure is that one man divides the cake and takes the last piece and others be allowed to choose before him. This example, Rawls argues gives two characteristics of perfect procedural justice. One, there is an independent criterion of what is fair division, a criterion defined separately from and prior to the procedure which is to be followed. Second, it is possible to form a procedure that can give the desired results. In arriving at this procedural justice there are certain assumptions we have to make like belief in the capabilities of the man to cut the cake in equal measures or to believe that the man wants biggest piece, etc.

Rawls gives example of imperfect procedural justice in criminal trial. In criminal trial, in many cases the criminal is not found guilty and an innocent man is found guilty. This injustice may not be done on account of human error but because of inherent weakness of criminal law where there is an independent criterion for the correct outcome but there is no full proof procedure to attain that. This inherent weakness of criminal procedural law is an example of imperfect procedural justice.

John Rawls further argues that difference principle has some merits worth noting.[25]

1. Difference principle includes principle of redress in the sense that natural inequalities like inequalities of birth and natural endowment are to be compensated in this. For providing fair equality of opportunity, a just society should pay more attention to those with less natural benefits like lower social births or should spend more money on education of those who are less intelligent or less privileged in economic or social sense. Thus those who are in better position because of their birth will get benefit from the society only when the lesser privileged will get benefit too.
2. Difference principle also denotes principle of reciprocity advocating mutual benefit. If we accept chain connection in difference principle, it automatically follows that all persons holding positions in between the best off and the worst off get benefit if one of them is benefitted. The system is thus egalitarian by nature. It is accepted that well-being of one

depends on social cooperation by others. The well off will also be willing to participate in such cooperation because they are sure that they will get help in their ventures by the less fortunate willingly. Here the question of desert also crop in. Rawls does not favour the notion of desert in his difference principle. According to desert doctrine, a man deserves to get benefit from society on the basis of what contribution he has made for society. Rawls, on the other hand, argues that the distribution of goods takes place in such a manner in which everybody gets benefitted and the maximum benefit should go to the least advantageous.

3. Difference principle also expresses one interpretation of principle of fraternity. French Revolution gave the slogan of liberty, equality and fraternity. But fraternity was never considered an important part of democratic theory. Fraternity was considered to represent a sort of civic equality and friendship with an overall sense of social solidarity. Any theory of justice does not seem to directly connect with the idea of fraternity. Difference principle believes in the idea of fraternity that a well off person will want benefits until and unless it benefits others who are less well off. Fraternity is normally interpreted as having elements of sentiments and feelings and that is why it does not feature in democratic theory. But if it is interpreted as something which incorporate social solidarity then 'justice as fairness' has a place for it. The traditional ideas of liberty, equality and fraternity are very well incorporated in Rawlsian justice. The first principle is about liberty. Equality is expressed in the first principle as well as in the second principle of equality of fair opportunity and fraternity corresponds to difference principle.

Rawlsian justice gives much importance to difference principle while applying it to the main subject of justice, namely, basic structure of society. Rawls also talks of justice for individuals along with social institutions.[26] He believes that it is necessary to choose principles of justice in a definite order as these principles denote not merely right, liberty and equality but also many unexpressed ideas innate in them such as mutual respect. Rawlsian justice for individuals also include obligations and duties on part of them as fairness requires that individuals must respect their social obligations and perform their natural duties so that social solidarity remains intact.

Conclusion

John Rawls's theory of justice is a major landmark in four traditional disciplines: Law, Economics, Political Science and Philosophy. In philosophy it displaced linguistic and analytical philosophy and made morality a central concern for philosophy and thus revived Immanuel Kant. In Political Science, Rawls not only revived liberalism with its basis of 17th–18th century social contract theory but also revived the concept of justice, which was overshadowed in political theory after Greeks by rights, sovereignty, state, power, etc. In economics the welfare theory and rational choice theory got new inputs from 'justice as fairness'. In law, Rawls extended the arguments of H.L.A. Hart in jurisprudence and interpreted justice, which is the basis of law with a new perspective.

The debate about social justice today is centred on John Rawls. If egalitarianism and social justice remains the buzzword of contemporary consciousness, Rawls will remain relevant.

Notes

1. John Rawls, *A Theory of Justice*, Cambridge, Mass.: Belknap Press of Harvard University, 1971, p. 11.
2. For a comparison of original position and state of nature, see, Allan Bloom, 'Justice: John Rawls Vs. Tradition of Political Philosophy', *The American Political Science Review*, Vol. 69, 1975, pp. 651–53.
3. John Rawls, op. cit., p. 3.
4. Aristotle, *Politics*, (ed.) and translated by Ernest Barker, Delhi: OUP, 1977, p. 7. *Nomos* means law and *dike* means justice in Greek language. For a discussion of Aristotle on justice, See W.F.R. Hardie, *Aristotle's Ethical Theory*, Oxford: Clarendon Press, 1968, ch. x.
5. Ibid.
6. After several years, John Rawls dared to venture into formulating theory of justice which is applicable to a specific ideologically based system like political liberalism and found suitability of his principles of justice in international law. See, John Rawls, *Political Liberalism*, New York: Columbia University Press, 1993 and *The Law of Peoples*, New York: OUP, 1999
7. See, John Locke, Second Treatise on Government, Rousseau, The Social Contract and Kant, The Foundations of the Metaphysics of Morals.
8. John Rawls, op. cit., p. 12.
9. Ibid., p. 18.

10. I have used individual and person interchangeably, Rawls also uses, party, man for this.
11. John Rawls, op. cit., p. 19.
12. See, Henry Sidgwick, *The Methods of Ethics*, London: Macmillan 1907.
13. For works of these thinkers see John Rawls, *A Theory of Justice*, Cambridge: Harvard University Press, 1971, p. 34 (footnote 18).
14. Lexical order is a shortened form of 'lexicographical' used by Rawls. The familiar example of such an ordering is that of words in a dictionary.
15. John Rawls, op. cit., p. 43.
16. Ibid., p. 60.
17. Ibid., p. 61.
18. Ibid., p. 62.
19. Primary social goods here means, in Rawlsian sense, things that every rational man is presumed to want, e.g. rights, opportunities, power, income, wealth, etc.
20. John Rawls op. cit., p. 65.
21. Ibid., p. 76.
22. Ibid., p. 82.
23. On this argument see, M. Lessnoff, 'John Rawls' Theory of Justice' *Political Studies,* no. 1, March 1971, p. 19. D. Lyons, 'Rawls versus Utilitarianism', *Journal of Philosophy,* no. 18, October 1972, p. 69.
24. John Rawls, op. cit., p. 85.
25. Ibid., pp. 100–106.
26. Later on John Rawls applies his principles of justice to existing state ruled by the ideology of political liberalism and also to the laws of nation-states. See his, *Political Liberalism,* New York: Columbia University Press, 1993 and *The Law of Peoples,* New York: OUP, 1999.

3

Rawls's Theory of Justice

Asok Mukhopadhyay

John Rawls (1921–2002), the most eminent political philosopher in the second half of the 20th century, has given new meaning and resonance to the theory of liberalism and the concept of justice. His watershed publication *A Theory of Justice* (1971) came at a time when serious questions were raised about the future of liberal political theory, especially in his own country United States in the context of the ongoing furious debate over the Vietnam war, the raging racial inequality and large-scale unemployment. In fact, he began his philosophical inquiry into the nature of the problem of realizing a just social order and political system in the late 1950s when many people had predicted the end of the political theory of liberalism and, for that matter, of political philosophy itself. Rawls, an academic philosopher, broke from the main current of modern philosophical thinking in terms of logical and linguistic analysis. His theoretical work helped stimulate a revival of interest in moral theory and political philosophy. His great theoretical contribution has been his sophisticated arguments for a new concept of justice.

John Bordley Rawls was born in Baltimore, Maryland, in the USA on 21 February 1921. His father William Rawls, without attending law school, learned enough to become a lawyer qualified to argue cases before the Supreme Court. His mother Anna Rawls was a participant in the women's movement for advocating voting rights for women. John attended the Kent school in western Connecticut and thereafter entered Princeton University in 1939.

There he was introduced to political philosophy by Norman Malcolm, a student of Wittgenstein. He graduated in 1943 and joined the US Army as a private. After initial training, he was sent to fight in the war in the Pacific, in New Guinea, in the Philippines and eventually in Japan.

His military service as a combat infantryman came to an end after the termination of the Second World War. He began his graduate studies in philosophy at Princeton in 1946. He wrote his doctoral dissertation on the moral knowledge and judgments on the moral worth of character. It was here that his interest in developing a theory of justice first developed. After teaching for two years in Princeton, he went to Oxford University on a Fulbright Scholarship for the academic year 1952–53 and joined Christ Church College. This one year in Oxford was one of the most formative periods of his long career. He was especially influenced by lectures of H.L.A. Hart on the philosophy of law as well as by seminars held by Isaiah Berlin and Stuart Hampshire.[1]

Returning to the United States in 1953, Rawls went to Cornell University as assistant professor of philosophy. Here he found his former teacher Norman Malcolm on the faculty, and his former Princeton classmates Rogers Albritton and David Sachs. He stayed at Cornell till 1959, was in Harvard University during 1959–60, and thereafter joined the Massachusetts Institute of Technology where he continued till 1962. Finally he took a teaching position in the standing faculty at Harvard where he held, since 1976, the John Cowles Chair in philosophy until 1979, when he succeeded Kenneth Arrow as James Bryant Conant university professor. In this post he continued till his retirement in 1991 (though he continued teaching until, 1995). By nature a quiet, witty and modest man, Rawls turned down hundreds of honorary degrees and accepted them only from Oxford, Princeton and Harvard, with which he was associated. He was awarded in 1999 the National Humanities Medal by the President of the US with the citation noting his success in helping women enter the ranks of a male-dominated world.[2] Rawls died of heart failure on 24 November 2002 at his residence in Lexington, Massachusetts, ending his suffering of a stroke in 1995.

From the outset of his intellectual career, Rawls's work was guided by the question 'what is the most appropriate moral conception of justice for a democratic society?' In his *A Theory of Justice* (1971), this question was pursued as part of a general investigation into the nature of social justice. This book was a sort of a wake-up call to the contemporary liberal theory of social and political justice and dazzled the world of philosophy till then dominated by utilitarianism, logical positivism, empiricism and linguistic analysis. By reviving the concept of social contract in defiance of the prevailing philosophical sensibility of the day, Rawls attempted to answer a single ethical question of how to construct a just society. *A Theory of Justice* (1971) was a stupendous success, which immediately sold two lakh copies and inspired over five thousand books and articles on related issues. This book has since been translated into 27 languages.[3]

Rawls turned to the liberal and democratic 'social contract' tradition built up by Locke, Rousseau and Kant. According to the doctrine of social contract, laws can be called 'just' when they could be agreed to by free persons from a position of equal right. This argument had the consequence that, to be just, laws must benefit not simply a majority but everyone, thereby promoting the common good.

In the 1960s, Rawls had to confront the socialist propaganda that socialism alone can cater to a just distribution of resources in society. So, in formulating his own theory of justice, Rawls elaborated the argument that the principles of liberalism and socialist egalitarianism can coexist. This attempt of critical moral philosophy to harmonize the principles of liberty and equality in his theory of justice is his greatest contribution to liberal political philosophy in the second half of the 20th century.

Rawls aimed to redress the predominance of utilitarianism in modern moral and political philosophy. Utilitarianism, which had grown out of the work of the British empiricists starting with David Hume (1711–76), was best developed by Jeremy Bentham (1748–1832) and has been the most influential moral conception for more than 250 years. Utilitarianism says laws are 'just' when they promote the greatest overall happiness of the majority members of society. But issues of just distribution have long been seen as problematic for utilitarianism, which seems to condone sacrifices of individual and minority welfare for the sake of the majority. Yet a compelling alternative conception of justice seemed to be lacking in moral philosophy.

To develop such an alternative, Rawls turned to the liberal and democratic 'social contract' traditions of Locke, Rousseau and Kant. According to social contract doctrine, laws are just when they could be agreed to by free persons from a position of equal right. This has the consequence that, to be just, laws must benefit not just a majority, but everyone, thereby promoting the common good. Utilitarianism, which was also extremely influential outside the academic world, seemed to provide a straightforward and rigorous method by which public officials could solve hard political problems. The utilitarian method is, for every policy alternative, to add up the social benefits, subtract the social costs, and implement the alternative that maximizes net benefits.

Alongside the dominance of utilitarianism, there was however the common intuition that the rights of individuals should not be sacrificed for the sake of social welfare. But the advocates for rights of individuals lacked systematic philosophical arguments against the Benthamite notion that rights are nothing more than 'nonsense on stilts'. There was also the Marxist critique of rights as the common sense of capitalists, confusing the class interests of the bourgeoisie with the universal interest of humanity. Rawls used the method of 'social contract' to overcome these intellectual challenges. Rawls followed the liberal tradition of thinking to defend a politics more explicitly egalitarian than Lockeanism and explicitly more libertarian than Marxism, and he constructed a theory of justice that proved to be the most systematic and coherent integration of liberal and socialist ideals.

Rawls adopted the hypothesis of 'social contract' also to counter the defects of intuitionism which is a sort of incoherent jumble of ideas and principles. Intuitionist theories consist of a number of first principles which may conflict with one another; they include no explicit method, no priority rules for weighing these principles against one another. Intuitionism has two defects. First, it is unable to explain as to why its principles should be followed. Rawls deals with this defect by proposing a contractual hypothesis as a method of arriving at principles of justice without relying simply on intuition. Secondly, intuitionism gives no guidance for decision when two or more of its principles point to conflicting courses of action in a particular situation. Here also contract resolves the disagreement on the substance of the principles of justice whether distribution should be according to merit or need. The contractual hypothesis would lead to the criterion of need. Rawls asserts that when intuitional approaches conflict with one another, necessary guidance comes from political theory. His theory of justice is meant to provide a political theory for finding out the principles of justice and a framework of a just society.

Rawls adopts the method of 'reflective equilibrium' for breaking the intuitional – utilitarian deadlock and constructing his theory of justice. As a method of thinking, reflective equilibrium goes back to Aristotle and was later used by Sidgwick. It is the intellectual technique which ensures coincidence of reasonable philosophical conditions on *principles* with considered *judgments*. It is an equilibrium because principles and judgments coincide; and it is reflective because people think about the principles conforming to people's judgments and the premises of their derivation. According to reflective equilibrium, if a practice derived from the principles conflicts with a conviction, then either the principle has to be reformulated or the conviction has to be changed. To decide which course to take, practical judgment has to be used to weigh a variety of considerations such as firmness and consistency of conviction, the certainty of the principles and of the evidence underlying the practice, and so forth. When philosophers sidestep this process of approaching reflective equilibrium, they act on faith rather than reason. This equilibrium is not necessarily stable. It is liable to be upset by further examination of the conditions which should be imposed on the contractual situation and by particular cases. The method of reflective equilibrium, as used by Rawls, challenges every critic to offer constructive revisions of justice as fairness.

The technique of reflective equilibrium is employed by Rawls as a method of testing rival moral theories and gauging which one is to be preferred. Rawls's defense of 'reflective equilibrium' as a method of justification is his distinctive contribution to the tradition of grand theory built up by Plato, Hobbes and J.S. Mill. In doing this, he is the wisest and most modest of grand philosophers.

Pursuing his 'social contract' idea, Rawls makes some assumptions to put forward a logical presentation of his theory of justice. First of all, he assumes an 'original position' with which he begins his discourse, and on which he focuses while developing his theory of justice. Rawls's 'original position' plays a role analogous to the 'state of nature' in earlier social contract tradition. He treats this as a hypothetical rather than a historical condition. In the original position persons live in a 'veil of ignorance'. They are bound by incomplete knowledge and limited judgment. In this original position 'no one knows his place in society, his class position or social status; nor does he know his fortune in the distribution of natural assets and abilities, his intelligence, strength and the like ... the parties (to the contract) do not know the particular circumstances of their own society'. They do not have their conception of the good or their special psychological propensities. The principles, of justice are chosen behind a veil of ignorance.

The concept of 'veil of ignorance' was not used by Rawls in his version of justice written first in 1957–58.[4] It is used in *A Theory of Justice* (1971)[5] to negate and nullify the influence of genetic endowments, superior talents and characteristics and social contingencies which may tempt the individual to exploit and tailor the principles according to his own advantage.

Secondly, it is assumed that parties to the contract are persons who, like 'negotiators' are 'rational agents', want to achieve common good in a just society and, at the same time, protect their individual liberty. Rawls has thus in an excellent manner combined the traditions of Locke (individual liberty), Rousseau (common good) and Kant (humans as moral personality). The contract is hypothetical but it is made to serve a logical purpose of establishing a well-ordered and just society which protects the values of liberal democracy. Rawls's logical presentation serves the purpose of reconciling the liberal ideal of political obligation with a redistributionalist conception of social justice. In his scheme of justice (distribution), both the individual and society benefit simultaneously. His theory of justice secures a place for normative theory in the face of behaviouralist theory in political discourse.

Thirdly, Rawls assumes that persons, while entering into a social contract, want to achieve benefits of 'primary social goods'. This category of primary social goods includes, in Rawls's thinking, 'liberty and opportunity, income and wealth, and the bases of self-respect'. These primary social goods are directly distributed by social institutions like powers, rights and liberties. They are distinguished from another kind of primary goods called primary natural goods which include health, intelligence, vigour, imagination and natural talents. These are affected by social institutions, but are not directly distributed by them.

While persons in the original position enter into contract to obtain the maximum of these primary social goods, they as negotiators have general wisdom but particular ignorance. They are wise enough to feel that they need these primary social goods as much as possible but living in a 'veil of ignorance' they are unable to distinguish their own interests from the interests of others insofar as they do not know what special qualities and talents they have. In denying the people the original position knowledge about their social location and their natural endowments, Rawls tries to ensure that the principles to which they agree are not distorted by those chance inequalities that in the real world might be thought to bias distributive outcomes. Justice requires a bargain made under fair conditions, and that is why knowledge of inequalities is ruled out.

The parties to the social contract in Rawls's original position do not know their conception of the good. This means that they do not know what their beliefs are about and how they should lead their lives. Just as justice requires that no attention be paid to the different talents of different members of society, so it requires that no attention be paid to the particular conceptions of the good held by them. Rawls says: 'The idea of the original position is to set up a fair procedure so that any principles agreed to will be just. The aim is to use the notion of pure procedural justice as a basis of theory.'[6]

Fourthly, it is assumed that deliberations or negotiations leading to the contract are conducted through the technique of reflective equilibrium. The principles of just distribution is thus the result of moral deliberations in the sense that the parties to the social contract rise above the considerations of personal interests, biases and prejudices. Rawls has explained the process in an ingenious manner. He says that when at a birthday party the members are asked to cut the cake into pieces and if they do not know which particular pieces they individually would get, then the invariable tendency would be to cut the cake in as fair a way as possible. Rawls's assumption is that if people do not know who they are going to be, then it will make sense for them to choose fair (i.e. just) principles for distributing the primary social goods and regulate the social order accordingly. The principles of justice arrived at in the original position by people living in a veil of ignorance has therefore to be the outcome of a *fair* agreement. Hence Rawls defines 'justice as fairness'.

There is a link between ignorance of conceptions of the good and freedom. The parties to the social contract in the original position are taken to be motivated above all by an interest in protecting their capacity to 'frame, revise and rationally to pursue' conceptions of good. Of fundamental importance in the Rawlsian scheme are not the conceptions of the good but something that lies behind such conceptions, viz. people's freedom to decide upon their own conceptions of the good, to act upon, and to change those decisions. Thus, Rawls builds up the substantive moral claim that, when thinking about justice, what matters is people's freedom to make their own choices and to change their mind, not whatever they choose.

The 'original position' conceived by Rawls is Kantian in essence. In the original position people are assumed to be *noumenal selves* in Kantian sense. This means that people are free, moral, equal, rational beings and hence autonomous. Such autonomous personalities do not have particular ends but they desire certain primary social goods, which are derived from their rationality and flow from their noumenal selves.

The idea of 'original position' is to set up a *fair* procedure so that any principles agreed upon would be *just*. The purpose is to nullify the effects of specific contingencies which put humans at odds and tempt them to exploit social and natural circumstances to their own advantages. Hence the assumption that parties to the 'social contract' in the original position are situated in a 'veil of ignorance'.

Rawls's general conception of justice as fairness consists of one central idea: 'All social values – liberty and opportunity, income and wealth, and the bases of self-respect – are to be distributed equally unless an unequal distribution of any, or all, of these values is to everyone's advantage.'[7]

The general conception, Rawls admits, is extremely vague and requires interpretation. It is not yet a full theory of justice, because the various primary social goods being distributed according to that principle may conflict among themselves. For example, income increase for some may be accompanied by loss of liberty for others; or unequal income may benefit everyone but may create inequality of opportunity, thereby disadvantaging those with less income.

Rawls suggests a solution of this problem by enunciating two principles of justice and two priority rules. He argues that the conception of 'justice as fairness' that is finally accepted by the contracting parties (i.e. people in the initial situation) consists of two principles and two priority rules.

Rawls's First Principle is about equal basic liberty for all. To quote him: 'Each person is to have an equal right to the most extensive basic liberty compatible with a similar liberty for other'.[8] The First Principle is the liberal core of Rawls's theory. It implies that each person is to have an equal right to the most extensive basic liberty compatible with similar liberty for others. The *basic liberties* of citizens, according to Rawls, include political liberty like right to vote and eligibility for public office, together with freedom of speech and assembly, liberty of conscience, freedom of thought, right to personal property, freedom from arbitrary arrest and seizure (that is, rule of law). Rawls maintains that justice should be understood in the light of an individual's liberty, and the individual's liberty should be understood in the light of general or common good. On this point, there seems to be a touch of Rousseauist concept of common good combined with Kantian concept of autonomy of the individual.

The Second Principle is about fair equality of opportunity for all.[9] This principle has two parts. First: the 'difference principle' – 'Social and economic inequalities are to be arranged so that they are reasonably expected to be to everyone's advantages and, in particular, to the advantage of the least well-off persons'.

This principle is called 'maximin' principle, that is, maximum benefit to the minimum advantaged. Rawls has not used the term in the mathematician's sense of the *maximum minimorum*. He uses the term 'maximin' as a shortened way to describe the 'difference principle'. He argues that principles of justice require the establishment of a social minimum. The 'maximin rule' is a single strategy that people in the initial situation would pursue in selecting one of the many possible institutional designs for society. It is introduced as a heuristic device to clarify the structure of the choice problem in the original position. The 'maximin' rule means maximization (or, at least, increase) of the incomes and advantages of the least advantaged group. As a strategy, it would always yield justice because it would always be just to impose any loss, however big, upon a better-off group in order to bring a gain, however small, to the least advantaged group. These two principles of justice are intended to serve as guidelines for how basic institutions are to realise the values of liberty and equality. In realizing these principles, it is necessary to conceive society, as Rawls does, 'as a fair system of cooperation'.

Second: social and economic inequalities are to be arranged so that they are attached to positions and offices open to all under conditions of fair equality of opportunity. That is, people with similar abilities and skills should have similar life chances ... irrespective of the income class to which they are born. Thus Rawlsian liberalism goes far beyond the classical liberal ideal of careers open to talents. The Second Principle constitutes the socialist core of Rawls's theory.

These two principles are accompanied by two Priority Rules. The first Priority Rule asserts priority of liberty over equality of opportunity. Accordingly the First Principle, according to Rawls, has lexical priority over the Second Principle (the correct term is 'lexicographical' but it is too cumbersome, hence Rawls uses the term 'lexical'). That is to say, liberty can be restricted only for the sake of liberty, and equal enjoyment of liberty must be pursued prior to the distribution of social and economic resources. Rawls rejects equalization at the expense of the basic liberties of any citizen.

The second Priority Rule asserts priority of fair equality of opportunity over efficient distribution for realizing the 'maximum' principle. Accordingly, the principle of fair equality of opportunity would have lexical priority over the principle of efficient distribution and welfare and that of maximizing the sum of advantages.

The priority problem is not that of how to cope with the complexity of already given moral facts which cannot be altered. Instead, it is the problem of formulating reasonable and generally acceptable proposals for bringing about the desired agreement in judgments. In general, a lexical order cannot be strictly correct, but it may be an illuminating approximation under certain special, though significant, conditions. It may indicate the larger structure of conceptions of justice.

Rawls, as we find him in *A Theory of Justice* (1971), had to confront a situation which saw the culmination of various movements in the United States, for example, Civil Rights movement, Black Liberation movement, movement for equal rights for the minorities, Great Society programme for alleviation of poverty, anti-Vietnam war movement, all of which raised questions about individual and minority rights, just and unjust wars, issues of social justice in policy formulation and execution. Rawls in his theory of justice seeks to unite the libertarian ideal of liberalism with the economic egalitarianism into a single theoretical structure. In the process he has brought back liberalism into the centre of political debates and discussions. He seeks to redefine the relationship between liberty, equality and fraternity. He rejects meritocracy and advocates *fair* equality of opportunity in order to correct morally arbitrary inequalities in society. He is uncompromising on the primacy of liberty but wants that society endeavours to equalize economic wealth, social status and political power.

Rawls admits that some sort of a basic structure of framework is needed to simplify the application of the two principles of justice. The main institutions of the basic structure are those of a constitutional democracy. The principles of justice define a workable political conception.

Rawls sets out a four-stage sequence that clarifies how the principles for institutions are to be applied. First, a constitutional convention is to be held; second, this convention is to choose the effective and just constitution; third, at the legislative stage, the provisions of the constitution are to be translated into laws; and at the fourth stage, laws and rules are to be applied to particular cases. He insists that at this fourth stage everyone should have a complete access to all the facts and information.

It seems that Rawls prefers the 'welfare state' which can be defined simply as one in which the government undertakes the responsibility for providing the essential social services, free or at subsidized rates, to all or, at least, to lower-income groups.

Rawls did not straightway conceptualize any theory of the state. However, his theory of justice subscribes to a particular kind of liberal democratic state with certain egalitarian principles. According to Rawls, the functions of the state is not only to maintain law and order but also to achieve distributive justice by putting the highest social value on the requirements of the disadvantaged. His notion of the state is that of a voluntary organization of rational individuals established for achieving general social welfare. He seeks to correlate the tradition of Lockean (personal liberties) and Rousseauist (common good) democratic thought, taking the Kantian idea of individual autonomy as the guiding thread. Since he wants his state to help the disadvantaged section of the society, his political theory can be called the theory of liberal democratic socialism putting importance on structuring of basic liberties which cannot be bargained with socio-economic gains. His political theory is informed by the ethics of humanitarianism and the concept of Man as moral personality who needs freedom as much as material goods.

Rawls's liberalism is not a patched-up compromise between conservatism and socialism; it is a distinctive creed with solid moral foundation. His liberal democratic socialist state is not directed towards achieving an equitable social policy. Rawls, like Max Weber, accepts social stratification and hierarchy as functionally necessary and inevitable. But Rawls insists on the state and society to secure 'the most extensive system' of equal basic liberty for all. He does not believe in steam-rolled equality and wants to protect the creative individuality through *fair* equality of opportunity. His concept of 'justice as fairness' is basically a concept of political culture and not a metaphysical one. Hence one of the most striking characteristics of Rawlsian liberalism is that the 'right' of the individual is prior to the aggregate social 'good'.

Rawls clarifies that his conception of 'justice as fairness' is apolitical conception of justice for a constitutional democracy. This conception avoids certain philosophical and metaphysical claims. He maintains that in a constitutional democracy the public conception of justice should be, as far as possible, independent of controversial philosophical and religious doctrines; hence the public conception of justice is to be political, not metaphysical.[10] He holds the view that the justification of a conception of justice is a practical social task rather than an epistemological or metaphysical problem. That is, this conception of justice can serve 'as a basis of informed and willing political agreement between citizens viewed as free and equal persons.'[11] Rawls avoids a metaphysical conception of 'justice as fairness because he thinks that 'philosophy as the search for truth about an independent metaphysical and moral order cannot provide a workable and shared basis for a political conception of justice in a democratic society.'[12] He insists that, to secure agreement, disputed moral and religious questions are to be avoided not because they are unimportant but because there is no way to resolve them politically, and the only alternative to a principle of toleration is the autocratic use of state power.

Since the publication of his *A Theory of Justice* in 1971, Rawls was criticized by a variety of liberal thinkers. One general area of agreement among liberals is that the government should be committed to tolerating the views and cultures of its people and, in general, committed to staying out of decisions by individuals regarding the best way to lead their lives. But they have differed, sometimes dramatically, in how they defend this commitment to toleration and limited role of the government. Throughout the 1970s and 1980s, Rawls wrote a few articles to meet the points of his liberal critics, thereby restating his position wherever needed.

In his second important book, *Political Liberalism*[13], Rawls accepted that in any free society, reasonable and fair-minded people are inevitably going to have different and conflicting religious and moral views. This poses a problem, since ideally a liberal constitutional democracy requires that the laws be justifiable to everyone if people are to be free and accorded due respect. This is not possible unless citizens do not share a common moral or religious view. Rawls no longer takes issue directly with utilitarianism or other moral conceptions. Instead he tries to show how democratic citizens with diverse moral and religious views can all affirm the same 'freestanding' liberal conception of justice on the basis of 'public reason'. He defends a form of political liberalism which is so thoroughly committed to toleration that it eschews any kind of metaphysical, moral or religious foundation for basic liberal principles.

Rawls recognizes the great importance of autonomy and of the moral doctrines of Kant, J.S. Mill, Emerson, Thoreau and Whitman, but he does not accept liberalism as a comprehensive moral doctrine because he wants to specify the value of full autonomy by a political conception of justice and not by a comprehensive moral doctrine. Rather he prefers to present his account of 'justice as fairness' as a conception of political justice rooted in 'the public culture of a constitutional democracy'. The Rawlsian conception of justice as fairness seeks to identify the kernel of an 'overlapping consensus', that is, the shared intuitive ideas sufficient to underwrite a just constitutional regime. Rawls firmly believes that the priority of the right over the good is characteristic of liberalism, a political doctrine, and this belief is essential to any conception of justice reasonable for a democratic state.

Rawls accepts that liberty and equality are the two ruling concepts in a liberal political regime. Nonetheless, in his *Political Liberalism* (1993), he affirms them merely as 'political' values and avoids endorsing them as part of some kind of metaphysical, moral or religious theory or 'comprehensive' view. Liberty and equality are supposed to be 'freestanding' values that are implicit in the political culture of the liberal society.

Most important is Rawls's view that a liberal society's commitment to these values should not depend on the society's belief in the truth of moral or religious arguments. These values are supported by what Rawls terms 'public reason' in a liberal society. This reason does not disclose universal moral truth or is not the vehicle to get access to moral values animating the liberal society. Instead, 'public reason' is something to all members of the society, because it is constructed out of commonly accepted values. Public reason involves appeal to reasons that are used by all citizens in their political arguments and that are concerned with the good of the public. The implication of Rawls's contention is that such public reasons are commonly accepted because no matter how they differ, all reasonable members of the liberal state accept that these reasons count in their society. To put it in Rawlsian terms, the members of the state have constructed 'an overlapping consensus' on them. Public reasons are supposed to be at the intersection of their differing comprehensive views.

Rawls says that reasons to which people appeal in a liberal society come from 'a conception of justice that may be shared by citizens as a basis of a reasoned, informed and willing political agreement.' He argues that his own two principles of justice turn out to be the conception that is shared at least in the United States, by all reasonable people. In any case, Rawls insists that such a conception, once constructed, expresses their shared and public political reason.

In Rawls's view, liberals are supposed to work together as reasonable people to develop an overlapping consensus. This democratic consensus yields plural results and looks for political values and policies that all reasonable people, despite their different starting points and moral views, can accept. Moreover, even though 'public reason' is constructed out of the beliefs of citizens, it is supposed to be vigorously non-partisan.

Rawls admits:

> To attain such a shared reason, the conception of justice should be, as far as possible, independent of the opposing and conflicting philosophical and religious doctrines that citizens affirm. In formulating such a conception, political liberalism applies the principle of toleration to philosophy itself. The religious doctrines have gradually given way to principles of constitutional government that all citizens, whatever their religious view, can endorse.[14]

Such non-partisanship makes a liberal state governed by this public reason tolerant and respectful of the competing moral views of all its citizens. Rawls's liberal state attempts to bind together people of disparate views via shared political conceptions and public reasoning. It is just a matter of interest to note that Rawls published his third book, *The Law of People,* in 1999, where he developed an account of international justice. Just and decent nations, he argues, have a right to intervene to protect the persecuted peoples of 'outlaw states'. Moreover, he maintains that all nations have a duty to assist impoverished nations so that they may become self-sufficient. Rawls also condemned the Allied bombing of German cities and American bombing of Japanese cities during the Second World War and especially the nuclear attacks on Hiroshima and Nagasaki, as these attacks amounted to violations of human rights of civilians.

In 1999, Rawls's Collected Papers were published. His lectures at Harvard on Kant, Leibnitz, Hume and Hegel, and those on his own work, were issued as *Justice as Fairness*: *A Restatement* in 2001.

What is intended in this section is to indicate briefly the main critiques, both liberal and non-liberal, of Rawls's theory of justice.

Rawls's concept of 'original position', constituting a strategic part of his theory of justice, has been the subject of enormous discussion. While many have supported Rawls's position, many others have criticized his arguments as well as conclusions. Some critics attack his arguments, paying less attention to his conception of justice, whereas some others simply attack his conclusions. There are some logical inconsistencies in Rawls's argument. First, there is the issue whether Rawls's theory of justice is really 'contractarian' at all. It seems reasonable to argue that it is the idea of 'veil of ignorance', and not the prospect of having to agree with any other person in the original position, that leads to the choice of the Two Principles of Rawlsian theory of justice. Since every person in the original position, insofar as he is subject to the veil of ignorance, is defined in exactly the same way, Rawls has no basis upon which to ground any kind of bargaining among these identically defined parties. The reason of the Two Principles being selected by each person in the original position seems to have nothing to do with such a contract. If the choice of the Two Principles is not a function of any contract in Rawls's hypothetical contract situation, Rawls's argument cannot be taken as contractarian.[15]

Secondly, Rawls advances some arguments to defend his 'difference principle' or the 'maximin' rule, but all of them are problematic. Rawls argues that the 'maximin' rule is appropriate in the original position because each person cares very little for what he might gain above the minimum. This argument contradicts Rawls's own earlier stipulation that in the bargaining process each person wants as many and as much primary social goods as possible. If a person is ignorant of his status and needs, it is not logically possible for him to bargain for as much social primary goods like liberty and opportunity, income and wealth, and bases of self-respect.[16]

Thirdly, some critics point out that Rawls's original position argument for the 'Two Principles' is fatally flawed. Rawls has used the assumption of the 'veil of ignorance' in order to kill off the possibility of having persons with genuinely different interests and nature, but this same assumption also kills off the possibility of having a 'real' contract argument providing a proper defence of his 'Two Principles'.[17]

So far as Rawls's conclusions are concerned, a plethora of criticisms of his theory of redistribution (justice) and of the nature of his liberal state have followed. These criticisms have been made by both the right-wing and the left-wing camps of contemporary liberalism.

Robert Nozick, a conservative liberal attracted to Lockean ideas, criticizes Rawls precisely because the Rawlsian conception of justice, in his view, fails to protect individuals as ends. Individuals need liberty to determine what they should do with what belongs to them. Nozick argues that individuals and their talents must not be made for, and supposed to serve, collective purposes. He prefers minimal state and creative individual, and is opposed to parentalism of the state.[18]

Ronald Dworkin, a conservative egalitarian, advocates a way to distribute resources whereby everyone will not have exactly the same amount, yet each person would be left both contented with his lot and be able to take responsibility for satisfying his tastes and securing his welfare. He advocates a thought experiment similar to a contractarian approach to defining Justice.[19]

Bhabatosh Datta, an economist of leftist persuasion, points out that the Rawlsian 'maximin' (maximization of the minimum) argument can be used by some to justify the enrichment of the rich so that they may spend something for the poorest. But raising the minimum does not necessarily mean a reduction of inequality. Rawls has not considered the possibility of income distribution in such a way that after redistribution of incomes and advantages, the gap between the rich and the disadvantaged may be reduced yet both sections may gain simultaneously. A variant of the Rawlsian position is the 'filtration theory' which has been empirically disproved practically everywhere.[20]

Amartya Sen, the welfare economist with egalitarian slant, has argued that equalizing 'welfare' will be impossible or extraordinarily expensive and difficult if there are some people in the society who suffer from natural disadvantages like ill health and diseases, mood disorders and disabilities negatively affecting their well-being, and from social disadvantages like illiteracy, environmental degradation, and gender bias.[21]

A major critique of Rawlsian position has been made by the 'communitarian' liberals like Charles Taylor, Alasdair McIntyre, Michael Walzer, Michael Sandel, and others. They have argued against different targets, some specifically criticizing Rawls and others being concerned with the contemporary moral culture of the liberals in general. The communitarian debate has covered a range of complex philosophical issues, for example, conception of the self (person), possibility or desirability of state neutrality vis-à-vis the individual, universal or culture-specific applicability of the principles of justice. The thrust of the communitarian attack on the Rawlsian position is that Rawls's view of 'unencumbered self' does not correspond with self-perception of humans; it ignores the embeddedness of the self in communitarian practices in particular time, place and culture. Sandel asserts that a sense of deep communality is created through 'shared self-understanding and affection', which is constitutive of a just society. Rawls has been charged for having completely missed this point.

The communitarians have questioned Rawls's unrelenting emphasis on the 'empty' individual and his ignoring the 'community' which ought to be the locus of concern for distributive justice. They argue that the community shapes the individual's sense of identity, talents and pursuits in life and hence the appropriate locus of concern for a political society must be what is good for the community, not what any particular individual should get.[22]

Rawls's theory of justice has also been attacked by many feminists who consider liberalism as a political approach totally inadequate to the needs and aims of women and, in some way, profoundly subversive of their aims. Some feminists believe that social or political systems of domination, such as that of males over females, distort society so severely that none of the theories of justice would prove acceptable unless these systems of oppression are overturned.[23] However, it needs to be noted that Rawls's theory of justice might be able to address at least some feminist concerns.

Marxists criticize Rawls and, for that matter, any theory of justice. They do not emphasize justice and indeed object to the idea that communism is based on a principle of justice. Marx was averse not only to the idea of justice but also to the concept of moral equality underlying it. Marxists see critical moral philosophy of the Rawlsian kind as totally irrelevant to the ideological framework of historical materialism and class struggle.[24]

In fact, Marxism has no theory of justice, because it believes in a law of social development and considers class struggle as the motif force of history. Marxism as well as Marxism-Leninism advocate complete socialization of the means of production and the channels of distribution. They do not bother about the kind of arguments indulged in by Rawls in order to build a just society. Marxists like C.B. Macpherson viewed the Rawlsian system as a defence of private capitalist enterprise. Marxists generally charge that Rawls's 'difference principle' is merely another version of the open market-oriented trickle-down effect.

Before the publication of Rawls's *A Theory of Justice* (1971), academic political philosophy was either the history of political thought or quasi-technical linguistic analysis of the meaning of political concepts. Since Rawls, there has been *systematic and substantive* argument about what society we live in ought to be like actually. His theory of justice invokes and incorporates ideas like liberty, equality and community, which are all interrelated among themselves and with the quest for building a 'just' society.

Philosophically Rawls's theory espouses and defends a case for a constitutional and democratic order with a social market economy that would be humane and compassionate. It advances a case for greater equality without sacrificing individual liberty. It revives the optimism of constant and uninterrupted growth, a faith of the early liberals. It hopes to ensure that its beneficial effects would not merely trickle down to the worse-off sections of the society but would continually and procedurally elevate them. It is a liberal theory with a humane face.

The publication of *A Theory of Justice* provides, for the first time in the 20th century, a direct link between a fairly abstract, philosophical theory and particular policy recommendations in both the areas of right and distribution. Rawls unites the libertarian ideal of liberalism with economic egalitarianism of democratic socialism into a single theoretical frame, and thereby brings back liberalism into the centre of political debates and discussions. He is seen as an integral part of a new movement (in the United States) called New Egalitarianism.

Rawls's theory dominates the field of liberal political philosophy, not in the sense of commanding agreement but in the sense that later liberal theorists have defined themselves in opposition to Rawls. Very few people agree with all of what Rawls says. But his theory of 'justice as fairness' established the terrain upon which subsequent theorists and policy-makers have fought with one another. The libertarian and communitarian theorists, his toughest critics, have formulated their position in terms that make explicit reference to Rawlsian arguments. In many ways Rawls simply did define the agenda and still continues to do so. Even Rawls's most severe critics have acknowledged their debt to him. Right-wing libertarians like Nozick claim that political philosophers now must either work within Rawls's theory or explain why they cannot. Nozick has hailed *A Theory of Justice* as 'a powerful, deep, subtle, wide-ranging, systematic work in political and moral philosophy which has not seen its like since the writings of John Stuart Mill' and considers Rawlsian thought 'a fountain of illuminating ideas'. Leftists admit that Rawls is profoundly wrong but almost perfectly relevant. Rawls successfully compels attention to the point that theories of socialism without a critical moral philosophy are as undesirable as they are impossible. Social and moral philosophers have since been following Rawls's methodological suggestion of searching for reflective equilibrium by considering theoretical alternatives to one's own considered judgements. Even in moving away from Rawls, contemporary scholars are fully engaged with him. Amartya Sen has admitted his greatest intellectual debt to Rawls. When Sen goes in a quite different direction in focusing more on the extents of freedom rather than on the *means* of freedom, that is, Rawls's primary goods, he has done so on an explicit critique of Rawls. This is the enduring significance of Rawls's theoretical contribution.

From the mid-1980s Rawls began using the political and pragmatic concept of 'overlapping consensus' which has found widespread acceptance. Rawls in the 1990s repositioned liberalism on one of its oldest and most controversial concerns, viz, peaceful coexistence. To some extent, this position taken by Rawls has led him to tie up his conception of justice more to order than to autonomy or individuality. Rawlsian overlapping consensus today serves a very practical purpose in the context of identity politics and the contemporary dichotomy of secularism versus religious revivalism. In this sense, Rawls has become quite relevant to the modernizing and turbulent societies like India. To Rawl, it is reasonable to disagree about comprehensive doctrine like Catholicism, Islam, utilitarianism and so on. That is partly why it matters that people be free to choose which of them to pursue. But it is not reasonable to disagree about the political values of autonomy, freedom and equality. Someone who denies these political values is indeed outside the overlapping consensus. The consensus that counts is the consensus of reasonable comprehensive doctrines. But the tragedy of the Rawlsian legacy is that his famous conceptualization of the 'difference principle' having profound implications for social welfare policies has been virtually ignored in the developing countries like India since the 1990s, thanks to the overpowering influence of neo-liberalism and economic globalization.

However, the impact of Rawls's theorization is distinctly felt. He is recognized as the most important English-speaking philosopher of the 20th century. Through a mixture of bold experiment in metaphysical thinking, conceptual rigour, historical imagination and a sense of pragmatism, Rawls has, more or less, invented analytic political thought. In the later years of his life, Rawls was increasingly interested in the history of the western world and American history. He became interested in Abraham Lincoln, whom he especially admired as a great stateman who refused to compromise with evil. These interests are evident in his later works on justice between nations.

Notes

1. Obituary note in *The Times* (London), 27 November 2000.
2. Obituary note by Douglas Martin in *New York Times,* reprinted in *Frontline,* 20 December 2002.
3. Nalini Rajan, 'John Rawls', *Economic and Political Weekly,* 7 December 2002.
4. John Rawls, 'Justice as Fairness', *The Journal of Philosophy,* Vol. 54 (1957); John Rawls, 'Justice as Fairness', *Philosophical Review,* Vol. 57 (1958).
5. John Rawls, *A Theory of Justice*, Cambridge, Mass.: Belknap Press of Harvard University, 1971.
6. *A Theory of Justice*, ch II, sec. 24.
7. Op. cit., ch. II sec. 11.

8. Ibid.
9. Ibid., for a re-statement of the Second Principle, see John Rawls, 'The Basic Liberties and their Priority', *Tanner Lectures on Human Values,* Vol. III 1982; and also John Rawls, *Political Liberalism*, New York: Columbia University Press, 1993.
10. John Rawls, 'Justice as Fairness: Political not Metaphysical' *Philosophy and Public Affairs*, Vol. 14,1985.
11. Ibid.
12. Ibid.
13. John Rawls, *Political Liberalism*, New York: Columbia University Press, 1993.
14. Ibid.
15. Jean Hampton, *Political Philosophy: An Introduction*, Delhi: Oxford University Press, 1998, pp. 141–43.
16. Ibid.
17. Ibid.
18. Robert Nozick, *Anarchy, State and Utopia*, New York: Basic Book, 1974.
19. Ronald Dworkin, *Taking Rights Seriously*, Cambridge, Mass.: Harvard University Press, 1977; R. Dworkin, *Sovereign Virtue*, Cambridge, Mass.: Harvard University Press, 2000.
20. Bhabatosh Datta, *Social Justice in a Mixed Economy* (Professor Monimohan Sen Memorial Lecture, 1980) Calcutta: Calcutta University, 1982.
21. A.K. Sen, *Inequality Re-examined*, Cambridge, Mass.: Harvard University Press, 1992.
22. A McIntyre, *After Virtue*, Notre Dame, USA: University of Notre Dame Press, 1980; M. Sandel, *Liberalism and the Limits of Justice*, Cambridge, UK: Cambridge University Press, 1982; C. Taylor, *Sources of the Self: The Making of the Modern Identity*, Cambridge, Mass.: Harvard University Press, 1989; M. Walzer, *Spheres of Justice*, New York: Basic Books, 1983.
23. Iris Young, *Justice and the Politics of Difference*, Princeton, NJ: Princeton University Press, 1990; Seyla Behnabib and Drucilla Cornell, *Feminism as Critique*, Minneapolis: University of Minnesota Press, 1987; Alison Jagger, *Feminist Politics and Human Nature*, Totowa: Rowman and Allanheld, 1983; Rosemaire Tong, *Feminist Thought*, Boulder: Westview Press, 1989.
24. Afton Buchanan, *Marx and Justice*, London: Methuen, 1982.

4

Theorizing Social Justice Beyond Distributive Principles

M.P. Dube

The questions of justice have been central to political life since time immemorial. John Rawls, the most important and influential liberal theorist of justice in recent decades, maintained that justice is the first of the virtues of social institutions in the way that truth is of scientific theories. It has been the subject of intense argument during the last quarter of 20th century and onwards. The idea of justice is generally distinguished between formal and substantive senses. In the formal sense, justice is correct weighting and proportion in judgments. The core element of the idea of justice is that like cases should be treated alike. It is a rule of logical impartiality. On the other hand, what counts as like cases and what involves equal treatments are domains of substantive principles. What substantive principles are appropriate in particular situations and what they imply has been debated since ancient times. Today the most significant kinds of justice are: procedural or unpatterned and distributive or patterned or social justice. Procedural theories of justice uphold the 'rule of law'; justice is concerned with rule-following. The main concern of justice for proceduralists is not a teleocratic order, rather maintaining procedural rules to provide conditions for individual freedom.[1] The most important procedural justice theories are Friedrich Hayak's commutative account of justice and Nozick's entitlement theories. But distributive justice has become the principal normative concern of modern political life. It has been defined as a question of equity in the distribution of social goods. Brighouse rightly claims that 'the fundamental question is this: how and to what end, should a just society distribute the various benefits. (resources, opportunities, and freedoms) it produces, and the burdens, (costs, risks, and unfreedoms) required to maintain it?'[2]

The most of the 20th century justice theorizing is concerned with the ideal rational conditions in which individuals come to a decision about the manner of distribution in society. Distributive principles dominated the scene specially since 1971 with the publication of John Rawls's book. Distributive justice deals with the distribution of benefits and burdens 'to each according to his due or fare allocation of burdens and benefits in society.' There are various principles that determine 'due'. Each principle can be formulated in the form of rights, deserts, needs, services, work, moral worth, ability, skill, or status, and so forth.[3] These principles can be sub-divided into desert and non-desert-oriented distributive principles. There is no problem with desert-oriented distributive principles because a person with merit worthy activity or a valuable quality should be rewarded in relation to that activity or quality. But most contentious are non-desert oriented distributive principles. Since the 1970s, much attention has fallen to these principles of which a larger bulk of contemporary justice theorizing is based on contractarian claims and needs.

The contractarian arguments have dominated the literature on social justice. There are two forms of contractarian arguments. They are justice as mutual advantage and justice as impartiality. Justice as mutual advantage arguments were advanced by Gauthier and Buchanan.[4] In theorizing distributive justice, they advance a sophisticated form of argument of rational choice. To them justice is an outcome of a mutual bargaining process among individuals in an initial position. They regard justice as mutual advantage. It is essentially a hypothetical social contract account. On the other hand, John Rawls, Barry and Scanlon[5] regard justice as impartiality. In Rawl's theory, justice is not seen as an outcome of a mutual bargaining process, as in Gauthier. It is the outcome of rational agreement between discreet individuals in an original position. To him justice is 'the appropriate division of social advantages'. However, Michael Walzer and Miller[6] attempt to establish a plural concept of justice.

John Rawls develops a fair way of developing such principles of distribution. Rawls thinks that an acceptable theory of justice must not depend on moral foundations which are widely disputed among reasonable people. To him utilitarianism and ordinary notions of merit are disputed among reasonable people. As such they cannot be considered as basis of a theory of justice. The basic idea in Rawls is 'to identify a fair arrangement in society for all parties to agree to without knowing how it will affect them.' It will cut out the possibility of arbitrariness in decision about justice.[7] For Rawls, justice should not reflect or re-enforce arbitrary chance or interests, but rather should aim to nullify them for the sake of basic fairness. His initial task, and primary innovation, was to evolve a device to achieve this nullification. For this he conceived an 'original position'. The 'original position' allows individuals to choose principles for organization of justice in society behind 'veil of ignorance' – a form of rational disinterestedness. Rawls's original contract is not 'as one to enter a particular society or to set up a particular form of government. Rather the guiding idea that the principles of justice for the basic structure of society are the object of the original agreement.[8] Thus, the principles of justice for basic structure of society are the object of the original agreement.

Rawls maintains that justice regulates the distribution of primary goods. The primary goods include basic rights and liberties, powers and offices, income and wealth, the bases of self-respect and leisure. The distribution of these goods is regulated by two principles, the first of which has lexical priority over the second.[9] The first principle holds that basic rights and liberties are distributed in a suitably fair way, income and wealth and the rest should be distributed equally unless the unequal distribution would increase the share going to the least well off.

Rawls's is an egalitarian vision of justice. It combines values of equality and liberty in a single conception. These principles are ones that free and equal persons could accept as a fair basis for social cooperation.[10] Brian Barry also follows John Rawls. He emphasizes the need for impartiality in the contractualist method of constructing principles of justice. His central argument is that we should agree on the rules of distributive justice while remaining impartial to different notions of the good life individuals have.[11] To both Barry and Scanlon, impartiality reflects a commitment to equality. To them impartiality is primarily a requirement on the moral and legal rules of society. Disagreeing with John Rawls,

Michael Walzer says that there cannot be a single distributive criteria which can be applied to different spheres of society. His theory of justice identifies different distributive criteria for different social spheres. Justice requires that spheres should not intermix or try to dominate other spheres. Walzer distinguishes between simple equality and complex equality. While in simple equality there is one dominant good which all spheres acclimatize to, in complex equality there is multiplicity or plurality of goods in different spheres. Plurality is maintained by preventing conversion between different goods. The dominance of any one good in all spheres must be prevented for the cause of justice. Walzer talks about relative autonomy of social spheres. He gives a plural and differentiated account of justice.

The liberal egalitarians have been attacked both by Robert Nozick and F.A. Von Hayak.[12] In their view, justice is not a matter of how benefits or burdens are distributed, but a matter of protecting individual rights to resources. To them justice involves extensive rights to private property, such that only very minimal taxation is ever legitimate. Moreover, its grounds must be related to the good of those who are being taxed. They maintain that the concept of distributive justice implies an agency entitled to achieve it, which is incompatible with the individual liberty. To them goods and opportunities are justly distributed when they are in the hands of their rightful owners.

Nozick advances an 'entitlement theory of justice in holdings'. His entitlement theory of justice consists of three principles:

1. A person who acquires a holding in accordance with the principle of justice in acquisition is entitled to that holding.
2. A person who acquires a holding in accordance with the principle of justice in transfer, from someone else entitled to the holding, is entitled to the holding.
3. No one is entitled to a holding except by (repeated) application of 1 and 2.[13]

He explains the principle of justice in acquisition that A is entitled to X, if nobody else is entitled to X and if in taking X, A does not make anyone else's condition worse. Here justice in acquisition and justice in transfer does not specify a pattern of distribution rather these specify a set of procedures for justice. Nozick's justice is concerned with historical entitlement theory. 'We have to know how that distribution came to be, that is, whether the principles of justice in acquisition and in transfer have been followed'.[14] To

Nozick principles of justice in transfer is that it must be based on consent of the parties and no one be coerced.

Hayek gives primacy to freedom of individuals. Justice is concerned with maintaining procedural rules to provide the conditions for individual freedom. Intentional acts of restraint, interference or coercion is injustice. The Hayekian scheme implies beliefs about the importance of individualism, the liberty and rights of individuals, the significance of the free market economy, and a more limited conception of the constitutional state.[15]

The distributive principles of justice have been challenged by various theorists during the 1990s and onwards; the sole emphasis on distribution without an examination of the underlying causes of the mal-distributions was not acceptable to several contemporary political theorists. Iris Young, Nancy Frazer, Axel Honneth and Charles Taylor[16] argue that while justice must be concerned with classic issues of distribution, it must also address the process that constructs mal-distribution. To them individual and social recognition, rather than simply fair process for the distribution of goods and benefits, are the key elements of attaining justice. They discuss the injustices in the real world. Their central concern is recognition. They argue that 'a lack of recognition in the social and political realms, demonstrated by various forms of insults, degradation and devaluation at both individual and cultural level, inflicts damage to oppressed individuals and communities in the political and cultural realms'.[17] To them it is the foundation for distributive injustice; therefore the social context in which unjust distributions exist becomes much more significant. Young says that the examination of social, cultural, symbolic, and institutional conditions, underlying unjust distribution is an important component of justice. She says that 'while distributional issues are crucial to a satisfactory conclusion of justice, it is a mistake to reduce social justice to distribution'.[18] A lack of recognition of group differences determines unjust distributions. She argues that 'distributional injustice comes directly out of social structures, cultural beliefs and institutional contexts. If distributional differences are constituted, in part, by social, cultural, economic, and political processes, any examination of justice needs to include discussions of the structures, practices, rules, norms, language, and symbols that mediate social relations.'[19] For Young, distribution is not the only problem; a concept of justice needs to focus more on elimination of institutionalized domination and oppression, particularly of those who represent difference and remain un-, mis-, or mal-recognized.[20]

Likewise, Nancy Frazer also argues that justice is 'bivalent'. It requires to give attention to both distribution and recognition. The distribution of resources and recognition both are equally and independently important. Both are distinct, though often linked in practice. She argues that culture is a legitimate and necessary terrain of struggle – a sight of justice in its own right, yet also deeply tied to economic inequality. She focuses on both the structural nature of the construction of the subordinate and disrespected identities and communities, and on the mal-distribution experienced by these subjects. To her the recognition – redistribution dilemma is centred on the problem of 'group differentiation'. In struggling against cultural injustice, the politics of recognition tends to promote the specificity of social groups, while the politics of redistribution works to undermine such specificity. While former is primarily affirmative the latter is transformative. Sometimes these two modes of politics create problems for social groups that have both the traits. Frazer tries to resolve this dilemma between conferring respect upon misrecognized groups (recognition) and transferring resources to the under privileged (distribution) by endorsing an across – the – board transformative approach. Thus, to examine the context of oppression, to understand and find remedy for existing injustices are the key issues of the Fazer's concept of justice. In the political realm, she calls for 'participatory parity' of all affected parties for justice. Frazer says that justice requires three conditions to be fulfilled:

(a) Formal legal equality: that is there must be no legal discrimination against women, ethnic minorities, homosexuals and so on.
(b) The distribution of resources must be such as to ensure participants' independence and voice.
(c) Institutionalized cultural patterns of interpretation and evaluation expressing equal respect for all participants and ensure equal opportunity for achieving social esteem.[21]

Understanding the social norms, language, and mores is key to the understanding of recognitional injustice in the social and cultural realm. She says that cultural injustice is 'rooted in patterns of representation, interpretation and communication'.[22]

For Frazer, misrecognition is an 'institutionalized relation of social subordination, rather than an individual experience.' She claims that a general practice of cultural domination, a pattern of non-recognition and disrespect are three processes of misrecognition. Unlike Frazer, Taylor and Honneth focus on the psychological nature of recognition. Taylor argues that self-worth comes from the recognition given by others. 'Misrecognition can inflict harm; can be a form of oppression imprisoning someone in a false, distracted, and reduced mode of being.' For Taylor, adequate recognition involves treating others in ways that confirm and affirm their distinctive identities. He argued that 'difference blind' liberalism is deficient to meet the human demand for identity. To him, 'Canon wars in higher education' and 'Canadian constitutional crises' are examples of the 'politics of recognition', in which 'people seek to transform the ways in which they are being seen and esteemed by others, and so to satisfy the deeply rooted human need to be recognized as the bearer of distinctive identity.'[23]

For Honneth, recognition involves valuable qualities of individuals or groups. And injustice is felt in the first instance as a denial of inter-subjective recognition that violently disrupts a subject's relationship to herself, whether through the violation of body, the refusal of basic moral respect or legal protection, or the denigration of individual or collective ways of life. What is crucial in the analysis of injustice is not the inflicting of the pain, but the perception of misrecognition on the part of the victim; that is, injustice is a psychological condition. For both Honneth and Taylor psychological recognition is crucial element of justice.[24]

In addition to distribution and recognition, there is a third dimension to the concept and practice of justice, namely procedural justice. Procedural justice is the fair and equitable institutional process of a state. Frazer, Honneth and Young insist on an integrated approach to the understanding of justice. Young argues that 'justice must focus on the political process as a way to discuss both inequitable distribution of social goods and the condition undermining social recognition.'[25] democratic and participatory decision-making procedures are both an element of, and condition for, social justice. Young argues that a concept of justice needs to focus on the elimination of institutionalized domination and oppression. For this justice must focus on institutions and political processes as a way to address injustices based on inequitable distribution and misrecognition.

Frazer also advocates integration of procedural justice with distributive and recognitional theory of justice. She argues that 'when patterns of disrespect and disesteem are institutionalized, for example, in law, social welfare, medicines, public education, and/or the social practices and group mores that structure everyday interaction, they impede parity of participation, just as surely as do distributive inequities.'[26] Frazer argues for 'parity of participation' She is of the firm conviction that 'to remedy mal-distribution we must focus on politico-economic restructuring; but such considerations will only come along with recognition, where the remedy is in cultural and symbolic changes in how we regard the presently misrecognized, only then will participatory parity and procedural justice be attained.'[27]

These notions of justice based on distribution, recognition and democratic participation are not contradictory, rather they are integrated. David Schlosberg rightly comments that 'both distributive inequity and misrecognition hamper real participation in political and cultural institutions. Issues of justice are not just bivalent but trivalent. Improved participatory mechanism can help meliorate both other forms of injustice; but those other forms of injustice must be addressed in order to improve participation.'[28]

Amartya Sen[29] and Martha Nussbaum[30] expand the conception of justice beyond John Rawls (distributive justice) by advancing the 'capability approach'. Rawls's conception of justice is the distribution of the social primary goods. For him social primary goods are the criteria for measuring well-being, where as economists measure relative wealth of different countries in gross domestic product, in terms of money or make interpersonal comparisons in terms of preference satisfaction. To them a person having a higher level of preference satisfaction is better off than those having less. As an alternative to above for measuring well-being, Amartya Sen and Nussbaum developed capability approach.

Sen says that people differ enormously in their ability to convert income or goods into welfare. He says that a good theory of well-being should take into account not only the primary goods the persons respectively hold, but also the relevant personal characteristics that govern the conversion of primary goods into the person's ability to promote her/his ends.[31]

Sen and Nussbaum have developed a theory of justice that focuses on the capacities necessary for individuals and groups to function and flourish. Along with distribution of goods, the focus is on how those goods are transformed into the functioning and flourishing of individuals and communities. The focus is to judge how those distributions affect our well-being and how we 'function'.

Amartya Sen objects to fair distribution on the ground that individuals born with different physical and psychological propensities will generally be unequally efficient transformers of resources into whatever goals they might seek. Therefore, we should look beyond distribution and see to what extent individuals are able to be and do with their primary goods allotments, given their circumstances. Capabilities are about a person's freedom to do and to be what they choose in the context of a given society; the focus is on individual agency, functioning and well-being, rather than more traditional distributive indicators. Our concern is not in what amount of goods we get, rather the capabilities that translate the basic goods into the functioning of human life. To Sen, capabilities rather than functionings are the proper measure of well-being. Functioning refers to various doings and beings. The concept of functionings ... reflects the various things a person may value doing or being – varying from the basic (being adequately nourished) to the very complex (being able to take part in the life of the community).[32]

Sen argues that while making normative evaluation, the focus should not be on what people can consume, or on their incomes, rather on what they are able to be and to do. He insists on taking note not only of the ownership of the primary goods and resources, but also of interpersonal differences in converting them into the capability to live well. Indeed, he has tried to argue in favour of judging individual advantage in terms of the respective capabilities, which the person has, to live the way he or she has reason to value. This approach focuses on the substantive freedoms that people have, rather than only on the particular outcomes with which they end up.[33]

According to Nussbaum, 'to see each thing flourish as the sort of thing it is', is the basis of capability approach. Here it is not important that how much we have, 'but whether we have what is necessary to enable a more fully functioning life as we choose to live it.'

There is indexing problem in capability approach because there are unaccountable numbers of capabilities that people may have. Sen has not prepared a well-defined list of capabilities. He insists on public discussion, flexibility, and context specificity in making a list of capabilities. On the other hand, Nussbaum tries to address the indexing problem. She proposes a list of 10 capabilities, which she claims as universal, although she is not against the contextual modification of the list. These 10 capabilities between them constitute a threshold below which it is particularly unjust for a society to let any individual fall. Her list includes:[34]

1. *Life:* being able to live to the end of human life of normal length.
2. *Bodily health*: being able to have good health, nourishment and shelter.
3. *Bodily integrity*: being able to move about freely, to have opportunities for sexual satisfaction, reproductive choices, and being able to be secure against physical violations.
4. *Senses, imagination and thought*: being able to imagine, think and reason in a 'truly human' way, and having the education necessary to exercise these capabilities.
5. *Emotions:* 'in general, (being able) to love, to grieve, to experience longing, gratitude and justified anger'.
6. *Practical reason*: being able to form a conception of the good and engage in critical reflection about the planning of one's life.
7. *Affiliation:* (a) being able to live with and toward others, to recognize and show concern for other human beings; (b) having the social bases of self-respect and non-humiliation; being able to be treated as a dignified being with equal worth.
8. *Other species*: beings able to live with concern for and in relation to animals, plants and the world of nature.
9. *Play*: being able to laugh, play and recreate.
10. *Control over environment*: (a) *Political:* being able to participate effectively in political choices that govern one's life; (b) *Material:* having real opportunities to hold property, seek employment on an equal basis with others, having freedom from unwarranted search and seizure.

The 'capability approach', distribution, recognition and participation are linked together. Robeyns[35] argues that the capability theory can accommodate both issues of re-distribution and recognition and yet is broader than even Frazer's bi-violent or tri-violent approach. However, she remarks that the capability approach is a framework of thought, a normative tool, but it is not a fully specified theory that gives us complete answers to all our normative questions. It is not a complete theory of justice. Theorists Wolff and de-Shalit[36] have tried to modify the approach. They argue that it also matters whether people can sustain their functioning, and that risk and vulnerability also need to be taken into account. However, the capability approach has been extremely influential in development economics and has added a new dimension to the concept of social justice.

In recent years, issues of environment have become an integral part of the discourse of justice. The reason is that the environmental issues are very much political in nature. Dobson[37], environmental philosopher, rightly remarks that 'the natural world – normally invisible in political theory – affects and is affected by political decisions in a way which makes it necessary to consider it a site for political activity.' Today, environmental and ecological justice have become very important themes of discussion for social and political theorists and movements. Central to environmental justice is the distribution of the goods and bads, but, at the same time, it is tied to some discussion of recognition, political participation and capabilities at both the individual and community level. In the USA, it is used to cover the antitoxics movement and the movement against environmental racism. Generally things like, sewage, industrial waste sites, municipal and hazardous waste dumps have been concentrated near the working poor, the minorities, deprived sections and politically disempowered groups. The movement against environmental racism in the USA popularized the term 'environmental justice'. It emphasizes that there is a connection between environmental risk and poverty, that there is also connection between race and environmental hazards. Generally, deprived sections bear the brunt of the pollution.

Today, the neoliberal model of globalization and development has turned the inequity from bad to worse, both between the North and the South, and between the elite and the impoverished in Southern nations. It creates a threat to food security and sustainable livelihood of deprived sections, specially tribals, women and children. It drains off natural resources for economic gains. Current development process has devastated natural resources and habitats, created environmental refugees and is posing a serious threat to the continuation of life on the earth itself.

Along with equity, demand for recognition and respect for cultures, tradition, local knowledge and expertise, and ways of economic, social and religious life, for authentic participation and capability of functioning of both affected individuals and communities, constitute the elements of environmental justice. In fact, demand for equal, informed and respectful participation in decision-making is central to environmental justice.

Prior to the development of the welfare state, many societies had made provision for the support of their vulnerable members through religious and charitable institutions. These provisions were not regarded as a requirement of justice, rather a matter of charity. It was during the 20th century that the argument for support centred around justice. Charity, such as assistance to the sick, the old, and those in poverty, are regarded as a duty. Such duties of charity are private and a matter of individual choice, whereas duties of justice are generally taken to be enforceable by the state. In traditional theories of justice, the subject of justice is basic structure of society, the way that major institutions, such as the political system, the economic system, and the family, interact to shape people's life prospects. As individuals, people are not bound by the principles in their everyday life, that is, people are free to behave in their personal life as they like. It is Gandhi who tries to synthesize tradition and modernity by presenting a very comprehensive view of justice. For Gandhi, not only political, social, economic and cultural institutions should be based on principles of justice, the personal behaviour of the individual also must conform to the principles of justice based on truth and non-violence. Gandhi's views on social justice support a programme of social action: 'the nature of man is divine; through service to mankind the individual may realize his divinity, and with that will come spiritual freedom and a sense of his unity with all being.'[38]

To Gandhi, institutions, in a civilization where there is multiplication of wants, lack of self restraint and declining of moral and spiritual depth, cannot be just. There is a need to cure the modern civilization. He was of the view that if human beings developed moral character, they may succeed in taking the craze out of technology, and making it into a means of freedom, equality, and universal happiness. To him, the development of moral character has to begin with self-reform or self-rule, i.e. *swaraj*. The truth and non-violence are the core of Gandhi's concept of *swaraj*. The truth instead of freedom is the Gandhi's starting point.

Gandhi believed that universe is regulated by supreme intelligence or principle that is Truth. It is embodied in all living beings in the form of self-conscious soul or spirit. The spirit constitutes man's essence. Gandhi believed in the doctrine of man's oneness with God and humanity. The moment a man awakens to the spirit within, he cannot remain violent; the passions, selfishness and violence do not belong to the immortal spirit of man. 'Since all men', argued Gandhi, 'partake in divine essence, they are ultimately one'. They are not only equal, but identical. Since all mankind in essence are alike, what one man is capable of achieving is possible for all to attain. As such, violence has no place in relations amongst mankind; love is the only proper form of relation between them. It is 'the law of our being', of 'our species'. Love implies care and concern for others and total dedication to the cause of 'wiping every tear from every eye'. The immediate service of all mankind becomes a necessary part of the activities of human beings. Negatively, it implies non-violence. 'In its negative form it means not injuring any living being whether by body or mind. In its positive form, *ahimsa* means the largest love, the greatest charity. The complete non-violence is complete absence of ill will and active non-violence is goodwill towards all life. He equated it with humility, forgiveness, love, charity, selflessness, fearlessness, strength, non-attachment, meekness and innocence.

Gandhi saw himself as 'philosophical anarchist'. He had intense distrust of political authority. He favoured 'enlightened anarchy where everyone is his own ruler, and there is no political power because there is no state.' To Gandhi, state is not an ideal association. It is an 'unfortunate necessity'. It represents violence in a concentrated and organized form. It speaks in the language of compulsion and uniformity. It weakens its subjects' 'spirit of initiative', freedom, creativity and self-help. Gandhi said, 'An increase in the power of the state does the greatest harm by destroying individuality, which lies at the root of all progress. The state represents violence in a concentrated and organized form. The individual has a soul, but as the state is a soulless machine, it can never be weaned from violence to which it owes its very existence,'[39] State, therefore, should be organized in such a way so as to have its activities employ coercion as little as possible and that as large an area of human life as possible is left to voluntary efforts. A truly non-violent state is composed of small scale self-governing and relatively self-sufficient, politically empowered village communities relying on moral and social pressure and running their own affairs on the basis of local resources and local needs. The police are not a means of coercion. They are basically social workers enjoying the confidence and support of the local community and relying not on brute force but on moral suasion and public opinion to enforce the law. Crime is not an offence requiring punishment rather it is to be treated as a disease requiring understanding and help. Decisions are to be taken by the majority but without overriding the minority. No one should be compelled to do things contrary to his/her conscience.[40]

A Gandhian state is committed to *sarvodaya*, the upliftment of all human beings. It is concerned for the downtrodden – the *daridranarayan*. His emphasis on *'daridranarayan'* and *'swadeshi'* was an outright rejection of capitalism as the instrument of development and modernization. This concern for the downtrodden gives Gandhi's thought its universal relevance in all times and climes. To Gandhi private property is immoral; it denies the 'identity' and oneness of all men. Roots of exploitation, sensual indulgence and contempt for one's fellow men lie in private property. In Gandhi's view, it is a sin against humanity to posses superfluous resources when others cannot even meet their basic needs. Since the institution of private property already exists and men are attached to it, it was suggested by Gandhi that the rich should take only what they need and hold the rest in trust for the community.

The tactics of *satyagraha*, non-violent resistance to injustice and wrong, can be used to develop the capability for functioning. It can be used to end human misery and degradation. Gandhi said:

> My humble occupation has been to show people how they can solve their own difficulties … . My work will be finished if I succeed in carrying conviction to the human family, that every man or woman, however weak in body is the guardian of his or her self-respect and liberty.

In realization of justice, distribution, recognition, participation, capability, and environmental and ecological components put together, Gandhian ideas need to be made the basic foundation on which just relations between man, nature and society should be founded and sustained. The need to create just order demands adherence to Gandhian ideas to enable man and nature to live in peace and harmony with mutual respect and recognition.

Notes

1. Andrew Vincent, *The Nature of Political Theory,* Oxford: Oxford University Press, 2004, pp. 113–14.

2. Harry Brighouse, *Justice*, Cambridge: Polity Press, 2004, p. 2.
3. David Miller, Social Justice, Oxford: Oxford University Press, 1979, p. 20.
4. James Buchanan, *The Limits of Liberty: Between Anarchy and Leviathan*, Chicago: University of Chicago Press, 1975; D. Gauthier; *Morals by Agreement*, Oxford: Oxford University Press, 1986.
5. John Rawls, *A Theory of Justice*, Cambridge, Mass.: Belknap Press of Harvard University, 1971; Brian Barry, *Justice as Impartiality*, Oxford: Oxford University Press, 1975; T., Scanlon, *The Significance of Choice*, in Sterling M. McMurrin (ed.), *The Tanner Lectures on Human Values* Vol. 8, Salt Lake City: University of Utah Press, 1989.
6. Michael Walzer; *Spheres of Justice: A Defence of Pluralism and Equality*, Oxford: Oxford University Press, 1983; David Miller, *Principles of Social Justice*, Cambridge, Mass.: Harvard University Press, 1999.
7. Rawls, supra, pp. 101–2.
8. Ibid., p. 11.
9. Ibid., p. 243.
10. Andrew Vincent, supra. pp. 124–26.
11. Barry Brian, *Justice as Impartiality*, Oxford: Oxford University Press, 1975
12. Robert Nozick; *Anarchy, State and Utopia*, Oxford: Oxford University Press, 1974; Friedrich von Hayek, *The Road to Serfdom*, Abingdon, UK: Routledge and Sons, 1944; *Law, Legislation and Liberty*, Abingdon, UK: Routledge, 1976.
13. R. Nozick, supra p. 151.
14. Brighouse, supra p. 96.
15. Andrew Vincent, supra p. 114.
16. Iris Young, *Justice and the Politics of Difference*, Princeton, NJ: Princeton University Press, 1990; *Inclusion and Democracy*, Oxford: Oxford University Press, 2000; Nancy Frazer, *Justice Interruptus: Critical Reflections on the Postsocialist Condition*, New York: Routledge, 1977; 'Social Justice in the Age of Identity Politics: Redistribution, Recognition and Participation' in Grethe B Peterson (ed.), *The Tanner Lectures on Human Values*, Vol. 19, Salt Lake City: University of Utah Press 1998; Axel Honneth, *The Struggle for Recognition: The Moral Grammar of Social Conflicts*, Cambridge, Mass.: MIT Press, 1995; Charles Taylor, *Multiculturalism*, Princeton, NJ: Princeton University Press, 1994.
17. David Schlosberg, Defining Environmental Justice, Oxford: Oxford University Press, 2007, p. 14.
18. Ibid., p. 14.
19. Iris Young, *Justice and the Politics of Difference*, Princeton, NJ: Princeton University Press, 1990, p. 22.
20. Ibid., pp. 2–5.
21. Nancy Frazer, 'Social Justice in the Age of Identity Politics: Redistribution, Recognition and Participation' in Grethe B Peterson (ed.), *The Tanner*

Lectures on Human Values, Vol. 19, Salt Lake City: University of Utah Press, 1998, pp. 30–31.

22. Ibid., p. 7.
23. *Oxford Handbook of Political Theory*, 2006, pp. 451–55.
24. Schlosberg, supra, pp. 17–18.
25. Iris Young, *Justice and the Politics of Difference*, Princeton, NJ: Princeton University Press, 1990, pp. 20–23.
26. Nancy Frazer, 'Social Justice in the Age of Identity Politics: Redistribution, Recognition and Participation' in Grethe B Peterson (ed.), *The Tanner Lectures on Human Values*, Vol. 19, Salt Lake City: University of Utah Press, 1998, p. 26.
27. David Schlosberg, *Defining Environmental Justice*, Oxford: Oxford University Press, 2007, pp. 27–28.
28. Ibid.
29. Amartya Sen, 'Well-being, Agency and Freedom', *The Journal of Philosophy*, 82(4), 1985, pp. 169–221; *Commodities and Capabilities*, Oxford: Oxford University Press, 1999; *Development as Freedom*, New York: Oxford University Press, 1999.
30. Martha C. Nussbaum, *Women and Human Development: The Capability Approach*, Cambridge, UK: Cambridge University Press, 2000; *Frontiers of Justice: Disability, Nationality, Species Membership*, Cambridge, Mass.: Harvard University Press, 2006.
31. Amartya Sen, *Development as Freedom*, New York: Oxford University Press,1999, p. 74.
32. Ibid., p. 75.
33. Sen's lecture delivered in Stockholm, 8 December 1998.
34. Martha C. Nussbaum, *Women and Human Development: The Capability Approach*, Oxford: Oxford University Press, 2000, pp. 78–80.
35. Ingrid Robeyns, 'Sen's Capability Approach and Gender Inequality', in *Capability, Freedom and Equality* (eds.) Bina Agarwal et al., Oxford: Oxford University Press, 2996, pp. 70–100.
36. J. Wolff and A. de-Shalit, *Disadvantage*, Oxford: Oxford University Press, 2007.
37. Andrew Dobson,*Green Political Thought*, London: Routledge, 1995.
38. Dennis Dalton, 'Hindu Political Philosophy', in George Klosko (ed.), *Oxford Handbook of the History of Political Philosophy*, 2011, p. 817.
39. M.K. Gandhi; *Democracy: Real and Deceptive*, Ahmedabad, Navjivan Press, 1969, pp. 28–29.
40. M.P. Dube, *Gandhi: The Practical Idealism and Strategies of Inclusion,* New Delhi: Pentagon Press, 2011, pp. 3–6.

5

Affirmative Action and Justice

Ramashray Roy

Inequality in the distribution of wealth, income and opportunity is one of the basic features of all societies irrespective of time and space. However, when inequality is considered to be unfair and unjust, the need to eliminate poverty, especially of the needy and the excluded, becomes urgent. When this happens, a problem, which was earlier subsumed under social and political category, assumes a political coloration; it becomes now subsumed under political category. As a political category, it prompts what we call affirmative action on the part of the state to address the problem of the needy and the excluded.

Affirmative action is inspired by the realization of essentially two factors: one, that inequality in the distribution of wealth, income and opportunity is arbitrary and two, that the needy and the excluded are unable to do very much on their own to improve their existential situation. It is so because by the very definition, they lack requisite resources, including political power to do so. These two realizations prompt the government to do something to correct the injustice and unfairness involved with unequal distribution of wealth, income and opportunity.

Both these inequalities are not only unjust and unfair but they also constantly engender further injustice. Thus, inequality stands in need of justification and the only possible justification for inequality is to improve the condition of the poor and the excluded. What is needed to improve the lot of the poor and the needy is, on the one hand, development and, on the other, extending a helping hand to them through affirmative action so that they can help themselves.

What affirmative action aims at, in effect, is to substitute one type of injustice with another; what is involved in affirmative action is to take recourse to distributive politics, which is the dominant characteristic of non-unanimous politics. It manifests in the everyday sense that taxes of some go to supplement the resources of others. It takes money out of the pocket of one person and transfers to another on the ground that the need of beneficiary is greater than the one who pays. A.S. Jasay (1997: 11) puts it: 'This forces us, sometimes with great severity, to do what we would not freely choose to do and forbear from what we would choose … . In particular, it takes the lion's share of individually earned and owned resources and uses them in ways that the individual in question would not have chosen'.

The individual, who is forced to abstain from doing what he urgently needed to do, would feel that injustice has been done to him. He would think so because he has been deprived from doing something with the help of what he has earned legitimately and to which he has a just title. Affirmative action then confronts us with two quite opposite and contradictory ideas of justice. We are faced with a frontal confrontation between two claims of justice: justice as conceived by those who have to empty their pockets to fill the pockets of others who they do not even know and justice as something that enables the needy and the excluded to be in a position to overcome the pains of deprivation and destination.

It is quite obvious, then, that what we encounter here is the collision between two rival conceptions of justice. One conception holds that principles of just acquisition and entitlement set limits to distributive possibilities. If outcome of the application of the principles of just acquisition and entitlement is gross inequality, the toleration of such inequality is a price that has to be paid for justice. In contradiction to this, another conception underlies the fact that the principles of just distribution set limits to legitimate acquisition and entitlement. If the outcome of the principle of just distribution is interference – by means of taxation or such devices as eminent domain – with what has, up till now, been regarded in a society as legitimate acquisition and entitlement, the toleration of such interference is a price that has to be paid for justice (MacIntyre, 2007: 253).

The confrontation between two very different conceptions of justice is real and poses a challenge to us all. The philosophic/theoretical problem caused by this confrontation needs to be resolved, it is true. However, it involves turning our back to the worldview in which the philosophy undergirding the idea of affirmative justice is embedded, whether it is possible right now to do so is a question that should not concern us here. What is necessary is to have a close look on how effective affirmative action has been.

There are several ways in which the principle of justices can be enunciated. One of these ways was the manner in which traditional societies approached the problem of justice. It was recognized that the idea of the justice was involved, on the one side, with nature of man and, on the other side, the actually observed inequalities in all societies. The traditional understanding underlined the fact that inequality was impossible to eliminate. What one could do was to find an approximately adequate solution to the problem that arises because of the dynamic interaction between the two referents of justice. Traditional societies found this solution in a distinctive conception of equality; they considered equality in terms of spiritual and moral equality by virtue of men being the children of God. This meant that while human beings are equal with regard to the potentiality of their nature, they are unequal through the mode of realization achieved in each individual case. Thus, individuals may be unequal in worldly possessions, but they were treated as equal in moral and spiritual terms.

However, the traditional worldview was jettisoned and was replaced by the modern worldview, which refused to recognize anything else but the visible world and its human residents. Men came to be engaged in the secular enterprise of creating a human order in which the question of God became obsolete. The obsolescence of the question of God did create a void. However, as Ackerman (1981) assures us, 'there is no need to be overwhelmed by the void. We may create our own meanings.' Thus allows, in a world devoid of divine presence, only a deontological approach to the question of justice. 'Only a world ungoverned by a purposeless order leaves principles of justice to human construction and conceptions of the good to individual choice' (Sandel, 1982).

And when human construction of the principle of justice with the aid of deontological approach takes form, it can only reflect difference of opinion even while they are couched in a theoretical language. Thus, when the idea of justice is robbed of its anchor in the transcendent entity, its formulation becomes various. This is well reflected by three different versions of the principle of justice by John Rawls, R. Nozick and Amartya Sen. Starting from the same common ground of man as a free and rational being, they come to different formulations of the principle of justice. Note for example, that all of them are opposed, in one form or the other, to utilitarianism; they all call for right-based ethic and aim to secure the liberty of the individual more securely; all of them insist on treating man as an end, not as a means and on seeking principles of justice that embodies it; they all deny any social entity above or beyond the individuals who comprise it; and by the aspiration of a well ordered society, they all emphasize plurality and distinctness of persons (Rawls), or ' separateness of our existence' (Nozick, 1974).

Despite these commonalities, they arrive at different theories of justice. If Rawls's conception of justice permits social and economic inequality only to benefit the least well off, Nozick rules out distributive policies altogether, and Sen rejects both and insist on capability building. He also questions the wisdom of giving priority to liberty over poverty. If deontological approach of the theory of justice underlines 'separate existence of man', as empirical characterization of society, the construction of theories of justice that it yields are highly coloured by the aspirations of a well regulated and harmonious social order. Such a social order reflects the primacy of altruism over egoistic concerns. And yet how the two can be reconciled remains unanswered.

Denied as it is of any anchoring beyond what is visible, deontological approach to justice must see its manifestation in the equalization of life condition in terms of equality, as far as is possible, distribution of wealth, income and opportunity. Such a distribution will, it is hoped, provide equal opportunity to all to enjoy equality, dignity and self-determination, factors that ensure human flourishing. We should add to it the modern belief that opens up the pathways to human development, including the growth in moral sensibilities. Human flourishing signifies both material well-being and a fully developed moral sense; in short, 'virtuous materialism' as the basis of comfortable and happy life. This, in effect, amounts to what T.S. Elliot characterizes as 'a system so perfect that nobody needs to be good.'

India too embraced this ideal after Independence and immediately engaged in the act of transforming the old and tottering social order in accordance with the vision of modernity.

India declared herself a liberal democratic republic and framed a Constitution to confirm it. The Constitution assured all the citizens justice, social, economic and political. This assurance was addressed particularly to those who have historically been excluded and therefore are the needy in the true sense of the term. Three social groups – Scheduled Tribes (STs), Scheduled Castes (SCs) and Other Backward Classes (OBCs) – were identified for special dispensation in the form of affirmative action.

These groups needed to be actively assisted, first, for releasing them from the constraints that the traditional society had put on them and which had kept them subdued for ages, making them unable to stand on their own feet. They were, thus, prevented from competing on equal terms with the advanced sections of Indian society in order to solve the problems that their economically adverse condition created for them. Affirmative action was in response to this situation. It was aimed at achieving basically two purposes: reservation of jobs for them in public offices and institutions, and providing certain concessions and the creation of certain facilities to promote their rapid advance in society.

In adopting the strategy of affirmative action, India committed herself to the principle of just distribution that sets limits to legitimate acquisition and entitlement. Two specific purposes have driven the Indian State to embrace this conception of justice. One had to do specifically with the question of how best to remove poverty, the national scandal, while the other involved the need to equalize life conditions, as a necessary precondition for enjoying the blessings of the good life of modern conception. Looked at from this perspective, the two dimensions of affirmative action, in the larger context of distributive justice, need to be examined. One of these dimensions is, of course, the extent to which the needy and the excluded have been enabled to overcome the pains of deprivation and the other concerns the question of how far inequality and disparity have been eliminated.

It is not necessary to stress the fact that these two dimensions are intimately interlinked. Development is considered *sine qua non* for increasing the stock of goods and services; the increasing stock is to benefit even those who stand at the lower rungs of the economic ladder; and redistribution becomes necessary for ensuring that the benefits of development do, in fact, reach the needy and the excluded too. However, redistributive policies, especially those that aim at helping the needy and the excluded, must be supplemented by certain other measures. Accordingly, India has adopted what Rawls characterizes as liberal equality. How has India performed with regard to both empowering the deprived and depressed social groups and causing reduction in inequality in the distribution of wealth and income.

Income is one of the vital sources for ensuring welfare. There is a direct connection between income and education, which in turn, enhances the chances of upward status mobility. And development is *sine qua non* of access to education and its concomitants. The magnitude of the income earned depends on the level of education one has achieved. Also, education constitutes the central axis around which modernity is constructed. Almost all the central values of modernity, such as democracy, equality, mobility and the ability to define oneself, depend upon access to education. Also, higher levels of education are related with better health practices.

How do different social groups –STs, SCs, and OBCs – the three groups that are the beneficiaries of affirmative action, compare with the upper castes? One would expect that after impressive economic development during the last six decades, coupled with a vigorous and intensive exercise of affirmative action, there would be not only a general rise in the levels of income among these three groups, but also a marked degree of reduction in inequality and disparity. What do economic facts tell us? What they tell us is the same old story now repeated after six decades of impressive economic development: 'India's demographic structure is still heavily tilted in favour of the upper castes – whether in terms of the income they earn and jobs they hold' (Shukla et al., 2010: 21).

The reflection of this tilt can be seen in three different patterns of inequality and disparity. These patterns are indicative not only of the present situation; they also carry the intimation of not much change in the future. The first pattern reveals that the higher we go in the caste hierarchy, the share of income of each caste group becomes larger. This is indicated by the fact that while the upper castes, who comprise 34 per cent of the population, earn 45 per cent of the total income of India, the STs comprising 8 per cent of the population earn only 5 per cent and the SCs amounting to 6.8 per cent of the population can claim only 11.8 per cent of the income.

The situation improves in the case of the OBCs who with 41.1 per cent of the population earn 37 per cent of income. To look at it from another vantage point, given their low income levels, SC and ST households form a larger share of the lower income quartiles in the country: they comprise 41.9 per cent of the lowest income quartile and 32 per cent of the one just above the lowest one. They form only 12.2 per cent of the total of the total in the top quartile.

This pattern engenders yet another pattern that is inequality within each of the caste groups (ibid., 22). Since SCs and STs earn lower incomes, their level of education would be low and, therefore, they would have mostly low paid, unskilled jobs. This creates a vicious circle to break out of which becomes very difficult, if not impossible. Note, for instance, that an illiterate ST earn ₹ 22,456 per annum as compared to ₹ 85,023 per annum for a graduate ST, a difference of almost four times. Also noteworthy is the fact that most of the SCs and the STs live in rural areas where low paying jobs abound. This too means lower income for the poor and the needy.

It is quite a reflection on India's development strategy that even now 42.1 per cent of all households are still engaged in agriculture; they contribute only 31.2 per cent to the total income of the country. STs have the highest proportion (61.2%) of households engaged in agriculture. To put it differently, of the total households, 5 per cent are engaged in agriculture; they have only a total disposal income of 2.7 per cent of all households. The situation of the SCs is not any better. If a person from the SC groups is engaged in farm-related jobs, his income amounts to almost one-third of what another person from the same group engaged in profession and technical jobs gets (₹ 34,843 versus ₹ 1,13,745). However, the proportion of the illiterate ST persons greatly outnumbers the highly educated ones. Note, for example, that only 12 per cent of ST households have at least one graduate as against 34.4 per cent of upper castes households.

The third pattern is associated with whether a person lives in urban areas or in states with high income. Drawing from the data provided by Shukla et al. (Shukla et al., 2010: 62), households in low income states tend to have, on an average, income levels that are around one-fifth lower than the national average of ₹ 65,041. These states account for 41.1 per cent of the total households in the country and around 32.3 per cent of the total income. A household moving from a low income state to a higher income state earns higher income.

Households in high income states account for 21.5 per cent of the total households but only 29.6 per cent of the income. A rural ST household earns much less than those in, say, first class towns (₹ 37,615 versus ₹ 85,023). Similar is the situation of the SC households: ₹ 38,622 for a rural household versus ₹ 82,650 for an urban SC household.

In view of the fact that different caste groups have realized the value of education for status mobility, inequality in access to education exists in two important sense – utilization of existing educational institutions and cost still remains highly skewed, despite great expansion at all levels. It is still the upper castes who have greater access to education; for instance, only 1.5 per cent of the upper castes persons are illiterate as compared to 8.6 per cent of both the STs and the SCs. In terms of graduate and above education, the difference is almost three times.

What is all the more distressing is that the children of ST/SC do go to schools; however, they have to drop out in large numbers under economic compulsions. Also, the poor are forced to spend for education out of their pockets over ₹ 5,000 annually even in urban areas where educational facilities are concentrated.

This signifies that the poor people, belonging especially to ST/SC castes save less and become, therefore, vulnerable to contingencies of life. Also, interesting is the fact that as the level of education rises, the proportion of educational expenses also go up.

An illiterate ST household spends 2.5 per cent of its income on education as compared to 10 per cent spent by a graduate ST household. Given the strong relationship between education and health, rise in the educational level is not accompanied by a comparable rise in the expenditure on health; expenditure on health falls proportionately but not in absolute terms. Thus, the age-old inequality and disparity still persists, even if some of their strings may have broken through the noose of poverty and deprivation.

The sufferings of the poor and the needy are, however, compounded by their vulnerability to malnutrition and morality.

As the National Family Survey (2005–06) reveals, there are sharp regional and socio-economic divides in health outcomes with the lower castes, the poor and the less developed states bearing the burden of morality and mal-nutrition heavily. High rates of infant mortality and under-five mortality rates are, in general, inversely related with income. This means that the occurrence of child mortality is higher in poor families. The risks of mortality before the age of five are higher in girls than in boys among the SCs. STs and OBCs as compared to others.

Other darker dimensions of inequality and disparity are there. However, what has been so for said is enough to underline their starkness. Clearly, then, the launching of a myriad of plans, projects and programmes to uplift the needy and the excluded have not yet made them capable of standing on their feet. The progress in securing justice to them is still very slow, tardy and hesitant. Moreover, as Vikram Pathak (2009) reports, 21 Dalit women are raped and 11 Dalits murdered every week. More than half of Dalit students drop out before they reach class VIII; and untouchability is still rampant; in many hostels built especially for Dalit students, children do not know how the milk tastes.

The National Human Rights Commission receives more than 70,000 complaints in a year; the National Crime Bureau registered 27,000 cases of violence against Dalits in 2006 (Saxena, 2009). On top of all this, the state administrative machinery seems to be indifferent to programmes of social justice. It is not surprising, then, that a JNU sociology professor ruefully comments that 'all talk of justice is just talk.'

It is against this background that the confrontation between the two conceptions of justice, referred to earlier, has to be taken seriously. The effectiveness of affirmative action in ameliorating the conditions of the targeted groups is seriously in question. The issue now is, or should be: should we continue with the principle of justice that prescribes limits to legitimate acquisition and entitlement? It can be argued that it is too early to put the idea of affirmative justice under the critic's scalpel and pronounce that it is in the state of inanimation because of factors internal to it; it may be in a condition of inanition. It can, however, be invigorated if the pace of development becomes faster. This argument is fallacious for three different reasons.

First, there is no relationship between development and welfare. It is true that development adds to the stock of goods and services that are considered to be vital for the good life of modern conception, But, as Hirsch (1977: 60) makes it clear. Increase in resources (and thereby in the availability of goods) does nothing to increase welfare since wants increase correspondingly. The extent to which existing demands are satisfied may never increase welfare because wants rise commensurably with resources. So, economic advance appears as one of those hoax races that leaves the participants in the same place.

Second, affirmative action becomes necessary when the inability of the poor and the excluded prevents their recourse to self-help. This becomes very important in view of the fact that in a liberal polity all men are alike and, therefore, they all are weak.

By the same token, they are equally powerless and poor in resources in taking care of themselves. In a situation where what Tocqueville calls 'permanents social revolution' has engendered a widespread passion for the equalization of power, property and status within the spheres of state and civil society. Unable to improve their lot by their own efforts, individuals *manque,* to use Oakeshott's phrase, have to depend on the state for getting what they consider necessary for their welfare.

Unable to carry forward the struggle for equality on their own, the dispossessed and the deprived depend on the state to secure equality for themselves. This creates a situation where the ideal of freedom from despotism is replaced, bit by bit, by the phenomenon of state-secured equality. The result is that 'day by day citizens fall constantly under the control of public administration in which they insensibly surrender even greater portions of their individual independence' (Tocqueville, 1956: II: 379). This situation permits the state to emerge as a titular head with its hands and eyes intruding more and more in the minutiae of the daily life of the people.

As a titular power, the state perpetuates in the social body a type of drowsiness which the heads of administration are inclined to call good order and public tranquility (Tocqueville, 1956: I: 158). This results in state-induced permanent childhood, especially in most of the poor and excluded, who, because of distributional faults, ever remain dependent on the state for protection. However, dependence on the state enervates their soul and noiselessly unbends the spring of action. Dependence on the state transforms poverty into a political colouration: demands for state protection escalate and multiply. This leads to what Hannah Arendt calls 'the overwhelming of the political by the demands of the social' the state finds itself unable to satisfy all the emergent demands. As a result, the pre-existing consensus breaks down.

The result is the breakdown of social peace, which becomes difficult to restore. And as MacIntyre notes, politics then turns into 'a civil war carried on by other means.' The best the state can do is to fire-fight and displace discontent at one place and put it at another place as well as grant more and more of 'manifesto rights'.

Third, it is true that the state is the agency that defines what happiness means as well as the one who does the provisioning. However, with the loss of the initial vigour, the state has now entered the stage of what Crouch (2004) calls post-democracy fully armed with the philosophy of neo-liberalism. 'This means that whatever the party identity of the government, there is steady, constant pressure for state policy to favour the interest of the wealthy – those who benefit from the unrestricted operation of capitalist economy – than those who needed some protection from it. (Perforce) It is presumed that individual freedoms are guaranteed by the freedom of the market (Harvey, 2005: 7).

This, Rahul Bajaj confirms when he says:

> The role of the participative plural governance is central to the inclusive growth model that India has instituted so effectively. It has led to a growth-oriented investor-friendly and sustainable climate for doing business, one that encourages individual creativity and fosters innovation. (2011: 20)

Thus, he finds that there is a virtuous positive correlation between economic freedom and political freedom.

This is indicative of the fact that there exists a collusion between the state and free market forces – a collusion that is poor-friendly only in sloganeering. Thus, affirmative action aimed at improving the lot of the poor and the excluded 'have little impact on the socio-economic status of Dalits, with a few exceptions. Even so Dalit initiative is bringing about change where the state has failed. The expansion of private capital in post 1991 India and the emerging market has helped the rise of a new class of Dalits who are overriding Manu's law that proscribed specific occupations for 'lowly castes'. Massive industrialization has also helped millions of Dalits to escape the countryside and farm work (Karup, 2011: 16).

The implication is very clear. If the worldly status of Dalits and other needy classes can be improved only by market forces, then, can we hope that freedom of capitalist economy will protect individual freedom and ensure the welfare of the poor and the needy? The onset of neo-liberalism has, as Harvey forcefully shows, led to the decline in the welfare of the poor and the excluded. Also, the migration of the poor and the needy to towns and the cities does add a bit to the income of the dispossessed and the deprived.

However, when they come to the towns and the cities, they face even worse living conditions.

The alternative of neo-liberalism does not offer any better and salubrious alternative. The fact remains that India still has a large number of people who are still deprived, if not dispossessed. This leads to widespread dissatisfaction and the resultant state of exception in Agamben's sense, on the one hand, and specularity, on the other. In conclusion, then, this forcefully argue for a new look on the principle of justice.

References

Ackerman, Bruce, *Social Justice in the Liberal State*. New Haven: Yale University Press, 1981.

Bajaj, Rahul, 'Just Path to Development,' *The Hindustan Times*, 22 January, 2011.

Crouch, Colin, *Post-Democracy*, Cambridge, UK: Polity Press, 1988.

Harvey, David, *A Brief History of Neo Liberalism*, Oxford: Oxford University Press, 2005.

Hirsch, Fred, *Social Limits to Growth*, London: Routledge, 1977.

Jasay, Anthony de, *Against Politics: On Government, Anarchy and Order*, London: Routledge, 1997.

Karup, Saira, 'For the People, By the People,' *The Times of India*, 24 February 2011.

MacIntyre, Alasadair, *After Virtue A Study in Moral Theory*. Notre Dame: Notre Dame University Press, 2007.

Nozick, Robert, *Anarchy, State and Utopia*, New York: Basic, 1974.

Pathak, Vikram, *Hindustan Times*, 27 July 2009.

Sandel, Michael, *Liberalism Limit of Justice*, Cambridge,UK: Cambridge University Press, 1982.

Saxena, Shibban, 'A Billion Indian and Millions of Injustices', *The Times of India*, 26 July 2009.

Shukla, Rajesh et al., *Caste in A Different Mould: Understanding the Discrimination*, New Delhi: B.S. Books, 2010.

Tocqueville, Alexis de, *Democracy in America*, tr. Henry Reeve,New York: Vintage, 1958.

6

Beyond Rawls

Conceptualizing Social Justice in a Varna-Based Society

T.R. Sharma

The kingdom of Pratishthan and Brahamavarta, as the whole Indo-Gangetic region was then called, was witness to the evolution of hierarchically structured *varna*-based social order during the later vedic and Brahaminic period, which Manu sanctified in his *Manusmriti* as *varnadharma*.[1] A series of intermittent historic battles between the Aryans while they were advancing from north-west India (the Saptsindhu region) to Madhyadesa (central India) and Brahamavarta, and the aboriginal non-Aryan communities which culminated in the decisive victory of the former were fought here. A large chunk of vanquished non-Aryans became *dasas* (slaves) of the victors; while the rest were pushed either to the north-east or to south of the Vindhyas or fled to the forests of central India.[2] In due course, the vanquished non-Aryans became the Sudras and Ati-Sudras, the lowest *varna* of the hierarchical Hindu *varna* order. This whole arrangement got legitimized and solemnized in the *pushsukta* of Rig Veda[3], more or less in the same way as the Greeks justified slavery in their society. Thus, it will not be far wrong to say that this region was the real theatre of the emergence of *varna*-based marginalization of the non-Aryans at the hands of the Aryans, which has been the most marked (and the most despised) feature of the Hindu social order ... . At the outset it would be appropriate to conceptualize the notion of social justice and marginality in the specific context of Hindu *varna* order which has become a pan-Indian phenomenon as other faiths have also, willy-nilly, adopted some of its discriminatory practices.

However, before doing so it would be useful to look at some of the most prominent aspects of the prevailing notions of social justice, particularly the Rawlsian notion because for the last 40 years it has been the dominant discourse on social justice in the western liberal political theory. For John Rawls[4], a just society is one in which each person has equal right to the most extensive total system of equal basic liberties compatible with a similar system of liberty for all and where social and economic inequalities are to be arranged so that they are both:

> (i) to the greatest benefit of the least advantaged and (ii) attached to offices and positions open to all under conditions of fair equality of opportunity.[5]

In other words any socio-political arrangement ought to be judged on how it promotes the good of individuals and groups constituting the given society. The core of Rawlsian conception of social justice lies mainly in his assertion that inequalities in the allocation of goods and positions is permissible only if they work to the benefit of the least advantaged members of society. In his, *A Theory of Justice* (1971) and his subsequent writings, Rawls has devised a meticulous political and economic arrangement to bring about a just society. It is pertinent to point out that the core of Rawlsian notion of social justice is a certain pattern of distribution of goods, resources, opportunities and offices. Hence it is 'economy-centric' or at best 'politico-economy-centric'. As such, it does not adequately address the issue of social discrimination, much less the issues of humiliation, insult and torture in social relations. In fact, Rawls is not the only one to do so rather in the whole liberal tradition ranging from ultra-individualists like Robert Nozick to ultra-collectivists like the communitarians, social justice has been understood in juxtaposition to individual justice as binary categories. The liberal theory distinguishes between 'social' and 'individualistic' conceptions of justice, where the former is directed at creating an egalitarian social order; while the latter is concerned with the claims of individuals vis-à-vis the society. However, both these assumptions remain 'money-centric' rather than 'socio-cultural-centric' one which is concerned with 'social' aspects of individual's life. As Reinman argues social justice ought not to take some form of distribution of things but dignified relations among persons and groups. Several scholars have convincingly argued that the concept of (social) justice can have various mutually exclusive connotations, depending on the societal context.[6]

The main contention of this paper is that for societies which are organized on the principle of social hierarchies, like the *varna*-based Hindu society or any other society which practices social apartheid or racial segregation in day-to-day interactions among people belonging to different ascriptive social stratums, social justice ought to have a much wider connotation. As such, the very meaning of social justice as well as its scope and form of struggle to secure it will vary among them. For example, in Hindu society where the *varnas* and *varnadharma* (duty) of each *varna* is projected as divinely ordained, the search for social justice may have to be more protracted and assertive, if not more aggressive as compared to the civil rights movement of the Blacks against racial segregation in America or the struggle of Blacks against apartheid in South Africa.[7] It seems that in all such societies it is not enough to ensure that the marginal groups get adequate share in political power and economic resources; rather it is imperative that they are able to live a life of honour and dignity as equal members of the social community. In short, the essence of social justice lies not only in having a politically and economically fair society but also a society which is what Margalit calls a decent society.[8]

In the following part of this paper an attempt will be made to spell out the contours of such a decent society. As Margalit tries to show, the search for a decent society can begin only if the current controversies in which the western liberal theory is struck are settled and a new catalogue of political and, more significantly, moral ideals is evolved. In this context it must be said that the cardinal principles of justice: social economic and political along with liberty, equality and fraternity which are constitutionally guaranteed in India and the various policies of positive discrimination enacted from time to time by the Indian State constitute the necessary conditions for the establishment of a decent society but they do not constitute the sufficient conditions. The various measures of political and economic empowerment of the people who are at the margins, particularly the Dalits, who alone constitute nearly one-third of India's population, will help usher in a more egalitarian society but it will fall short of ensuring a decent and humane society because the linch-pin of social justice in a *varna*-based society or any other society so organized lies in ensuring equal respect and honour to these groups in their day-to-day life on the social plane. Such a notion of social justice seeks to transcend the prevailing strategies which are being followed by the Indian State for political and economic empowerment of the socially excluded groups. In essence it calls for change in the mindset and stereotypes of those segments of society who are at the apex of *varna* hierarchy towards the *varna* order itself.

Thus, the main theatre of a decent society lies on the social and cultural plane rather on the political and economic plane. To put it in sharp terms, one can say that while a Rawlsian type just society organized fully around his two principles of justice may not qualify to be called a decent society, even a utilitarian liberal democratic society or even an unequal society which is on the face of it unjust, according to the Rawlsian parameters, may be a decent society. This is so because the concept of decent society is not necessarily concerned with the concept of rights. So much so that even a society without any concept of rights may be a decent one. This is so because the essence of social justice lies not merely in eliminating class dominance (in economic sense) which inevitably gets reflected in the modes of rulership (political sense) but in eliminating the modes of social dominance and social apartheid which no amount of political and economic empowerment can fully address. In other words, social justice is more a matter of social behaviour and practice rather than political enactment and economic arrangement. It is not merely a matter of providing a legal framework and evolving economic strategies of inclusive growth; it centres around rules of inter-personal behaviour. It is more than the Kantian stipulation that law should treat every citizen equally. The notion of social justice goes beyond the contemporary western notion which entails fair distribution of resources and opportunities where fairness hinges on multiple criteria of merit, desert and need. The whole argument in this paper hinges on the assumption (which may appear to some to be questionable) that probably there cannot be a single conception of social justice which is universally valid. For instance, the western liberal conception of social justice with its emphasis on equal distribution of goods and resources (money liberalism as some prefer to call it) has only a limited relevance in a *varna*-based society where the emphasis ought to be on egalitarian social relations across the *varnas*. In this regard, David Miller's notion of 'people's equal standing in public life' captures the essence of social justice. In fact, Miller goes so far as to say that inequalities in market income may well be fair if they are broadly proportionate to people's contribution. However, these inequalities, while being fair in themselves may undermine the desired sense of fellowship underlying a society of equals. He further adds that a classless (one may say a casteless) society is not necessarily more just in the sense of distributing resources more fairly, but is attractive for reasons other than distributive justice such as community.[9] R.H. Twaney's conception of a just society is one which has a common tradition of respect and consideration. To paraphrase him, some classes (one may say castes) should not be excluded from the heritage of civilization which others enjoy and the fact of human fellowship should not be obscured by economic contrasts which are trivial and superficial.[10] Here Anthony Crosland asserts that social justice ought to weaken the deep-seated existing stratification, with its concomitant feelings of envy and inferiority and its barriers to uninhibited mingling between classes (castes in the Indian case).[11] In the same vein Walzer talks of spheres of justice where one sphere concerns the acquisition of money and commodities which result in inequalities but these inequalities should not be allowed to cross the boundary and contaminate other spheres of justice, more particularly public honour.[12] This would imply that even if economic inequalities between different social strata are sufficiently bridged, it may not itself lead to corresponding weakening of caste prejudices. Hence, in a society like India the concept of social justice cannot be limited only to distributive equality; rather it ought to aim at equality in social and cultural spheres of life, more particularly in the sphere of social relations among individuals and groups based on mutual respect. That constitutes the real essence of social justice. At this point it seems relevant to spell out, in greater detail, different dimensions of a decent society. The concept has positive as well as negative dimension and it is only by taking the two dimensions together that its full import can be comprehended. In positive sense a decent society is based on centrality of honour in the lives of people; while in negative sense it is absence of humiliation or absence of deliberate infliction of insult. In positive sense it is a society that respects all its members and all social groups; while in negative sense it is a society whose individuals and institutions do not humiliate any of its members individually and any of its clusters collectively, particularly the latter. Of course, this positive-negative binary is more conceptual than real because humiliation itself is a condition where a person or a group feels that his/her self-respect and honour is being injured; while respect itself is a condition sans humiliation. In order to elaborate the above formulation it is necessary to discuss, on the theoretical plane, the concept of decent society and bring into sharp focus its different dimensions. At the outset it needs to be pointed out that decent society has a negative as well as a positive dimension and it is only by taking the two dimensions together that the full importance of a decent society can be comprehended. A decent society is based on the centrality of honour and humiliation in the lives of people. Humiliation is deliberate infliction of insult. Negatively, a decent society is one whose individuals and institutions do not humiliate any of its members individually or any of its clusters collectively, more particularly the latter. Positively, it is a society that respects all its members and social groups. In short, a decent society is one which accords respect and honour and avoids humiliation to any of its members and any of the social groups that constitute it. It is a society which safeguards human dignity. Of course, this binary is more conceptual than real because humiliation itself is a condition where a person or a group faces that his/her self-respect and honour is injured.

Here it needs to be recognized that while it is a two-phased process, there is weighty asymmetry between eradicating evil (humiliation) and promoting good, i.e. ensuring respect. It is quite possible that a society may not humiliate any of its members but may also not treat them honourably. There may be an attitude of indifference without being humiliating. It also seems reasonable to argue that transformation of a humiliating society into a decent one must begin by eradicating humiliating practices and it must be followed by creating an environment of honour and respect. This is so because, as Margalit rightly argues, it is easier to identify humiliation than respectful behaviour just as it is easier to identify illness than health. Humiliation like illness involves attack in which there is one who is attacker and the other who is attacked. Humiliation arises as a result of behaviour of others towards you. In a hierarchically structured *varna*-based society like the Hindu society humiliation is in-built in the very existential conditions of life because of the over-all structure of society even if no one intends to do so intentionally. Here, a decent society is one which consciously fights the social conditions which breed the *varna*-based humiliation. In this sense, a decent society is a macro-ethical concept concerned with the structure of the society as a whole.

It follows from the above argument that in certain religious denominations like Hinduism a decent society is possible only if the *varna*-based edifice of institutions with their built-in humiliating paraphernalia is demolished. Of course, this position should not be equated with nihilists or anarchists who hold the extreme view that a society founded on ruling institutions is by definition a humiliating society and further that no society with permanent institutions can be a decent society because all such institutions do exercise coercive power over its members. In other words, there is a need to distinguish between the institutions that humiliate and the ones that do not. Moreover, there are institutions which are essential for orderly human existence and there are others which only facilitate humiliation which have potential to do so (this is like Herbert Marcuse's notions of necessary repression and surplus repression where the former is necessary but the latter is not). The whole issue is, indeed, very complex because one can quite legitimately argue that even the *varna* order was based on the logic that allocation of different functions to different *varnas* is necessary for holding the society together. The deformity in the *varna* order entailing humiliation occurred when a particular *varna* which was assigned the duty of doing the unclean social jobs began to be looked at with disdain by the other *varna*'s performing other functions. So much so that the situation of Dalits was rendered beyond redemption because the functions assigned to the different *varnas* began to be justified in terms of one's *karmas* (actions) in the previous life. Because of historical rootedness of the *karma*-based *varna* theory, it is very difficult to imagine a non-humiliating society so long as the *varna* order in which humiliation is deeply imbedded persists. Here it is necessary to discuss the various ways in which humiliation manifests itself. For one thing, the phenomenon of humiliation can be contrasted with virtues of honour and dignity. In so far as humiliation violates human dignity it violates social justice.

The litmus test of social justice is that all members of the given society are accorded due respect and honour in equal measures on the basis of a primary consideration as to what they are (human beings qua human beings) rather than what they do or how well they do what they do.

Unfortunately, the primary consideration in dealing with the Dalits has not been what they are (human beings), but what they do (unclean jobs). Being a human being is matter of belonging but being a superior human being is a functional concept. Honour and respect accorded in the latter sense is a secondary trait but that which is accorded in the former sense is a primary trait. The notion of upper and lower *varna* is a ranking concept and, hence, unequal in intent entailing respect to some and disrespect to others or honour to some and humiliation to others. On the other hand, Hindu (without any adjective good or bad, upper or lower) is an egalitarian concept implying the absence of grounds that generate and sustain humiliation. Social justice lies in recognizing the fact that every one in the society is entitled to equal honour.

Theoretically, one can argue that social injustice may manifest in different ways. For example, it may manifest itself in treating humans as non-humans; treating some as gods or angels (deification) and others as devils or demons (demonization); or treating some human beings as mere objects or machines or animals (dehumanization and objectification). However, the social injustice that the Dalits have suffered in India does not fall in any of these categories. If it were so then the very basis of injustice would disappear. After all, physical objects, machines and probably, to some extent, even animals do not nurse a feeling of injustice if some cruelty is done to them, nor would the one who is inflicting such injustice think that he or she is being unjust to them. History bears testimony to the fact that despite a lot of cruelty to which they were subjected, the Greek or American slaves were not ever thought to be mere physical objects. Further, although they were bought and sold and the buyer often examined their teeth to see how healthy they were but nobody, neither the buyer nor the one who was bought ever thought that they were non-humans. Rather, they were considered human beings but of inferior quality. Seeing human beings as human beings according to Sartre would involve seeing them as free to make decisions bearing on their lives. Seeing them as objects or things involves seeing them as unfree. *Varna*-based social injustice is somewhat akin to it yet not exactly so. While the Dalits were not free in some respects (choosing vocation for example), they were free in some other respects. Hence, they were not viewed as things or objects or animals but inferior members of human commonwealth which amounts to humiliation and injustice of the worst order. In other words, injustice that the Dalits suffered in India for several millennia did not arise out of treating them as non-humans but rather by treating them as human beings of inferior quality. It is only by doing so that the perpetrator of injustice (upper caste) could demonstrate his/her absolute superiority over the humiliated (the Dalit). Such superiority can be achieved only over humans. The *varna*-based humiliation and injustice was such that the humiliator did not only humiliate his victim but also made sure that the victim recognized and accepted the legitimacy of the humiliator to do so. Such recognition amounted to conceding that the victim is a thinking being sensitive to and capable of deciphering the feelings of honour and dishonour. Here the victim felt dishonoured by one's life condition because of the attitude of others towards him/her.

Such recognition is possible only in intra-societal relations among groups of human beings. After all, the phenomenon of treating some people as unseeables, unapproachables and untouchables had a clear implication that they were not considered as objects or animals or non-humans but as human beings of inferior quality, intellectually as well as physically. To emphasize the point even at the risk of some repetition it must be said that injustice that the Dalits suffered in India did not imply that they were not the members of human commonwealth, rather it implied that they were integral parts of human commonwealth but unequal and inferior parts. In this respect the denial of equal status to the Dalits in India was of quite a different order in a very subtle sense than the humiliation that the Jews suffered at the hands of Anglicans earlier and at the hands of the Nazis in recent times. Of course, the Jews drew some solace in the belief that all the human beings are children of God and hence they were as good (or bad) children of God as any other community. However, the Indian Dalits could hardly argue like this because the divinely ordained *varna* order stipulated that different *varna* clusters of Hindus are born out of different parts of the Almighty: Brahmans from mind, Kashtriyas from arms, Vashyas from thighs and the Sudras from feet. It further implied that they had different social roles and their roles were irreversible.

The worst part of it was that the Dalits felt this humiliation and injustice even in the absence of a humiliating agent, be it an upper-*varna* humiliating agent or the *varna*-based humiliating social order as such. To put it differently, if a just society is one which gives equal respect to all its members qua human beings then humiliation arises when some members are perpetually considered lower-quality human beings in the social hierarchy and are not allowed any escape route from this order. To assign a dirty or unclean job to a person and make him believe that only he/she is meant to do it lowers one's self-image which may lead to shame (as external reaction) and guilt (as internal reaction). When a society makes people feel ashamed of their low social origin then it is not a just society. A society is not just and decent if it compromises the integrity of some of its segments. Jews were subjected to ridicule, Nazis to hatred, proletariat to exploitation, minorities to discriminations but dalits in India suffered humiliation and injustice of quite a different nature. They were subjected to social exclusion, moral debasement and spiritual degradation which lowered their self-image. Such humiliation and the resultant injustice rested on the basic premise that human beings do not only feel the physical pain but also understand its symbolic and psychic meaning. While the humiliator feels pleasure in the very act of humiliating others, the humiliated feels the very anguish of it. In this sense, humiliation is cruelty, cruelty not in the physical sense but more so in the psychological sense. Both realize fully that while the scars of physical pain heal with passage of time, the scars of psychological pain (insult) never heal, particularly if such insults are repeated day in and day out in the existential situation.

The most fundamental question here is this: if one is seeking to establish a decent, non-humiliating, socially just society in a *varna*-based community like Hinduism then what moral and scientific justifications can one offer for it. In other words, what justifies according to persons of all colours, creeds and *varnas*, including the Dalits, respect and honour. The whole edifice of a socially just society hinges on this question. The oft repeated and the most obvious answer to this question is that all human beings deserve honour and respect because they have common (human) traits. Their bodies are constituted of same chemical elements: *jal* (water), *vayu* (air), *prithvi* (earth), *aakash* (sky), and *antriksh* (space). Since humiliation is a sort of cruelty that is inflicted on human beings by human beings, the remedy lies in repentance by the inflictor for such acts of cruelty. It requires one to live and behave differently and recognize that one's unjust conduct all along has been utterly wrong and undesirable. Further, the denial of the right to choose a vocation of one's liking is not only an issue of distributive justice but it is socially unjust. Hence, social justice lies in giving this right to all. Finally, a word may be said about the culture of a society rooted in social justice. A society whose work of art commits the sin of systematically humiliating certain individuals or certain groups is not a just society particularly if such a work has institutional support. A just society is one whose works of art do not inflict stigmas on individuals and social groups, stigmas which may refer to repulsive physical traits like black or brown skin, flat nose, thick lips, foul smell of one's sweat or stigmas relating to social practices like denial to the sudras the freedom to read or even listen to the *Vedas*, or freedom to wear the sacred thread, or to support a *tilak* (mark on the forehead). Such institutional humiliation is more painful than individual acts of humiliation because institutions are more powerful and hence more damaging. As such, social justice lies in negating all such stigmatizing practices both individual as well as institutional.

Notes

1. See, G. Buhler, *The Laws Manu*, Delhi: Motilal Banarsidass, 1988.
2. See, Max Muller, *Chips From a German Workshop*, London: Longman Green and Co., 1865.
3. See, Ralph T.H. Grifith, *The Hymns of Rig Veda*, Varanasi: Chowkhamba Sanskrit Series, 1963, (in two volumes), Vol. II, p. 75.
4. John Rawls, *A Theory of Justice*, Cambridge,Mass.: Belknap Press of Harvard University, 1971.
5. Ibid.
6. See, for example, Emmanuel Levinas, *Totality and Infinity*, Pittsburg: Duquesne University Press, 1969; Will Kymlicka, *Contemporary Political Philosophy*, New Delhi: Oxford University Press, 2005.

7. Buhler, op cit.
8. For a detailed exposition of a decent society see, Avishai Margalit, *The Decent Society,* Cambridge, Mass.: Harvard University Press, 1996. The present paper is an attempt to understand the relevance of Margalit's theoretical formulation in the context of Indian empirical reality as it has existed since remote antiquity.
9. David Miller, *Social Justice*, Oxford: Oxford University Press, 1976. Also see Jeffrey Reiman, 'Moral Philosophy: The Critique of Capitalism and the Problem of Ideology' in Terrell Carver (ed.) *The Cambridge Companion to Marx,* London: Cambridge University Press, 1991. Also see, Miller, 'Equality and Market Socialism' in Pranab Bardhan and John Roemer (eds.) *Market Socialism: The Current Debate,* New York: Oxford University Press, 1993; and 'What Kind of Equality the Left Pursue' in Jane Franklin (ed.) *Equality,* London: Institute for Public Policy Research, 1997.
10. R.H. Tawney, *Equality,* London: Allen and Unwin, 1964.
11. Anthony Crosland, *The Future of Socialism,* London: Jonathan Cape, 1964.
12. Michael Walzer, *Spheres of Justice: A Defence of Pluralism and Equality,* Blackwell: Oxford, 1983.

7

Justice for Groups

Multiculturalist Critique of Rawls's Theory of Justice

Papia Sengupta

> Justice is the first virtue of social institutions as truth is of systems of thought. A theory, however elegant and economical must be rejected or revised if it is untrue; likewise laws and institutions no matter how efficient and well arranged must be reformed or abolished if they are unjust. (Rawls, 1971: 3)

John Rawls's, *A Theory of Justice* published in 1971 revolutionized scholarship on justice. It can rightly be termed as one of the most influential work in political philosophy of the 20th century. Rawls asserted that 'until recently liberal theories of justice have regarded the reconciliation of equality and difference as relatively straight forward. According to them, rights and benefits, privileges and power should be distributed in a manner that is blind to social difference' (Rawls, 1971: 31).

Rawls theory was criticized by the libertarians like Robert Nozick, who wrote his famous work *Anarchy, State and Utopia* as a reaction to Rawls's *A Theory of Justice* in 1974. Nozick is not the only person who criticized Rawlsian justice, feminists, communitarians and multicultural theorists have also challenged Rawls theory on various grounds. In this paper, I analyse the multicultural critique to Rawls's theory of justice. Rawls principle of justice was endorsed by liberal democrats as a theory which answered issues of social welfare within liberalism. Hence, his theory comes under liberal school.

Critique of John Rawls Theory of Justice

Multiculturalists, as well as feminist and communitarians, criticized liberal position of justice as difference blindness which is in turn based on the liberal conception of 'formal equality' which treats every citizen equally and gives them universal rights. The underlying principle is 'uniformity of treatment'. This, in turn, rests on the liberals' emphasis on 'individuals' as the holders of equal rights and duties irrespective of (social and cultural differences) race, creed, caste, religion, class and language. In doing so, liberals recognize individuals and not groups, as holders of rights, whereas multiculturalists, communitarians and feminists believes that individuals are not abstract and are deeply embedded in their culture, community and group identity. The identity of an individual is shaped by the language, cultural groups, religion, class, gender, etc. she is born in. And since all groups are not on an equal footing in the society, treating them equally invariably leads to *'treating unequals equally'*. This breeds injustice not justice.

By defining justice through a process of reasoning which totally abstracts from social particularities, liberals have inadvertently built biases into their principles of justice themselves. This can be seen in the work of liberal theorists, including Rawls, Ackerman, Dworkin, and so on. Rawls original position, Ronald Dworkin's desert island with its insurance scheme, Bruce Ackerman's spaceship journey to a new planet, all serve the purpose of enduring that ascriptive group difference and play no role in the definition of justice.

In the light of this critique, how is the task of defining political communities' just obligations towards members of marginalized groups to be pursued? What is the multicultural notion of justice? Does it adhere to the principle that to treat people equally means treating equal cases alike and unequal cases differently? Or does justice imply that not only a person's individual characteristics but her group or community identity must also be taken into consideration for a truly unbiased conception of justice? To understand the multicultural notion of justice as different from Rawlsian conception of justice, it is important to first understand Rawls position on justice.

Rawlsian Conception: Justice as Fairness

John Rawls's *A Theory of Justice* is one of the most influential contemporary works on the subject. For Rawls, what is directly relevant for social ethics and justice is the individual's means to pursue their own ends to and to live whatever 'good life' they choose for themselves. His argument makes use of the idea of a hypothetical social contract, applied not to the nature of state's authority over the people but to the nature of justice.

Rawls believed that the contract takes the individual seriously. He was greatly influenced by Kant who treated people as ends and not merely means. Criticizing utilitarianism as conflating individuals, Rawls argues that an adequate theory of justice must morally respond to and preserve the distinction of persons.

Rawls theory of justice as fairness consists of two primary principles:

(i) First, each person is to have an equal right to the most extensive scheme of equal basic liberties compatible with a similar scheme of liberties for other.

(ii) Second, social and economic inequalities are to be arranged so that:
  (a) they are to be of the greatest benefit to the least- advantaged members of society (the difference principle).
  (b) offices and positions must be open to everyone under conditions of fair equality of opportunity.

Rawls basic premise is that the primary goods are to be distributed by the state equally, unless an unequal distribution would be to everyone's advantage. Whereas unequal distribution of liberty is never desirable, he does accept that it may be possible that unequal distribution could be desirable in so far as giving more to some will result in their using these resources in a way that yields more for everyone.

Multicultural Notions of Justice

There is no single version of justice on which multiculturalists agree. In general terms, multiculturalists argue for a view of justice as accommodative of the concerns of the marginalized. Most of them provide a defense of collective rights for minority cultures. Multicultural theorists claim cultural membership as an essential component of individuals' moral agencies, their ability identify and pursue a way of life that can be affirmed as good. Cultural membership is such an important prerequisite of individuals' ability to pursue a conception of the good, that it should be regarded as a primary good in the Rawlsian sense, a good whose equal enjoyment by all citizens should be assured by a conception of justice which is fair to all (Kymlicka, 1989: 4).

According to multicultural theorists, Rawls's theory of justice fails to satisfy the ideal of fairness because of the hidden assumption that those who are to be regulated by a conception of justice belong to a single homogeneous culture. They argue persuasively that some birth-given attributes should be taken into account in any reasoning about justice, as they have a profound significance for the bearers' ability to pursue meaningful lives in terms of equality with other members of their political communities.

One group of multicultural thinkers argues that the state plays a vital role in fostering a sense of justice. Its role is even greater in any multicultural society in which it is one of the sources of unity, it provides a focus to the shared life, and is expected to set an example of how to rise above narrow communal prejudices and point of view. It is, therefore, of the utmost importance that the institutions of the state should be impartial in their treatment of members of different communities. The state, as the source of legally secured justice in society, needs to ensure that its citizens enjoy equality of treatment in all significant areas of life such as employment, criminal justice, education, health, public services, etc. Negatively equal treatment involves absence of direct and deliberate or indirect and institutionalized discrimination. The former occurs when those in charge of decision-making are guided by prejudices against certain groups of people. The latter occurs when the rules and procedures they follow contain unnoticed discriminatory biases and works to the systematic disadvantage of particular communities or groups (Parekh, 2000: 210).

According to this group of multiculturalists, the basic structure is not only economic and political as Rawls maintains but also cultural. Hence, principles of justice should deal not only with liberties and material resources but also with cultural rights and opportunities. Since culture is an integral part of an individual's sense of identity and well-being, cultural rights are part of human rights and a good society should guarantee them. Besides, the cultural tone in every society is generally set by the majority community. Justice requires that the same opportunities should be extended to the minority communities as well. Thus, only guaranteeing individual rights of citizenship is not enough to eliminate discriminations based on cultural identities. The state needs to take special care in formulating laws and policies so that they do not discriminate against any one on the basis of culture. The politics of recognition is, therefore, part of a wider and nuanced theory of justice, with the crucial difference that unlike liberties and resources, recognition on cultural grounds cannot be individually enjoyed or centrally distributed.

Iris Marion Young criticized Rawls's theory of justice, specifically his original position and treatment of justice, as being 'impartial' to anyone. She asserts that one cannot be impartial or neutral because the person who defines justice constructs it in a way that reflects one's social location. Moreover, the task of defining what is just is often performed by individuals of privileged groups. She argues that any attempt to reduce the task of defining justice to a procedure is inherently flawed and she describes this as 'impossibility of impartiality' (Young, 1989: 104). To avoid this, she suggests the direct introduction of the perspectives of marginalized groups into the institutional context in which conceptions of justice are defined and enforced. According to her, what we require is a participatory structure in which actual people, with their geographical, ethnic, gender, culture, linguistic and occuptaional differences, assert their perspectives on social issues within institutions that encourage the representation of their distinct voices. Her approach to defining justice enjoins the creation of public spaces in which group differences can be recognized, affirmed and can contribute to formulation of policy.

Joseph Carens, another multicultural theorist, advocates the idea of justice as 'evenhandedness'. According to him neutrality can be replaced by a conception of justice as 'evenhandedness'. 'Evenhandedness' as a principle to defining justice is one that makes no one worse off but at the same time does not always aim to define justice in a manner that works for the betterment of the advantaged. Anne Phillips argues for the 'mirror' or proportional representation of different social groups, at least as a step along the way to a difference-blind society and politics (Phillips, 1991: 77).

Despite the differences between them, each of these arguments rests on the view that justice remains unfulfilled so long as some groups remain silenced. We cannot understand what it means to treat others as equals until we have understanding of how existing practices affects their most fundamental interest. And, because of the partiality of our own experiences, it is impossible to understand that through projecting ourselves into others' point of view in a process of abstract reasoning.

This is reflected in Seyla Behnabib's recent work on a 'communicative ethic of needs interpretation', whose aim is to formulate a procedure of discourse which represents our respect for the dignity of the individual and also created a space in which the needs that attach to particular social circumstances and differences be expressed (Behnabib, 1992: 148–77). She draws from Hannah Arendt's reading of Kant's theory of judgment, that by a simultaneous regard for both the generalized and concrete other can be realized in a discursive process in which individuals exercise their capacity for the 'reversibility of perspectives'. Such a model redefines the standpoint of moral judgement i.e. 'enlarged thinking'. This is parallel to Ronald Beiner's discussion in 'political judgement' (Beiner, 1983: 82). His argument may be summarized as 'to judge is to judge-with and to judge-with is to be a friend'. Likewise Behnabib insists that justice and empathy or 'ethic of care', are not antinomies but complement each other.

Defining a Group

If the group identity of an individual is to be taken into consideration while defining justice, then how is a 'group' to be defined? Is it cultural, occupational, regional, language, religious, ethnic, gender and do all these groups deserve to be considered in conceptualizing justice?

Many political philosophers defend collective rights or group rights. Their position differs in their defining group or collectivity and which criteria should be fulfilled by a group to be eligible for group rights. Joseph Raz (1986), Ian MacDonald (1989), Nathan Brett (1991), Allen Buchanan (1993, 1994), Leslie Green (1991), Vinit Haksar (1998), Will Kymlicka (1995), Peter Jones (1999), Susan Moller Okin (2002), many of them, especially the feminists, have criticised group rights and the impact it will have on intra-group equality.

Joseph Raz argues that a collective right exists when the following three conditions are fulfilled:

(a) it exists because an aspect of the interest of human beings justifies holding some person(s) to be subject to a duty.
(b) the interest in question are the interests of individuals as members of a group in a public good and the right is a right to that public good because it serves their interest as members of the group.

(c) the interest of no single member of that group in that public good is sufficient by itself to justify holding another person subject to a duty (Raz, 1986: 208).

I argue that the ascriptive group identities of an individual must be given due importance in a notion of justice. This position should not be misconstrued as defending group rights. Being just to an individual implies that the individual's cultural, social, religious, ethnic, gender background should be considered and any discrimination one would have faced because of belonging to a particular group needs to be addressed. To have a will to do justice to others, one must have some effective commitment to them that leads one to prefer just obligations over one's selfish interests. Habermas calls this 'solidarity' (Habermas, 1983) while Melissa Williams calls this 'trust' (Williams, 1995: 186).

The concept of justice in multiculturalism is that we not only let cultures survive and recognize them as equal but what is of greater concern is the acknowledgement of their worth. People need the respect and approval of others in order to develop self-esteem. As argued by Honneth, 'human integrity owes its existence to the patterns of approval and recognition' (Honneth, 1998: 131). A theory of justice must be based on the idea that all humans are equally worthy of respect. Kant uses the term 'dignity', as what commands respect in us is our status as rational agents capable of directing our lives through principles. Thus, what is worthy is the universal human potential, a capacity that all human individuals share. In the case of politics of difference and recognition, the universal potential for forming and defining one's own identity as an individual is embedded in one's culture and, hence, this must be equally respected in everyone.

John Rawls is one of the greatest political philosophers of our times and his *A Theory of Justice*, one of the most influential woks of the 20th century. Even though the multiculturalist view criticizes Rawls theory of 'justice as fairness' as based on individualism, it should not be forgotten that the most important theories of justice in political theory emerged either as criticism or appraisal of Rawls's theory.

References

Ackerman, B.A., *Social Justice in the Liberal State*, New Haven, Conn.: Yale University Press, 1980.

Behnabib, Seyla, *Situating the Self: Gender, Community and Postmodernism in Contemporary Ethics*, New York: Routledge, 1992.

Beiner, Ronald, *Political Judgment*, Chicago: Chicago University Press, 1983.

Brett, Nathan, 'Language Laws and Collective Rights', *Canadian Journal of Law and Jurisprudence*, 1991, Vol. 4(2), pp. 347–360.

Buchanan, Allen, 'The Role of Collective Rights in the Theory of Indigenous People's Rights', *Transnational Law and Contemporary Problems,* 1993, 3(1): pp. 89–108.

——, 'Liberalism and Group Rights', in *In Harm's Way: Essays in Honour of Joel Feinberg,* Jules L. Coleman and Allen Buchanan (eds.), Cambridge: Cambridge University Press, pp. 1–15.

Carens, Joseph, 'Justice as Evenhandedness', *Seminar,* December, 1999, pp. 49–52.

Dworkin, Ronald, *Taking Rights Seriously*, London: Duckworth, 1977.

Green, Leslie, 'Two Views of Collective Rights', *Canadian Journal of Law and Jurisprudence,* 1991, Vol. 4(2), pp. 315–327.

Habermas, Jurgen, *Reason and the Rationalization of Society*, Boston: Beacon, 1983.

Haksar, Vinit, 'Collective Rights and the Value of Groups', *Inquiry*, 1998, Vol. 41(1), pp. 21–43.

Honneth, Axel, *The Struggle for Recognition: The Moral Grammar of Social Conflicts,* translated by Joel Anderson, Cambridge,UK: Polity Press, 1998.

Jones, Peter, 'Group Rights and Group Oppression', *Human Rights Quarterly*. 1999, Vol. 21(1), pp. 80–107.

Kolm Serge, Christophe, 'Distributive Justice', in Robert E. Goodin and Philip Pettit (eds.), *A Companion to Contemporary Political Philosophy*, Oxford, UK: Blackwell, 1993.

Kymlicka, Will, *Liberalism, Community and Culture*, Oxford: Oxford University Press, 1989.

Kymlicka, Will, *Multicultural Citizenship: A Liberal Theory of Minority Rights,* Oxford, UK: Clarendon, 1995.

MacDonald, Ian, 'Group Rights', *Philosophical Papers*. 1989, Vol. 18(2), pp. 117–136.

Okin, Susan Moller, 'Mistresses of their Own Destiny: Group Rights, Gender and the Realistic Right of Exit'. *Ethics*, 2002, 112(2), pp. 205–230.

Parekh, Bhikhu, *Rethinking Multiculturalism: Cultural Diversity and Political Theory,* London: Macmillan, 2000.

Phillips, Anne, *Engendering Democracy*. Philadelphia: Pennsylvania State University Press, 1991.

Rawls, John, *A Theory of Justice*, Cambridge Mass.: Belknap Press of Harvard University, 1971.

Raz, Joseph, *The Morality of Freedom*. Oxford: Clarendon Press, 1986.

Williams, Mellissa, 'Justice Towards Groups: Political not Juridical'. *Political Theory*, 1995, Vol. 23(1), pp. 67–91.

Young, Iris, 'Politics and Group Difference: A Critique of the Ideal of Universal Citizenship'. *Ethics*, 1989, Vol. 99, pp. 250–274.

8

The Question of Justice in the Contemporary Global Order

Some Guiding Considerations

Anand P. Mavalankar

In the contemporary global order, the question of justice has acquired greater prominence in the wake of growing 'economic globalization' across the planet earth, and cultural and other diversities prevailing in different national societies within the contemporary world.[1] Why has the justice question figured as the dominant concern in the present times, remains a matter of reflection on the nature and dynamics of the contemporary global order. The Latin root of the word 'justice' is 'suum cuique tribuere', which means 'to allocate to each his own'. The quest for restoring and reaffirming the value of justice is indeed quite relevant and extraordinarily significant in the contemporary social discourse. Both corrective justice and distributive justice are posited as the essential endeavours on the part of sovereign states as well as the international community as a whole. The idea of corrective justice due to a person as punishment has been refined and reformulated in past few decades, although there is disagreement about the justification of the punishment. Similarly, the idea of distributive justice as due by way of benefits and burdens other than punishments has occupied centre stage in policy debates across the political spectrum in contemporary democratic societies. At the same time, there is no agreement about the content of just principles for the distribution of benefits and (non-punitive) burdens.

The main objective of this essay is to explore the question of justice in the contemporary global order. How do we approach the problem of justice from the analytical level of the global order itself? Where does justice figure in the hierarchy of values that shape the contemporary global order? How do we differentiate different kinds of justice, and what are the implications of coming to terms with the changing contemporary global order? We shall address these questions by referring to certain guiding considerations that should shape our exploration into the question of justice in the contemporary global order. In the subsequent sections of this essay, we shall discuss them at some length.

I

At the outset, it is important to recognize that the value of justice in contemporary international relations is not acknowledged as overriding one by certain scholars working in the domain of international or global studies. According to them, given the absence of a global sovereign authority, conditions for bringing about justice in the contemporary global order do not exist at the present juncture. The implicit suggestion here is that the state constitutes the maximal moral authority.[2]

This line of thinking is, however, contested by those who advance the idea of fundamental human equality, the belief that in some sense human beings are of equal value. As Andrew Linklater, one of the leading scholars wedded to this idea, contends that the idea of humanity needs to be 'reconstituted within a theory of history which is able to avoid the inadequacies that were endemic in traditional and modern theories of natural law'.[3]

At the level of the sovereign nation-state, the emphasis on social justice has been historically acknowledged, since it relates to the basic condition of inequality among communities, groups and individuals within the territorial confines of the state. The idea of the welfare state was meant to reduce disparities in income and wealth among its citizens. In a sense, it was meant to ensure credibility of the government of the day, in terms of meeting certain basic requirements of its people by fulfilling their minimum living standards.[4]

At the level of the sovereign state-system, however, some scholars wedded to an enlightened state-centric view of the international community prioritize the value of order over the value of justice. Hedley Bull's argument in the Anarchical Society was based on his contention that order is considered to be more fundamental than justice. According to him, 'order is a condition for the realization of other values'.[5] Clearly, order is recognized here as prior to justice. While this was articulated as such by way of a general statement, Bull did qualify it by saying that in any particular case, justice may come first. In this connection, Bull gave the example of international justice of self-determination and state sovereignty for colonized people in Asia and Africa. It was widely regarded as morally prior to the international order of Western colonialism in the colonized societies of Asia and Africa.

Bull's argument, however, does not squarely address the political economy context of the contemporary global order as it evolved since the late 19th century. The divide between the 'North' (advanced industrial states of the Western world) and the 'South' (less developed, erstwhile colonized countries of Asia, Africa and Latin America) in the contemporary international economic order, fundamentally challenges the political conception of Bull which establishes the overriding salience of order vis-à-vis justice in the contemporary international society of states.

The nature of the contemporary international economic order remains highly inequitable, as certain elements of the relationship between the developing and the developed countries are particularly irksome. In his perceptive appraisal of the contemporary order, W. Arthur Lewis outlined those elements in the following manner:

> First, the division of the world into exporters of primary products and exporters of manufactures.
> Second, the adverse factorial terms of trade for the products of the developing countries.
> Third, the dependence of the developing countries on the developed countries for finance.
> Fourth, the dependence of the developing countries on the developed for their engine of growth.[6]

Although these underlying elements have undergone change in the past two decades, the thrust of his argument does point towards an inherently restrictive political conception of Bull on justice, to the extent that it fails to take into account the injustice-producing structural make-up of the contemporary global order.

By way of conclusion, Lewis had pointed towards domestic change in the prevailing international economic order. As Lewis puts it, 'the engine of growth should be technological change, with international trade serving as lubricating oil and not as fuel. The gateway to technical change is through agricultural and industrial revolutions, which are mutually dependent.'[7] He went on to say that 'the most important item on the agenda of development is to transform the food sector, create agricultural surpluses to feed the urban population, and thereby create the domestic basis for industry and modern services'.[8]

These ideas of Lewis enable us to focus on the underlying economic variables that produce conditions of injustice in the developing countries. They sensitize us to the sources of inequitable international economic order that give rise to the unjust economic environment for the countries of the 'South'.

Be as it may, the question of justice in the contemporary global order from the standpoint of the sovereign state-system has to be considered in detail from Bull's perspective, as it focuses upon international justice. We may now briefly turn to Hedley Bull's conception of justice. Bull makes a distinction between 'commutative justice' and 'distributive justice' in the realm of the world of sovereign states. Cumulative justice refers to procedures and reciprocity in the international community of sovereign states. According to him, it is a process of claim and counter-claim among states. Accordingly, justice is fairness of the rules of the game – the same rules are applied in the same way to every state. Such rules of the game are expressed by international law and diplomatic practices.[9]

Bull's notion of commutative justice posits that states are socially responsible actors and they have a common interest in promoting international justice. Although complying with certain rules and norms create basic framework for society of states, it does not necessarily lead to justice among states.

As regards 'distributive justice', Bull examines the issue of how goods should be distributed among states, as exemplified by the idea that justice requires a transfer of economic resources from rich countries to poor ones.[10] The suggestion here is that the poor and weak states deserve special treatment, such as development aid. The notion of distributive justice does indicate what the developing countries are legitimately entitled to in the first place, both positively and negatively, the appropriate distribution of benefits and (non-punitive) burdens within a political order.

In the latter half of 20th century and early 21st century, issues of distributive justice have been vociferously presented by a whole range of groups and organizations from international civil society. The call for establishing a 'New International Economic Order (NIEO)' in 1974 was a clear expression for realizing distributive justice on part of the developing countries as a united bloc to influence the workings of the prevailing global economic order.

Bull's framework on justice differentiates three distinct levels of justice in world politics. The first level refers to 'international or inter-state justice' which basically involves the notion of sovereign equality of states and removing unfair and unjust barriers to their economic growth. The second level refers to 'individual or human justice', which basically involves justice pertaining to human rights. The third level refers to 'cosmopolitan or world justice', which basically involves 'what is right or good for the world as a whole'. Applying global environmental standards across the board among all nations of the world would be a case in point here.

II

Considering the question of justice from the standpoint of the wider planet earth or globe enables us to look at it in the holistic manner. There are principally two broad ways to examine the question of justice in the contemporary global order, which would capture the range and complexity of the justice problematic itself.

The distinction between 'international justice' and 'global justice' remains vital to the discourse of justice in the contemporary global order. In the present age of economic globalization, the globe itself has become the reference point to assess the workings of the globalized world. Hence, with regard to global justice, the guiding consideration must be humanity as a whole as the referent object of justice. Clearly, it is conceptually quite distinct from the so-called 'international justice'. Bull's proposition that states are bound by various norms and practices is instructive in this regard. It also indicates the extent to which violence and conflict are not prevalent in the international society. In the Westphalian order, international justice rests on an ethic of co-existence of sovereign states. This being a procedural view of justice, it does not address the substantive issues relating to the nature and implications of justice in the contemporary world. In this connection, it is worthwhile to recall Terry Nardin's[11] proposition that the society of states is analogous to an association of citizens (cives) as opposed to an 'enterprise association', which is devoted to the pursuit of some substantive common goal of nations.

The main difficulty with the notion of international justice is that it overestimates the degree of order in the Westphalian system. In the 21st century, this notion is ineffective due to several reasons. First of all, in a predominantly non-European contemporary global order, state will impose its own culture and provide its own support for a legal system based on coexistence among nations. Secondly, the growing trend towards democratization of the present order has undermined old diplomatic culture.

On the other hand, 'global justice' focuses on humanity as a whole. In such conceptualization, interests of the entire humanity are best served by the normative principles that underlie inter-state relations. Broadly speaking, there are three distinct sets of arguments for the notion of global justice. First of all, Charles Beitz took the view that under contemporary conditions of interdependence, national societies are not sufficiently discrete to justify their being treated as separate, self-contained entities.[12] In other words, the world has to be seen as, in certain respects, a single society and therefore the Rawlsian idea that differences in outcome vis-à-vis the distribution of social and economic goods must be justified, applies. Rawls's 'difference principle' can be applied to the effect that such inequalities must work to the benefit of the least advantaged should be applied internationally which would, of course, require wholesale distribution of wealth and income between different national societies[13]. Its implications for the contemporary global order are quite clearcut. As Beitz puts it, a Rawlsian society is to be understood as a cooperative scheme based on mutual advantage and it is by no means clear that the current world economic order could be seen in this light[14]. As Beitz states that the principle that states own the raw materials found on their territory is indefensible, since they have done nothing to deserve this wealth and thus resource-poor countries should be compensated by the equivalent of a global wealth tax. The implicit assertion is that existing international economic inequalities are actually created by, rather than reflected in, the contemporary international economic order.

The second set of arguments for the notion of global social justice refer to the basic assertion that rich countries of the contemporary global order are responsible for the poverty of poor countries. The argument says that rich countries have extensive obligations to the poor and weak countries. This broad line of argumentation is echoed in post-Leninist theories of imperialism, dependency theory and centre-periphery analysis.[15]

Another variant of the approach is that of Thomas Pogge.[16] His work highlights that the problems of environmental degradation, mass poverty, malnutrition and starvation are the price paid by the poor to support the lifestyle of all the inhabitants of the advanced industrial world. He advocates global redistribution via a tax on the use of natural resources, which is a requirement of global social justice. This line of inquiry is, however, contested by certain economists who contend that genuine free trade would do more to help the poor.[17]

Both of these arguments, referred above, are challenged on the ground that they contain incorrect empirical propositions about the state of affairs in the actual global order that prevails in the contemporary times.

The third set of arguments favouring social justice is based on the Kantian principle that a wrong done anywhere within the contemporary global order is felt everywhere in it. The Kantian view entails a priori moral principles which envisage all individuals as deserving of equal respect independent of boundaries of nation-state. Kant's formulation of categorical imperative forms the basis of Beitz's (1983) account of cosmopolitanism, and Onora O'Neill's account of our obligations to distant strangers.[18] Peter Singer's utilitarian framework regarding obligation of the rich to the poor is another attempt to conceptualize the question of the global justice.[19]

Brian Barry's espousal of the principle that the basic needs of all should be met before the non-basic needs of anyone are satisfied is essentially a cosmopolitan one, which derives from the idea of justice as impartiality (Barry, 1994, 1998).

In the third set of arguments, there is recognition of the prevailing social reality that such extremes of wealth and poverty in itself (that are found in the contemporary global order) create obligations on the part of the rich to help the poor.

Here the debate has revolved around certain key considerations. To begin with, it is important to determine the extent of such obligations on the part of the 'haves' towards the 'have-nots'. Secondly, it is vital to figure out whether these obligations are necessarily fulfilled by full-blooded state intervention to redistribute resources in an inequitable contemporary global order. John Rawls, in his work, *The Law of Peoples*[20] advances the proposition that our obligation extends only to helping societies that are not capable of sustaining internal schemes of social justice to reach the point at which they would be so capable. Rawls was of the view that the transfer of actual wealth is not necessary to put burdened societies on the road to social justice. According to him, what such societies require is the right kind of civil society and socio-political values. The real assistance, though, of a different order was suggested by economists in the form of free trade and access for less developed countries to developed world markets.[21]

Rawls invokes the idea of public reason that 'specifies at the deepest level of the basic moral and political values that are to determine a constitutional democratic government's relations to its citizens and their relation to one another. In short, it concerns how the political relation is to be understood'.[22] This should serve as the basis for initiating systematic efforts to address the problem of justice in the given national society. According to Rawls, 'such reason is public in three ways: as the reason of free and equal citizens, it is the reason of the pubic; its subject is the public good concerning questions of fundamental political justice, with the questions being of two kinds, constitutional essentials and matters of basic justice; and its nature and content are public, being expressed in public reasoning by a family of reasonable conceptions of political justice reasonably thought to satisfy the criterion of reciprocity.[23] Rawls relies upon the effectiveness of deliberative democracy, as the best way to address the question of justice. He goes on to say that there are 'three essentials of deliberative democracy. One is an idea of public reason; ... a second is a framework of constitutional democratic institutions that specifies the setting for deliberative legislative bodies. The third is the knowledge and desire on the part of citizens generally to follow public reason and to realize its ideal in their political conduct.'[24]

The arguments in favour of global justice are, however, subject to certain criticisms regarding the status of global justice as a feasible and desirable line of argumentation in the contemporary global order. First of all, social democracy and a strong welfare state in Western Europe have come under sustained scrutiny as a sound political economy option in the past few decades.

Commitment to one's fellow citizens and high taxes are being questioned as credible propositions. Secondly, the Westphalian assumption that power would be divided amongst a plurality of national actors no longer holds true. Thirdly, anti-global capitalist movement such as 'Occupy Wall Street' agitation have fundamentally critiqued the bases and motivations of global justice framework. Thirdly, changes of policy in national units in response to the demands of global justice are visible, rather than the development of effective global institutions of governance. Fourthly, the Westphalian states have not been able to cope with problems thrown up by environmental degradation or the management of the global economy.

III

While addressing the question of justice in the contemporary global order, the above sets of guiding considerations impinge upon the problem of justice at the present juncture. The idea of global justice emerges as the most credible way of inquiring and acting upon the sources and nature of injustice in the contemporary global order. Since the globe remains the reference point for conceptualizing the nature and dynamics of the contemporary global order, the question of justice has to be addressed from the vantage point of the globe itself and its necessary implications will have to be taken into account for forging an effective strategy of countering injustice across the global spectrum.

As regards human rights violations and its impact on world politics, former or even sitting heads of states are brought before various national and international courts or tribunals. In 1998, General Augusto Pinochet, the former ruler of Chile, was arrested in London on an extradition request by a Spanish Court seeking to try him for crimes committed during his military dictatorship. Later, Slobodan Milosevic of Yugoslavia and Charles Taylor were indicted for war crimes. Due to shifts in international legal standards and practices, human rights prosecutions have taken place. Sikkink has called the rise and spread of a set of ideas and norms as 'justice cascade'.[25] The question of justice in contemporary global order is indeed multi-dimensional. Under present political conditions, the obligations derived under conceptions of international and global justice are so stringent that compliance cannot be ensured in the foreseeable future.

Notes

1. Globalization, essentially refers to the shrinking of geographical distance. It means compression of both time and place in that events in one location can be visually and aurally experienced, through the grace of modern technology, virtually instantly around the globe. See Anthony Giddens, *BBC Reith Lectures 1999: Runaway World* and *Runaway World: The Reith Lectures Revisited*, November 1999.

   Economic globalization indicates convergence in regard to income levels, social structure and behaviour across the planet earth. But its critics point towards sections of society, which are not benefitted by economic globalization. As regards cultural diversities, the point is that their differences must be so acknowledged. Protecting their cultural diversity means ensuring justice to them.

   Sweden's Deputy Foreign Minister at the Council Meeting of the Socialist International in New Delhi had made the following observation:

   'Globalization without a global political and ethical framework cannot be a driving for combatting poverty and creating peace, democracy and development'.
2. This remains the essence of the realist thought in international relations.
3. See Andrew Linklater, *Critical Theory and World Politics*. London: Routledge, 2007, p. 29.
4. On the question of welfare state, see Clause Offe in John Keane (ed), *Contradictions of the Welfare State*, London: Hutchinson, 1984.
5. See Hedley Bull, *The Anarchical Society: A Study of Order in World Politics*. London: Macmillan, 1977, p. 93.
6. See W. Arthur Lewis, *The Evolution of the International Economic Order*. Princeton: Princeton University Press, 1978, p. 3.
7. See Lewis, p. 74.
8. Lewis, p. 75.
9. See Bull, 1977.
10. See Bull, 1977.
11. See Terry Nardin, *Law, Morality and the Relations of States*. Princeton, NJ: Princeton University Press, 1983.
12. See Beitz, 1983.
13. See John Rawls, *A Theory of Justice*. Cambridge, Mass.: The Belknap Press of Harvard University,1971.
14. See Charles Beitz, 'Cosmopolitan Ideas and National Sovereignty', *Journal of Philosophy*, 1983, 80, pp. 591–600.
15. See A.G. Frank, *Capitalism and Underdevelopment in Latin America*, Harmondsworth: Penguin, 1971; See Johan Galtung, 'A Structural Theory of Imperialism', *Journal of Peace Research*, 1971, 8(2), pp. 81–117; See Immanuel Wallerstein, *The Modern World System*, Vol. I, II and III, London: Academic Press, 1974/1989, 1989; See Bill Warren, *Imperialism: Pioneer of*

Capitalism, London: New Left Books, 1980; See Anthony Brewer, *Marxist Theories of Imperialism: A Critical Survey*. London: Routledge, 1990.

16. See Thomas Pogge, *World Poverty and Human Rights,* Cambridge: Polity Press, 2002.
17. See M. Desai, *Marx's, Revenge: The Resurgence of Capitalism and The Death of Statist Socialism,* London: Verso, 2002; Also see J. Bhagwati, *In Defense of Globalisation*. Oxford: Oxford University Press, 2004.
18. See O. O'Neill, *Faces of Hunger,* London: Allen and Unwin, 1986; and also see O. O'Neill, 'Transnational Justice', in David Held (ed.), *Political Theory Today,* Cambridge: Polity Press, 1991.
19. See Peter Singer, 'Famine, Affluence and Morality', in C.R. Beitz, et al. (eds) *International Ethics*, Princeton: Princeton University Press, 1985.
20. See John Rawls, *The Law of Peoples,* Cambridge, Mass.: Harvard University Press, 1999.
21. See R. Cassen, *Does Aid Work?* (2nd Edition), Oxford: Clarendon Press, 1994.
22. See Rawls, 1999, p. 132.
23. Ibid., p. 133.
24. Ibid.
25. See Kathryn Sikkink, *The Justice Cascade: How Human Rights Prosecutions Are Changing World Politics*, New York: Norton, 2011.

Part II

Social Justice and Marginalized Sections in India

9

Social Development through Social Justice

The Indian Context

S.V. Pande and Archana Srivastava

It is a well known fact in the domain of social sciences that the primacy accorded to the understanding and explanation of the process of economic development/growth led to the widespread belief that it also implied social development. However, two approaches to development could easily be distinguished from each other, namely, the functionalist and the Marxist approach. Based on them, two broad conceptions of development have been formulated, *viz.*, social development meaning an increase in the life chances, and economic development meaning an alteration of resource allocations, respectively. Both these conceptions and the operational indicators derived from them, however, suffer from a predominantly economic basis.

Almost until the middle of the 20th century, sociologists and political scientists were somewhat inhibited to take up the idea of development in the right earnest due to the powerful influence of Weber's doctrine of value-free social sciences, leaving the scope to be almost entirely used by economists. But due to the interplay of various social forces (not requiring a detailed description right now), the hold of the Weberian doctrine of objectivity in the social sciences started to be reviewed and revised in a critical frame, resulting in its slackening and, thereby, justifying or confronting the question of social development.

Social Dimensions of Development

Though economic development in certain ways seems to be a pre-requisite to social development, yet it does not lead to their being synonymous. At least four non-economic dimensions of development have been well established by social scientists, namely the political, social, cultural and the human dimensions (Sharma, 1980). It is true that the economists themselves were the first to recognize the importance of human factors in economic development; it was to the credit of sociologists who systematically brought into focus the social dimensions of development, beginning with an analysis of social determinants and consequences of economic development (Hoselitz, 1960; Eisenstadt, 1961; Smelser, 1965; Barringer et al., 1965). It was only from their sustained interest and effort in the sociological bearings of economic development that the notion of social/societal development was established in its own right (Blumer, 1966; Drewnowski, 1967; Kim, 1973). However, the idea of social progress held almost the same appeal to social philosophers in the late 17th and early 18th centuries as the idea of development today. But that could not last long, and it is not necessary for the present purpose to go further into its comprehensive ramifications either.

The concept of economic development has, however, broadened over the years as evident from the following conceptions which have, according to Sharma (1980), emerged in that order: economic development as economic growth; economic development as change in the social and political structures accompanying economic growth, and economic development as a trinity of economic growth, economic equity and economic self-reliance. The conceptualization of economic development as economic growth measured by the rate of increase of per capita income or product fell into disrepute because of common criticism of GNP statistics. It also implies the economist's apprehension that development includes much that cannot be specified in purely economic terms, the broadening of the above-said concept of economic development notwithstanding.

The functionalist perspective of social development tends to view it as a movement in the 'upward and forward' direction: Parsons (1966, 1971, 1974), Smelser (1966) and Eisenstadt (1961, 1966) have all portrayed it as a process of social differentiation, integration and adaptive upgrading. Such a view of development, according to Sharma (1980), has proliferated in the current themes of modernization all of which share at least one attribute in common, i.e. European ethnocentrism. Consequently, this perspective explains 'underdevelopment' as a state of non-development caused and perpetuated by ignorance and inaction rooted in traditionalism.

The dialectical (Marxist) perspective of social development contends that the underdevelopment of the 'developing' societies is the result of the development of what are known today as 'developed' societies. Following the historical materialist point of view, social scientists like Baran (1967), Frank (1967) and Amin (1976) have variously elaborated this theme by tracing the dialectics of development and underdevelopment from the period of merchant capitalism through colonialism to neo-colonialism. This perspective conceives development as liberation of the underdeveloped/developing societies from their dependency on the developed ones, thereby implying a rejection of economic aid, technical assistance and model emulation as a strategy of development. It, therefore, suggests the 'original' path of development with technical cooperation as its strategy.

These conceptions of development have been criticized both for their logical imperfections and their empirical distortions, apart from their ideological predilections. Attempts have also been made to reconcile the two perspectives, but that is not our purpose right now, and we leave it here at that.

A Normative Concept

It has now come to be almost accepted among all sorts of social scientists and on all hands that development is essentially a normative concept. Seers (1970: 1–2) clearly asserts: 'Development is inevitably treated as a normative concept, as almost a synonym for improvement. To pretend otherwise is just to hide one's value judgements'. Social development as normative category, however, includes two broad conceptions: one, as increase in life chances of people and, two, as egalitarian alteration of society's resource allocation or distribution. The first one essentially is a utilitarian conceptualization which implies a move towards a better social life, aptly understood by Streeten (1971) as 'change towards social state judged desirable'. The UNO (1975) also stressed the same view: 'As the ultimate purpose of development is to provide increasing opportunities to all people for a better life, it is essential to expand

and improve facilities for education, health, nutrition, housing, social welfare and to safeguard the environment'. All this amounts to a welfare-based conception of social development with its emphasis on the ever-increasing scale of social services to be organized by the state.

However, this most common kind of conception of social development suffers from two limitations: first, it reduces a better quality of life to a better standard of living, and second, it generates dependence on the state to provide necessary social services which to some extent blunts the individual's sense of responsibility for the good of other individuals besides the fact that the state itself may suffer from lack of adequate financial resources to fulfil these expectations of all the people.

The second part of the normative conception of social development, as pointed out above, is egalitarian in that it relates to alteration of resource allocation/distribution, the sharpest formulation of which came from Kim (1973: 468) who, treating it as a value concept, identified the following indicators as core development values of all human societies: social and economic justice, economic prosperity, political freedom, health and education. As a measure of societal development, he proposes the concept of 'structural flexibility' by which he means 'the degree to which the structure of society allows the deprived and alienated majority not only to demand their just (or equal, ideally if possible) share of resources but also to actually obtain such goals'.

This (egalitarian) conception of social development emphasizes the view that as long as the structure of society changes in the direction that enhances the opportunity for the deprived masses to obtain a greater (or equal) share of resources, that structure is in the process of development. The goal of social development here is, obviously, to create a just and non-exploitative social order rather than a mass-consumption society.

This view has, however, been criticized for its lack of internal conceptual consistency, that is, its core development values are not self-consistent because a certain amount of strain inheres in their interrelations with the result that pursuit of one may impede the realization of another. The problem of compatibility may arise, for example, between national sovereignty and individual autonomy, or between freedom and justice. These are not contrived value dilemmas but are genuine problems of coherence among the development values. The experiences of the socialist societies, past and present, bear testimony to the limitations of the egalitarian formulation of social development: apart from lack of freedom in them, political repression has been their characteristic feature.

The Contextuality Issue

Whichever the conception of social development – utilitarian or egalitarian – to be operationalized, the issue of contextuality, i.e. the question of place-time dimension, cannot be escaped or ignored. Two perspectives can easily be discerned in this regard – the uniformitarain/universal and the relativistic. The former stipulates a uniform set of indicators of social development supposed to be universally applicable, while the latter asserts society-specific differential sets of such indicators. Seers (1972: 22) takes the former position when he asserts: 'The realization of the potential of human personality is the universally accepted aim of social development (which) spells out its necessary conditions'. On the other hand, Mukerjee (1975: 120) expressed his opinion by maintaining that 'at the present state of our knowledge in the social sciences, we are not in a position to standardize the concept of social development and evolve 'universally' applicable social indicators on that basis'.

Without, however, going into the details of this aspect of our discussion, let it suffice to say that both the welfare-based and the egalitarian conceptions of social development delineate specific sets of its indicators ranging from equalitarian distribution of natural and economic resources to acquisition of education, better quality of life, availability of nutritious food, longevity and medical facilities, ecological balance and communitarian solidarity, confident personality and other cultural indicators, etc. It is noteworthy that the most critical and crucial indicator of social development, namely a spontaneous adoption and prevalence of the spirit social-justice principle has either remained only implicit in the earlier formulations or it has skipped their advocates' attention altogether. That is reason enough to clearly, though briefly, articulate it in any discussion of this theme, which is what has been attempted here.

Social-Justice Approach to Social Development

The concept of social justice is rooted in and directly opposed to the phenomenon of social inequality. It is hypothesized that there exists in society a dominant minority which enslaves the majority of people for perpetuating its own interests, that is, for keeping itself in positions of power and maintaining its social and cultural supremacy. Therefore, the groups of people experiencing various forms of humiliation, and who constitute the majority of any given population, will, at some time or the other, start making efforts to come on par with their superiors. Social justice as a goal is said to have been achieved when this minority of social, economic, cultural and political superiors come to terms with the majority (inferiors), and willingly agree to treat them as their equals in all these respects.

The social-justice approach to development aims to socially enable those who were socially disabled because of tradition or for other reasons. The social development through social-justice approach gives precedence to the development of the human material or human resource coming particularly from the underprivileged or the downtrodden sections of society. Also that it precedes the development of material elements. Conditions of exploitation and oppression are detected and liquidated at each level, apparent or subtle, to restore social justice.

This approach postulates changes in social structures. The character of changes contemplated in particular depends on two factors: (a) which section of society treats itself as oppressed and demands changes in the prevailing social structures; and (b) how far such 'unjust' structures are considered to be alterable. Both these factors are variable and their variation gives rise to the corresponding changes in the demand of social justice. For instance, the early liberal theory articulated the demand of the new industrial-commercial middle-class against mercantilism: 'social justice' was then identified with the 'laissez faire individualism'. In the 19th century, the socialist theory pressed the claims of the working class for social justice as it was directed against the excesses of the capitalist system. Today 'social justice' signifies claims of all the oppressed and exploited sections whether they comprise economic classes (e.g. workers vs. employers, consumers vs. traders, etc.), races (e.g. black vs. white), nations (e.g. underdeveloped/developing vs. developed ones), groupings like those based on gender (female vs. male), and castes (lower vs. the upper castes, particularly in India).

Advancement of science and technology, increased spread of democracy and of freedom of the intelligentsia, of social mobility and of educational opportunities are all common features of the present-day society; they are also the factors which have successfully changed the social consciousness of people. Consequently, the demand of 'social justice' continues to be articulated in newer and newer forms for the achievement of the goal of social development. It is significant that the demand for changes in social structures in the direction of social justice is first raised by or on behalf of the oppressed sections. In due course such demand is recognized as a just claim of those sections; and it gradually becomes part and parcel of the current social consciousness.

Some authors regard social justice purely as a problem of distribution of wealth, offices, opportunities, and other resources available in society, thus equating it with distributive justice. Miller (1976) identifies various models of social justice according to the different views regarding such distribution eg. according to rights and needs. When we speak of 'economic growth with social justice', we mean it in the sense of distributive justice, implying thereby that the benefits of economic growth are justly distributed among various sections of society, particularly so that they percolate to the lower strata of society. In fact, the process of securing social justice cannot be divorced from the process of securing social development.

Social justice represents the developmental concept in another sense also. For instance, Rawls's (1973) concept of social justice as fairness comprehends for it a regulated free-economy, with a reasonable 'concentration of wealth'. Here justice is treated as a matter of adjustment between the conflicting claims of the contending parties in a 'political situation'. On the contrary, developmental concept of social justice represents a humanist aspiration, treating justice as a matter of improving the conditions of the oppressed and underprivileged social groups not by placing them in a competitive situation but by creating more congenial conditions for the downtrodden. Thus, developmental concept of social justice covers all its essential aspects; it represents social justice as the voice of the oppressed, as a humanist philosophy and also as a force behind structural changes in society.

For securing an effective change in the direction of social justice, two conditions must be fulfilled: (a) there should be a general awareness of the goal, i.e. there has to be a mass support for the proposed change; and (b) there should be an enlightened and energetic group with a firm determination to achieve this goal. And Ambedkar (1936) would have us believe, particularly in the Indian context, that social democracy must precede political democracy in order to achieve real social development.

The Indian Context

In the Indian context, it precisely means equal treatment to be meted out to the dalits, tribals, women, minorities, and various other weaker sections of society. The policy of social justice adopted by the Union Government and its states is based on the ideology of protection of human dignity. It has been unambiguously asserted that liberty, equality and fraternity are those primordial values on which the notion of social justice rests, and the Constitution of India guarantees all of them as the fundamental human rights for all the citizens of India. Abolition of social disabilities like untouchability and exploitation in all its forms provide further testimony to this policy. These fundamental rights and their explanations are spread through Articles 13 to 23, of the Constitution, and in order to protect them, the judiciary has been kept independent of state control. Thus, all forms of social, economic, political and cultural disabilities from which the former Shudras suffered have been meticulously sought to be abolished by the state.

The practical implications of the policy of social justice in India operate through Articles 330 to 335 of the Constitution, which guarantee reservation of seats to the members of the scheduled castes/tribes in the Lok Sabha and the state legislatures, and also ensure reservation to them for appointments in jobs of various kinds. Now this policy has to a large extent been extended to the members of 'other backward castes' after the government's acceptance of the Mandal Commission's Report (1990).

However, the real success of the policy of social justice as the crucial indicator or requirement of social development depends more on the attitudinal changes marked by a sense of fraternity between and among various castes when exhibited spontaneously in the behavioural patterns of both the upper and the lower castes, that is when the upper castes start treating the lower as their natural equals and the latter start treating the former with brotherly trust. There is evidence to show that the caste system does not inherently lack in the required resilience and the desired adaptability. Mutual tolerance and intercaste marriages are likely to increase in conjunction with the other forces of modernization like education, science, technology, mass media and democratization of the public mind through various means and measures.

This observation can be further elaborated by pointing at the fact that in India, the planned economic development blended with the spirit of social justice has led to various social-structural changes. A few examples as following ones would suffice to bring out the present-day changing reality in so far as the landed aristocracy stands abolished as a class; the power structure in the villages has passed almost completely from the traditional rural elites to a new rural middle-class. A new class structure has emerged in the villages and a peasant middle-class, which is aggressively entrepreneurial, and has quickly adopted scientific methods and techniques of agriculture. The monopoly in higher education, previously a privilege of the upper castes and classes, has now slowly started percolating to the middle and lower classes and castes in the villages.

These changes, according to Singh (1993), are a result of legislation and other reform measures. The reservations which the Constitution accorded in the legislatures, government services, and schools for the underprivileged have now successfully spawned a new generation of educated youth. All of them have together contributed to the increasing mobilization in the social structure. To quote him (1993: 120):

> India has deliberately chosen a path of development and social change which promotes social mobility, opportunity, and well being of the deprived sections of society in a nation which is no doubt dominated by the rich and the elite. It does, however, employ a method of legal consensus which is based on a reconciliation model. In such a model, the responsibility of the dominant classes becomes acute because reconciliation implies, almost in a Gandhian style, the voluntary accommodation of the demands of the poor, the weak and the deprived, and the underprivileged. Its logical compulsion is more pragmatic than ethical; the privileged should know that such accommodation is also in their self interest. In Marxist terminology, it is the tactics of the intelligent national bourgeoisie who, forewarned of revolutionary potential, attempts to contain it. On the contrary, the specificities of the Indian social structure and its historicity would show imperfections both logical and historical in the nature of alternative paths of development and modernization.

However, the state policy of caste-based quotas or reservations in government services, legislatures, educational institutions and elsewhere (mistaking it as the panacea of social justice and development) has been decried by eminent social scientists long since (Kothari, 1970; Srinivas, 1959, 1962; Mayer, 1967; Beteille, 1965; Rudolf and Rudolf, 1960; Rao, 1968) mainly due to the fact of its politicization and creation of vote-banks politics by unscrupulous political forces. An example reflecting the views of Andre Beteille (2009) would be apt in the present context: 'Recourse to quotas for addressing every perceived social imbalance has become a habit of mind among leaders of every political party. The habit has become so deeply ingrained in our political culture that even to raise a question in public about its wisdom is to risk causing a scandal in the political establishment. It is in this environment remarkable for any single political leader, no matter how high his standing in his party, to question the advisability of quotas for his own community … . If serious thinking has begun in political circles about the limits of numerical quotas and the need for affirmative action in the case of Muslims, should there not be the same kind of thought given to policies relating to women?'

So it seems apropos here to emphasize that the equal-opportunity principle must be allowed to work through creation of abilities and personality development of the historically deprived populations, not only by the negatively-oriented legal removal of the disabilities. Social justice being the mainstay of the culture of democracy is the surest index of all social development.

Conclusion

In the foregoing analysis, an attempt has been made to formulate a more adequate construct of social development by including in it the normative dimension of social justice as its supreme indicator: the more we achieve it, the higher the level of social development achieved in any specific society. The normative upgrading of this non-material aspect of social life is more crucial to social development than improvement on material conditions insofar as it directly ensures a better quality of life which is a function not only of the objective characteristics of anyone's situation but also of his (subjective) expectations and aspirations aimed to lead a dignified life. It is because of this assumption that measures of material welfare are deemed inadequate unless supplemented by this measure of life quality, for one's life satisfaction might be found to decrease even as per capita income/GDP might be rising.

So what is needed is the internalization of the norm of social justice, that is, 'others before self' in the personality integration of the members of society. It is this sentiment that leads us to the importance of normative upgrading of society (as a measure of its development). From limiting oneself to self-seeking to intense humanitarian concern for others is a sure index of the operation of the principle of spontaneous social justice, and therefore a clean index of normative upgrading/social development. Needless to assert that it is all the more required in modern times in view of its preference for an unbridled indulgence in material pleasures and consumerism, having lost in large measure its sensibilities towards others' sufferings. Surely, a society devoid of its concerns for social justice cannot be regarded as a developed society.

It is, thus, concluded that the process of social development consists in the rise or evolution of a society from less just to more just or less human to more human stage. That is where the crux of the truly social dimension of social development lies.

References

Ambedkar, B.R., *Annihilation of Caste*, Bombay: Bharat Bhusan Press, 1936.

Amin, S., *Unequal Development*, New York: Monthly Review Press, 1976.

Baran, P.A., *The Political Economy of Growth*, New York: Monthly Review Press, 1967.

Barringer, H.R. et al., *Social Change in Developing Areas*, Cambridge, Mass.: Schenkman, 1965.

Beteille, A., 'Break The Quota Routine: Push Social Uplift Through Affirmative Action' New Delhi: *The Times of India*, 15 June 2009, p. 12.

——. *Caste, Class and Power*, Berkeley: University of California Press, 1965.

Blumer, H., 'The Idea of Social Development', *Studies in Comparative International Development*, 1966, Vol. 2, pp. 3–11.

Drewnowski, J., 'Indicators of Social Development', *Social Change and Economic Growth*, Paris: Development Centre, 1967.

Eisenstadt, S.N., *Modernization: Protest and Change*, Englewood Cliffs, NJ: Prentice Hall, 1966.

——. *Essays on Sociological Aspects of Political and Economic Development*, The Hague: Mouton, 1961.

Frank, A.G., *Capitalism and Underdevelopment in Latin America*, New York: Monthly Review Press, 1967.

Hoselitz, B.F., *Sociological Aspects of Economic Growth*, New York: The Free Press, 1960.

Kim, Kyong-Dong, 'Towards a Sociological Theory of Development: A Structural Perspective', *Rural Sociology*, 1973, Vol. 38, No. 4, pp. 462–476.

Kothari, R., *Caste in Indian Politics*, Delhi: Orient Longman,1970.

Mayer, A.C., 'Caste and Local Politics in India' in Philip Mason (ed.), *India and Ceylone: Unity and Diversity*, New York: Oxford University Press, 1967.

Miller, D., *Social Justice*, Oxford: Clarendon Press, 1976.

Mukerjee, Ramkrishna, *Social Indicators*, Delhi: Macmillan, 1975.

Parsons, T., *Societies: Evolutionary and Comparative Perspectives*, Englewood Cliffs, NJ: Prentice Hall, 1966.

——. *The System of Modern Societies*, Englewood Cliffs, NJ: Prentice-Hall,1971.

——. 'Evolutionary Universals in Society', *American Sociological Review*, 1974, Vol. 29.

Rao, M.S.A., 'Political Elite and Caste Associations' *Economic and Political Weekly,* 18 May 1968.

Rawls, J., *A Theory of Justice*, London: Oxford University Press, 1973.

Rudolf, L.I. and S.H. Rudolf, 'The Political Role of India's Caste Association', *Pacific Affairs*, 1960.

Seers, D., 'What Are We Trying To Measure?' *Journal of Development Studies*, 1972, Vol. 8, No. 3, p. 22.

——. 'The Meaning of Development', *The Agricultural Development Council*, Reprint, September 1970, pp. 1–2.

Streeten, P., 'How Poor are the Poor Countries?' in Seers, D. and Joy, L (eds.), *Development in a Divided World*, Harmondsworth: Penguin, 1971.

Sharma, S.L., 'Criteria of Social Development', *Social Action*, January–March, 1980,Vol. 30.

Singh, Y., *Social Change in India*, Delhi: Har-Anand Publications, 1993, p. 120.

Smelser, N.J., 'Modernization of Social Relations' in M. Weiner (ed.), *Modernization: The Dynamics of Growth*, New York: Basic Books, 1966.

——. *The Sociology of Economic Life*, Englewood Cliff, NJ: Prentice Hall, 1965.

Srinivas, M.N., 'The Dominant Caste in Rampura', *The American Anthropologist*, 1959, Vol. 61.

——. *Caste in Modern India and Other Essays*, Bombay: Asia Publishing House, 1962.

10

Transformation of Caste System into 'Caste' in Contemporary India

K.L. Sharma

The question about caste as a 'system' has always remained in vogue as it has been projected as a sort of absolute institution relating to prescription and proscription of practice and behaviour of people, particularly among Hindus in Indian society. Available authentic sources indicate that caste system has always been resilient and dynamic as it has been affected by its inner logical inconsistencies and contradictions on the one hand, and it has also affected economy, polity, culture and religion on the other, and due to this dual process, it has never been a static and stagnant system. The main objective of this paper is to understand and analyse continuity and change in the caste system as a social force, having varying forms, manifestations and activities. Caste system has always engaged people, often directly, with varied functions and obligations. Based on a set of norms, which acquired a sort of meta-legal approval, people have been grouped as *Jatis*, and arranged as higher and lower entities.

Caste system has never been monolithic and undifferentiated since ancient times. No generalized caste ideals have ever existed. It has been 'elaborate' in south India, and it has not been so in north-west and north-east parts of India. Susan Bayly (2000: 4) has stated that today manifestations of caste are far more generalized than before. Caste as a system has been endangered, shaped and perpetuated by recent political and social developments. The persisting traditional elements of caste have their roots in the early 18th century. The British rule (ibid., 1–24) significantly expanded and sharpened caste norms and conventions, recreated many manifestations of caste language and ideology as a source of power and authority. Nicholas B. Dirks (2003) also considers, like Bayly, caste as a modern political phenomenon, a creation of the British colonialism. Before the British advent, there were more of caste-like elements rather than a rigid and static caste system.

Even ethnosociologist Ronald B. Inden (1990: 213–62) is of the view that castes were as political assemblages or 'subject-citizens' within medieval kingdoms. Each region had its specific schemes and groupings, hence no uniform all embracing scheme of caste gradations. Caste was a dynamic, diverse and multidimensional reality of Indian society. Bayly vehemently argues that there is nothing like an orientalist fiction or monolithic culture code regarding origin and functioning of the caste system (op. cit., 6). Caste has become a system of oppression, a scheme of social disabilities and hindrances, like any other system of inequities, mainly due to incorporation of the element of power in its sociocultural fabric.

II

Today, caste is a reality, though of a different kind than what it was before the British rule in India. It has become a crude means of political mobilization, of discrete use for specific goals, and more for seeking 'representations,' 'reservations' and 'favours' in public domains. Caste has become a weak-strong phenomenon. As a system, it has eroded its legitimacy and appeal, and as a phenomenon, it has reincarnated itself as a way of reckoning and identity.

The Indian State has played a dual role in shaping and reshaping of the caste system. As we have stated earlier that the state has twisted and mutilated caste in innumerable ways, it has also recognized significance of the caste system by way of accepting caste as the basis of socio-cultural and economic standing of people as higher and lower. In the 1891 census, social groups were named as 'agricultural and pastoral', 'artisans and menials', 'professionals', and even 'vagrants'. Rankings were made based on local evidence of 'social precedence'. Before this, in the 1881 census, profiles of over 400 'races' and 'tribes' were presented. The series of 119 volumes of imperial gazetteers also reflected 'titles', 'races', 'stereotypes' in the context of caste. The 1901 census ranked all castes in terms of specific *varna* context. 'Ritual distance' was the main criterion of caste ranking in 1901 census, and the 'functions' performed by the caste system was accorded primacy in the 1931 census (Census of India, 1891, Vol. I; Census of India, 1901, Vol. I, Part I; Census of India, 1931, Vol. I, Part III).

The first post-Independence census conducted in 1951 did not include enumeration of caste, except counting of the Scheduled Castes (SCs) and the Scheduled Tribes (STs). However, reservations based on caste (in case of the SCs) kept the caste in vogue in social and political domains. Though, even without enumeration of caste in the post-Independence censuses, caste has remained the centre of Indian politics. Caste-based reservations were granted the Other Backward Classes (OBCs) in 1993. Caste is being accepted by the State as the basis of social standing. The Constitution of India pronounces India as a secular, democratic and socialistic State, free of caste, creed and religion. Such an ambiguity and dualism have provided scope for unethical and undemocratic appropriation of caste in the field of politics and power, in particular. The inclusion of caste enumeration in the census of 2011 speaks about the weak-strong Indian state and flexible nature of Indian politics. We have today 'caste parties' and 'caste leaders' in political parties.

Before we explain in somewhat detail the nature and functioning of the caste system in general, and also in some particular contexts, it may be desirable to mention that within each caste, in principle, all members are equal, but in reality, individuals and families have also been distinguished and differentiated based on their achieved status, despite equal ascribed ritual status, that is, birth in the same caste. Thus, along with ritual hierarchy of castes, intra-caste and inter-caste distinctions based on non-ritual criteria, were given due consideration and weightage. Clearly this implies that caste incorporated class and the congruence of these two, further implied inclusion of power in the orbit of caste. Though birth in caste could not be mutilated, but at the same time, it did not rule out a noticeable play of extra-caste considerations. Thus, caste was always more than a simple hierarchy based on the notions of 'pure' and 'impure' or a set of values and ideas (Dumont, 1972; Srinivas, 1952; 1962), which encompassed the entire matrix of socio-economic and political relations.

The propagation of caste system as an absolute and rigid system has done more harm to the Indian society than the caste system itself. Projection of caste as an ideology itself became an ideology of its propagators. This became, no doubt, even before the advent of British rule in India, however, the British granted an added impetus to both caste and feudalism for the reasons best known to them. Writings by James Tod (1990) Herbert Risley (1909), J.H. Hutton (1963) and many others are a clear evidence of the glorification of feudalism and caste as institutions of highest merit and for good of the Indian people. Such a doctored blasphemy helped the British in pacifying the agitating souls against their rule and also sealed revelation of full facts relating to demerits of the caste system.

The British created two histories: (1) which they desired to create and produce; and (2) which they did not like to be written and desired but to remain dormant or dead. For example, at times, the functionaries of lower castes withdrew their services rendered to higher castes when they were not paid their just dues, wages, and rewards. A barber, being dissatisfied, declined to do his job of cutting hair, and other multiple services. So was done by a potter, who refused to supply earthen posts. A carpenter denied supply of ploughs and other wooden implements required in agriculture, when he was dissatisfied with his patrons. Under a hierarchical system, these were the systemic provisions for seeking 'fair justice', if not 'absolute justice' (Rawls, 1999). After a tug of war, which ensued because of injustice done to the lower caste functionaries, under public pressure and because of non-availability of alternatives to the services rendered to the patrons, often the higher caste patrons acceded to the legitimate demands of their service castes.

III

Today, the practice of caste can be seen in two domains: (i) politics, and (ii) rules of marriage. Caste is being appropriated in elections from Panchayati Raj institutions to Lok Sabha (Lower House of Indian Parliament). Even elections for trade unions and students bodies are not free from the caste virus. Candidates are nominated by political parties and groups based on combinations/alliances. Muscle, men and money power of contesting candidates belonging to different castes are also equally heavy considerations. Caste as a phenomenon and caste as a notion of reckoning can be seen in political mobilization, atrocities, violence, exploitation and in other similar contexts and situations.

Another practice of caste is seen in the so-called concern and anxiety regarding violation of rules of marriage. In the present form, such a concern and anxiety have attained notoriety in the form of 'honour killings' of young men and women on the pretext of violation of rules of marriage, namely, caste endogamy and clan exogamy. The perpetrators of such a heinous crime have become self-appointed *thekedars* (protectors) of honour of their castes/communities. Such a mischievously assumed notion of the purity of descent or blood group is, in fact, a blasphemy, a crime against humanity. *Gotra* has mythical origin, and as such it is not within the possible range of relatives by blood and lineage. There is nothing in the sanskrit texts to object to clan endogamy. Marriage was allowed within the same *gotra* or between those who recited the same *pravara (mantra)* (Kapadia, 1986: 127).

It is also pertinent here that ritual hierarchy was not absolute even in principle as it has been made out to be, mainly because of propagation of a certain imagery of the caste system by the British. For example, certain rituals could not be performed/completed, which were in the ritual purview of the lower caste functionaries, such as sweepers, shoemakers, barbers, potters, blacksmiths, etc. These lower caste ritual-performers were treated as 'pious' on given occasions, such as birth, marriage, death, etc.; and they were paid customarily like the Brahmin priests. Harold Gould (1967: 26–55) has addressed the lower caste ritual performers as 'contra-priests'. A message of equality in an inequalitarian system is quite implicit here.

In this way, caste system was not absolutely rigid, but flexibility was considerably less than its rigidity. There were mechanisms and devices which prevented openness in the system. It became an insulated system of intercaste relations. Endogamy and exogamy became the cardinal norms of marriage. Violation of rules of marriage, hereditary occupations, commensality, etc. was taken as an offence, and invited punishment, including ostracization from the caste, heavy fines and hardships. Even today, stray instances of punishment are reported from some parts of India, but the way in which such punishments are carried out is quite different from what it used to be. The modalities are very different and so are the motives behind such incidences of the so-called violations, and so are the agencies which take upon themselves to punish the 'offenders'.

Today, intercaste relations, which were the bedrock of the caste system, do not persist. The hierarchy, which was an overarching phenomenon, has given a way to stratification. Caste has become one of the several other criteria in status determination. *Jati* (group) is being replaced by family (Beteille, 1998: 435–451; Sharma, 1974: 125–168) and individual. The two imply less rigidity, more flexibility, mobility and achievement. Family and individual are also not completely devoid of ascription. Caste is devalued to a certain extent, and achievement becomes a desired goal. Values and norms related to caste system have, thus, shown increasing tendency towards their decline. The system has become considerably weak, it is hardly in existence as it used to be in the beginning of the 20th century or even upto India's Independence in 1947. However, caste persists, not as a system so much, but as a means of reckoning and identity-making (Sharma, 2001: 17–43). Caste as a system has been 'questioned' and 'interrogated' (Gupta, 2000). Then, what is caste? In our view, caste is more of a notion, being appropriated by a select few, eclectically and discretely. The so-called leaders and strongmen of a given caste appropriate it for their specific aims and gains. It is used/misused as a plaything to have a mileage in community, politics, and to extract monetary benefit, out of the incidences of the so-called violations of the rules of marriage.

Another domain of appropriation of caste is elections at all levels, from Panchayati Raj institutions (village civic bodies) to Lok Sabha (Lower House of Indian Parliament). Even elections of the Students' Unions are not free from the caste virus, and nor are the trade unions. In all these elections, candidates are nominated by political parties and groups based on caste considerations, particularly in terms of their numerical strength in a given parliamentary/legislative constituency, and the muscle, men and money power of the contesting candidates of particular castes. Jawaharlal Nehru, the first Prime Minister of India, often argued in his public utterances that caste was antithetical to democracy and merit. On the contrary, some scholars are of the view that caste is not against democracy and development (Kothari, 1970). It has a representative character, because an elected person would care for the interests and welfare of those fellowmen who have voted for him/her.

Caste as a system is seen in terms of the ideology of pure and impure, division of labour, connubiality, commensality, caste panchayat or *biradari*, intracaste and intercaste relations, etc. Caste as a phenomenon and a notion of reckoning can be observed in political mobilization, atrocities, violence, exploitation, etc. In a nutshell, the journey is though several centuries old, transformation of its systemic character into a discrete phenomenon is particularly a 20th century incarnation, and that too, mainly after India's Independence in 1947. In view of these observations, K.L. Sharma (2001) has suggested a comprehensive study of caste with a view to understand: (1) caste-class nexus: its continuity and change, (2) changing character of intercaste and intracaste relations, and (3) levels of practice and mobility in caste.

IV

The main motive behind these points is to see how and to what extent ideas and values are basic for knowing actual and observable behaviour of people. To what extent Louis Dumont's thesis of special type of inequality based on caste system is in practice? We have mentioned earlier that the idea of pure and impure is central to Dumont's notion of caste hierarchy. But in our view, caste is in class and in other systems of social stratification, hence taxonomic problem persists relating to the distinction of caste from other stratificatory systems. Elsewhere, I have stated: 'Caste is increasingly becoming a matter of interpretation rather than substantialization. Caste refers to a purposive rationality, and at the same time, it provides a description and explanation of the pathologies of modern polity and economy. It is no more an absolutised system as it was characterized by punitive acts like ostracization and social neglect. Caste obstructs, which occur occasionally by a way of killings and torture of the violators of caste ethics, are incongruent with the dwindling of the caste system in recent times' (Sharma, 2001: 7).

Secondly, cliches such as tradition and modernity, continuity and change, hierarchy and stratification, organic and segmentary structures have led to unfounded dichotomies/antinomies of a resilient and harmonic society. A continued emphasis on caste as a homo hierarchicus, culture-bound and change resisting system (Dumont, 1972) has undermined the very semblance of continuity and change. However, the encompassing capability of caste system has been questioned by several scholars, including Ram Krishna Mukherjee (1957), Andre Beteille (1966: 224–46; 1969: 219–35), K.L. Sharma (1974), and Dipankar Gupta (2000). Beteille has focused on the emergence of 'differentiated institutional structures of various kinds', and the role of 'interests' along with ideas, in shaping of social stratification. Further, he observes that a new 'caste free occupational structure' and modern education have created a non-traditional basis of social relations weakening intercaste and intracaste relations. Gupta is of the view that ultimately 'individual' matters a lot in the caste system. A reconceptualization of caste system is clearly evident in the notions, such as 'multiple status hierarchies', 'attributional' criteria of caste ranking, 'new castes', 'levels of social mobility', 'downward social mobility', 'obverse structural process of social change', 'structural criteria of dominance', 'new status images', etc. (Sharma, 1974; 1977; 1980; 2010). These are expressions and articulations, relating to change of the conventional constructions and orientations. Obviously, there is today a new discourse in vogue, reflecting distantiation from caste as the basis of social relations and stratification, by the alert and articulate sections of the upper, middle, and even the erstwhile depressed sections.

Thirdly, we also see a revival of a culturological framework (Marriott, 1989) to look once again at Indian society through caste and religious categories. Such an approach considerably underrates the relevance of structural criteria in effecting change in the caste system. Historical and contextual contexts (Singh, 1994: 28–59) of change cannot be sidelined in understanding of the changing face of intercaste and intracaste relations and emergence of individual and family as more effective institutions and units of social stratification. When caste becomes weak, then family and individual emerge as stronger agencies of reproduction of equality and inequality. The two, separately as well as in conjunction, attack the traditional impediments to social mobility, and become significant units of status-evaluation.

Thus, 'caste for itself' and caste as an everyday life phenomenon are two different aspects, generally unrelated to each other. In the first case, caste is an episodic, metaphoric and goal-oriented phenomenon; and in the second sense, it is a discrete, personalized, and family-specific behavioural/interactional phenomenon. Both the interpretations are not in tune with the 'caste model' (Beteille, 1966: 224–246) of Indian society. Caste-free relations, new patterns of alliances and configurations across *biradaries*, levels of mobility, downward mobility, etc. are reflected in new status dynamics and power equations. However, discrete use of caste identity, as a resource in mundane personal spheres and as a symbolic entity in not-so-essential social domains, remains a reality of our society.

V

In my study of six villages in Rajasthan (Sharma, 1974: 125–168), I have analysed three levels of mobility in caste structure, that is, of a family, of a group, and of an individual. In no case, mobility of an entire group, that is, of a caste/sub-caste was evident. At none of the three levels mobility was there in equal measure. Mobility of members of a given family was attributed to the family, but it did not engage all the members in the act/process of mobility in an equal measure. When a noticeable number of families moved upward, socially, economically or politically, it was commonly referred as caste mobility. Such a misnomer of caste/group mobility persists even today, though no efforts, by a *jati*/group as such, are there in sight. No doubt, family facilitates mobility of its potentially capable members, concrete instances are that of mobility of individuals in any given context.

Social mobility has brought about intrafamily, intracaste and intercaste status-distinctions and cleavages, which are neither determined by ritualistic considerations, nor they have created a new ritual hierarchy. Class-like differences of a high magnitude could be seen today in a given caste, due to multifarious mobility of its individual members and families. Resultant social distinctions from mobility have significantly weakened hereditary occupations, connubiality, and commensality. Let us make it clear here that no uniform pattern of mobility is evident among different castes, families and individuals, and it is not in congruence with the traditional caste hierarchy or with the notion of pure and impure. Downward mobility of some families and groups from among the higher castes, and upward mobility of the previously disadvantaged families and *jatis*, are a stark reality of the present system of social stratification (Sharma, 1974; 1997).

Increasing emphasis on the study of structural aspects of caste exposes the preeminence of caste as a unique cultural phenomenon, and brings out analytic and empiric distinctions between caste, class and power. Beyond caste, lies caste-class nexus and its ramifications, negating 'caste alone' approach to the study of Indian society. Earlier, regarding caste, K.L. Sharma (2001: 7–8) has observed: 'Increasingly, caste is becoming a desideratum, a state of mind, a plastic and malleable institution. No more hyper symbolization is manifest to express caste differences and typifications on a continuing basis'. Though, the 'essential' of caste is largely delegitimized, yet some sporadic caste-based pronouncements and religious and metaphysical interpretations of caste and its divinity pose a challenge to secularism and democracy in Indian society.

Alongwith the role played by family and individual in weakening of the caste system, political and economic factors have contributed immensely in shaping the dynamics of Indian society. Historian Irfan Habib (1995: 161–179) strongly denounces Louis Dumont's theory of caste as Homo Hierarchicus (Dumont, 1972). He observes: 'The caste system, in its classical form, could therefore function with as much ease in a natural economy as in a market-oriented one. In either case, it helped essentially to maintain not a fabric of imagined purity (if it did, this was incidental), but a system of class exploitation as rigorous as any other'. In medieval India, caste system remained a means of a system of class exploitation, and the British colonized the caste system by their policy of 'divide and rule', and by propagating the norms of social distance. The census of 1901 by Herbert Risley (1969) and the census of 1931 by J.H. Hutton (1963) are unambiguous examples of sheer politicization of caste by the British.

Some western scholars, namely, Louis Dumont (1972), McKim Marriott (1989), Ronald B. Inden (1990), and Akos Ostor (1984), have advocated a renewed culturological approach to the study of caste in particular. Emphasis is on application of ethnosociology and use of indigenous concepts and categories, with a view to revive the understanding of caste as a cultural aspect of Indian society. While distancing from such a rejuvenated culturology, Ursula Sharma (1999) explains that caste needs to be studied in the context of its setting and surroundings. More or less in a similar way, Dipankar Gupta (2000: 224–264) pleads emphatically for an intersubjective sociology/anthropology against typification to study the caste system. He is of the view that castes need to be seen as discrete entities, being all abiding and durable identities. Gupta also looks for 'individual' in caste, as we did look for 'family' and 'individual', and Andre Beteille did look for 'family'. According to Gupta, individuals interrogate their own social existence, reflect on it, and maximize their options. By locating 'individual' in caste, Gupta reinforces our earlier hypothesis of 'levels of mobility' in caste structure, and demythologize the rigid and closed supersymbolizations, typifications and binary oppositions as vehemently proposed by Louis Dumont. Received knowledge and socio-cultural recipes are being questioned increasingly by 'individual'.

VI

Thus, in our view, caste is becoming more of a state of mind of an individual rather than continuing as an ideology, directing collective actions and practices. A pre-given ideology is being questioned for caste identity and mobilization. In a recent comprehensive analysis, Susan Bayly (2000) argues that caste has been for many centuries a real and active part of Indian life, and not just a self-serving orientalist fiction. Contemporary political and social developments have shaped it. Bayly adopts a middle path as she is of the view that caste is not reducible to the realm of imagination or discourse. Caste or caste-like identities have been there in changing and often threatening circumstances. The titles, symbols, and lifestyles of caste have proved to be remarkably durable and adaptable. Thus, according to Bayly, caste is neither an orientalist fiction or a shameful crime to be disguised or ignored in discussing India's history. 'Caste is not and never has been a fixed fact of Indian life' (Bayly, 2000: 25).

Caste has been made and remade over a long period of time. Fluidity of caste has existed and persisted because of India's remarkable cultural diversity and physical environment, and the diversity of its states (provinces) and political systems. A sequence of complex but intelligible changes in Indian life have brought about changes in India's religion, state power and material environment. Caste is not just a coded way of communication or expression of differences in power and wealth. It is also not giving way to purely class-based social differences. It needs to be understood against the background of India's political and social experiences, that is, patterns of statecraft, religion and economic life (Bayly, 2000: 366–367).

Why caste has become for so many the core symbol of community in India? Nicholas B. Dirks (2003) addresses this question quite differently compared to Susan Bayly's analysis. Dirks explains that caste is not some single system that reflects a core civilizational value, and not a basic expression of Indian tradition. According to Dirks, caste is a modern phenomenon, that, it is, specifically, the product of an historical encounter between India and western colonial rule. Dirks writes: 'It was under the British rule that 'caste' became a single term capable of expressing, organizing, and above all, 'systematizing' India's diverse forms of social identity, community, and organization' (ibid., 5). He further states: 'In short, colonialism made caste what it is today' (ibid., 5). Caste has been continuously reinvented. Under colonialism, it was made out to be far more pervasive, far more totalizing, and far more uniform, and was made a fundamentally religious order.

Dirks consider caste as a political phenomenon in the British as well the post-British periods. Today, it is denied and accepted at the same time. Caste groups are asking for creation of social conditions essential for their development and progress. However, in everyday life, caste has become nearly non-existent and passive. Recent incidences of the so-called violation of rules of marriage present a horrifying picture of caste in some parts of India. A couple of times, for example, in the state of Haryana, some self-appointed 'caste leaders' have punished the violators of the rules of marriage, that is, caste endogamy and clan exogamy. *The Times of India* (28 October 2009) reported that under the pretext of purity of descent or blood group, a boy, who married, ignoring Sagotra sanction, the so-called caste leaders imposed death penalty on the violator. Obscurantism, orthodoxy, cognitive blindness, inhuman and cruel acts, emanating from the so-called violators, reflect a totally blurred and opaque picture of the caste system.

Another manifestation of 'caste' is observable in congregations of *biradaris (Jati Samaj)*. Today, a couple of the so-called leaders of their respective castes have been engaged in mobilization of support of their fellowmen for political gains, in the name of realization of the demands, such as reservation, as it is available to the SCs, the STs, the OBCs, etc. The B.P. Mandal Commission's Report (1978–80) and its acceptance by the Government of India drastically changed the Indian political scene in 1991–92. Aftereffects of the mandalization of Indian politics can be seen even today after two decades in the caste-based mobilizations for reservation by the upper castes, and in the demand for inclusion of some castes in the OBCs/STs/SCs categories.

VII

While concluding this paper, we agree with Ishita Banerjee – Dube (2008: XV) as she observes: 'Caste, elusive yet enduring, retains a critical importance as concept and practice in India today'. Caste has really a diverse and chequered career in history of India. Caste has become an imprecise and vague system. Today, caste is an episodic expression and articulation rather than a systemic institution. It is not, therefore, seen in everyday life. Because of such a blurring nature of caste, manipulations for its appropriation have surfaced, and its social and cultural fabric has been relegated to the background. Caste as an ideology of pure and impure is redundant in the present-day India.

Today, caste as a system, due to its resilience and dynamics, inconsistencies and contradictions, has endangered its systemic form and substance. The Indian State, before and after Independence, has politicized the caste system, by way of superimposed social and ritual divides. As a result of such a tendency, caste has become a discrete phenomenon, a state of mind, and a means of political play. In everyday life, intercaste and intracaste relations have become a casuality, and caste-based permutations and combinations and calculations, in terms of alliances or non-alliances for political gains, have gained currency. Appropriation of caste is an open fact. Khaps (caste panchayats) have acquired a new form and functioning for ulterior motives by the select so-called caste leaders. Caste needs to be understood now, not in terms of caste endogamy, clan exogamy, hypergamy, pure-impure divide and *jajmani* system, but it requires to be probed as a means/mechanism of political mileage. At the time of finalization of this paper, results of elections held in Bihar for State Legislature poured in, which reflected a landslide victory of the JDU-BJP alliance. Newspapers reported the victory as 'Development beats caste politics' (*The Hindustan Times*, 28 November 2010), and 'Caste politics in passé' (*The Times of India*, 25 November 2010). We have to wait and watch for the eclipse of caste. Caste is quite elusive and slippery phenomenon. It has never died in toto. It has a tendency to revive itself and regenerate in multiple ways, as a phenomenon, though not as a system.

References

Baines, J.A., *Census of India, 1891: General Report*, London: Eyre and Spottswood, 1893; H.H. Risley and E.A. Gait, *Report on the Census of India, 1901*, Vol. I, Calcutta: Office of the Superintendent of Government Press, 1903, and H.H. Risley, *The People of India*, Calcutta and Simla: Thacker, Spink and Co., 1909 was published based on this Census, that is, J.H. Hutton, *Census of India, 1931*, Vol. I, Part 3, Delhi: Manager of Publications, 1935, and J.H. Hutton, *Caste in India: Its Nature, Functions and Origins*, Cambridge: Cambridge University Press, 1948 was published, based on this Census.

Banjerjee-Dube, Ishita, 'Introduction: Questioning of Caste', Ishita Banerjee–Dube (ed.), *Caste in History*, New Delhi: Oxford University Press, 2008, pp. XC-LXIV.

Bayly, Susan, *Caste, Society and Politics in India,* Cambridge: Cambridge University Press (First Indian Edition), 2000.

Beteille, Andre, *Caste, Class and Power,* Bombay: Oxford University Press, 1966.

——, 'Closed and Open Social Stratification in India', *European Journal of Sociology,* 1966, Vol. VII, pp. 224–246.

——, 'Ideas and Interests: Some Conceptual Problems in the Study of Social Stratification in India', *International Social Science Journal*, 1969, Vol. 21, No. 7, pp. 17–31.

——, 'The Reproduction of Inequality: Occupation, Caste and Family', in Patricia Uberoi (ed.), *Family, Kinship and Marriage in India,* Delhi: Oxford University Press, 1998, pp. 435–51.

Dirks, Nicholas B., *Castes of Mind: Colonialism and The Making of Modern India,* Delhi: Permanent Black, 2003.

Dumont, Louis, *Homo Hierarchicus: The Caste System and its Implications*, London: Paladin, Granada Publishing Limited, 1972.

Gould, Harold A., 'Priest and Contrapriest: A Structural Analysis of Jajmani Relationships in the Hindu Plains and the Nilgiri Hills', *Contributions to Indian Sociology*,1967, New Series No. 1,pp. x26–55.

Gupta, Dipankar, *Interrogating Caste: Understanding Hierarchy & Difference in Indian Society,* New Delhi: Penguin Books, 2000.

Hutton, J.H., *Caste in India: Its Nature, Functions and Origin*, Bombay: Oxford University Press, 1963.

Inden, Ronald B., *Imagining India*, Oxford: Basil Blackwell Ltd., 1990.

Kapadia, K.M., *Marriage and Family in India* (Ninth Impression), Oxford: Oxford University Press, 1986.

Kothari, Rajni, *Politics in India*, New Delhi: Orient Longman Ltd., 1970.

——.*Caste in Indian Politics* (ed.), New Delhi: Orient Longman Ltd., 1970.

Mandal, B.P., The Backward Classes Commission, New Delhi: Government of India, 1978–80.

Marriott, McKim, *India Through Hindu Categories* (ed.), New Delhi: Sage Publications, 1989.

Mukherjee, R.K., *The Dynamics of a Rural Society*, Berlin: Academie Verlag, 1957.

'New Introduction', *Review of Caste in India*, Jaipur: Rawat, 1974, pp. I-XXIX.

Rawls, John, *A Theory of Justice* (Revised ed.), Oxford: Oxford University Press, 1999.

Risley, H.H., *The People of India* (2nd ed.), Delhi: Orient Books, 1969. First published in 1909 from London.

Sharma, K.L., *The Changing Rural Stratification System*, New Delhi: Orient Longman., 1977.

——.*Essays on Social Stratification*, Jaipur: Rawat, 1980.

——.*Reconceptualising Caste, Class And Power*, Jaipur: Rawat, 2001.

——.*Perspectives on Social Stratification,* Jaipur: Rawat, 2010.

Singh, Yogendra, *Modernisation of Indian Tradition*, Jaipur: Rawat, 1986, reprinted 1994.

Srinivas, M.N., *Religion and Society Among the Coorgs of South India*, Oxford: Clarendon Press, 1952.

——.*Caste in Modern India and Other Essays*, Delhi: Oxford University Press, 1962.

The Times of India, 28 October 2009.

Tod, James, *Annals and Antiquities of Rajasthan* (3 vols.), London: H Milford, 1920; repr. Delhi: Low Price Publications, 1990. The first edition of Tod's seminal work on Rajasthan was published in 1829.

11

Politics of Social Backwardness and Empowerment of Other and Economically Backward Classes

D.K. Verma

Theoretical understanding of the paper is based on equality and justice dimensions of sustainable development juxtaposing B.R. Ambedkar's vision of egalitarian society. After a thorough review of existing approaches, strategies and priorities, ongoing programmes and their implementation, persisting and emerging problems and on the basis of a socio-historical analysis of emergence, identification, status characteristics generalization, and assessment of aspirations of Other Backward Classes (OBCs) and Economically Backward Classes (EBCs) from various sources, including Supreme Court judgments, reports of National and State Commissions, reports of National Sample Survey Organization (NSSO), National Family Health Survey (NFHS) and empirical research studies conducted by the author, following policy recommendations are being made for empowerment of OBCs and EBCs:

(i) *Separate Ministry for OBCs and EBCs:* Like SCs and STs, which used to be a synonym of caste-tribe politics during pre-Mandal era, OBCs and EBCs have become synonym for socio-economically-backward politics in post-Mandal era. At present, OBCs affairs are being looked after by the Ministry of Social Justice and Empowerment alongwith Scheduled Castes.

Earlier, Tribal Affairs got separated from SCs and OBCs. Concerns for EBCs are of recent origin. There should be a separate ministry for concerted efforts and focused programmes for empowerment of OBCs and EBCs.

(ii) *Sub-categorization of OBCs and EBCs according to their differential economic and educational empowerment needs:* OBCs are socially and educationally backward, within OBCs all castes/communities are not equal, and higher income status (creamy layer) may dissolve materialistic obstacles but do not ensure their economic and educational empowerment. Social stigmatization of being OBC continues and thus empowerment of OBC will not be sufficient through achievement of physical targets (reservation and representation) only. Their sustainable empowerment would require social and educational empowerment in terms of elevation in their social status and strengthened capabilities, for which besides reservation, social upliftment, discarding ascriptive status characteristics (removing stigmatized caste/community identities) and accelerated educational mobility by enhancing achieved status characteristics (through quality education and capability/skill development) would be more effective. Similarly, EBCs also have their differential economic needs.

(iii) *Provision of divisible budget for OBCs and EBCs:* Like provisioned for Scheduled Castes and Scheduled Tribes, overall (Central as well as State level) and sectorial divisible budget should be earmarked for OBCs and EBCs in terms of their population in respective states/Union Territories. And within this divisible budget, prioritized demand as per sub-categorization at different need-based levels, both physical and financial empowerment must be ensured.

(iv) *Sustainable empowerment:* This should be done through capability enhancement rather than making OBCs and EBCs passive beneficiaries and target orientation of functionaries. In this regard, National Commission and existing institutional arrangements should be reoriented to work as *change agents* acting like social bridge between state and society, particularly for economic, educational and ecological needs of OBCs and EBCs.

Adopting our Constitution on 26 November 1949, We, the People of India aspired to become egalitarian society disposing off the caste-based social stratification.[1] The *varna* model of stratification existed for centuries, evolved and imposed various means and ways to discriminate certain castes leading to their social and educational backwardness. In order to compensate for historical social and educational backwardness, certain categorized sections are being positively discriminated in independent India by providing reservation particularly to Scheduled Castes, Scheduled Tribes and OBCs. The basis of such categorization is mainly because of social backwardness of certain castes or communities followed by educational backwardness of individuals belonging to those caste or communities. Besides, 'Socially and Educationally Backward Classes', the Constitution of India also contains directives to states (Article 46) for protection of economically and educationally 'Weaker Sections' as well. Empirical studies confirm that, though *prima facie*, 'OBCs are not economically backward but they are socially and educationally backward. But recently issues concerning Economically Backward Classes have also surfaced demanding reservation and welfare schemes for this new category of EBCs.

As a corollary of the equality before law (Article 14) and the general assurance of absence of discrimination by the State on the grounds only of religion, race, caste, sex, place of birth or any one of them (Article 15, 29), the Constitution of India contains directive (Article 46) that the State shall promote educational and economic interests of weaker sections.[2] Besides these Articles, particularly Articles 38, 39, 41, 42, 43, 45, 47 and 48 under the Directive Principles of State Policy Mandate the ideal of socio-economic justice and embody the aims and objectives of the State to functions as a 'Welfare State'.

As for the term 'weaker sections', it finds expression in Article 46 under Part IV (directive principles of state policy) of the Constitution of India which state that 'the state shall promote with special care the educational and economic interest of weaker sections of the people and in particular Scheduled Castes and Scheduled Tribes and shall protect them from social injustice and all forms of exploitation'. It may be noted that while Article 16(4) had referred only to social or educational backwardness, Article 46 mentions 'economic interest' to be promoted by the state for 'weaker sections'.

The expression 'weaker sections' has not been defined under the Constitution. However, the Supreme Court in Indra Sawhney case differentiated the term 'Backward Classes of Citizens' mentioned under Article 16(4) from 'weaker sections' under Article 46. The Apex Court clarified that the expression 'weaker sections' is of people is wider than expression 'backward classes' of citizens, which is only a part of weaker sections. Backward Classes comprise only those which are socially and educationally backward. Weaker section connotes all sections of the society which are rendered weaker due to various causes, e.g. poverty, natural calamity or physical handicap. [*Indra Sawhny v. Union of India*, 1992(3) SCC 217].

Thus, Article 46 of the Constitution of India, which declares that the objective of the State to promote educational and economic interests of the weaker sections extends to cover all needy people (other than SCs and STs also). Accordingly, 'OBCs and EBCs are 'weaker section' which also meant a group/groups of people or a family/families or a part/parts of a caste/community from other than SCs and STs. And without reference to any particular caste or community but as a dynamic open group of acquired status of OBCs and EBCs also get strengthened from Article 39 which states that 'the citizens, men and women, equally have the right to an adequate means of livelihood'.

Identification of Backward Classes: A Socio-Historical Analysis

Expression of Backward Classes first appeared in 1870s in Madras residency where the British Government had grouped scheduled castes and untouchable castes under the label of Backward Classes and gradually their number increased from 39 in 1870 to 131 in 1920. Though the term 'backward class' has appeared more than once in the Constitution of India but it has not been defined adequately in order to adopt suitable criteria and identify those who come under backward class category. Several commissions/committees were set up at national and state level to identify backward classes.

Justice L.C. Miller Committee, Mysore in Karnataka, was constituted during 1918–20. In Karnataka, four other commissions of backwardness include Naganna Gowda Commission (1961): L.G. Anna Havenoy Commission (1972–75); T. Venkataka Swami Commission 1986 and Chinnappa Reddy Commission (1989–90). In Kerala also a commission on backwardness was constituted in the colonial period during 1935 under the chairmanship of Justice C.D. Nokes. Thereafter, three commissions were constituted in Kerala including V.K. Vishvanathan Commission (1961–63), J.

Kumar Pillai Commission (1964–66), M.P. Damodran Commission (1967–70).

Backward Classes Commissions constituted in Tamil Nadu include A.M. Sattanathan Commission (1969–70) and J.M. Ambasankar Commission (1982–86). In Andhra Pradesh also three Backward Class Commissions constituted include Manohar Pershad Committee (1968–69), Ananta Raman Commission (1970), Murlidhar Rao Commission (1982). Mungeri Lal Commission was set up in Bihar during 1971–76. In Gujarat, A.R. Bakshi Commission (1972–76); Justice C.V. Rane Commission (1981–83); Justice R.C. Mankad Commission (1987) were constituted. Justice Gajendragadkar Commission (1967–68); Justice J.N. Wazir Commission (1969); Justice Adarsh Anand Commission (1976–77); and Gurnam Singh Commission (1990) were set up in Haryana.

O.H.B. Starte Committee (Bombay Presidency, 1928–30); B.D. Deshmukh Committee (1961–64) in Maharashtra; Brish Bhan Committee (1965–66) in Punjab; Chhedi Lal Sathi Commission in Uttar Pradesh and Mahajan Commission (1989–1983) in Madhya Pradesh were constituted to identify backward classes.

In the year 1932, Madan Mohan Malviya, the signatory on behalf of caste Hindus and B.R. Ambedkar on behalf of the depressed classes, signed the Poona Pact. That was the first occasion when British Government recognized the depressed classes as a separate element in Indian politics.

The debate remained focussed on social and educational backwardness which had its roots in the *Pax Britanica*. The initial construction of the larger criteria of social and educational backwardness was in negative terms wherein the Madras residency all sections, apart from Brahmins, were by definition, considered backward. Thus, no technical or scientific definition of backwards was evolved but non-Brahmins and later on non-upper castes, continued to be included under a larger umbrella 'socially and technically backward classes'. Community-based census of 1931 was mainly exploited to identify the population of (such) backward classes.

Thus, two categories emerged whereby caste and tribe were together constructed into a homogenous mass for the purpose of public policy irrespective of understanding of social reality, all families and communities belonging to upper caste and lower caste were categorized as non-backward and backward.

While the question of identifying Scheduled Castes and Scheduled Tribes was settled before Independence, largely due to efforts of B.R. Ambedkar, who composed them as a backward class[3] in the Constitution but the question of 'other backward classes', as Jawaharlal Nehru quoted was 'left for subsequent generations'. Thus, the criteria and identification of Backward Class other than Scheduled Castes and Scheduled Tribes remained a more political and less academic debate in the past in Independent India.

Under Article 340 of the Indian Constitution, it is obligatory for the state to promote the welfare of the Backward Classes.[4] The first attempt to identify those Backward Classes other than SCs and STs at national level was made in 1953 when the first Backward Class Commission was set up by a presidential order on 29 January 1953 under the chairmanship of Kaka Kalelkar which submitted its report on 30 March 1955. The first commission included 2399 castes or communities as backward and among them listed 837 as the 'most backward'. The commission recommended *CASTE* as the criteria to determine the backwardness and all women as a class was considered backward. The main aim of such identification was to provide maximum opportunity to backward classes, with a major means of reservation policy. The reservations policy was largely criticized as often preceded independently of ethical basis, practical efficacy and sustainability, particularly in response to contingent political compulsions.

Though the first commission indicated that caste was an important measure of backwardness, however, five out of 11 members of the commission including the chairman himself, raised strong objections on considering caste as a criteria to identify backwardness. In his dissent-note annexed with the report of the first Backward Class Commission, its chairman expressed that 'the caste system is the greatest hindrance in the way of our progress towards an egalitarian society, the recognition of the specified class backward may serve to maintain and even perpetuate the existing distinction on the caste basis' (GOI: Backward Class Commission Report, p. 2). The then Central government rejected the report of the first Backward Class Commission on the grounds that the commission had not applied more objective criteria such as income, education and literacy to determine backward status.

Thereafter, a number of state commissions were constituted to devise methods for identifying backwardness. In 1978, the second Backward Class Commission was constituted on 20 December

1978. As many as 3743 castes/communities, representing over 52 per cent of Indian population, were identified as backward. During 1970s and 1980s, a number of castes including Yadavs, Kurmis, Koris and Bokkaligas emerged as important political forces and launched political agitations in the name of OBCs and when Janata Party came to power in 1977, many of them represented their respective communities or the castes in governance. That was the background under which the second Backward Classes Commission was set up.

On 7 August 1990, the then Prime Minister announced the government's acceptance of the Mandal Commission Report in the Parliament reminding the nation that the Constitution envisaged that social and educational backwardness be identified, their difficulties removed and their conditions be improved in terms of Article 340(1) read with Article 314(4) as well 16(4).

The government decided to adopt in the first phase the castes common to both the Mandal list and lists prepared by various states to introduce 27 per cent reservation in services for Socially and Educationally Backward Classes, SEBCs (the Constitutional term for OBCs); but that policy was not extended to educational institutions. Though the Mandal Commission had recommended reservation in educational institutions but the commission also stated that:

> The initial part of the battle against social backwardness is to be fought in the minds of backward people in India … . Government services have always been looked upon as (status) prestige and power by increasing the representation of OBCs in government services, we give them an immediate feeling of participation in the governance.

In 1992, the apex Court gave its approval to the legitimacy of the government order to empower the Mandal report subject to the exclusion of the social advanced sections (creamy layer) amongst identified as Backward Classes. However, the parliamentary standing committee on personnel, public grievance, law and justice in its eighth report on the SC/ST/OBCs (Reservation in Posts and Services Bill, 2004) found that many of the castes, tribes and classes among the SC/ST/OBCs had been deprived of the benefits of reservations in services as these were restricted to certain upper sections among backward classes. It was expressed that 'exclusion of some castes from the benefit of reservation has pushed them far behind which is violation of the principles of social harmony and social equality as embodied in the Indian Constitution'.

The above analysis makes it clear that there was no thinking about Backward Classes other than SCs and STs in the pre-independence period at central level yet in provinces such as Bombay, Madras and Mysore residencies there were some reservations of jobs and seats for them in the field of education. The recognition of the first backward class commission were not accepted and before accepting recommendation of second Mandal Commission report, some states had already given reservation to OBCs, for example, in 1970 on the basis of recommendations of the Manohar Pershad Commission, Andhra Pradesh Government reserved 25 per cent of seats in colleges. Inclusion of Sikhs and Buddhists opened a new debate because Sikhism, Buddhism and Jainism emerged as protests/movements against the institution of caste. The lists for SCs and OBCs were prepared on the basis of caste as the major criteria. Christianity and Islam were also opposed to the recognition of caste, but only backward Muslim were included among OBCs by Mandal Commission. Thereafter, emerged the issue of SC converts to Christianity and Islam, as the two faiths were not included in the list for SCs. The confusion was confounded with conversion itself and when that was compared on caste or tribe basis.

The confusion was further confounded if the issue of conversion itself was raised and when that was compared with the caste and tribe. If a Scheduled Caste converted to Christianity or Islam such a person was automatically deprived of SC benefits. In the case of *Soosai v. Union of India*, SC, 1996, the Supreme Court ruled that SC members converted to Christianity were not eligible for benefits granted to them, as their disability did not continue after conversion as per the meaning of the 1950 presidential order.

However, if the convert was a Scheduled Tribe, he or she continued to take advantages of ST benefits because those benefits were ethnicity based and not religion-centric. In several studies in the country either Muslims in general or Muslim OBCs as part of the General OBCs are on the positive discrimination list. In Madhya Pradesh, Joshi and Verma (1998) conducted empirical studies to investigate the social, educational and economical conditions of Muslim communities whose applications were received by the Government of Madhya Pradesh for inclusion in the OBC List. The main criteria adopted for identification of backward communities among Muslim, was comparison of their socio-economic status with that of a local community already included in the list of OBC. For that study referent community elected was Patidar. Based on the findings, 32 Muslim communities were studied and recommended for inclusion in the list of OBCs. Therefore, philosophically and in democratic social set-up, the concept of backwardness needed to be understood in the context of issues like justice and equality irrespective of caste, race, religion and gender. Accordingly, the concept of backwardness was extended to non-Hindu communities by the Mandal Commission which declared over 80 Muslim groups as backward and, in fact, half of the Muslim population was identified as backward (Galanter, 1984). Thus, it was a major policy shift to consider backwardness on religion basis. However, Mandal Commission refused to declare Muslims as a whole a backward community enjoying the same status as SCs and STs. Though backward communities among Muslims have been included in the OBC list but they were not getting actual benefits as was evident in the representation at various levels (Momin, 2004).

- Two levels of equality, namely, intra-group and inter-group became important, further inequality of gender and region also brought many disadvantages to religious minorities. Therefore, the concept of specific balances of institutionalized inequalities was unless transcended the empirical context carried little utility. The problem of reservations for backward classes assumed a new dimension because of the massive socio-economic change and resultant change in the perspective about quality. The classes which got themselves excluded from the list of depressed/backward classes started movements to get themselves included in the list of backward sections so as to get share in the power, employment and education.

On behalf of all Dalit Christians, All India Christians Council sought immediate steps to amend the Presidential Constitutional Scheduled Castes Order 1950 so as to include Christians of Scheduled Caste origin for the benefits under Articles 330, 332, 334, 335, 338, 341 and 366(24). Dalit Christians constituted more than 75 per cent of the total Christian population in the country. However, their social and educational status had not changed since their conversion. The National Commission for Minorities also recommended statutory benefits to Dalit Christians as Scheduled Castes.

The Karnataka Backward Class Commission 1952 observed that a Scheduled Caste might have made some progress after embracing Islam or Christianity and thereby the disability, he or she suffered might not disappear but the fact remained that such castes and tribes and racial groups still continued to suffer under other social, educational and other economic backwardness. Kumar Pillai Committee 1965 of Kerela Government stated that 'we were convinced that in practice a convert to Christianity from SC is treated as socially backward. Mandal Commission also observed that Christian community was not only divided into various denominations on the basis of beliefs and rituals but also into various ethnic groups on the basis of their caste background.

Mandal Commission report took note of suggestions made by Madhu Dandwate who stated that conversion from one field to another did not change the socio-economic status of a person and the Mandal Commission concluded that among Indian Christians caste was a reality and reported that social and educational backwardness among them was more or less the same as among Hindu communities.

B.R. Ambedkar also noted:

> Has Christianity been able to save the converts from the sufferings and ignominy which is the misfortune of everyone who is born an untouchable? Can an untouchable after his conversion to Christianity take water from a public well? Are his children admitted to a public school? ... Will a barber shave him? Will a washerman wash his clothes? Will the Hindus take water from him? Will they dine with him?

Caste-based exclusion and discrimination had been a long debate in economics and sociology of the caste system. In fact, in terms of consequences, the economic theory of the caste system clearly predicted negative outcome of caste-based market discrimination (Akerlof, 1976). Therefore, it was established that the backwardness in Indian society could not be understood irrespective of caste system.

Caste remained a major force in Indian politics too, however, it remained to explore whether caste indicated the degree of backwardness actually suffered by its adherents. Most of the times, the relation between the caste and backwardness were discussed at a wider and macro level. Most of the times the sufferers from the link between caste and backwardness were families and individuals at micro level. However, there was no direct evidence of wealth and caste linkages. Similarly there was no direct link between literacy and caste as there were wide variations in the literacy ratio within so-called upper castes as well. Thus, as understood traditionally to workout degree of backwardness in terms of ritual ranking gathers a very little ground in the present post-modern era. There should be transformation strategy in dealing with socially and educationally backward classes so that the focus could shift from caste and community (Roy Burman, 2006), primarily to caste and income and secondarily to community only.[5]

I.P. Desai was associated as a member of the Expert Committee constituted by first socially and educationally Backward Class Commission appointed by the Government of Gujarat in 1972, popularly known as Bakshi Commission. He expressed that some members of the Expert Committee including him were left with a certain dissatisfaction, particularly when Bakshi Commission made caste as a unit of identification for a collectivity being included in the socially and educationally Backward Classes and that their dissatisfaction enhanced when the Mandal Commission (1978–82) said that the survey had no pretension of being a piece of academic research and that had been used as rough and readymade tool for evolving a simple criteria for identification of socially and educationally Backward Classes. Desai also observed that leaving aside SCs and STs, the Constitution left us with an option to consider backwardness on the basis other than caste or on secular basis.

The Mandal Commission was assisted by three bodies *viz.*, a panel of experts led by M.N. Srinivas, a research planning team of sociologists, and a support committee of experts constituted by technical committee. The commission mentions (in Part 11.1, p. 50, Vol. I) that the experts panel agreed with the observations of the research planning team that the task before the commission was to lay down the criteria for identifying recognizable and persistent collectivities and not individuals. By that it was meant that those groups, which followed low and impure occupations, were socially backward and also educationally backward. They had low income also. In other words, all these backwardness were related to the concept of pollution and impurity. This is an important consideration to identify the criteria and indicators about social and economic backwardness among religious minorities, whether to consider collectivities or individuals. The Backward Class commissions so far constituted in the country or in various states, referred to collectivities. The view that backwardness referred to a class or a group or a collectivity was also widely accepted by the judiciary.

However, the beneficiaries of the schemes and programmes meant for the welfare and development of so identified backward classes are in fact the individuals. Reservations are made in favour of individuals. In other words, the state creates a class of individuals who get benefits under the schemes designed for the purpose and, thus, it is difficulty to categorize them under traditional understanding of social status in terms of ascriptive or achieved status. Verma (2003) described such new emerging class as affirmed status of groups and explained the process of social devolution. Therefore, it is proposed that the criteria and indicators for backwardness should focus on the individuals and level of their affirmed status should be taken as indicator of backwardness.

The research planning team of the Bakshi Commission gave due consideration to the problem of ascriptive and achieved status and felt it necessary to consider the problem of relationship between social backwardness and educational backwardness, while the former referred to ascriptive status and the latter to the achieved status. They considered that the social backwardness could change over a length of time while faster change was possible in the case of educational backwardness.

Therefore, while criteria of social and economic backwardness should be considered as a critical element and educational backwardness a linked element, though not necessarily derived from the former. It was also observed that once the collectivities were identified in terms of the traditional framework, one was to examine the changes that had taken place in their social and educational status under the impact of various forces in modern society.

Desai also observed that what was true of the caste in its vertical relationship in a village, may not be true of the caste as horizontal and segmental division of society spread over different parts of the region or the whole state, particularly the urban area. It was recognized by the Mandal Commission that reservation for a few thousand jobs was not going to solve the problem of backwardness. But the chief merit considered was that it would erode the hold of higher castes. Desai (ibid. p. 87) mentioned that if caste was abjured as a unit of identifying socially and educationally backward classes, it was important to suggest the alternative and certain broad indications were: the unit must be completely secular, it must be in consonance with the new society that had emerged and was developed, the new society was based on the individual as a citizen and his rights and obligations were defined by secular political authority, the class to which the individual belonged could be identified by the activity, he engages himself in for earning a livelihood and the social relations in which he entered in the course of his activity were governed by the contract into which he entered out of his free will and which could also be annulled by the will of either party, and the backwardness of the class was to be judged by the existence or non-existence of various impediments in exercising the choice in selecting the activity for earning the livelihood and in entering into the contract.

The impediment collectively characterizes the backwardness of class. The understanding of Desai, academically could be elaborated but it becomes difficult at the policy making and implementation level. Caste remained the easy and readymade choice though a rough and academic improper criteria to identify backwardness. This takes us to the position where research for the policy making does not remain merely an academic piece of exercise but deeper and greater implications on the society need to be given much consideration.

Sub-Categorization Among OBCs and EBCs

Caste and caste-based disabilities are usually considered as criteria and indicators to identify social backwardness. The Constitution of India, in its Article 17 has abolished untouchability, which was the most important manifestation of caste-based social backwardness. The Constitution also prohibits a discrimination based on caste. The sociological understanding also confirm that the economically and politically empowered caste at lower ranking break away to form new caste and claimed high ritual status. For example, during pre-Independence period, Kayastha and Jat who were close to Sudras in ritual ranking became powerful after Independence and claimed a higher ritual ranking nearer to Rajputs. However, in post-Independence, even after claim of a higher ranking, Jats made a demand to be identified as OBCs but to avail the reservation facilities and even certain sections of Brahmins are also raising their voices for such demands.

Thus, caste and its association with the social backwardness does not establish a direct link. In the era of privatization, globalization and liberalization, market affairs have become dominant, concept of welfare state has weakened and religion has also become a part of market. Professionals who have less concern for ritual ranking of individuals or caste groups are managing the religious functions and structures. In the professionally managed religious discourses in the name of personality development and peace like art of living, yoga, commune, *satsang*, people from all walks of life irrespective of their caste background are invited to attend. There is no discrimination or segregation on the basis of caste.

Caste is more important as a political agglomeration for a particular type of voting behaviour rather than deciding the ritual ranking to segregate people. In other words, the politicization of caste has less focus on social equality but more interest for enblock voting. Thus, caste appears to be a very weak indicator for socio-economic backwardness among religious minorities, which do not, in fact recognize caste system. Empirical research for its practical utility in terms of acceptance at various levels including legislature, executive and judiciary is important. Very scientific and objective indicators can be worked out but looking at the level of present democratic set-up and capability of implementing measure, that is going to create more problems in handling backwardness than providing opportunities to backward people to develop. However, giving due consideration to diversity in Indian society and pluralism of culture and religion, it would not be proper to evolve a uniform criterion to identify the backwardness. It would be required to provide a space to respective communities to accept and assimilate such identified criterion so that no further segmentation takes place within the society. Thus, the above analysis brings to the position that caste has been a controversial and debatable criteria to identify backwardness even among the communities belonging to the majority religion, where caste-based social disabilities are much pronounced.

However, when OBCs and EBCs are considered, in principle, caste cannot be the basis for identification of backwardness among them because graded inequality is embedded in the caste system. Theoretical analysis though indicate that caste structures have close linkages with the knowledge and economy but for identification purpose, they are related to the structures only. Therefore, OBCs and EBCs cannot be treated as a monolithic block referring to a homogenous structure. In other words, backwardness cannot be identified on the basis of castes or communities but we will have to come down at the level of individual and family. Thus, the analysis of the backwardness makes a departure in terms of identifying backwardness among communities on the basis of age-old academic debate on collectives versus individuals. Therefore, sub-categorization of OBCs and EBCs would be required on the basis of differential empowerment needs of individuals/families rather than the entirety of a caste/or community among OBCs and EBCs.

Socio-Educational Backwardness: Status Characteristics

In India, both during pre- and post-Independence period several attempts have been made to identify indicators for measuring backwardness among various sections of the society. In Andhra Pradesh, Backward Classes were categorized into four major groups namely Ab-origin tribes; Vimukti Jati; Nomadic and semi-Nomadic tribes, occupational and service class; Scheduled Castes who were converted to Christianity; and Other communities.

In Karnataka, a different approach to the problem of backwardness and determination of backwardness was followed by Havanor Commission. The Commission first of all prepared a list of educationally backward classes on the basis of indicators wherein 'a caste or a community whose student per thousand of its population passing out SCLC examination was below state average'.

Then on the basis of the list of educationally backward classes so drawn, further categorizes identified were: backward communities identified on the basis of criteria as 'student average per thousand of population was below state level', backward caste identified with the indicator as 'whose student average per thousand of population was below 50 per cent of the state average', and backward tribes identified with the indicator as 'whose student average per thousand of population was below 50 per cent of the state average except Dombars and Voddars (nomadic and denotified tribes). The commission under the chairmanship of L.G. Havanor did not take caste as the criteria to identify backwardness. However, the emphasis remained on caste, tribes and communities.

Later, Justice Chinappa Reddy Commission constituted by the state government in 1989–90, however, again considered caste as the 'sufficient criteria' to identify backward classes. In Bihar, two categories of Other Backward Classes were prepared, one containing 79 castes who were deemed more backward than the other list of 30 castes. However, the Patna High Court declared those two lists of backward castes as unconstitutional. Therefore, the Bihar government appointed a Backward Classes Commission under the Chairmanship of Mungeri Lal which remained in office during 1971–76. Based on the indicators like social status, educational backwardness, representation in government service and adequacy of share in trade, commerce and industry, the Mungeri Lal Commission prepared two lists of other backward communities and most backward classes, the later contained 93 castes.

A backward class commission was set up in August 1972 under the Chairmanship of A.B. Bakshi by the Gujarat Government. The Commission considered the following 10 factors in determining the social and educational backwardness in Gujarat: social backwardness in general; poverty and economic backwardness; illiteracy and educational backwardness; occupational factors; representation in public sector services; social status in general; mode of living, customs and beliefs; caste only as one of the relevant factor; nomadic way of living and backwardness in other ways. The Bakshi Commission identified 82 castes as socially, economically and educationally backward.

As per the National Commission for Backward Classes guidelines for inclusion in the central list of OBCs include indicators[6] that are modified indicators adopted by the Mandal Commission.

However, such indicators cannot be used for identification of backwardness mainly because the target is individual or family but not any caste or community as a whole. Therefore, above mentioned caste or community-based criteria or indicators would not be effective for OBC. Further, identification of EBCs is yet to be established. Therefore, National and State Commissions and institutional arrangements would need to be reoriented to act a change agents rather than identifying and confirming identities of OBCs and EBCs.

The basic understanding and the conceptual framework for measuring multiple deprivation is reflected in the writing of Alpock 1997, 'we must know what poverty is before we can identify where and when it is occurring or attempt to measure and before we begin to do anything to alleviate it. The office of the Deputy Prime Minister of London commissioned the Socially Disadvantaged Research Centre at the Department of Social Policy and Social Research at the University of Oxford to update the indices of deprivation for the country. The index of multiple deprivation (2004) was published in April 2004 in which domains and indicators for measuring multiple deprivation are discussed. And the account of poverty in UK in which Townsend (1979) sets out the case for defining poverty in terms of relative deprivation has 'individuals, families and groups can be said to be in poverty if they lack the resources to obtain the type of diet, participate in the activities and have the living conditions and amenities which are customary or at least widely encouraged or approved in the societies to which they belonged. Following seven domains of deprivation were considered: Income deprivation; Employment deprivation; Health deprivation and disability; Education, skill and training deprivation; Barriers to housing and services; Living environmental deprivation; and Crime. Each domain contained a number of indicators totalling to 37 in all.

In any case, sustainable empowerment through capability enhancement is needed rather than making OBCs and EBCs passive beneficiaries and target orientation of functionaries. In this regard National Commission and existing Institutional arrangements should be reoriented to work as *Change Agents* acting like social bridge between state and society, particularly for women and children belonging to OBCs and EBCs.

Welfare Measures for Empowerment of OBCs

According to the Article 46, the welfare measures that are directed to State for weaker sections include:

(i) promote with special care their economic interests,
(ii) promote with special care their educational interests,
(iii) protect them from social injustice, and
(iv) protect them from all forms of exploitation.

It would be appropriate to understand economic interest of OBCs and EBCs. For poverty has been a much debated phenomenon. East and West have remained divided on conceptualizing poverty. Is poverty simply about the level of income obtained by households or individuals? Is it about lack of access to social services? Or is it more correctly understood as the inability to participate in society, economically, socially, culturally or politically?

In western world, the understanding about poverty could be traced back to the codification of poor laws in medieval England, but the empirical studies appeared, at the turn of the century. Rowntree (1901) was the first to develop a poverty standard for individual families, based on estimates of nutritional and other requirements. In the 1960s, the main focus was on the level of income, reflected in macro-economic indicators like Gross National Product per head. In the 1970s, poverty became prominent, notably as a result of Robert MacNamara's celebrated speech to the World Bank Board of Governors in Nairobi in 1973, and the subsequent publication of Redistribution with Growth.

Townsend, in particular, helped redefine poverty: not just as a failure to meet minimum nutrition or subsistence levels, but rather as a failure to keep up with the standards prevalent in a given society. The second shift was to broaden the concept of income poverty, to a wider set of 'basic needs', including those provided socially. New layers of complexity were added in the 1980s with the incorporation of non-monetary aspects, particularly as a result of Robert Chambers' work on powerlessness and isolation which helped to inspire greater attention to participation.

Thereafter, theoretical work by Amartya Sen, emphasized that income was only valuable in so far as it increased the 'capabilities' of individuals and thereby permitted 'functioning' in society. Finally, the 1980s was characterized by a rapid increase in the study of gender. In 1990s the idea of well-being came to act as a metaphor for absence of poverty, with concomitant emphasis on how poor people themselves view their situation. At the same time, inspired by Sen, UNDP developed the idea of human development: 'the denial of opportunities and choices to lead a long, healthy, creative life and to enjoy a decent standard of living, freedom, dignity, self-esteem and the respect of others. Thereby, ecological concerns also got much attention' (Verma, 1994, 1995). Further broadening of the concept of poverty to a wider construct, livelihood appeared in the report 'Our Common Future' (Brundtland Commission on Sustainability and the Environment, WCS, 1987) which popularized the term sustainable development (Adiseshiah, 1990). Besides, concerns for intergenerational equity (Verma, 1993) and intra-generational equality (Verma and Sohrot, 2003) were also included for sustainable empowerment of backward classes.

The social sciences offer a wide range of theoretical literature on the causes of poverty. This debate has been broadly distinguished between the individualistic and the structural perspectives. The focus on the individual approach is on the behavioural and cultural factors. Poverty is seen as a result of internal factors, such as undesirable behaviour of the poor, lack of intelligence or living an indecent way of life. Such a lifestyle generates a culture of poverty characterized by various interacting social, economic and psychological features. These include lack of education, poor financial situation, suspicion, deviant values and lack of participation in society or in any other social functioning outside the immediate family (Lewis, 1965, 1969).

An essential feature of this approach is the intergenerational transmission of poverty. A strong nuclear family that creates strong ties and dependence between family members ensures the transmission of poverty, as the younger generations inherit values and customs from their parents (Lewis, 1969). In addition, families on welfare become trapped in poverty because receiving welfare benefits often changes the values and behaviour of both parents and children (Mead, 1992). While the individualistic approach emphasizes individual reasons as an explanation for poverty, the structural approach focuses on the external factors (Merton, 1968; Wilson, 1987, 1996).

The structural approach emphasizes that the poor are in an unfavourable position in structural hierarchies. It regards poverty as a result of external forces, such as lack of education or low income. The poor are victims of social structures. For example, in his study of inner city ghettos, Wilson (1987) argues that poor public transport and loss of manufacturing jobs in inner cities are reasons for poverty and the urban underclass, and that these factors reduce the chances of escaping poverty.

In Indian perspective, despite rapid economic growth in our country and in spite of surviving against global recession because of strong economy, achieving global poverty reduction remains a major challenge. While accelerated growth in India has been widely attributed to the reforms of the early 1990s, their impact on poverty is still much debated among scholars with regard to three main issues: the divergence between the NAS and NSS consumption expenditure, the adjustment procedure to make the 55th round comparable to the previous rounds and the choice of the poverty line. (Siggel, 2010).

Some social scientists (Lal, Mohan and Natarajan, 2001; Bhalla, 2003; Sundaram and Tendulkar, 2003; Datt, Kozel and Ravallion, 2003; Kulshreshtha and Kar, 2003; Deaton and Cozel, 2005) believe that poverty has been reduced in post-reform period (evident from NSS rounds) as accelerated growth is likely to lead to rapid poverty reduction. While Sen and Himanshu (2004) hold that it did not decline as sharply as the official numbers claimed, and that the worsening situation of inequality is to be held responsible for that.

Historically also, it has been observed that economic growth leads to improved living conditions for most, but not all individuals. The notion of poverty is usually taken to mean lack of material well-being, but it does equally apply to non-material aspects of well-being, especially education and health.

It has been found useful to measure poverty by counting the number of individuals that are lacking in well-being. Human Poverty Index (HPI) is an indicator of deprivation in the three categories of average income, education and health. The Planning Commission reports the HDI for each Indian state as well as a ranking according to the HDI. Among the 15 large states, Bihar maintained the lowest position for 1981, 1991 and 2001. At the other end, Kerala occupied the highest rank over the whole period. A basic and promising fact is that the composite HDI has increased for all-India as well as for all states. Although all the states have improved their performance over time, but at different rates, their rankings have not changed much.

Bihar, Madhya Pradesh, Uttar Pradesh, Rajasthan, Orissa and Assam were, and are, still the poorest and the lowest ranking states. Kerala, Punjab, Tamil Nadu, Maharashtra, Gujarat and Haryana, on the other hand, have remained the richest and the highest-ranked states.

Further, human development finds a counterpart in the current debate about social exclusion. The focus is on multiple deprivation (low income, poor housing, poor access to education and health), but also on the process by which multiple deprivation occurs. The key arenas for exclusion include democratic and legal systems, markets, welfare state provisions, and family and community: rights, resources and relationships are all important.

The Approach Paper to the Eleventh Five Year Plan (2007–12) chose 'faster and more inclusive growth' as its central theme. It recognized the need to make growth 'more inclusive' in terms of benefits of growth accruing to those sections of population, which have been bypassed by the high rates growth achieved in recent years. But both exclusive and inclusive models will take us to the domain of caste and ascribed status characteristics.

However, in the theoretical frame of present context, poverty needs to be understood first and foremost as a problem at the individual rather than caste or community level. Also, 'being in poverty' is a temporary status as people move in and out of poverty. In designing poverty programmes, it is wise to respect the vision of poverty articulated by poor people themselves. For many decades, the concept of poverty has been mostly identified with economic deprivation. People are considered as poor when they lack sufficient purchasing power (Akindola, 2009). In the individualistic view, poverty is the product of factors operating at the individual level, such as personal traits and behaviour of the poor themselves as against the social explanation that poverty is a result of structural factors (economic, political and/or cultural) operating at the supraindividual, social level (van Oorschot and Halman, 2000; Gallie and Paugam, 2002).

Conclusion

In conclusion, the Directive Principles of State Policy lay foundations for a 'Welfare State' which need to work for weaker sections of society. Accordingly, there is a need to identify specific groups among OBCs and EBCs for whom specific welfare measures could be designed and ensured. For policy making and programme implementation, there is need to have a separate ministry for OBCs and EBCs.

Provision of Divisible budget for OBCs and EBCs, like provisioned for Scheduled Castes and Scheduled Tribes, overall (Central as well as State level) and sectorial divisible budget should be earmarked for OBCs and EBCs in terms of their population in respective states/Union Territories. And within this divisible budget, prioritized demand as per sub-categorization of OBCs and EBCs at different economic, educational and ecological need based levels, both physical and financial, need to be ensured for sustainable empowerment of Backward Classes.

Notes

1. The *varna* model comprises *Brahmins, Kshatriays, Vaishyas*, and *Sudras* and those outside *varna* as *Avarna*.
2. Weaker sections of the people, and, in particular of Scheduled Castes and the Scheduled Tribes and shall protect them. The Article 46 states: the State shall promote with special care the educational and economic interests of the weaker from social injustice and all forms of exploitation.
3. B.R. Ambedkar was elected to Constituent Assembly of India from Bengal and later from Bombay and on 29 August 1947 became the Chairman of the Drafting Committee of the Constitution of India. On 21 February 1948, Ambedkar submitted the Draft Constitution and in the revised Draft Consti-

tution of November 1949 term 'backward class' was incorporated as suggested by him. In the Constituent Assembly, Ambedkar stated that India was a society based on the principle of graded inequality that meant elevation of some and degradation of others. He apprehended that the free India might revert to the old traditions and downtrodden sections of the society might get further marginalized in absence of proper state intervention

4. Article 340(1) states: 'The President may by order appoint a commission consisting of such persons as he thinks fit to investigate the conditions of socially, economically and educationally backward classes within the territory of India and the difficulties under which they labour and to make recommendations as to the steps that should be taken by the Union or any state to remove such difficulties and as to improve their conditions and as to grants that should be made and the order appointing such commission shall define the procedure to be followed by the commission.' Article 340(2) states: 'A commission so appointed shall investigate the matters referred to them and present to the President a report setting out the facts as found by them and making such recommendations as they think proper.'

5. B.K. Roy Burman in his letter (Reference No. CHCRESP/BKRB/57/OBC/2006 dated 7 June 2006) sent to the author, enclosing his paper entitled 'How much reservation in favour of OBCs' published in the *Mainstream* on 2 June 2006, in which he has mentioned that when he was chairman of the technical committee of the second Backward Class Commission, he found lack of transparency and many aberrations and congruities in the functioning of the commission. He expressed that he firmly believed in formative action in favour of socially and educationally backward classes. He also mentioned that Mandal Commission did not make use of available information to correctly quantify the numerical strength of the population belonging to the socially and educationally backward classes. Besides, there was a question of developing a strategy to prevent casteism being more deeply entrenched through formative action. He expressed that for a long time he had held that there should be transformation strategy in dealing with socially and educationally backward classes so that the focus could shift from caste and community, primarily to caste and income and secondarily to community only.

   In his aforementioned article, he mentioned that the state governments were asked to undertake *ad hoc* survey with a major focus shifted away from caste after the refusal of the Government of India to accept the recommendations of the first Backward Class Commission. As Incharge of the Cultural Research Institute, Government of West Bengal, Roy Berman suggested that 50 per cent or more of persons depending on any non-agricultural occupation belonging to the scheduled castes or the scheduled tribes, and at the same time, the persons whose dependent having less than 50 per cent average literacy of the State could be considered as socially and educationally backward.

   On behalf of the Government of West Bengal that was presented to Government of India and was accepted with a rider that per capita income limited to ₹ 1,000 per annum was also to be kept in view. That was considered to be a deft interlacing of caste and or community and occupation to go beyond casteism.

6. A. Social:
   1. Castes and communities, generally considered as socially backward.
   2. (a) Castes and communities, which mainly depend on agricultural and/or other manual labour for their livelihood and are lacking any significant resource base.
      (b) Castes and communities, which, for their livelihood, mainly depend on agricultural and/or other manual labour for wage and are lacking any significant base.
      (c) Castes and communities, the women of which, as a general practice, are for their family's livelihood, engaged in agricultural and/or other manual labour, for wage.
      (d) Castes and communities, the children of which, as a general practice, are, for family's livelihood or for supplementing family's low income, mainly engaged in agricultural and/or manual labour.
      (e) Castes and communities, which in terms of caste system, are identified with traditional crafts or traditional or hereditary occupations considered to be lowly or undignified.
      (f) Castes and communities, which in terms of the caste system, are identified with traditional or hereditary occupations considered to be 'unclean' or stigmatized.
      (g) Nomadic and semi-nomadic castes and communities.
      (h) Denotified or *Vimukta Jati* castes and communities
   3. Castes and communities having no representation or poor representation in the State Legislative Assembly and/or district-level Panchayati Raj institutions during the 10 years preceding the date of the application

   B. Educational:
   1. Castes and communities, whose literacy rate is at least 8 per cent less than the state or district average.
   2. Castes and communities of which the proportion of matriculates is at least 20 per cent less than the state or district average.
   3. Castes and communities of which the proportion of graduates is at least 20 per cent less than the state or district average.

   C. Economic:
   1. Castes and communities, a significant proportion of whose members reside only in *kachha* houses.
   2. Castes and communities, the share of whose members in number of cases and in extent of agricultural lands surrendered under the Agricultural Land Ceiling Act of the state, is nil or significantly low.
   3. Castes and communities, the share of whose members in State Government posts and services of Groups A and B/Classes I and II, is not equal to the population-equivalent proportion of the caste/community.

References

Adiseshiah, Malcolm S., 'Sustainable Development: What it is and its Coverage', in Sustainable *Development: Its Content, Scope and Prices*, New Delhi: Lancer International in association with India International Centre, 1990.

Akerlof, George, 'The Economics of Caste and of Rat Race and Other Woeful Tales', *Quarterly Journal of Economics*, 1976, XC 4.

Akindola, Rufus B., 'Towards a Definition of Poverty: Poor People's Perspectives and Implications for Poverty Reduction', *Journal of Developing Societies*, 2009, Vol. 25(2), pp. 121–150.

Bhalla, Surjit S., 'Recounting the Poor: Poverty in India', 1983–1999, *Economic and Political Weekly*, 2003, 37(4), pp. 338–49.

Bullock, H.E., 'Attributions for Poverty: A Comparison of Middle-Class and Welfare Recipient. Attitudes', *Journal of Applied Social Psychology*, 1999, 29, pp. 2059–82.

Bullock, H.E., 'From the Front Lines of Welfare Reform: An Analysis of Social Worker and Welfare. Recipient Attitudes', *Journal of Social Psychology*, 2004, 114, pp. 571–88.

Corson, Walter H., 'Priorities of a Sustainable Future: The Role of Education, the Media and Tax Reform', *Journal of Social Issues*, 1995, Vol. 51(4), pp. 37–62.

Datt, Gaurav, Valerie Kozel and Martin Ravallion (2003): 'A Model-based Assessment of India's Progress in Reducing Poverty in the 1990s', *Economic and Political Weekly*, 2003, 37, pp. 355–61.

Deaton, A. and Jean Drèze, 'Poverty and inequality in India: A Reexamination', *Economic and Political Weekly*, 7 September 2002, pp. 3729–48.

Deaton, A. and Valerie Kozel, 'Data and Dogma: The Great Indian Poverty Debate', *The World Bank Research Observer*, 20, 2005, pp. 177–99.

Dworkin, R., What is Equality? Part I: equality of Welfare and Part II: Equality of Resources. *Philosophy of Public Affairs*, 1981, 10, pp. 185–246 and 283–345.

Ferro, M., D. Rosenblatt and N. Stern, Policies for pro-poor growth in India. In Basu, K., (ed.) *India's Emerging Economy*. Oxford: Oxford University Press, 2004, pp. 153–81.

Fukuoka, M., *One Straw Revolution: The Natural Way of Farming*. Emmaus, Pennsylvania: Rodale Press, 1978.

Galanter, Marc, *Competing Equalities: Law and the Backward Classes in India*, New Delhi: Oxford University Press. 1984.

Gallie, D. and Paugam, S., 'Social Precarity and Social Integration', A Repot, October 2002.

Garrett, Hardin, 'The Tragedy of the Commons', *Science*, 13 December 1968, 162, pp. 1243–48.

Ghosh, Madhusudan, 'Dynamics of Agricultural Development and Rural Poverty in Indian States'. *Margin: The Journal of Applied Economic Research*, 2009,3(3), pp. 265–295.

Gillen, Martie and Kim Hyungsoo, 'Older Women and Poverty Transition: Consequences of Income Source Changes from Widowhood'. *Journal of Applied Gerontology*, 2009, Vol. 28(3), pp. 320–341.

Government of India, *National Human Development Report 2001*. New Delhi: Oxford University Press, 2002.

Halman, L. and W. van Oorschot, 'Popular Perceptions of Poverty in Dutch Society'. *WORC Paper* 16. Tilburg University, 1999, geywww.kub.nl:2080/greyfiles/worc/1999/doc/16.pdf

Hussain, Monirul and Lipi Ghosh, *Religious Minorities in South Asia: Selected Essays on Post-Colonial Situations*, New Delhi: Manak Publications, 2002.

Indra Sawhny v. Union of India, 1992. (3) S.C.C. 217.

Khan, Rahman K., 'Report of High Power Committee on Socio-Economic and Educational Survey: 1994 of Religious Minorities in Karnataka', Karnataka State Minorities Commission, 2005.

Khoshoo, T.N., 'Environmental Priorities in India and Sustainable Development' Presidential address, Indian Science Congress Association, 73rd session, 1986.

Kulshreshtra and Kar, 'Estimates of Value Added per Worker from Enterprize Survey, *Economic and Political Weekly*, Vol. 38, No 51–52, 27 December 2003.

Lal, Deepak, Rakesh Mohan and I. Natarajan I.: 'Economic Reforms and Poverty Alleviation: A Tale of Two Surveys', *Economic and Political Weekly*, 2001,36(12), 1017–28.

Leekok, Lee, *Social Philosophy and Ecological Scarcity*. London: Routledge, 1989.

Lewis, O., 'The Culture of Poverty', in D.P. Moynihan (ed.) *On Understanding Poverty*, New York: Basic Books, 1969, pp. 187–200.

McGarry, K. and R. Schoeni, 'Medicare Gaps and Widow Poverty',*Social Security Bulletin*, 2005a, 66(1), pp. 58–74.

McGarry, K. and R. Schoeni, 'Widow(er) Poverty and Out-of-Pocket Medical Expenditures Near the End of Life. *Journals of Gerontology: Psychological Sciences and Social Sciences*, 2005b, 60B(3), pp. S160-S168.

Mead, L.M., *The New Politics of Poverty: The Non-Working Poor in America*. New York: Basic Books, 1992.

Merton, *Social Theory and Social Structure*, New York: Free Press, 1968.

Misturelli, Federica and Claire Heffernan, 'The Concept of Poverty: A Synchronic Perspective'. *Progress in Development Studies*, 2010, 10(35).

Momin, A.R., *The Empowerment of Muslims in India: Perspectives*, Contexzt and Prerequisites', New Delhi: Institute of Objective Studies, 2004.

Moon, Vasant, *Dr Babasaheb Ambedkar Writings and Speeches: Philosophy of Hinduism*, 'The Hindu Social Order – Its Essential Features'. 1987, Vol. 3, pp. 1–94.

Narake, Hari, M.L. Kasare, N.G. Kamble and Ashok Godghate, B.R. Ambedkar (2003): Dr Ambedkar and His Egalitarian Revolution', in *Dr Babasaheb Ambedkar Writings and Speeches*, 2003, Vol. 17 (parts 1,2,3).

Olson, Robert L., 'Sustainability as a Social Vision', *Journal of Social Issues*, 1995, Vol. 15(4), pp. 15–36.

Palmer, J.A., *Environmental Education in the 21st Century: Theory, Practice, Progress, and Promise*, London: Routledge, 1998.

Parameswara, S., Development of Backwardness, Coexistence or Confrontation? A Study of Leather Workers of Karnataka, New Delhi: Reliance Publishing House, 1990.

Rowntree, B.S., *Poverty: A Study of Town Life*, London: Macmillan, 1901.

Sandell, S. and H. Iams, 'Reducing Women's Poverty by Shifting Social Security Benefits from Retired Couples to Widows', *Journal of Policy Analysis and Management*, 1997, 16(2), pp. 279–297.

Sen, A., *On Economic Inequality*. Delhi: Oxford University Press, 1973.

Sen, A., 'Radical Needs & Moderate Reforms' in Jean Dreze and Amartya Sen *Indian Development: Selected Regional Perspectives*', Delhi: Oxford University Press, 1996.

Sen, Abhijit and Himanshu, 'Poverty and Inequality in India', *Economic and Political Weekly*, 18 and 25 September, 2004, pp. 4247–63 and pp. 4361–75.

Siggel, Eckhard, 'Economic Reforms and their Impact on the Manufacturing Sector: Lessons from the Indian Experience', *Asia–Pacific Development Journal*, 2007,14, pp. 73–104.

Siggel, Eckhard, 'Poverty Alleviation and Economic Reforms in India. *Progress in Development Studies*, 2010,10, 3, pp. 247–59.

Siggel, Eckhard, The Indian Informal Sector under the Influence of Globalization and Reforms, *International Labour Review*, 2010, 149, pp. 93–105.

Sundaram, K. and S.D. Tendulkar, 'Poverty has Declined in the 1990s: A resolution of Comparability Problems in NSS Consumer Expenditure Data', *Economic and Political Weekly*, 25 January 2003, pp. 327–37.

Sundaram, K. and S.D. Tendulkar, 'Poverty in India in the 1990s: Revised Results for all-India and 15 Major States for 1993–94', *Economic and Political Weekly*, 15 November 2003, pp. 4865–72.

Thorat, S.K., 'Ambedkar on Economics of Hindu Social Order: Understanding Its Orthodoxy and Legacy' in Walter Fernandes (ed.), *The Emerging Dalit Identity*, Delhi: Indian Social Institute, 1996.

Thorat, S.K. and R.S. Deshpande, 'Caste and Labour Market Discrimination', *Indian Journal of Labour Economics*, Conference Issue, November, 1999.

Townsend, Peter, *Poverty in the United Kingdom: A Survey of Household Resources and Standards of Living*, New York: Penguin Books, 1979.

United Nations (2005): Poverty and Economic Growth: Challenges to Human Rights, Economic and Social Council.

van Oorschot, W. 'Who Should Get What, and Why? On Deservingness Criteria and the Conditionality. of Solidarity among the Public', *Policy & Politics*, 2000, 28: pp. 33–48.

van Oorschot, W. and L. Halman, 'Blame or Fate, Individual or Social? An International Comparison of Popular Explanations of Poverty', *European Societies*, 2000, 2: pp. 1–28.

Verma, D.K. and A. Sohrot, 'The Concept of Social Justice in Post-modern Society: Some Reflections on Sustainable Development', in B.R. Purohit and S. Joshi (eds.) *Social Justice in India*, Jaipur: Rawat, 2003, pp. 174–197.

Verma, D.K., 'Concept and Dimensions of Social Environment Needed for Sustainable Development', in Y.G. Joshi and D.K. Verma's (eds.), *Social Environment & Sustainable Development*, Jaipur: Rawat, 1999.

——, 'Dr Ambedkar's Views on Planning, Development and Conservation of Environmental Resources', *AJSDJ*, 1997, Vol. 5, pp. 1–8.

——, 'Ecoethical Approach for Sustainable Development and Justice',*AJSDJ,* 1994, Vol. 2, pp. 37–59.

——, 'Ecological Sustainability in Social Development' in R.G. Singh and R.D. Gadkar's (eds.), *Social Development & Justice*, New Delhi: Radiant Publishers, 1995, pp. 225–229.

——, 'Intergenerational Equity: Environmental Right of the Child', *AJSDJ*, 1993, Vol. 3, pp. 163--168.

——, 'Role of Environmental Education in Social Development and Justice' (in Hindi), *Dr Ambedkar Samajik Vigyan Shodh Patrika*, 1993.

——, 'Sustainable Development'. *Madhya Pradesh Journal of Social Sciences*, 1999, Vol. 4 (2): pp. 37–59.

Wilson, *The Truly Disadvantaged*, Chicago: University of Chicago Press. 1987.

World Bank, *World Development Indicators*, Washington, D.C.: World Bank, 2000.

World Bank, World Development Report: Poverty, Washington D.C.: The World Bank, 1990.

12

Social Inclusion through Exclusive Provisions in India

The Glass is Half Full

P.K. Chaubey

Social inclusion of excluded groups and communities in societal processes of political and economic significance is a very good idea expressive of modern ethos across the globe, yet not without ambiguities. However, I do not set out here to carry out a scholastic discourse on what its nuances could be, but propose to discuss how it has been attempted and being attempted in India as it is broadly understood.

Social inclusion for this paper does not mean mainstreaming the excluded, partially excluded, and secluded sections of the people in any narrow sense but does mean bringing in some kind of integration among diverse social groups and some kind of fusion between them by addressing the perceived causes of divisive, fissiparous and fissionary tendencies. Two things we need to keep constantly in mind. One, the notion of inclusion presupposes a societal core to which diverse groups may wish to be included in certain senses and yet not in many others. Two, inclusion should not mean intrusion in areas which the sections (to be included) wish to preserve simply because the latter is uninvited. Broad understanding is that in most secular matters they wish to be included and in most religious matters they may not wish to be included. For example, communities not professing Hindu religion may not like to have common civil code and may seek seclusion.

India, that is Bharatvarsha, was perhaps for pretty long stretch of time a cultural identity without well-defined geographical boundaries or with shifting political boundaries. India, that is Bharat, is now a modern political State with more or less well-defined boundaries. India is unique where within the historically given boundary there is so much diversity and plurality that some scholars have chosen to call it most complex nation in the world. Yet, except very small countries and Bangladesh, all countries in the South Asia have a good measure of diversity, even within the majority religions which people in different countries happen to practice. But I shall, however, dwell on India with which I am more familiar much like in the fashion of a well-known litterateur late Rahi Masoom Raza who wrote in his celebrated novel *Adha Gaon* that he is speaking of that half of the village which he understood better.

The modern State of India is home to people of many religious faiths and castes and classes, within several of them, but they have a broad cultural affinity too. It has, therefore, been possible for the people to hold together despite lack of justice in certain spheres to certain sections. Even before Independence several reforms were carried out by various social reformers, generally within a given religion and particularly within Hindu fold, and at times with the State support. After Independence, many of the social grudges and grievances were addressed in the making of the Constitution. In a dynamic society like India with evolving aspirations and ethos, there could be no single permanent optimum mix; but cohesive forces were tried to be so built as to contain divisive tendencies in the society.

In this paper my general approach is to view the Indian social scenario as the 'glass is half full' rather than that of the 'glass is half empty' and my judgement is that the 'glass will never be full up to the brim' given the contradictions that exist between, say, notions of caste justice and gender justice, as is exemplified by the recent controversy over the bill for reservation of parliamentary and legislative seats for women or between gender justice and freedom to profess religion, as came to the fore a quarter century ago in the famous Shah Bano case.

Despite the fact that we Indians (which may be true of all the people in the South Asia) are quite argumentative, it goes to our credit that we have a great capability to develop broad consensus over many issues and move ahead in a positive direction. Both of these, argumentative tendency and capability to building consensus, are healthy signs for a democracy to thrive and not only to survive.

In post-Independence India, we seem to have been broadly pursuing a course of harmony without imposition of homogenization, unity without imposition of uniformity and diversity while mitigating disparities. To paraphrase: harmony sans homogenization, unity sans uniformity and diversity sans disparity. Jawaharlal Nehru had articulated the idea long ago and characterized Indian social fabric as 'unity in diversity'. Though at times mainstreaming was thought to be the best form of inclusion, the idea was shelved for good and preserving diversity and plurality rather than tolerating it became the dominant thinking. Some scholars have preferred to call this ethos as 'union' rather than 'unity'. I would prefer to articulate it as union of minds, unity of purpose and harmony of relations.

Yet justice demands doing away with disparities. It is quite a difficult task to live with diversities and pluralities, while trying to do away with disparities. Quite often it is not even easy to distinguish between diversity and disparity. Preserving cultural diversity yet doing away with social disparity, preserving religious diversity yet doing away with political disparity, and preserving local traditions and doing away with economic disparity, could not be an easy task. It is rendered difficult because in most of the religions, matters ecclesiastic have not been clearly separated from matters secular, with the exception of Christianity. In fact, it is a bit surprising that almost all people(s) in India have accepted the separation of secular domain from ecclesiastic domain even while the two major religions and, of course, many minor religions (minor-major division in numerical sense) had never articulated, let alone concluded, the separation of the two domains.

India chose to be a sovereign, socialist, secular, democratic, republic in 1949, though the words secular and socialist were added in the Preamble of the Constitution of India through an amendment in 1976 only. The Preamble pronounced to all Indian citizens the liberty of thought, expression, belief, faith and worship and also aimed to secure to all of them justice – social, economic and political. A fine balance has, thus, been attempted between preservation of traditional cultural values and promotion of modern secular values. In fact, the Preamble does not only aim at the liberty of belief and faith, it provides to secure it to the citizens. The state is in a pro-active mode in both the domains even though it is professedly secular.

Before we proceed further, it would be appropriate to bring forth the two streams of thoughts that prevailed in pre-Independence India. Gandhi wanted to achieve social harmony through a course of social reformation without State intervention and thus promote unity, especially among Hindus and between Hindus and Muslims where he could see some discord; at the same time, Ambedkar, on the other hand, wanted a political solution through State intervention to bring justice to disadvantaged groups, particularly within Hindu fold, and thus preserve the union. Gandhi thought achieving social harmony through social movement and change of heart would be a permanent solution to attain social justice without unwanted repercussions, while Ambedkar thought State affirmative action would be not only expedient but the only possible course in the given circumstances. In a sense, they believed in two different theories of relationship between State and society. It was Ambedkar line that we finally chose to pursue in the making of the Constitution of India, although original Ambedkar line was itself modified as a compromise that was evolved in the Poona Pact between Gandhi and Ambedkar in 1932 and was incorporated in the Government of India Act 1935 passed in the British Parliament for political dispensation in the Dominion of India.

It is true that Ambedkar line proved expedient but it occasionally gives rise to dissonance in certain quarters and disruption in social and economic life of the people, leading to backlashes and clashes at times. The domain of reservation, the most visible form of positive discrimination, went on expanding its coverage and dimensions from Scheduled Castes/Scheduled Tribes to Other Backward Classes to Minorities and from political representation to employment/jobs (also within that from initial recruitment to promotion and accumulation of vacancies) to admission in educational institutions. If some people have reservations on these reservations, it is because, they feel, the game is being played in a zero-sum fashion, particularly in the economic domain. In a zero-sum game, inclusion of one implies exclusion of another and this is what people are against, though opposition is often articulated in terms of efficiency and merit. Present policy of inclusive growth in some way addresses to this issue by emphasizing on participation of people, better distribution of growth and eradication of poverty instead of redistributing existing stocks, containing concentration and removing inequality. Converting policies into positive-sum games is the real issue, but some games cannot be easily turned into positive-sum games.

What Constitutes India?

In most of the countries with capitalistic economic framework, which the Constitution declares India to be one through its Articles 39(b) and 39(c), theoretical backdrop of the Constitution revolves around the relationships between State and individual and market. State's duty to individuals remain a major goal of a modern democratic Constitution. The State shall generally be required to oversee the conduct of a citizen vis-à-vis another citizen or entity or even the State itself. But reality is much more complex because many other institutions have to be reckoned with and regional aspirations have to be respected. More importantly, in countries like India, group identities have generally been accepted and have also been constitutionally recognized. These groups are in terms of races, religions, castes, classes, regional affiliations and gender. While we have inherited many practices which are considered bad today, we have also inherited a positive trait for appreciation for variety and traditions.

India with a population of more than 1210 million is more than three times larger than the rest of the SAARC countries and, therefore, more diverse and plural. It has the geographical area of about 3.3 million square-kilometres, which is twice as large as that of the remaining of the SAARC countries. With an area of one-third of the US or China, it is quite dense in terms of population density, more dense than any other SAARC country, except Bangladesh. It is also home to seven major religions viz. Hinduism, Islam, Christianity, Sikhism, Buddhism, Jainism and Zoroastrianism and 200 minor religions/sects. There are estimated 3,500 castes, of which about 500 castes excluding duplication across states, are scheduled for special treatment and another 1,000 castes for differential treatment. With 114 languages, of which 22 are recognized as 'national' languages (including the official languages of her three neighbours – Bangladesh, Nepal and Pakistan), India has around 1600 officially accepted spoken languages though mother tongues returned in the census of 2001 were around 10,000. There are several culturally different tribes in India , again with some duplication across States, which are (about 550) scheduled for special treatment. There are also several primitive, de-notified, semi-nomadic and nomadic tribes in India, 75 of them have been identified. Criminal Tribes Acts of 1871 and 1924, under which some of the castes and tribes that were considered 'criminal tribes' were repealed in 1952, though for a while they were considered as habitual offenders. De-notified tribes exist in all categories of classification. We had had stories of thugs and pindaries committing theft and robberies. Now, no castes are considered outcastes and no tribes are considered criminal.

Hindus constitute the majority, whose percentage has come down from around 85 in 1951 to 81.5 in 2001. Muslims constitute the major minority whose percentage has increased from 10.4 in 1951 to 13.4 in 2001. The two religious groups put together constitute more than 95 per cent of the population. Christians and Sikhs constitute 2.3 per cent and 2.0 per cent respectively. Buddhists and Jains are around 0.8 per cent and 0.5 per cent respectively. While Buddhism, Jainism and Sikhism are considered as having been originated in India, Islam and Christianity are not considered likewise. Growth rate of Hindu population is the smallest, after Sikhs, and that of Muslims is the highest among the major religions.

An overwhelming majority of people in any religion are converts from Hindus and as a result, Scheduled Castes are accepted to exist in every major religion in India. Officially scheduled castes are accepted to exist only among Hindus, Sikhs, and Buddhists. It may be noted that the original Constitutional Orders issued by the President on 10 August 1950 and 20 September 1951 restricted these castes to exist among Hindus only. It was only after amendments that people professing Sikhs and Buddhists were accepted to be belonging to Scheduled Castes if they originally came from such castes, races or tribes as were scheduled. Highest incidence of Scheduled Castes is found among Sikhs. Some scholars feel that freedom of religion should permit the converts (to Christianity and Islam) to be accepted as belonging to Scheduled Castes, if by origin they were from such castes, races or tribes.

Scheduled Tribes people are in all religions except among Muslims though there are such converts (numerically not very large) among Muslims as well. The Constitutional Orders issued by the President on 6 September 1950 and 20 September 1951 do not restrict their existence to any religion.

It may reiterated that Muslims, Buddhists, Sikhs and Christians are treated as religious minorities, but only followers of Buddhists and Sikhs could belong to Scheduled Castes while Scheduled Tribes people could profess any religion. However, they are found empirically almost absent, but not nil, among Muslims.

However, there are also socially and educationally backward classes, often called 'Other Backward Classes', which exist in all religions in India, including Islam and they account for a huge majority. As the census of India is not conducted on caste basis, and there is some difference between castes and classes, estimates of their numbers are controversial. Their numbers vary from well below 30 per cent to well over 50 per cent.

Castes and Exclusion

History is replete with cases of ostracism, isolation, segregation and apartheid – some of which is racial in nature. People have often been suppressed and oppressed in many civilizations. Slavery, widely extant in Greece in the ancient period, re-emerged in recent past centuries. America and South Africa both practiced apartheid till late in the passing centuries. Institution of private property and market forces, much useful as they are, have been analysed as causing exploitation and deprivation as well. Jajmani system, where institution of private property was well entrenched but money mediation was not the dominant mode of exchange, is now being increasingly defended because activities of production and distribution were taken care of simultaneously in that system.

Occupational castes exist everywhere in all societies, exception being non-State societies, with certain degree of division of labour. So is the case with discrimination. But exclusion from accessing certain amenities and privileges, performing certain functions and carrying out certain occupational activities has been an exclusive specialty in the caste system of Hindu society. Apart from this, there prevailed the curse of untouchability of certain castes doing cleaning jobs. The other characteristic of the casteism, as it is called, had been forbiddance of marriage and dining across castes. Even when occupational rigidity has melted away to a great extent, the other social practices still continue, particularly in the rural areas. Exclusion from accessing amenities, an extension of untouchability, is still prevalent in some parts of the country and in the neighbourhood though in a diluted form. Some scholars have, therefore, chosen to call it Indian Caste System. The system is so well ingrained and entrenched in the society that members belonging to certain low castes continue to be in the same low social status, in the eyes of others, even though they have converted to such religions which do not permit social hierarchy based on castes. In other words, they could not lose their castes even after conversion. And vocal sections have now started asserting castes, even after conversion, if their ancestors came from low castes. Almost all religions in India are found practicing casteism in marriage, if not in dining. Not to accept the existence of Scheduled Castes (and Scheduled Tribes) among Muslims, some scholars and leaders argue, is the discrimination practiced by the State.

While the State is supposed to intervene generally in the market processes for securing economic justice to the poor and labour, it has to do some extra efforts for ending exclusion of people belonging to certain castes and tribes from participation in the societal processes by ensuring their inclusion in those processes – accessing amenities, performing rituals, and carrying out activities.

There had been traditionally excluded castes – some of which were untouchable and in some parts of the country even unapproachable and unseeable. Obviously, these were the castes engaged in unpleasant lowest level occupations or cleaning occupations. There has been a sort of hierarchy within the groups as well as between the groups. Some of the groups can easily be identified with the *varnas*, but for others it is not easy. To these *varnas* were assimilated certain tribes, as they became part of the larger society, which can be seen as a process of inclusion. These tribes were not considered untouchable even while followers of other religions were called *mlechhas* and treated so. Tribal people were, however, considered low in skills, which they actually were as they came in contact with the larger society much later and were expected to take time to learn skills already developed. Low castes were considered quite adept in their various occupations as they have been a part of society always and had been naturally learning their skills and innovating for a long time. They actually made what is called as the exterior of civilization!

But there are also areas within the territory of India, which have been called scheduled areas. There are also exclusive tribal areas. Some areas got politically assertive and special arrangement has been made for them, for example, in the shape of Darjeeling Gorkha Hill Council. Then, there are marginalized sections like women, minorities – religious and linguistic, nomadic and migratory tribes, and physically handicapped persons as also ex-servicemen for whom some differential treatment has been provided.

The Constitution of India does take care of what it calls Scheduled Areas and Tribal Areas. Scheduled Areas, as provided for in the Fifth Schedule of the Constitution, were originally declared through Constitutional Orders issued on 26 January and 7 December of 1950. They are the areas/regions/pockets with tribal concentration that exist within the states/Union Territories except four states in the North-East viz. Assam, Meghalaya, Mizoram and Tripura. There is provision in the Fifth Schedule [under Article 244(1)] for a Tribes Advisory Council, mostly consisting of Scheduled Tribes representatives in the Legislative Assembly of the State, to advise the Governor on matters pertaining to the welfare and advancement of the Scheduled Tribes in the state. The Governor is empowered to disallow application of, or modify, any particular Act of Parliament or of Legislature of the State and may prohibit, restrict and regulate market transactions particularly with reference to transfer/allotment of land.

The Sixth Schedule [under Articles 224 (2) and 275 (1)], applicable to Tribal Areas in the states of Assam, Meghalaya, Mizoram and Tripura, makes provision for autonomous districts, and within them autonomous regions if there are different Scheduled Tribes, and District Councils (and Regional Councils) with powers to make laws, rules and regulations with respect to certain matters related with land, forest, water courses, taxes (including land revenue), social customs (including marriage and divorce), etc. The District and Regional Councils are largely bodies with members elected for a term of five years on the basis of adult suffrage. They are endowed with powers, subject to certain limitations, to constitute village councils and courts and to establish/construct/manage primary schools, dispensaries, markets, cattle ponds, ferries, fisheries, roads, waterways. They may prescribe the language of instructions and the manner in which primary schools would be run. They have been empowered to collect land revenue and impose taxes on land and buildings as well as tolls on persons resident in their jurisdictions. District Councils have powers to levy and collect taxes on professions, trades, callings and employments; on animals, vehicles and boats; on entry of goods for sale; and for maintenance of schools, dispensaries and roads. As of now there are nine such districts – two in Assam, three in Meghalaya, one in Tripura, and three in Mizoram.

One can notice that the provisions in respect of Scheduled Areas and Tribal Areas as well as Article 371A to 371C and Article 371F to 371H, pertaining to the states in the North-East, are reflective of inclusion in one sense, exclusion in another and seclusion in still another sense. However, in a broad sense, these dispensations have been accepted as part of inclusion policy, because these interventions are intended to take care of those groups in the secular realm without intruding into their personal and cultural spheres where they prefer a kind of 'seclusion' or 'self-exclusion'.

Constitution: Framework and Working

In the Constitution of India, particular and specific provisions for furtherance of welfare of the weaker sections besides general provisions have been made in the Parts dealing with Fundamental Rights (of the citizens vis a vis the State), Directive Principles of State Policy (about intervention in economic and social life), Fiscal Matters (Finance, Property, Contracts and Suits), and Special Provisions Relating to Certain Classes. It needs to be mentioned that the State has been defined in Article 12 of the Constitution to include 'the Government and Parliament of India and the Government and the Legislature of each of the States and all local or other authorities within the territory of India or under the control of the Government of India'. The word State has been used in the Constitution of India in several senses and we shall be using it in this paper in three senses viz., for the Republic of India, the Union of India and each of the states and UTs.

There are two kinds of measures adopted. One set is preventive and protective in nature and the other is that of promoting the interest and welfare of the weaker, marginalized and disadvantaged sections of the citizenry. Both types of these measures are provided in the Constitution.

Enshrining great principles in the Constitution is one thing but making them work is another. Howsoever anti-discriminatory, anti-exploitation, anti-oppressive and anti-exclusionary the Constitution is in its formulation, the issue is how much progress we could make in that direction. Making a good Constitution is the necessary condition but it is only the first step. Acts have to be legislated, rules have to be framed, institutions have to be established, and mechanisms have to be put in place. It has to be seen that dilution is not brought in the steps following the Constitution mandate. Also programmes/schemes/missions/ projects have to be planned, implemented, and monitored.

We shall first deal with the provisions in the Constitution, then with the steps taken to execute them and thereafter the outcomes. Yet, it is difficult to know clearly about how much change is autonomous and how much is on account of State interventions, more so when State interventions trigger societal change, which is what it ought to do, and when State intervenes because of societal and sectional pressure.

Constitutional Provisions for Positive Discrimination

Constitutional provisions could be grouped in certain broad areas like civil, political, economic, educational, cultural, employment and administrative. In the section dealing with Right to Equality (Article 14 to Article 18) in the Part III called Fundamental Rights, it has been made clear that, on the grounds of religion, race, caste, sex and place of birth, neither the State shall discriminate against any citizen in any sphere nor shall it permit others to impose any restriction on access to public amenities and facilities. Abolition of untouchability is specifically mentioned and its practice is declared as an offence in the Constitution itself. But it seeks exemption for the State to make special provisions for women and children as well as for advancement of any socially and educationally backward classes of citizens, in addition to the Scheduled Castes, the Scheduled Tribes. This affirmative exemption has been termed as positive discrimination. It further declares equality of opportunity in matters of public employment and makes it clear that nobody shall be discriminated on the grounds of religion, race, caste, sex, or place of birth. But it again seeks exemption for the State to make laws in favour of any backward class, which is under-represented in the services of the State. The Constitution also permits the State to make laws regarding domicile situation in certain classes of employment.

In fact, the Constitution was tested soon after its promulgation. While Article 16(4) had made provision of reservation by the State in the employment under the State, there was no exception for the State to make provision of reservation of seats in admission in educational institutions. The State of Madras (then comprising present four Southern States of Andhra Pradesh, Karnataka, Kerala and Tamil Nadu) had reserved seats for certain communities based on certain religions and castes in state medical and engineering colleges, which the Supreme Court of India had found violative of Article 15. Article 15 asserts non-discrimination but seeks exemption for making special provision only for women and children, not for castes, classes or communities. In the very first amendment of the Constitution a clause (4) was added to the Article 15, making room for the State to make special provisions for the Scheduled Castes, the Scheduled Tribes, and what came to be known as the OBCs later on through clause (5) added in 2005.

Civil

In order to operate the Constitutional provisions, laws were enacted quite early like Protection of Civil Rights Act, 1955 and Untouchability Offences Act, 1955. However, when they did not prove enough, some further protective provisions were made like Scheduled Castes and Scheduled Tribes (Prevention of Atrocities) Act in 1989, Employment of Manual Scavengers and Construction of Dry Latrines (Prohibition) Act in 1993, and Scheduled Tribes and Other Traditional Forest Dwellers (Recognition of Forest Rights) Act in 2006. In recent years there has been made amendment in the Hindu Succession Act 1955, where word Hindu has been defined to consist of Hindus, Sikhs, Buddhists and Jains. There has also been enacted the Indecent Representation of Women (Prohibition) Act in 1987 and the Protection of Women from Domestic Violence Act in 2005. There already existed Dowry Prohibition Act, 1961 and Pre-Conceptual and Pre-Natal Diagnostic Techniques (Prohibition of Sex Selection) Act, 1994. Recently there has been enactment of the Sexual Harassment of Women at Workplace (Prohibition and Redressal) Act (2007). There is also an Act to take care of physically handicapped persons, namely, The Persons with Disabilities (Equal Opportunities, Protection of Rights and Full Participation) Act, 1995.

The Constitution has also provided for appointing Special Officers, or Commissions for undertaking studies and recommending remedial measures to the State for protecting the interests of the SCs, and the STs, and later on for the OBCs and the Minorities, etc.

It is important to note that Uniform Civil Code, a central provision in the Directive Principles of State Policy (Article 44), impinging upon women's status in civil matters, has been kept in abeyance for indefinite period, despite positive nod from the Supreme Court. It is because such an enactment, thought a section of intelligentsia, might militate against religious rights of certain minorities. An Act professing uniform civil code could of course be enacted yet making certain exceptions and exemptions. No enactment is ever made without a proviso or two and certain practices for example, among the tribal communities could always be accommodated in the Act. But, even the mere mention of enacting any legislation in the matter itself creates a psychosis in the mind of protagonists as well as in that of antagonists and thus the operation of the provision has been postponed for an indefinite period.

Political

With regard to political inclusion, there is a Part (XVI) in the Constitution wholly devoted to Special Provisions relating to certain classes (Article 330 to Article 342). India is said to be unique to make political reservation for representation even in its legislative bodies. Seats are proportionally reserved for Scheduled Castes and Scheduled Tribes in the House of the People, in the Parliament, and in the Legislative Assembly of every State, with some distinction in the case of Scheduled Tribes in the Tribal Areas in the states of Assam, Nagaland, Meghalaya, Mizoram and Tripura. They are, however, not to be represented in the Council of States, in the Parliament, or Legislative Councils of States, wherever constituted. Special representation is ensured through nominations for Anglo-Indians in the House of People, as also in State Legislatures, if not adequately represented through election.

The provision of reservation of the seats in the House of People and the Legislative Assemblies was originally intended to end after ten years but the relevant Article has been continually amended every 10 year to extend the limit and by an Amendment in 2009 the limit has been extended till 25 January 2020. Presently 79 seats for Scheduled Castes and 42 seats for Scheduled Tribes out of total 543 seats are reserved in the House of People of the Parliament. In the Legislative Assemblies of the states, out of total 3961 seats, 543 and 527 seats would be reserved for Scheduled Castes and Scheduled Tribes respectively. Given the circumstances, the provision is likely to be extended again and again.

It is important to note that there is only one general electoral roll for each of the territorial constituencies and there are no special constituencies on the basis of religion, race, caste, or sex. But in certain constituencies only candidates belonging to Scheduled Castes or Scheduled Tribes, as the case may be, can contest for being elected to the House of People, Legislative Assemblies or local bodies. Here, candidacy is qualified but electorate is not. In autonomous districts, all constituencies are to be represented by a member of Scheduled Tribes.

According to original provisions, after each census, the allocation of seats in the House of People to the states has to be readjusted to keep them in proportion to their populations in relation to national population, and also the number of seats to be reserved for candidates belonging to Scheduled Castes/Scheduled Tribes depending upon their populations in relation to the population of the state in question. A Delimitation Commission has to be constituted to decide the above matter but also to determine the territorial constituencies within states and as to which constituencies will go to Scheduled Castes/Scheduled Tribes candidates. A similar provision exists for Legislative Agencies of the states. However, after three such commissions were constituted in 1952, 1962 and 1973 and which completed their exercises as per constitutional provision of proportionality, an amendment was brought in 1976 freezing the number of seats (as well as their territorial divisions) till the first census after 2000 so that the states do not have an incentive to go slow on family planning measures. Reference population composition thus remained as returned by 1971 census. However, by the time census was taken in 2001, it was discovered that even within states there was a wide variation in the size of constituencies. It was pointed out that in the National Capital Territory of Delhi, while Chandni Chowk constituency had a population of barely 0.35 million, outer Delhi constituency had a population of over 3.0 million. An amendment was brought in 2001 to freeze the number till the census after 2026. But by an Act a Delimitation Commission was also constituted in 2002 to rationalize the territorial constituencies within each of the states. Here the word state also includes Union Territory.

A little history would be of some importance here. Under Government of India Act of 1919, there were created separate electorates for representation for Muslims and Sikhs (and later on also for Indian Christians and Anglo-Indians under Government of India Act, 1935). The British rulers decided to review, under political compulsions at home, the working of the Government of India Act, 1919 and constituted Indian Statutory Commission of British MPs in 1927 under John Simon to make an assessment and propose changes in the governance of the country. The next five years were tumultuous in a sense. During this period, Ambedkar demanded a separate electorate for Depressed Classes (as the

Scheduled Castes communities were known in those days) on the pattern of Muslims and Sikhs. The Indian National Congress, the most important political party of the day, would not agree to the proposal but Ramsay Macdonald, the then Prime Minister of Britain, announced separate electorate for them in 1932. Ambedkar and Gandhi took two different and divergent positions. Gandhi undertook fast unto death. Finally, a compromise was brokered into what is popularly known as 'Poona Pact' between Gandhi and Ambedkar, which decided for single (joint) electorate for Hindus but doubling the number of the seats for Depressed Classes within the quota of the seats for Hindus.

It is significant to note that there was constituted an Advisory Committee on Minority Rights which, in order to safeguard the political interest of the minorities, proposed to recommend to Constituent Assembly reservation for minorities in the legislatures on the basis of population. It was a little before Independence. But it came for debate in the Constituent Assembly a fortnight after Independence, the sense of the House was against such a move. In fact when the Advisory Committee met again in mid-1949, a Christian member H.C. Mukherjee moved a resolution saying that 'the system of reservation for minorities other than SC in legislatures be abolished'. It was supported by all forty members, irrespective religions they belonged to, barring one Muslim member. Majority of Muslim members held that 'all these reservations must disappear and that it was in the interests of the minorities themselves that such reservations (as proposed on 8 August 1947) in the Legislatures must go'. Tajamul Hussain, a vocal member in the Constituent Assembly, even said:

> The term minority is a British creation. The British created the minorities. The British have gone and the minorities have gone with them. Remove the term minority from your dictionary. There is no minority in India … . I would like to tell you that in no civilized country where there is parliamentary system on democratic lines; there is any reservation of seats … . We want to merge in the nation.

It appears that to begin with, political representation for Scheduled Castes and Scheduled Tribes was 12.5 per cent and 5.0 per cent respectively as was in the case of jobs. Subsequently, it was raised to 15.0 and 7.5 per cent for national representation, roughly in proportion to their population, with varying degrees across the states and UTs, depending upon their numerical strengths. Though their share in population has increased, the number remains frozen as part of embargo imposed on the number of seats in 1976. This was with regard to representation in the House of People and the Legislative Assemblies in the states.

In the Constitutional provisions made in 1993 for panchayats and municipalities, seats have been reserved for membership and chairpersonship for Scheduled Castes and Scheduled Tribes in proportion to their population in each constituency. It is here that political reservation has been started for women in the Indian democracy and the Constitution mandates at least one-third positions for them (Article 243D and Article 243T). Following Bihar, many a state has raised it to the mark of 50 per cent, a little over-representation than their proportion in the population. Recently, the Union Cabinet has also decided to propose for an amendment in the Constitution to raise the reservation of seats to 50 per cent in panchayats and municipalities. These reservations have a further complication. No single constituency can perpetually be represented exclusively by a woman candidate and likewise no particular chairpersonship can be assigned to a woman representative on a permanent basis. So, a rotational basis is evolved to carry out the provision of reservation, not based on residential dominance of the section.

Government of India under different party coalitions made several attempts to make reservation of women in the Parliament and State Legislatures, but has failed so far. An articulation is now being attempted to show that it is not the removal of disabilities through Constitutional provisions, but creation of abilities through sensible affirmative action that intended results can be obtained even without invoking reservations which often provoke people against reservations. At the same time, it has to be noted, the same political parties which have favoured a higher representation of women in panchayats and municipalities are opposing this reservation in the House of People and Legislative Assemblies. Day will not be far away when there would be reservation for women in the Parliament and the Legislative Assemblies.

However, with reservations in local governments, India has around one million women as panchayat members, more than the population of several countries. However, women are occupying only around 11 per cent seats in the present House of People, which has been steadily rising at least from the mid-1980s of the past century from 5.5 per cent and before that the number fluctuated between 3.5 per cent and 7.7 per cent. The situation compares well with the same percentage in Japan, around 14 per cent in France, Ireland and Russian Federation, 16 per cent in Italy as well as the US, and around 19 per cent in the UK and Switzerland. In our Council of States also women parliamentarians are around 10 per cent. In many other countries where they have two houses, women representation is quite good as high as 40 per cent. India is far below in the ranking of the countries in terms of percentage of women representatives. It is below 100! All our neighbours have done better, except Sri Lanka and Bhutan.

To begin with it was in Scandinavia that reservation/quota for women came up in the political parties as pressure from within. Their quota crosses the mark of one-third and reaches two-fifths in Sweden, Norway and Demark. In many modern States, some quota has been reserved for women in their national legislature. They vary from Argentina to South Africa, from Uganda to Tanzania and Bangladesh, in some countries only notionally. Though there has been expressed some reservations in certain quarters by holding that 'in some ways, quotas are a remedy to a disease, but in some ways they can lead to another disease', but by and large such a move is considered progressive and inclusive and empowering.

It appears that we will be able to make a law, in near future, for reservations for women, with quota for SC and ST women within it, in the House of People and the Legislative Assemblies.

Cultural

The Constitution of India has provided, in its Part III belonging to Fundamental Rights under section 'Cultural and Educational Rights' (Article 29 and Article 30), for protection of cultural and educational rights of the minorities and non-discrimination in granting aid to educational institutions on the ground that its management is in the hands of a religious or linguistic minority. Also nobody shall be denied admission in the institutions run or aided by the State.

There is also a provision in Part IV relating to Directive Principles of State Policy under Article 46 for the State to promote the educational and economic interests of the Scheduled Castes, the Scheduled Tribes and other weaker sections of people.

Under Fundamental Rights dealing with non-discrimination on grounds of religion, race, caste, sex, descent and place of birth and residence, Article 16(5) guarantees that the affairs of a religious or denominational institution can be administrated by a person professing a particular religion or belonging to a particular denomination.

There are permanent Commissions to look after interest of the Linguistic Minorities, Women, the Scheduled Castes, the Scheduled Tribes and Religious Minorities. Recently, in pursuance of entry 15 mentioning 'vagrancy, nomadic and migratory tribes' in the Union List of the Seventh Schedule of the Constitution, there has been constituted a National Commission for De-notified, Nomadic and Semi-Nomadic Tribes.

Economic

Directive Principles of State Policy, the Part IV of the Constitution, though not enforceable by any court of law, are said to be 'fundamental in the governance of the country and it is the duty of the State to apply them in making laws' (Article 37). They are said to be forerunner of the UN Convention on Right to Development as an inalienable human right. These are the principles which make India a welfare State as is suggested in Article 38 that the State shall strive to secure a social order for the promotion of welfare of the people, echoing the Preamble, through ensuring that justice – social, economic and political – informs all the institutions of national life. In 1978, it was added that the State shall strive to minimize the inequalities in income, and endeavour to eliminate inequalities in status, facilities and opportunities, not only among individuals but amongst groups of people residing in different areas or engaged in different vocations.

Without using the modern phrase inclusion, it says a lot. Article 39, which accepts the primacy of private property and market forces, indicates the conditions for the State intervention. It specifically mentions equality among men and women about their right for adequate means to livelihood and equal pay for equal work. Article 39A, brought in as an amendment in 1976, provides for equal justice and free legal aid so that justice is not denied to anybody on account of economic or other disabilities. There are general indications for inclusion of men, women, children and workers, who are in need, in the matter of education, employment and public assistance, and there is a specific mention in Article 46 for promotion of the educational and economic interests of the weaker sections of the people, particularly of the Scheduled Castes and the Scheduled Tribes.

Under Article 275, the Union can provide each year from the Consolidated Fund of India such sums as grant-in-aid of the revenues of such states as may be in need of assistance to enable them to meet the costs of such schemes of development as are carried out to promote welfare of the Scheduled Tribes or to improve the level of administration of the Scheduled Areas.

In pursuance of these provisions, one notices that there has been created in the Five Year Plans special component plan for Scheduled Castes since 1978 and Tribal Sub-Plan since 1976, wherein is placed 15 per cent and 7.5 per cent of total plan budget respectively for the purposes. They are at the disposal of National and state authorities created for development of SCs and STs. There have been established the National Scheduled Castes Finance and Development Corporation in 1989 and (State) Scheduled Caste Corporations much before in 1978 as a Centrally Sponsored Scheme with 49:51 equity shares. In 1997, National Safai Karmachari Finance and Development Corporation was also established. For Scheduled Tribes there are again two bodies, viz., National Scheduled Tribes Finance and Development Corporation and Tribal Cooperative Marketing Development Federation of India. The National Backward Classes Finance and Development Corporation was also created in 1992 with an authorized capital of ₹ 200 crore, further raised to ₹ 700 crore and the National Minorities Development and Finance Corporation was constituted in 1994 with an authorized capital of ₹ 500 crore.

There are several schemes such as Post Matric Scholarship Scheme for Scheduled Castes (since 1944), Mahila Samriddhi Yojana (Women Prosperity Scheme), Adivasi Mahila Sashaktikaran Yojana (Tribal Women Empowerment Scheme), etc. There are exclusive girls schools, girls colleges and women polytechnics. There are several Gandhi, Ambedkar and Valmiki yojanas as well.

Employment

Employment and opportunity for employment is a crucial parameter in any society trying to transit from a feudal order to a capitalist order in the emerging technological scenario. People are dispossessed of means of production and wage employment is scanty and whatever wage employment is available is in the informal sector where wages are quite low because the demand for the goods and services produced in that sector is generally low, and elastic. Most people are still in 'forced' self-employment, somehow making out their living, barring few professionals who by definition are part of informal sector.

The State cannot normally force private employers for employment and wages at the same time in any economy, let alone in an economy where self-employment is the order and wage employment is at best intermittent and casual. Private organized sector is too small from the angle of employment as it employs barely two per cent of the total labour force. Therefore, the State stipulates employment of people under its wings, where it is at most 5 to 6 per cent. Accommodating huge number of aspirants in such a small opening is not possible and complications also arise because of competencies required for the jobs available. Therefore, there has occasionally been raised demand for reservation for weaker sections in private sector also, which is least likely to be finally conceded.

Since there exists a general shortage of jobs, one talks of equalization of opportunity, which is supposed to be just enough. Under Fundamental Rights, Article 16 guarantees equality of opportunity to all citizens in matters relating to employment or appointment to any office under the State and holds that no discrimination can be made on grounds of religion, race, caste, sex, descent, birth-place or residence for any employment or office under the State. The provision implies that if there is one vacancy and a hundred applicants, every applicant should stand equal chance of getting selected in the process of recruitment. However, in the same article, it is stipulated that nothing shall prevent the Parliament from making any law prescribing, in regard to a class or classes of employment or appointment to an office under the Government of, or any local or other authority within, a state or Union Territory, any requirement as to residence within that state or Union Territory prior to such employment or appointment. So, discrimination can be built between two or more categories of employment (say class IV) and of people (say, domicile). Not only this, it further makes exception for the state to make provisions for the reservation of appointments or posts of any backward class of citizens, which in its opinion is not adequately represented in the services under the state. That is, jobs are reserved for Scheduled Castes, Scheduled Tribes and Other Backward Classes. Then, the principle of equality of opportunity of employment would be applicable within each class but not between classes.

However, the facts of under-representation and backwardness of the castes/classes did not prove adequate for promotion of SCs and STs in jobs and it had to be specifically provided for by insertion of Article 16(4A) in 1995, which says, after amendment in 2001, 'Nothing shall prevent the State from making provision for the reservation in matters of promotion of any class or classes of posts in the services under the State in favour of Scheduled Castes and Schedules Tribes which, in the opinion of the State, is not adequately represented in the services under the State'. A further clause (4B) in Article 16 was subsequently added in 2000 to cumulate unfilled posts in any year and carrying them forward in subsequent years.

The Supreme Court of India had suggested a ceiling of 50 per cent for reservations of all categories and has indicated income criterion for creamy layer in the case of members of other backward classes. Article 16(4B) makes it clear that 50 per cent ceiling will apply only for fresh vacancies caused, not to unfilled SC/ST vacancies in the past.

It is a duty of the state, under Article 46 of 'Directive Principles of State Policy', to promote the educational and economic interests of the weaker sections of the citizens and in particular of the Scheduled Castes and Scheduled Tribes. The same article also asks the State to protect them from social injustice and all forms of exploitation. In the Part XVI, dealing with Special Provisions Relating to Certain Classes, Article 335 maintains that the claims of the members of the Scheduled Castes and Scheduled Tribes shall be taken into consideration, consistently with maintenance of efficiency of administration, in the making of appointments to services and posts in connection with the affairs of the Union or of a state. There is thus an issue of efficiency versus reservation. A recently introduced bill in the Council of States (on 23 December 2008), known as the Scheduled Castes and Scheduled Tribes (Reservation in Posts and Services) Bill restricts the reservation in 47 institutes of national importance to the lowest level of grade 'A' posts only. This has been seen by some quarters as a case of 'apartheid'. There is a genuine concern that reservation in employment in the category A at all levels (Lecturer, Reader and Professor; Scientist at levels A, B, C, D, E, F, etc.) would compromise the quality of work that is expected of the organization.

As of now there is reservation in the case of employment under the Government of India, generally speaking at entry level in all categories, 15 per cent for the Scheduled Castes and 7.5 per cent for the Scheduled Tribes, and 27 per cent for the Other Backward Classes, thus totaling to 49.5 per cent, over which there is supernumerary reservation of 3 per cent for physically handicapped persons in all categories. The states are free to determine their own quota for the Other Backward Classes. Creamy layer of the OBC, defined by an income limit, is debarred from enjoying opportunities under reservation. Income is not a criterion for non-discrimination.

Education

The most significant ethos of the day and an important factor for equalizing opportunities in employment is understood to be education. Under Article 46, in Directive Principles of the State Policy, the state undertakes to promote with special care the educational and economic interests of the weaker sections of the citizens, and in particular, of the Scheduled Castes and Scheduled Tribes. There are scholarships, hostels, special coaching institutions, etc. for these sections, but for a long time, there was no reservation in admission. Post-matric scholarship existed from 1944, pre-matric scholarship was introduced in 1977, remedial and special coaching to remove deficiencies in school subjects so as to help them enter professional and technical courses started in 1987 and Rajiv Gandhi Fellowship to help them pursue higher studies and research degrees was provided in 2005. They are given help to prepare for competitive examinations conducted by the Union Public Service Commission through coaching and hostel facilities. All this which is available to Scheduled Castes is also available to Scheduled Tribes. But in addition, for Scheduled Tribe students, there is a special focus for providing textbooks and uniforms and free tuition, etc.

Reservation in admission in most courses in all states is now available to the Scheduled Castes, the Scheduled Tribes, and physically handicapped and to the Other Backward Classes in the institutions funded by the Union Government. Some differential treatment is also meted out to girls and women in the matter of education.

In the wake of passage of Right to Education Bill in 2009, a good fillip is likely to be given to the provisions for scheduled and backward sections.

Administrative

In some way even administrative mechanism of ensuring inclusion has been provided for in the Constitution. It provides for, especially in the states of Bihar, Madhya Pradesh and Orissa, a Minister in charge of tribal welfare who may also be simultaneously in charge of the welfare of Scheduled Castes and Backward Classes. And there is specific provision for administration of Scheduled Areas and Tribal Areas and formation of autonomous state within Assam with full legislative and executive functions.

Though there is no specific direction for the Union to create such ministries yet it has been over time creating several ministries to look after interests of vulnerable sections. To begin with there existed several divisions in the Ministry of Home Affairs to look after interests of excluded sections, like Scheduled Castes Development Division, Tribal Development Division and the Minorities and Backward Classes Welfare Division. The Ministry of Law had a Wakf Division. All these divisions were moved to form a Ministry of Welfare. Department of Woman and Child Development, which was a part of the Ministry of Human Resource Development created in 1985, with main constituent as the Department of Education, was made part of the Ministry of Welfare. The Ministry of Welfare had two main Departments: Department of Welfare and Department of Woman and Child Development. Department of Welfare was upgraded to the level of Ministry and renamed as Ministry of Social Justice and Empowerment in 1998 while the Division of Tribal Development was taken out in 1999 and made the Ministry of Tribal Affairs. Minorities and Backward Classes Welfare Division/Department was again divided in 2007. While there was created a Ministry of Minority Affairs in 2007, Backward Classes Welfare Division was retained in the Ministry of Social Justice and Empowerment; Department of Woman and Child Development was also upgraded to the level of Ministry in 2006.

The Ministry of Social Justice and Empowerment as the name suggests is to ensure equitable treatment to such sections of society who have suffered social inequalities, exploitation, discrimination and injustice. The Social Defence Bureau of the Ministry caters to the requirements of neglected and marginalized people, abandoned destitute, neglected and delinquent juveniles who need care and protection for want of support or are in conflict with the society or the law. The Disability Division is supposed to empower the physically handicapped.

Current State of Affairs in Terms of Inclusion

Finally, the taste of pudding is in eating. How were provisions in the Constitution implemented and how much resources – financial and administrative – were actually committed, and how well were they utilized? How were other sections of the society taken along? How was the morale of the people, excluded and marginalized, boosted? What was the end result in terms of outcomes?

Political

As far as political representation is concerned, we know that the constitutional provision of reservation of seats exists for the Scheduled Castes and the Scheduled Tribes at all levels – national, state and local, including autonomous district/regional councils and tribes advisory councils wherever they exist, are followed *in toto*. However, for women, constitutional provision is only at local level and it is strictly followed. There exists no reservation for other backward classes and their number is not exactly known as there is no constitutional order declaring castes/classes in various states or parts thereof as is the case for Scheduled Castes and Scheduled Tribes. Various states have declared certain castes, including those among Muslims, as OBC but their number cannot be ascertained as the census does not enumerate people by caste. A variety of caste census is being attempted. There is no political reservation for them though they have emerged politically strong across the spectrum.

The reservation for SCs and STs was made to begin with for 10 years only, but it has been extended time and again and currently it exists up to 2020, and before its expiry it is certain that it will be further extended. Their seats are reserved in proportion to their population at national, state and local level, as the case may be. There has been no deviation, and the provision was implemented in toto. The Constitution has made provision for reservation of at least 33 per cent of the seats for women in each type and level of local government. The state of Bihar reserved 50 per cent seats for women and following Bihar, many other states have also enhanced the reservation quota. The Government of India is also contemplating an amendment for raising the quota from one-third to half of the seats at local level. The most important fact in this context is that political reservation at local level is permanent, as against at other levels. It has also been implemented in toto.

Women are increasingly coming to the legislatures, thanks to societal understanding. Their number has increased from 5.5 per cent in Ninth Lok Sabha to 11 per cent in Fifteenth Lok Sabha, which is one-third (or less) of what Scandinavian countries have for women but about two-thirds of what other developed countries may have but more than what many other countries have fixed for women.

We have at the moment a woman President and a woman Speaker in the House of People. We did have a woman Prime Minister earlier. We have been having woman Chief Ministers, Governors, Ministers and Legislators at all levels across the country.

Other Backward Classes have politically done quite well. They have come on their own. They may be even over-represented in terms of their numerical strength, as legislators, if not as ministers.

Practically every religion and caste/tribe group had at some point of time occupied one or the other top constitutional/political position. Even today the President is a Hindu, the Vice-President is a Muslim and the Prime Minister is a Sikh. And they are there often by their merit. No negative discrimination has been done to them on the grounds of race, religion, caste or gender.

Education

What is there in terms of education? Literacy is the simplest case to reckon with, which has been attempted through formal and non-formal institutions. We find from Table 1 that literacy level has increased from mere one-sixth in 1951 to about two-thirds in 2001, while the number of illiterates exceeded that of literates till 1990 or so. The SCs and STs still do not fare that well though increase in their proportion is somewhat better due to the efforts made by the State. It is true that the differences between overall literacy rate and those of Scheduled Castes and Scheduled Tribes have increasingly come down. But, it is a sorry state of affairs that literacy rate, with so much modern value attached, was still not two-third by 2001. It has improved to 74 by the census in 2011 for the country as a whole and that for weaker sections to cross the mark of 65 per cent and 60 per cent respectively.

But when we study literacy by religion across gender in Table 2, we observe that Muslims are the least literate and Christians are the most literate, followed by Buddhists and Sikhs. The disparity between male and female is the least among Christians followed by Sikhs while it is the worst among Hindus followed by Muslims. It is, in general, a reflection of prosperity and poverty and, of course, of culture and exposure. It seems that situation would have been far worse had the promotional measures not been undertaken.

Table 1

*Literacy Rates of SC and ST and Changes Over Time (in %)**

Year				*Difference*	*Difference*	*Ratio*	*Ratio*
	All	*SC*	*ST*	*SC*	*ST*	*SC*	*ST*
1951	16.7	—	—	—	—	—	—
1961	24.0	10.2	08.5	13.8	15.5	42.7	35.5
1971	29.5	14.7	11.3	14.8	18.2	49.5	38.4
1981	36.2	21.4	16.4	14.9	19.9	59.0	45.1
1991	52.2	37.4	29.6	14.8	22.6	71.7	56.7
2001	64.8	54.7	47.1	10.1	17.7	84.4	72.7

SC = Scheduled Castes; ST = Scheduled Tribes * Difference in Per cent Points

Table 2

Literacy Rates Across Religion in 2001 (in %)

Religion	*Male*	*Female*	*Persons*	*Male-Female*	*Female/Male*
All	75.4	53.7	64.8	21.7	71.2
Hindu	77.8	54.7	66.2	23.1	70.3
Muslim	67.6	50.1	59.1	17.5	74.1
Christian	84.4	76.2	80.3	08.2	90.3
Sikh	75.2	63.1	69.4	12.1	83.9
Buddhist	83.1	61.7	72.7	21.4	74.2

M-F = Per cent point difference between male and female literacy rates; F/M= Ratio of female literacy rate to male literacy rate, in per cent.

Economic

People's life depends a lot on how they are employed. Despite the fact that India is presently growing fast and contribution of its agriculture has fallen below 17 per cent, a preponderant majority, close to two-thirds, of labour force is still working in the agriculture sector either as self-employed cultivators or as agricultural wage labour insofar as its rural scene is concerned. More than 76 per cent of SC labour force and 85 per cent of ST labour force is still on farms. The major difference between the three categories is the division between cultivators and agriculture wage labour though, given the fact that more than three-fourth holdings are small and marginal, they are all labourers. For appreciating the division, we may peruse Table 3.

Table 3

Participation Rate of Population and Distribution of Workers in 2001 (in %)

	Participation Rate of Population			Workers as Cultivators			Workers as Agr Labour		
	All	SC	ST	All	SC	ST	All	SC	ST
India	39.10	40.41	49.06	31.65	19.99	44.71	26.55	45.61	36.85
Rural	41.75	42.50	50.37	40.24	23.47	47.07	33.05	52.23	38.37
Urban	32.75	33.14	34.56	02.81	01.76	06.55	04.71	11.03	12.38

While all workers are divided in the ratio of 5:4 as cultivators and agricultural labour in rural areas, where all workers include all religions and all forward and backward classes/castes, the Scheduled Caste workers are divided in the ratio of 5:11 and the Scheduled Tribes workers are in the ratio of 5:4 again. Scheduled Caste people are most dispossessed of land. This is the rural scene. Urban scene is different: the ST in the ratio of 1:2, the SC in 1:6, and all in 3:5. But again, Scheduled Castes people are most dispossessed of land though land may not be the most important possession in the cities.

But does ownership mean much? Not much. Let us look at the poverty incidence by social division for which data is readily available (Table 4). When compared to all population, the STs are worse off than the SCs in rural areas though they are better off in terms of land possession. The order of poverty incidence is just reverse in urban areas. When we concentrate on change between 2004–05 and 1993–94 (that is, during the years of so-called liberalization) reduction in poverty rate is better in the case of the Scheduled Castes irrespective of the area of residence (rural: 11% points, and urban: 10% points), while the Scheduled Tribes do not do better whether in rural areas (less than 8% points) or in urban areas (less than 8% points). If the STs fare better in urban areas (7.8% points) than the aggregate (6.7% points) their number is not large. Further, the gap between 'all' and 'STs' has increased between 1993–94 and 2004–05, as shown in Table 4.

Table 4

Poverty Head Count Ratios (in %) and Differences and Reduction (in % points)

Category	*1993–94*	*1993–94*	*2004–05*	*2004–05*	*Reduction*	
	Rural	*Urban*	*Rural*	*Urban*	*Rural*	*Urban*
All	37.2	32.4	28.3	25.7	09.0	06.7
Scheduled Castes	48.1	49.5	36.8	39.9	11.3	09.6
Scheduled Tribes	51.9	41.1	47.3	33.3	04.6	07.8
Difference: All – SC	10.9	17.1	08.5	14.2	02.3	02.8
Difference: All – ST	14.6	09.8	19.0	07.6	–04.4	01.1

Employment

For economic well-being, but more importantly for status, in India, government jobs matter a lot, particularly for those who are very well-off. The Constitution provided, to begin with, two things: political representation in legislative bodies without exceptions and job reservation in government employment with some riders. Other things were added later. It is worth having a look at the job position in the government. Our database supports information about the employment in the Government of India. But similar and a better position exists in the case of employment under the state governments, including their parastatal bodies, if we cannot say the same about local governments. For 2004, we also have information on the Other Backward Classes as well. First, let us see how the composition is across groups in Tables 5, 6 and 7.

We observe from Table 6 that proportion of the Scheduled Caste and the Scheduled Tribe employees in each category of service under the Government of India is improving except in the D category where the Scheduled Castes are a bit over-represented while the Scheduled Tribes are under-represented. There is some moderation in D group in the proportion of Scheduled Castes in last 10 years and Scheduled Tribes in last five years. In the government jobs as a whole, their proportions have reached or are reaching their share in population despite lag in literacy/education. Other backward classes are dismally represented in bureaucracy – the best they do is in the C category followed by that in the A category. We can note that in politics they seem to be doing quite well on their own without reservation.

Table 5

Employment of Scheduled Castes and Scheduled Tribes in Government of India

Group	*1994*			*1999*			*2004*			
	All	*SC*	*ST*	*All*	*SC*	*ST*	*All*	*OBC**	*SC*	*ST*
A	59,016	6,046	1,727	93,520	10,558	3,172	80,011	3,088	9,744	3,311
B	103,198	12,442	2,902	104,963	13,306	3,512	135,409	3,127	19,602	6,274
C	2,381,613	374,758	128,228	239,426	378,115	145,482	2,040,970	106,334	344,865	136,630
D	1,023,285	209,423	62,945	949,353	189,761	66,487	802,116	26,149	147,212	53,776
Total	3,567,112	602,670	195,802	3,544,262	591,740	218,653	3,058,506	138,698	521,423	199,991

* Backward calculations

Table 6

Share of Scheduled Castes and Scheduled Tribes and Other Backward Classes in the Employment in Government of India (in per cent)

Group	1994			1999			2004		
	OBC	SC	ST	OBC	SC	ST	OBC	SC	ST
A	—	10.24	2.93	—	11.29	3.39	3.86	12.18	4.14
B	—	12.06	2.81	—	12.68	3.35	2.31	14.48	4.63
C	—	15.74	5.38	—	15.78	6.07	5.21	16.90	6.69
D	—	20.47	6.15	—	19.99	7.00	3.26	18.35	6.70
Total	—	16.90	5.49	—	16.70	6.17	4.53	17.05	6.54

How is each group (Scheduled Castes, Scheduled Tribes and Other Backward Classes) distributed across categories? Most of the employees are in C group and their proportion is staying put and more than three-quarters of OBC employees are in this group while in the case of Scheduled Castes and Scheduled Tribes, employees are in the vicinity of two-thirds as is the overall composition. It implies that general category is little less represented. Group D is coming down across the social categories while shares of groups A and B is improving. OBC is less represented in group B than SC/ST while they are doing better in group A, suggesting a little better representation of general category. It may be noted that though OBC are numerically fewer in government jobs, their own composition is on the better side. (Table 7).

Table 7

Share of SC, ST and All in Government Employment (in %)

Group	1994			1999			2004			
	All	SC	ST	All	SC	ST	All	OBC	SC	ST
A	1.65	1.00	0.88	2.64	1.78	1.45	2.62	2.22	1.87	1.66
B	2.89	2.06	1.48	2.96	2.25	1.61	4.43	2.25	3.67	3.14
C	66.77	62.18	65.49	67.61	63.90	66.54	66.73	76.66	66.14	68.32
D	28.69	34.75	32.15	26.79	32.07	30.41	26.23	18.85	28.23	26.89

One side window we can afford to open here is that share of employees in A plus B categories is improving largely at the cost of D category employees while that of the C categories remains almost constant at two-thirds. Calculations can be made from Table 4 where one can observe that the number of employees in groups A and B is on increase whereas that of those in groups C and D is on decrease.

However, all euphoria evaporates when one notices, in Table 5, stagnancy in number of all employees between 1994 and 1999 and attrition in absolute numbers in 2004 over 1999. Five lakh less people, from 35 lakh to 30 lakh, are in the Union government jobs. That is a reduction of around 15 per cent in number of employees in the employ of Government of India. That is the impact of downsizing and rightsizing policies given effect to during this period. Had there been increase in private sector, we might have ignored the attrition. But the fact is in terms of employment, organized/corporate sector is not performing well. There is a tremendous work load and pressure on young generation in certain sectors of the corporate world. If we move down from *jobless to job-loss scenario*, inclusion policies will suffer a great blow. Reservation has much meaning when there is accretion in jobs but it loses significance when there is absolute attrition in the face of increase in the size of labour force. Sphere of wage employment, which frees one from a variety of bondage, has to increase in the present circumstances.

This scenario is expected to be reflective of the government employment in general though our database is limited to Union Government, except in the North-East states where major employment is in the government sector.

We can recall when Dadabhai Naoroji studied poverty, he did not blame the distribution but the lack of growth due to British drain policy. Likewise, talk of inclusion loses significance if opportunities are shrinking. *Ensuring equality of opportunity is not enough, growth of opportunities is even more important.* If recruitment is zero, 100 per cent reservation is useless. If, on the other hand, recruitment increases by 10 per cent instead of 5 per cent, a little more than half the stipulated reservation will work better.

Conclusion

Social inclusion of excluded, partially excluded and secluded communities and groups in secular domain of societal processes of political and economic significance has been attempted in India without intrusion in the privacy domain. Given the diversity and plurality that makes India, it was not an easy task to carry out inclusion agenda because removing disparity at times bumps into some notion of diversity and plurality. There has been a broad consensus about pursuing a course of harmony without imposition of homogenization and unity without imposition of uniformity of any kind, rather preserving diversity and plurality, yet doing away with or at least moderating the magnitude of disparities. However, it should be noted that in economic field we have done away with, along with the rest of the world, the idea of reducing disparity (often called inequality) and concentrated on poverty and in political and social arena we are stuck with reducing disparities. It means we shall not make attempt to do away with economic disparities but shall make attempt to do away with social disparities. In a way that is what existence of capitalist economic order and political democratic dispensation calls for! However, we are also witnessing interest, in countries like India, in reducing what has come to be known as horizontal disparity but losing interest in vertical inequality. Reduction in vertical inequality was no guarantee of reduction in horizontal inequality but overly emphasis on reducing horizontal inequality sans vertical inequality will not go a long way. Yet, on balance, social inclusion has improved – partly by autonomous movement of society and partly by State activism.

India as a State pursued Ambedkar line and perpetuated by practice political reservation for Scheduled Castes and Scheduled Tribes in the Lower House of the Parliament and Legislative assemblies, which was a temporary arrangement in Ambedkar formulation. When it came to reservation in local government, it was made permanent in the same Constitution. Reservation for women in local government is at least one-third of the total seats of members in each local government and of total number of chairpersonships in the state. But there is no reservation for women in the Parliament or State Legislature. Political success in what was proposed in the Constitution is total. In the civil matters success is more than half of the completed journey. In educational and economic matters the success is far from satisfactory. But it is not only in the case of excluded groups alone, but even in the case of so-called included. The State of India does face backlashes and clashes on reservation count.

For long growth of the economy and employment was very sluggish, but good enough not to badly impact on population growth. Now, when rate of growth of the economy has picked up fast and population growth is stabilizing, employment elasticity is on a declining curve. Neither employment growth is picking up nor is the quality of employment, in terms of productivity improvement. *Reduction of poverty though a bit higher for excluded sections, is not big enough to give a feeling of inclusion to those who were traditionally excluded, yet causing a feeling of exclusion in those who are supposedly included.*

In economic sphere, India seems to have been playing a zero-sum game leaving people on both the sides of inclusion-exclusion line dissatisfied. *The real challenge for India is to turn economic games into positive-sum ones so that fruits in terms of job and livelihood reach everyone.* Jobs just do not entitle an individual for livelihood, but also empower him/her socially and psychologically. Equality of opportunity which reservation policy seems to be promoting at best should be construed as an assignment problem of who gets what rather than an allocation problem in which some get and some do not. Unfortunately, that is not happening as employment is formulated as a derivative of growth strategy which looks for acceleration *per se*. Of late, realizing the failure of growth process to translate into employment of the socially excluded and exclusion of the socially included we have attempted strategy of inclusive growth in the recent past. Preliminary results are not very encouraging.

APPENDIX

Scheduled Castes and Scheduled Tribes

The word 'scheduled' in the context of the Scheduled Castes, Scheduled Tribes and Scheduled Areas is little confusing to many scholars. Therefore, the following explanation is offered.

There are twelve schedules in the Constitution of India, two of which viz., the Fifth and Sixth Schedules refer to similar matter. While the Fifth Schedule provides for a Tribal Advisory Council in a State with Scheduled Areas and also in a State with Scheduled Tribes but not Scheduled Areas, the Sixth Schedule provides for administration of the Tribal Areas, each with autonomous District Council and Regional Councils, if there are different Scheduled Tribes, with powers to make laws in respect of certain matters, in certain States like Assam, Meghalaya, Mizoram and Tripura. In the latter schedule, there is a Table with parts showing 78 *Journal of Social and Political Studies* certain districts as Tribal Areas. However, the word 'scheduled' in the above three expressions has nothing to do with these twelve schedules except that matters related to 'Scheduled' Areas are dealt with in the Fifth Schedule. In short, word 'scheduled' is different than a 'schedule' of the Constitution. Some of the Constitutional schedules are not in a strictly scheduler form. Some scholars have unfortunately attributed existence of scheduled castes and scheduled tribes to schedules appended to the main Constitution.

The President is supposed to issue an order, under the Fifth Schedule of the Constitution dealing with Part X, to declare the certain areas as Scheduled Areas. By the Constitutional Order No. 9 issued on 26 January 1950, the President actually declared four areas in Bihar, now in Jharkhand; ten areas in Bombay, now in Gujarat; eleven areas in Madhya Pradesh, now in Chhattisgarh except one that is in Maharashtra; and two in Madras, now one in Andhra Pradesh and one is Lakshadweep; two in Orissa; and one in Punjab, which is now in Himachal Pradesh. They were all listed under the relevant State.

Article 366 of the Constitution gives definitions of certain terms, which include Scheduled Castes and Scheduled Tribes. Scheduled Castes are defined as castes, races, tribes or parts of, or groups within, such castes, races, tribes as are deemed under Article 341 which empowers the President to specify with respect to a State (in consultation with the Governor) or a Union Territory by public notification. Likewise Scheduled Tribes are defined as tribes or tribal communities or parts of, or groups within, such tribes or tribal communities as are deemed under Article 342 which empowers the President to specify with respect to a State (in consultation with the Governor) or a Union Territory by public notification. These notifications are called Constitutional Orders. The Constitutional (Scheduled Castes) Order 1950, numbering 19 was issued on 10 August 1950 and the Constitutional (Scheduled Tribes) Order 1950, numbering 22, was issued on 6 September 1950, supplemented by the Constitutional (Scheduled Castes) (Union Territories) Order 1951, numbering 32, issued on 20 September 1951 and the Constitutional (Scheduled Castes) (Union Territories) Order 1951, numbering 33, issued on 20 September 1951. Of course, the words Union Territories were substituted for other words as certain category of States were redesignated as Union territories in 1956 only. Both the sets of orders were modified and amended several times only to include more castes and tribes or enumerate them under the newly formed/carved out States.

The word 'scheduled' has origin in Government of India Act of 1935, in which Depressed Classes were given these 'neutral' expressions. Gandhi used to call the people belonging to lower castes as Harijan, a term earlier used for Brahmins say writers like saint Tulsidas. Since most of tribal people used to live on the hills, they were given a term of Girijan by certain scholars. Word 'depressed' was the translation of Hindi/Marathi word 'Dalit', which is emerging in recent years in literature and is subsuming both Scheduled Castes and Scheduled Tribes; but the *adjective* is getting attached with Muslims and Christians as well.

References

Ministry of Law and Justice, Government of India, *The Constitution of India*, various editions.

Planning Commission, Government of India, *Eleventh Five Year Plan 2007–2012 Volume I: Inclusive Growth*, New Delhi: Oxford University Press, 2008.

Publication Division, Government of India, *India: A Reference Annual,* various issues.

13

Social Justice and People at the Margins

M. Kistaiah

John Rawls theory of justice as fairness is primarily based on public interest which can be discerned in most situations by applying two principles of justice (1) that 'each person is to have an equal right to the extensive basic liberty compatible with similar liberty for others' and (2) that 'social and economic inequalities are to be arranged so that they are both (a) reasonably expected to be everyone's advantage and (b) attached to positions and offices open to all', leading ultimately to the dignity of man as the paramount goal.

It also envisages that inequalities of wealth, authority and social opportunity 'are just only if they result in compensating benefits for everyone, and in particular for the least advantaged members of society. These principles rule out justifying institutions on the ground that the hardships of some are offset by a greater good in the aggregate. It may be expedient but it is not just that some should have less in order that others may prosper'.

In fact Rawls specifically states Aristotlian formulation of refraining from *Pleanexia*, that is, 'from gaining some advantage for oneself by seizing what belongs to another or by denying a person that which is due to him and so on'.

These formulations have inspired some of the Western thinkers in public administration and economics to question the validity of the classical theories. Without going into the rigour of enumerating different developments in the discipline of Public Administration and Economics during the last 50 years, encompassing cross cultural synthesis, it is appropriate to identify the emergence of 'the New Public Administration' and 'the New Economics'.

The emergence of New Public Administration, as we are well aware, was the result of the proceedings of a conference which were subsequently published as a book in 1971, edited by Frank Marini and entitled *The New Public Administration: The Minnowbrook Perspective*. The emphasis is normative in theory, philosophy and activism. It deals mainly with values, ethics leading ultimately to the development of the individual member in the organization and the relation of the client with the bureaucracy. Its focus is on morality.

Among other things the moral tone of New Public Administration is oriented towards the client. How is he to be treated? What is the purpose? What is fair? In an effort to conceptualize the usefulness of Rawls theory of justice as fairness, attempts were made by contrasting it with other philosophies such as *Intuitionism, Perfectionism* and *Utilitarianism*. Of the three, the utilitarianism advocated by Bentham, Adam Smith, J.S. Mill and Hume appears to be both democratic in values and systematic in thought. It provides a basis in which a Public Policy will be in the Public Interest provided that everybody is slightly better off, even if some individuals left slightly worse off in other ways as a result of a particular policy ultimately leading to an increase in the net balance of social satisfaction.

Based on this analysis it is suggested that the bureaucracy has to be trained in such a way that a sense of ethics is imbibed through proper education to meet the modern day challenges. Similarly in the discipline of economics, the echo of Rawls theory of justice as fairness is felt in which a new trend has taken shape which like discipline of public administration questioned the classical theories. A new concept called 'a theory of human needs' has been advocated which signifies the attention of critics about the whole range of basic needs of the people. This is relevant in view of the global meltdown, climate change, food shortage, and water scarcity, widespread suicides of farmers at the margin due to several man-made and natural calamities in the developing societies.

Rawls theory of justice as fairness envisages provision of 'primary goods' in which (1) basic liberties would be protected, insuring a democratic mode of political organization; (2) social inequality would only be tolerated to the extent that it would benefit the least well off through expanded production. In other words, it should ensure an equitable distribution of production. Finally equality of opportunity would be instituted.

In the final analysis it is argued that only if above mentioned principles are met then primary goods would be maximized in quantity and justly distributed and the society will be progressive. For this redistribution, some type of state responsibility and control are a necessary pre-requisite – which are in turn preconditions for basic individual needs to be met in practice. In addition, one point concerning the ecological constraints on the limits of economic production needs to be noted. Ecological strategies for conserving and protecting the environment from needless waste and pollution need to be looked into an international level for satisfying basic needs. In view of the technological advancements, the international strategies for their success must conform to the national strategies to meet the basic needs of the people. Thus, the vision of a more humane, need-oriented society must be realistic. Socially useful production or production to meet the basic needs should be the ultimate goal of a state.

After a brief description of Rawls theory of justice as fairness, let us look at a few public policies initiated by the modern states such as India to ameliorate the socio-economic problems of the people living at the margin. It may be noted that a large number of farmers, specially the marginal and small cultivators, for instance, committed suicides in Andhra Pradesh and Vidharba region of Maharashtra due to financial difficulties arising out of heavy investments in commercial crops such as cotton. According to the National Crime Records Bureau, between 1997 to 2008, about 1,99,132 farmers committed suicides mostly in cotton cultivated states called 'suicide belt' – Maharashtra, Andhra Pradesh, Karnataka, Madhya Pradesh and Chhattisgarh. Unable to wriggle out of the debt trap, almost one-fourth of the farmers get entangled, they reluctantly indulge in such an extreme step. One of the reasons for their indebtness has been the unavailability of inputs like institutional credit, appropriate seed at reasonable cost, fertilizers at affordable price and unadulterated pesticides and finally remunerative price for the produce. Sometimes the vagaries of monsoon complicated the situation and compounded their misery. In such a scenario, one factor which is very crucial deserves our attention that is availability of appropriate seed which will ultimately result in either profit or loss to the cultivator.

For centuries, the farmers in India depended on indigenous traditional seed which they adopted but the yield was low and many a time unremunerative. However, in recent times with commercialization of agriculture, dwarf varieties have been introduced thanks to bio-technology and genetical engineering. Cotton seed is no exception to this experience. Being adept in introducing the latest, the multinational corporations have grabbed the opportunities to enter the market. Taking advantage under the concept of intellectual property rights and the patent rights, the transnational corporation, Monsanto, has introduced a new product called Bacillus thuringiensis (Bt) cotton all over the world.

Being a monopoly commodity, the price was fixed arbitrarily and sold through a network of well established outlets. A pocket of 450 grams seed, which is just enough to cover one acre, was sold at ₹ 1,700 in India where as it was three dollars in US and one dollar in China, making it most expensive input in terms of investment to the farmer. Over a short period, a decade or so, the corporation made enormous profits. It is nothing but monetary hegemony through cross border economic terrorism. Since Bt Cotton is pest resistant and dwarf variety the farmers in India were tempted to prefer the seed hoping that the 'White Gold' as it is popularly called would bring a windfall of fortune to wipe out their poverty and miseries. But ultimately that was not to be.

During his Padayatra covering every nook and corner of the state before 2004 general elections to the Assembly in Andhra Pradesh, Y.S. Rajashekar Reddy noticed widespread suicides mostly in cotton cultivated pockets of the state. Being a pro farmer, after coming to power, he initiated several developmental programmes such as Jalayagnam on a massive scale to improve assured irrigation facilities, permanent housing to the homeless, Arogyasri to help the medical needs of the white card holders, monthly pension to the old age eligible persons, minimum rate of interest from Women Self Help Groups at 25 paise, called 'Pavala Vaddi', Crop Insurance Scheme, etc. These schemes were taken up in addition to centrally sponsored Rural Employment Guarantee Scheme. In this context it is pertinent to note that at the instance of Reddy, the minister for agriculture with the active support from bureaucracy and wise counselling from legal advisor, who came from farming family with indepth experience of agricultural problems, the exorbitant rate at which Bt cotton seeds were marketed was taken up. The confrontation between the state and the multi national corporation, Monsanto, over the issue of price fixation of Bt cotton was not against any body depriving their legitimate share but against the MNC for its unreasonable exploitation under the cover of intellectual property rights and patent acts. It took several twists and turns when the state approached the High Court, the Monopolies and Restrictive Trade Practices Commission and the Supreme Court and finally succeeded in bringing the price from ₹ 1,700 per 450 grams pocket to ₹ 700. It was a great relief to the cotton growers across the nation. Monsanto explored all the tricks of the trade with the legal luminaries at its disposal to defend its policy but ultimately agreed to bring down its price. However, the very next year, the corporation introduced a new variety called Bt II Cotton seed with some modifications and improvements and marketed the same at old price.

In a quick response, the state enacted a law to regulate the pricing policies of seed production of private enterprises. Monsanto was compelled to fall in line accordingly. The concept of public interest could be realized to a large extent if only there is political will and the resolve without succumbing to financial inducements coupled with administrative empathy towards the clientele who are mostly small and marginal.

There is another dimension to the concept of public interest when the people's representatives at the helm of affairs indulge in partisan ways resulting in deprivation of shelter to the people living at the margin. The state government in Andhra Pradesh in 2005 issued several government orders directing the State Housing Board to alienate a piece of land, which was notified as a slum and meant for housing scheme located adjacent to Gandhi Bhavan, State Congress Party Head Quarters, in favour of the Indian National Congress. This was contested by a voluntary organization in the High Court. The court set aside all the government orders stating that 'the action of the government is contrary to the act. When a public body exceeds or abuses power vested in it, the court interferes to correct the infraction and it is in larger public interest to set it aside'. It is an illustration only. There may be several such instances all over the nation. Vigilant voluntary organizations, civil society groups, human rights activists, committed intellectuals like Harsh Mandhar, late K. Balagopal, Aruna Roy, Binayaka Sen, Medha Patkar, Anna Hazare, Sunderlal Bahuguna of Chipco

Movement, Colin Gonselves of Human Rights Network, and several other unknown activists, who sacrificed their comfortable careers and took up the cause of the ignorant, hapless, illiterate people leading a life of misery, needs appreciation.

There are several others whose cause is yet to be taken up such as Dadaji Ramaji Khobargade in Maharashtra who developed a new strain of paddy. Being a small farmer and unaware of its use in multiplying paddy production some agricultural scientists and commercial seed companies cheated the poor farmer and made lakhs of rupees as profit. Several companies based in Nagpur and Chandrapoor minted money from his HMT seed but never thought of sharing even a small portion of their profit with him. This is an illustration in which the multinational corporation with their widespread network might successfully secure intellectual property rights and get patent rights depriving the small farmer who was the original inventor of the strain.

In India the political executives instead of being trustees, in true Gandhian spirit, of precious natural resources such as coal, gas, iron ore and mineral wealth, circumvent the public policies to suit their personal benefit at the slightest opportunity. Since citizens are sovereign in an independent sovereign democratic state, the national resources should be utilized carefully keeping the future needs of the society for the benefit of all.

The state policy regarding generation of power, distribution, tariff, etc. is included in the concurrent list of the Indian Constitution. The generation of power in Andhra Pradesh through hydel and renewable sources such as wind, solar, biomass account for about 15 per cent, the remaining is accounted for utilizing coal, natural gas as raw material. Bulk of the power is generated by the state undertakings. In addition, there is National Power Corporation located in the state to generate power. However, in view of the large scale shortage of power, gap between demand and supply being unmanageable, the state adopted a liberal policy of permitting the private sector to enter the field. The private sector units after fulfilling its obligation to the state by providing a certain percentage of power and as per agreement with the government, the remaining power is sold to any other state or industry in any part of the country utilizing the existing conductors established by the state undertakings. The rate at which the power is sold depends, however, on demand and supply, through a few licensed agencies. It's something like stock exchanges where commodities are delivered to the highest bidder. It's purely commercial proposition and depends on market economy. Therefore, there is a clamour from private sector, such as Ambanis, Hindujas, to enter into this very attractive and lucrative venture.

The private sector with considerable political clout, connivance of political executive, shortage of power being a perennial problem, cleverly manage to negotiate with the government and get uninterrupted coal, natural gas at a fixed price, but allowed to sell the product in the market without any regulatory mechanism. Similarly, the extraction of other minerals such as iron ore has become controversial in AP where allegations of illegal mining had prompted the state to suspend the export of precious iron ore. The matter is now sub judice.

It is a sad commentary on our public policy regarding national resources permitting unbridled exploitation by the private sector in which literally we find people from rags to riches controlling the state politics, and perhaps if left unchecked it may ultimately subsume the national government, surreptitiously through ill gotten wealth.

In this context it is relevant to note that a report of the National Sample Survey has revealed that more than 50 per cent of peasantry is willing to give up cultivation if provided an alternative. Between 1991 and 2001 it appears some 8 million cultivators quit farming. The number may increase between 2001 and 2011. They might have been 'inspired' by the 'role models' who with the help of political elite and dubious means become rich in the shortest possible time by exploiting natural resources of the nation. Now the time has come to seriously evaluate the public policies and examine to what extent they serve public interest, failing which we may have to confront Hobbesian state of nature which is not very far as things stand today.

14

Issues of Social Justice and the Marginalized

Contextualizing Scheduled Castes in J&K State

Ashish Saxena

Development involves complex processes and procedures of institutional changes and the redistribution of economic and political power for better egalitarian society. According to Amartya Sen, development requires the removal of major sources that hinder freedom and to see the 'instrumental' perspective of freedom. From a developmental point of view, social justice appeals a pertinent question of how social arrangements are made and social institutions to be chosen, and in turn, what social realization is to be achieved. Causally significant exclusion can have great instrumental importance, they may not be impoverishing in themselves, but they can lead to impoverishment of human life through their causal consequences. Like, landlessness is an instrumental deprivation. It is in this context, the role of state becomes extremely significant and the ability of reasoning plays crucial role to make a just society.

Theory of social justice to be driven by two cardinal principles; guaranteeing fundamental individual liberties and ensuring social and economic equalities. There are, thus, two ways of conceptualizing justice; at one spectrum a 'well-ordered society and at the other end a 'moral person'. Well, in retrospection one needs to ask a question of, do we have 'just society' with 'moral persons'? A well ordered society, perhaps, deemed to represent the realm of universality through citizenship. An ethical question arises – are all citizens objectively equal?

Perceiving the question of marginalization, one may visualize it with a group of people who sat on the borders of two cultures existing within a society, but were fully members of neither culture. In other words, marginalization is socially excluded persons who ostensibly have no significant role in society. It has manifested in the following forms such as: less access to the state institutions; degree of violence; and exclusion from the special treatment by society; and reaction to varying degrees of violence.

In recent years, the use of equal opportunity policy in the form of reservation, as a means of inclusion of socially excluded groups in India has become a subject of lively discussion. It covers a wide range of issues ranging from the characterization of Indian society, problem of socially excluded groups in India, possible remedies against discrimination and deprivation. An enduring form of social life can thus be visualized, by nurturing fair treatment among human beings that imprints equality and social justice. A just society is grounded on the principles of its pragmatism. In other words, social justice is realized through political justice, which guarantees distributive justice to all. A society, well aware about its setbacks, certainly would find remedial measures and desirability of advantage, for the marginalized would also be taken care of. Unfortunately, a State has an increased interest in compensation. In this context, a number of questions have been raised: what policies are warranted to overcome the problem arising out of historical denial of equal rights? What should be the nature of such policies?

It is reflected through various studies and government reports that socially excluded Scheduled Castes don't yet get justice at the hands of the government as well as society. Various studies on the Scheduled Castes show that they do not get *fair share* in the services, their representation in higher categories of administration is negligible, and their political representation does not confer *an effective form of power*. The significance of the social development and empowerment of marginalized groups thus entails sincere demolition of the structure of subordination imposed on them and sharing power with the powerless lots. Still, the anxiety is – are the marginalized groups in India still deprived of social and economic justice?

Belonging to the discipline of sociology, I too realize that conventional paradigms of sociology in India have largely ignored the persistent phenomenon on marginals and the minorities and have not changed the focus of sociology in India from its consensual model of Hindu India. Dissenting voices were heard later on with the research on social movements of backward classes and Dalit, caste and class violence in the aftermath of Green Revolution, and feminist concerns with the invisibility of women in sociology in India.

One may observe that quest for social justice in the era of globalization is assumed less relevant in the Third World countries. The modern welfare state, for instance, apart from maintaining law and order, has also subordinated and marginalized groups. However, various strategies and initiatives are notionally espoused by the state in different nomenclatures such as 'emancipation', 'development', 'empowerment', etc. Sadly to note that empirical studies found that due to the neo-liberal logic of the state, the notion of social justice in India become most abused concept especially for the economically and socially marginalized groups. Social and economic discrimination are continued to be a reality in Indian society today, which multiply the causes of deprivation and poverty questions, thereby, social exclusion. In corollary to this, worse form of marginalization is still continued in the old format such as untouchability and atrocities against Dalits, cultural deprivation among the women folk and they are still the victims of segregation (See works of Gail Omvedt; Nandu Ram; S.K. Thorat).

Although the significance of social development and empowerment of marginalized groups entails sincere pursuits for perceptive cognition and analysis of the composite processes of new identity formation, followed by conscientisation of these groups for the demolition of the structure of subordination imposed on them and sharing power with the powerless lots. Still, the anxiety is – are the marginalized groups in India still deprived of social and economic justice? Have Dalits been studied objectively by the Indian social scientist? Has India overcome from the subordination and control of women? Will the institutional initiatives be able to provide a space for the marginalized groups for their empowerment? Can we begin to listen to the subaltern voices? Can the marginalized be empowered without demolishing the institutionalized structure of subordination? What are the possible alternatives of empowerment available to the marginalized? Can we speak of social and national integration of the marginal? These and many such questions that are to be debated and examined in the interdisciplinary domains while dealing with the empowerment and social development of the marginalized groups.

Idea of 'Justice' and 'Social Justice'

We might note at the outset that we would choose to be governed by two principles of justice, the first guaranteeing fundamental individual liberties (of speech, association and worship, among others), and the second ensuring that social and economic inequalities are arranged to offer the greatest possible benefit to the worst-off in society, while upholding fair equality of opportunity.

The concept of social justice is an essential part of the broader concept of justice. In general, Greeks used the term 'justice' equivalent to 'virtue', while in modern times it is used as 'getting ones due'. The pertinent question here is how to determine what is a man's due and this brings us to the relationship between justices in general and social justice. In particular, social justice concerns the distribution of benefits and burdens throughout a society, as it results from the major social institution – property system, public organization, etc. Thus, broadly distribution of power allocation of benefits, material as well as tangible such as wealth, prestige and self-respect, have to be the most important concerns of social justice.

Historically speaking, the birth of the concept of social justice coincided with shifts in human consciousness: the 'death of God', the rise of science and the rise of the ideal of the 'command economy' leading to scientific socialism, i.e. reasons and intellectuals were supposed to rule. The roots of social justice thus lie in the thought process of enlightenment. The development of a scientific and rational viewpoint led to corresponding changes in the social thought process, which, in turn, initiated radical changes in the political and social structure of Europe, especially during the Renaissance. Thus, social justice, both as a concept and as a socially cherished goal, came into prominence during the French Revolution (1789) as far as Europe is concerned.

Significant philosophers had propounded there own ideas of justice. John Stuart Mill gave anthropomorphic approach by stating: 'Society should treat all equally well who have deserved equally well of it, that is, who have deserved equally well absolutely. This is the highest abstract standard of social and distributive justice; towards which all virtuous citizens, should be made in the utmost degree to convergence'.

J.J. Rousseau was a dreamer of an ideal just society. He wanted to build a genuine and humane community. He argued that men are equal by nature but the institution of private property has made them unequal and further perpetuated inequalities. Therefore, the perfection of man lies in the improvement of society that can be done by remaking man by cultivating natural feelings and sentiments which guarantee equality and social justice. He argued that the institution could be re-moulded in such a way as to realize a just and democratic society (Tilly, 2000).

For William Frankena, the concept of just society should emphasize on the principle and practical aspect of it. Therefore, he conceives social justice as part of political justice that emphasizes to create just society. Charles Evans says that justice is giving every man his due and conceptualizes justice as deserved treatment. For Robert Nozick historical entitlement is an important element of distributive justice where the society is aware of its wrongs and has an increased interest in compensation. Therefore, for him, backward-looking concepts are important that address the distribution of goods in society as social justice.

John Rawls conceptualized 'justice as fairness' where there is desirability of advantage for the marginalized groups in some respect. It includes the First Principle that each person is to have an equal right to the most extensive total system of equal basic liberties compatible with a similar system of liberty for all; Second Principle that social and economic inequalities are to be arranged so that they are both – (a) to the greatest benefit of the least advantaged, consistent with the just savings principle, and (b) attached to offices and positions open to all under conditions of fair equality of opportunity. To Rawls (1971), justice as fairness tries to uncover the latent ideas of freedom and equality, of ideal social cooperation, and of the person, by formulating two 'model conception', one of a 'well-ordered society' and another of a 'moral person'.

There can be no single application of theory of social justice and no definite prescription of justice can be made. For Miller (1976), therefore, a concept such as justice may possess sociological investigation awareness of cultural diversity and conceptual change.

Fundamentally, the basic premise of social justice remains to be the emancipation of the underprivileged, exploited, and oppressed section of society. Its main aim is to liberate mankind from traditional bondages of social and economic exploitation and discrimination. It postulates a social order which can guarantee freedom, mobility and equal rights to all section of society.

Social justice is a specific habit of justice that is 'social' in two senses:

- The skills it requires are those of inspiring, working with, and organizing others to accomplish together a work of justice. These are the elementary skills of civil society, through which free citizens exercise self-government by doing for themselves what needs to be done.
- It aims at the good of the society and not as the good of one agent only.

Here Tocqueville rightly says: 'the principle of association is the first law of democracy, and then social justice is the first virtue off democracy, for it is the habit of putting the principle of association into daily practice'.

In brief, justice in broader sense includes: principle of equality; principle of utility; principle of compensatory justice; justice as fairness; social justice.

Ambedkar on Hindu Social Order and Social Justice

- 'Freedom of mind is the real freedom. A person whose mind is not free though he may not be in chains, is a slave, not a free man. One whose mind is not free, though he may not be in prison, is a prisoner and not a free man. One whose mind is not free though alive, is no better than dead. Freedom of mind is the proof of one's existence'.
- 'His social philosophy may be said to be enshrined in three words: liberty, equality and fraternity'.
- 'Democracy is not merely a form of government. It is primarily a mode of associated living, of conjoint communicated experience. It is essentially an attitude of respect and reverence towards our fellow men'.
- 'Caste cannot be abolished by intercaste dinners or stray instances of intercaste marriages. Caste is a state of mind. It is a disease of mind. The teachings of the Hindu religion are the root cause of this disease. We practice casteism and we observe untouchability because we are enjoined to so by the Hindu religion. My religious conversion is not inspired by any material motive. This is hardly anything I cannot achieve even while remaining an Untouchable. There is no other feeling than that of a spiritual feeling underlying my religious

conversion. Hinduism does not appeal to my conscience. My self-respect cannot assimilate Hinduism'.

Locating Ambedkar's vision of social justice one finds that he pleaded for 'just society' and 'casteless society' having the element of liberty, equality and fraternity. His attitude towards justice was humanistic as well as nationalistic. The basic premise of social justice thus remains to be the emancipation of the underprivileged, exploited and oppressed section of the society and a guarantee for their freedom and mobility.

One centrally pervading theme of the writings of Dr B.R. Ambedkar was the attainment of 'social justice' and the establishment of a 'just society'. He not only provided a ruthless criticism of the existing social order but also came up with an alternative vision and alternative model of social order based on justice, liberty, equality, fraternity and annihilation of caste. Ambedkar was convinced that for ensuring social justice, it was essential to demolish chaurnavarna system.

He was the architect of the present reservation policy, and can be considered a pioneer who introduced the concept of a reservation policy at the all India level in early 1930. In fact, the articulation and systematic framing of various types of remedies against discrimination, including reservation/affirmative action policies for discriminated groups, internationally emerged only during the 1950s and 1960s, and Ambedkar developed a framework for such policies and got them implemented as early as 1930s (Poona Pact). He, thus, could be considered a pioneer of inclusive policies in the world.

For Ambedkar, understanding the nature of the institution of caste and untouchability were essential for recognizing the consequences for the excluded groups. He believed, in its classical form, the caste system involved in itself social, economic, cultural and political frameworks of governance of Hindu society. The caste system also draws justification from some elements of Hindu religious philosophy. It is not so much the existence of classes or segmentation, rather the idea of isolation and exclusiveness, which is inimical to a free social order.

Isolation and exclusion of Untouchables is a unique feature of the Hindu social order. Denial of equal access to education is another core feature of the caste system. In Ambedkar's view, the concept of formal education in the Hindu social order was quiet narrow. Formal education was confined to the study of the *Vedas*.

To put it in brief, Ambedkar's interpretation of the Hindu social order as a system of governance in general, and a system of productive organization and distribution in particular is based on three inter-related elements. These included fixed rights, unequal and hierarchical division of social and economic rights across castes, and provision of strong instruments of social and economic ostracization to sustain the rigid system with a philosophical justification in Hindu religion. To him, the religious intervention in social and economic sphere, however, was not positive in nature such that it promoted or facilitated social and economic justice. Unfortunately, Hindu social philosophy as a form of social governance of human society, far from promoting just order, promoted the opposite.

Ambedkar's Efforts Towards Social Inclusion and Justice

- It was in 1919 that Ambedkar for the first time submitted a statement to the Southborough Committee, including demands of the Untouchables in the political sphere in the legislative Council.
- In 1928, he submitted a memorandum to the Simon Commission to safeguard the interest of Depressed Classes. Later, appearing at the Round Table Conference in 1930–32, he once again demanded social and political safeguards to protect the interests of excluded groups.
- Ambedkar presented a memorandum on the safeguards of SCs to the Constituent Assembly on behalf of the All India Scheduled Castes Federation in 1946. It meant for the protection of common citizenry, and attempted to establish social democracy and state socialism.
- During a debate on the report of the commissioner for SCs/ST 1953, Ambedkar commented comprehensively on the functioning of the safeguards for these sections in the Republican India. He maintained that as the government has not taken land into its own hands and created land proprietors. Hence, it could not take away land and distribute equally among the masses. Therefore, the only way out was to amend the Constitution and put the cultivation of wasteland within the purview of the central government so that it was utilized for the benefit of the landless.

Various interventions by Ambedkar during 1919–54 capture his understanding about the problem of deprived castes. He reiterated his position that the problems of Untouchables are rooted in the historical denial of basic human rights. So the remedies against discrimination were placed within the framework of citizenship rights. He addressed the problems of 'structural inequalities' and suggested following policies for social inclusion and justice:

- Claim for equal rights: Ambedkar demanded political representation; however, he started with a claim for equal rights to the Untouchables that he called 'citizenship rights'.
- Measures for equal opportunity and participation.
- Policies for empowerment to compensate for historical inclusion and denial of equal rights like to resources, education and employment.

Jammu and Kashmir State and Scheduled Castes[1]: Present Endeavour

The J&K state has seen more radical social reform[2] than in many other states in the country. Even it has been referred by the various economic surveys that J&K represents lower poverty index. To quote few are, data of India Economy Growth 1995, which reflects that poverty is most prevalent in the states of Orissa, Bihar, Uttar Pradesh, and Madhya Pradesh, and least prevalent in Haryana, Punjab, Himachal Pradesh, and Jammu and Kashmir. Achin Chakraborty's (2001) work 'The Concept and Measurement of Group Inequality' attempts to measure the disparity among the three groups – the Scheduled Tribes, the Scheduled Castes, and others – in terms of the incidence of poverty. The extent of poverty in a group has been loosely measured here, as the percentage of people belonging to the group whose monthly per capita consumption expenditure (MPCE) does not exceed ₹ 190. The choice of ₹ 190 may be justified by the fact that it is the 30th percentile of the all India rural MPCE distribution. As per 5th quinquennial survey of 17 major states in consumption expenditure (NSS 50th Round, 1993–94) conducted by the National Sample Survey Organization (NSSO) and reported in NSSO (1997) the degree of association between poverty and social groups and the other between poverty and occupational groups reveal an important fact about the nature of association in the Indian context. The degree of association between poverty and occupational groups is definitely stronger than the other kind of association in all the states except Jammu and Kashmir. Although in J&K only 7 per cent population are below MPCE less than ₹ 190 but only 6.2 per cent of SC are below MPCE. This makes J&K stand second in all over ranking after Punjab but first with regards to Scheduled Caste's MPCE (with Punjab as second, having 7.9% MPCE). It is also further stated that the difference between the two varies across the states. The degree of association between poverty and social group identity is relatively weak in Kerala, West Bengal and Assam and Tamil Nadu comes next. The association is high in Orissa, Haryana, Madhya Pradesh and Rajasthan. The relative disadvantage that the two groups – SC and ST – experience vis-à-vis others again varies quite a bit across the states. Even within a state, the difference between SC and ST can be large. For example, whereas in Uttar Pradesh and Karnataka the Scheduled Tribe populations are much less disadvantaged compared to the Scheduled Castes, in Jammu and Kashmir (40.3% Scheduled Tribe below MPCE below ₹ 190) and Orissa a reverse scenario is apparent. Currently, the *India Social Development Report* (2006: 221) reflects that J&K's ranking on six component indices (demography, healthcare, basic amenities, education, unemployment and poverty, social deprivation), 1991 for rural and urban areas is fourth and third respectively (first being Kerala).

Keeping in view the overall developmental prospect, it is an apparent impression that the SCs[3] of J&K are well off than many other Indian states. Considering the prospective scheduled castes population of the state, the troublesome issue to be debated is the contemplation of Scheduled Castes as an active player (Dalits) vis-à-vis development process in the state. A hypothetical response to the partial lack of emergence of prominent 'Dalit' assertion among the SCs of the state may be attributed to significant role played by external agencies, especially the past liberal policies by the rulers or even radical state interventions meant for upliftment of scheduled castes of the state. Further, the historical situation as well as the geo-strategic position of the state too has diluted the sharp caste contradiction in the state. Keeping in mind these hypothetical situations, it becomes important to investigate and analyse the objective reality of the Scheduled Castes in the state. It further seeks to analyse the implications of the state intervention on the SC population. Nonetheless, the role of democratic politics[4] can't be underestimated in shaping and organizing the Scheduled Caste population in this state, like the other states of India.

In other words, the present attempt is to describe the status of rural SC population and their own endeavours to challenge the humiliation, if any. Drawing upon historical and empirical evidences from J&K state, the work depicts the process of change and challenges for social mobility among SCs in the Jammu division[5] of the state.

Prevailing *Varna* Composition in Jammu and Kashmir

Commenting on the socio-economic system of Jammu, the Census Commissioner of J&K in his report on the 1911 census has remarked: 'The caste system in its true sense exist only in the '*Duggar Illaqa*'. Here the influence of Brahmanism has always been the strongest and there the complete hierarchy of castes and sub-caste is met with its perfection (Gupta and Prabhakar, 1988).

All the *Varna* of the ancient period were found, in this region:

> *Sudra:* It consisted of 'serving castes' having access to higher castes. It includes various caste like Lohar, Tarkhans, Kumhar, Nai, Jhewars and others. They have been characterized as Weak and under Privilege Category by the State government.
>
> *Harijans*[6]: They are the depressed castes people and termed as '*harijans*' by the high caste Hindus. Prominent among them were *Megh, Doom, Chamar, Chura, Wattal, Ratal, Saryara, Jolaha, Koli, Barwal, Basith, Mussali, Halalkhor, Dhuyar, Gardi and Munchi*. During the first quarter of the 20th century, all such people came to be known as '*Harijans*'.

Characteristics, occupation and population of few prominent '*Harijan*' communities in Jammu region were as follows:

(i) *Megh:* They constituted the largest segment of the 'Harijan' community. The position of '*Megh*' in the social hierarchy of Harijans was somewhat like that of the Brahmins among the high castes. They acted as the priest of *Harijans* and considered themselves distinctly superior to other Harijans. Their main occupation was agriculture and weaving (Singh and Balouria, 1929).

(ii) *Chamars/Ramdasis*: They were leather workers usually called *mochis* in the plains of Jammu region. There were two categories of *chamars* – one that skinned the dead animals, tanned the hides and ate carrion, while the others were shoemakers. The second were superior in status than the first.

(iii) *Others:* Other prominent groups in Jammu region were *Dooms/Mahashas* (who were scavengers, basket makers and musicians) and *Barwalas*.

According to Soodan (1997) the numerical strength of the depressed classes, treated as Untouchable, was recorded by the census report of 1931 as 1,70,928 person, i.e. 23.31 per cent of the entire Hindu population of the state, while in 1941, their total population in Jammu province was 1,13,422. The *Barwals* were most numerous in the Jammu and were found in Jammu province only; the *Basiths* predominated in Reasi and Mirpur districts, the *Chamar* mainly in Jammu district, the *Chura* in Poonch Jagir, the *Dhiyar* caste in all districts of Jammu province, the *Jolahas* in Reasi district only, the *Ratals* in Udhampur and Reasi and *Wattals* in Srinagar district of Kashmir.

S.D.S. Charak's work viz. *History and Culture of Himalayan States*, Vol. VIII, have explained the relatively heavy concentration of depressed classes in Jammu region. To him, it may be attributed to the fact that here they could easily get land from Rajput and other high castes as tenants, and they could earn their earnings by labour and other traditional occupations. Earlier, they were not allowed for social intercourse. However, they were granted access to temples, other public places and admissions to government schools only in 1931–32 AD.

Trends Leading to Changes Among the Scheduled Castes of 'Durgra Desha'

It is an established fact that historical background must have had its impact in the shaping of socio-cultural aspect of present society. The socio-religious reforms, economic gains, role of the rulers and state and other dominant agent has resulted into the flexibility in the caste system and thus upliftment of scheduled caste population in the state (Saxena, 2007; 2009) are as follows:

Socio-Religious Reform Movement and the Scheduled Castes

The social reform in J&K has a long history. According to S.C. Sharma (1985), the proximity of Jammu to Punjab helped the spread of Arya Samaj movement in this state and a branch of the Arya Samaj was established at Jammu in 1891. In Jammu province it had branches at Mirpur, Kotli, Bhember, Rajouri, Nowshera, Reasi, Rramban, Bhaderwah and Kishtwar.

Mainly a branch of the Arya Pratinidhi Sabha known as the 'Shuddhi Sabha' carried out the proselytization programme of the Arya Samaj. Being in constant touch with the centre of the Arya Samaj, the 'Samajist' of the Jammu and R.S. Pura tehsil did commendable work as far as proselytisation among the depressed classes was concerned. Consequently, the number of Arya Samajis in the state rose to 93,944. In 1931, out of these, 93,374 were in Jammu province (Census of India, 1931: 290–91). Here the movement had taken a deep root particularly in Jammu and Kathua district because of the fact that these areas were situated near the Punjab border and people inhabiting these areas were highly influenced with the activities at main centre of Sialkot. Moreover, these two districts were permeated by a good number of depressed class like Megh, Dooms, Chamar and Bashiths, who easily accepted the Shuddhi movement to cut the shackles of untouchability. The credit for such proselytisation work in the district of Kathua goes to Rambhaj Dutt of Gurdaspur. He arranged a big Shuddhi Yajna at Kathua where thousands of Harijans were given the sacred thread. This raised the strength of the Arya Samaj in the district from 7,930 to 16,271 at end of 1931 (Census of India, 1931: 296). In continuation with the mission, the Samaj spread education among the depressed class. It started primary schools, *pathshalas*, for depressed classes at Rehari Mohalla, R.S. Pura in Jammu district and Garh Andral and Kal Kur in Kathua district. The role played by various 'Singh Sabhas' and newspapers like *The Ranbir* is also significant. However, it may be mentioned that the period between 1921–30 has witnessed a fierce crusade against the institution of caste. The movement against caste gained further momentum in 1931, when the *Jat-Pat-Todak Mandal* (organization to break caste) has been founded at Lahore and Punjab, which extended its activities to Jammu region. The most striking feature of the whole cause of social regeneration was the awakening on the part of depressed caste, which started organizing themselves with a view to demanding their due share in all lifestyles. In 1932, they submitted representation to Maharaja Hari Singh requesting for removing social evils. The first major steps that Hari Singh took in 1931 was throwing open all public educational institutions, temples and wells into public services (Census of India, 1931, 319). He also ordered that the proclamation be published in the Gazette Extraordinary of the government, which later amended, that any kind of obstruction to the use of public tanks, wells and so on by Harijans be taken as a penal and cognizable offence. In 1928, a provision was made for the grant of ₹ 4,000 in the form of scholarship for depressed class; unfortunately, three-two 'Harijan' students were there in the Prince of Wales College of Jammu during 1936–37 and 1938–39 respectively. Even the seats were reserved for their representation in local bodies and state legislature called 'Praja Sabha'. Later his wife Maharani Tara Devi (1910–67) too emphasized that all the temples be opened to Harijans. Thus, untouchability was abolished in the state long before Mahatama Gandhi took up the same.

Contextually, spread of sufism too emerged, not only as moral force but also as a comprehensive socio-religious force. Sufism reached the state of J&K almost simultaneously with the foundation of Muslim rule in 1320 A.D. and also after it had entered the last phase of its history. Existence of various important shrines in J&K such as *Hazratbal, Charar-e-Shrief, Panch Pir, Rishi*, etc. prompted the belief of both Hindus and Muslims on their teaching of brotherhood and amity. Under such circumstances, orthodox Hinduism too became flexible. It may be inferred that inter-religious tolerance might have led to decline of intra-religious and intra-caste rigidity in the state.

Land Reforms and the Scheduled Castes

As far as the agrarian social structure of Jammu and Kashmir and its changing land relations are concerned, land reform in J&K is considered a success story. Its implementation can be divided into two phases – reform introduced between late 1940s and early 1950s (Khatama *chakdari* in Samvat, 2007) and the reform introduced in 1970s (Zariah *Islahat* introduced in 1971 and implemented in 1973). Later, Agrarian Reforms Act 1976 (Amendment) was promulgated and it was based on the recommendations of the various commissions (Wazir Commission, 1953, Land Commission, 1963, Gajandragadkar Commission, 1967). The underlying fact was – the actual cultivators on the lands of high castes were prominently scheduled castes so they were hopeful of getting benefits owing to land reforms in rural areas. According to the estimates of the J&K Land Commission (1968), there were 9,19,212 'owners' holding 24,70,960 acres of land in the state in 1949–50. The number of owners in 1962 was 11,53,328 holding 22,95,610 acres of land. Thus, the number of owners increased by 25.47 per cent and area held decreased by 7.09 per cent in 1962 over 1949–50 (Bhatt, 1993).

According to the oral history extracted from the field, before independence, cultivatable land was mainly owned by Rajput zamindars and the Mahajans acted as owner cultivators. The SCs and OBCs acted as tenants (*mazhara*) and practised sharecropping (*galla batai* practiced by 80% of SC tenant). They had to give half of the produce to the owner but after tenancy reform they had to pay one-fourth of the produce. Moreover, earlier they were 'tenants at will' and were at the mercy of the landlord, but after Tenancy Act 1980 they are categorized as 'Protected Tenant' (*Mazhara Mafoos*).

Role of Social Organizations

Historically, many organizations, like Mahatama Phule's 'Satyashadok Samaj', M.K. Gandhi's 'Harijan Sevak Sangh', Ambedkar's Scheduled Caste Federation, Mahrshee Shinde's Depressed Class Mission, played an important role to change orthodox Indian social structure. Similarly, in Jammu province by the beginning of 20th century, important social, religious and regional groups had begun forming their own organizations and their efforts did have some influence in reforming the lives of the people. As quoted in Kanchan Sharma's (1995: 54–58) work, the prominent organizations directly or indirectly working for the welfare of Harijans were:

- The Dogra Sadar Sabha (1904).
- All J&K Harijan Mandal (1920).
- Harijan Mandal (1951).
- Depressed Class League (1962).
- Scheduled Caste Employees Federation (1972).
- Dalit Sudhar Federation (1979).
- Backward and Minority Community Employees Federation (1979).
- Emerging New Organizations: J&K Batwal Council; Scheduled Caste Welfare Association; J&K Dalit Sena; All India J&K Ravi Das Sabha; J&K Mahasha Sabha; Guru Ravi Das Sabha, Udhampur; Bhartiya Dalit Sahitya Academy, Roopnagar; Peoples Republican Party of India.

Governmental Efforts in Enhancing the Status of Scheduled Castes

In exercise of the proviso, conferred by clause (i) of Article 341 of the Constitution of India, the President, after consultation with Sadar I – Riyasat of J&K, is pleased to make order, namely – 'The Constitution of J&K Scheduled Caste Order, 1956'. This includes, *Barwala, Basith, Chamar, Batwal, Chura, Dhyar, Doom/Mahasha, Garddi, Jolaha, Megh/Kabirpanthi, Ratal, Saryara, Watal* as Scheduled Castes with condition that no person who profess a religion different from the Hindu or Sikh religion shall be deemed to be a member of the Scheduled Caste.

Efforts through Social Welfare Department

Initially, this department carved out of the erstwhile 'State Dehat Sudhar' Department in 1960 with a limited purpose for the welfare of SCs and OBCs. The department has since expanded extensively all over the state, taking care of various welfare programmes. The department launched schemes in two phases: I from 1960–75 and the II from 1975–96. Several schemes launched in the first phase include, grant of pre-matric scholarships to the students belonging to SCs and OBCs. It included free books and uniform for these students from first to third class. The department also provided legal aid under the scheme 'financial assistance' to SC families, facing litigation for eviction from land holdings, untouchability and other atrocities. The unemployed youth of SC/OBC category were also trained in different trades like, carpentry, leatherwork, craft making, etc. The department in the areas thickly inhabited by SC communities established social welfare centres. In the second phase, the scholarship rate was raised, post-matric scholarship were sanctioned in 1978 for pursuing their studies from higher secondary to post-graduation level. The J&K SC/ST/OBC Development Corporation came into being in 1986 for the socio-economic upliftment of weaker sections (Information Department, J&K Government, 1998).

According to Gajendragadhkar Commission of inquiry report, 1968 and Social Welfare Department, J&K, 2006: The status of recruitment of Scheduled Castes in the state from 1961–65, it is observed that the first intake in gazetted posts was observed in 1965. In gazetted post we find an increase from 0.4 per cent in 1967 (Gajendragadhkar Commission of Inquiry Report, 1968) to 6.25 per cent in 2002. This signifies trend of occupational mobility among Scheduled Castes (Table 1).

Table 1

Overall Socio-Economic Profile of Scheduled Castes in Jammu and Kashmir

Parameters	*1961*	*1971*	*1981*	*2001*
Population# (%)	7.98	8.26	8.31	7.59
Sex ratio (per 1000 males)	—	—	—	910
Literacy* (%)	4.72	11.97	49.2	59.0+
School going children in age group 5–14 years (%)	—	—	—	69.8
Work participation rate**	T: 41.06 M: 56.32 F: 23.90			36.7 (All India 40.4) M: 50.3 (A.I. 50.7) F: 21.7 (A.I. 29.4)
Category of workers***	Cultivators: 23.0 Agr. Labourers: 2.0 HHI workers: 1.0 Other workers 6.0			Cultivators: 49.7 Agr. Labourers: 8.7 HHI workers: 1.7 Other workers 39.8
Ownership of agricultural land****				Percentage of landless: 0.5 per cent Percentage of land upto 0.4 hectare: 70.8 per cent
Rural Poverty Ratio*****				7.1
Net change in disparity ratio (1983–2000)##				All India: 0.95 J&K: 2.02

#Out of 13 SCs, Megh is the most populous caste having a population of 300,980, constituting 39.1 per cent of the total SC population. They are followed by Chamar with 187,277 population (24.3%) and Doom having a number of 159,908 (20.8 per cent).

*Level of Education: Literate without education (3.0%); below Primary (21.8%); Primary (29.0%); Middle (27.7%); Intermediate (16.3); Technical (0.1%); Graduate and above (2.0%). Further, among all SC's Chamars have shown the highest literacy rate (65.5%) highest proportion of matriculates, followed by Megh. Dooms have registered the lowest percentage of matriculates preceded by Batwal.

** Among the major SCs, Megh have registered higher overall (37.2%) as well as female WPR (23.5%) than those of all SCs at the state level.

*** Almost half of total SC workers are engaged in cultivation[7] and this percentage is more than twice that of the national average (20%) in respect of all SCs. 'Other Workers' also have a significant share of 39.8 per cent showing higher proportion than that of the country (30.5%). 'Agricultural labourers' constitute 8.7 per cent which is significantly lower if compared with the national average (45.6%). At the individual caste level, Megh and Chamar have maximum proportion of 'cultivators' whereas Batwal and Doom have the highest percentage of 'Other Workers' in their total working population.

**** It has lowest landless rural household percentage at all India level during 1999–2002 (Source: Department of Statistics, NSSO, GOI, October 2002). Even cultivated land upto 0.4 hectare is second highest in India, after Himachal Pradesh (Rural Labour Enquiry, 1999–2000, MoL).

***** Lowest rural poverty ratio at All India level (NSS 55th Round, July 1999 – June 2000).

Second highest after Punjab having 2.24 (Thorat and Senapati. 2006. 'Reservation Policy in India', Working Paper Series, Vol. I, No. 2, IIDS).

+ This figure is higher than the national average of 54.7 per cent in respect of all SCs.

@ Hinduism is the predominant religion of the Scheduled Castes (98.7%) of Jammu and Kashmir. The SCs professing Sikhism are 1.3 per cent (10,159). Buddhist SCs are 194 only.

Contemporary Affirmative Actions by SCs of Jammu Region

The Scheduled Castes of Jammu region have contemporarily shown their assertion for Dalithood on the following grounds:

(i) *Religious congregations and procession:* The Scheduled Castes of Jammu region come together for the celebration of birth anniversaries and 'shoba yatras' of great persons of their community. Celebration of anniversaries or '*prakash divas*' of the personalities like Ambedkar, Ravi Dass, Kabir, Nabha Das and others are significant because this collectivity and its demonstration is in public sphere, i.e. the main city area and they are allowed now without any obstacles and also sometimes with the support of few political leaders.

(ii) *Reservation issues:* Recently, various Scheduled Caste organizations have come together to represent their protest against reservation policies framed by the government. State regulation order (SRO) – 294 passed by the government is one such issue. The concerned SRO has become the bone of contention owing to the due reservation and also to exclude the state formed reserved areas out of the purview of the reservation policies. There demand is to increase reservation seats from 8 per cent to 9 per cent and to enhance overall reservations in the state from 43 per cent to 50 per cent as practiced in other states of the country. For raising theses demands even they are trying to develop alliances with ST and OBC organizations for showing more strength and, thus, putting effective pressure on the existing government. This dimension not only leads to horizontal mobilization of the SCs but also their vertical linkage with the other downtrodden or marginalized categories of the society.

(iii) *Inter-district recruitment bill:* Passing of amended inter-district recruitment bill (The J&K Civil Services Decentralization and Recruitment Bill, 2009) by the state government, for thinking about institutional representation and recruitment as part of a radical democratic politics for the underprivileged, in light of recent reconsideration of pluralism and recent concerns about the J&K state as an institutional site for such politics. Evaluating the bills against Ambedkar vision on minority representation, he rightly said that equal treatment of all the minorities in the matter of representation is only a part of the problem of the representation of minorities.

My final words of advice to you are educate, agitate and organize; have faith in yourself. With justice on our side, I do not see how we can loose our battle. The battle to me is a matter of joy. The battle is in the fullest sense spiritual. There is nothing material or social in it. For ours is a battle not for wealth or for power. It is battle for freedom. It is the battle of reclamation of human personality.

Conclusion

It is observed that the changing position of Scheduled Castes in Jammu region has been because of multiple factors. Prominent among them are the land reform measures in 1950s and 1970s, the Arya Samaj movement from 1891 onward, activities of the voluntary organizations, governmental efforts through Dalit ameliorative policies and reservations. Combinations of all these factors have resulted in a pattern of the assertion of Dalit identity to minimal extent. Lower castes, permeated by the values of individual rights and dignity, find themselves in a flux. In the process of modernization, they are constantly adding new layers of complexities to Indian identity. Presently, each Scheduled Caste out of the 13 listed SCs in the state tries to distinguish themselves (in terms of superiority) from one another, as evident through the formation of multiple SC organizations in the state. This practice is more visible among the numerically and economically well-off SCs namely Megh, Mahasha and Chamar, which are not contributing towards construction of a larger Dalit identity in Jammu region. The lack of horizontal mobilization among SCs in Jammu region thus impedes the quest for concrete Dalit mobilization and their macro-identity construction in J&K state. Unfortunately, the so-called SCs of J&K are more or less satisfied with their identity from above and have failed to mobilize their identity from below.

Notes

1. According to 2001 census, the Scheduled Castes are mainly concentrated in the Jammu region and their population in the state is 770,155 which form 7.6 per cent of the total population of the state. At district level, Megh, Chamar and Batwal are primarily concentrated in Jammu district whereas Dooms have the highest proportion of the total SC population in Kathua district.
2. It can be judged through the implementation of democratic decentralization in 1935 by Raja Hari Singh and later the historical document called 'The *Naya* Kashmir', which became the inspiring source of National Conference policies and programmes. The implementation of Land Reforms (1948–1953) and later Agrarian Reforms of 1970s are such radical attempt in this direction.
3. Maharaja Hari Singh granted SCs access to temples and other public places and admissions in government schools in 1931–32. This removal of legal restrictions on the Harijans' entry in public places was probably the first in princely states of India. The grant of this right without any strong struggle of the Harijans or absence of any public reaction against this grant by the upper castes shows the non-rigidity of untouchability and discrimination against the Harijans in this state. The removal of restrictions by the Maharaja resulted in gradual end of denial and discrimination and improvement of their social situation.
4. Regarding the influence of political parties on the Scheduled Castes in the state, one finds that the National Conference (prominent regional party since independence) had a bigger say for the under-privileged. Unfortunately, BSP could not impress upon the underprivileged of the state, may be because of its late emergence in the state. The data on general election to the J&K Assembly election-2002 depicts BSP contest for 33 seats, out of which it could get only one seat.
5. Jammu Division, having 17.3 per cent of SCs population, as compared to the Kashmir Division having negligible SC population of 0.059 per cent (J&K State Census, 2001). In Jammu Division, Scheduled Castes population is mainly concentrated in the following districts, namely – Jammu, Udhampur and Kathua district. Further, at district level, Megh, Chamar and Batwal are primarily concentrated in Jammu district. Dooms have the highest proportion of the total SC population in Kathua district.
6. In Jammu and Kashmir, the depressed classes constituted nearly one-fourth of Hindu population of Jammu province, but stood at the base of the Hindu social hierarchy. The members of the depressed classes were put into the category of caste Hindus but latter humiliated and maltreated former in

almost all fields. High caste Hindus avoided contact with the Harijans and the touch of the Harijan obliged them to purify themselves with the bath (*Census of India, 1961*). They were, in fact, debarred from free social intercourse. So much so, they had no access to temples and public places, like wells and tanks. The condition of this section of society was indeed pitiable. (*Census of India, 1931*). Having been denied the basic rights, the depressed classes were forced to lead a precarious life in isolated localities. However, they were granted access to temples and other public places and admission to government schools only in 1931–32 AD (*Fortnightly Reports*, September, 1930).

7. Verifying that land reform initiatives worked in favour of SCs of the state.

References

Bhatt, M.S., 'Land Distribution in Rural J&K: An Inter-Temporal Analysis', in B.K. Sinha and Pushpendra (eds.) *Land Reform in India: An Unfinished Agenda*, vol. 5, New Delhi: Sage Publication, 1993, pp. 139–69.

Chakraborty, A., 'The Concept and Measurement of Group Inequality', Working Paper, Thiruvananthupuram: Centre for Development Studies, 2001.

Charak, S.D.S., *History and Culture of Himalayan States*, vol. VIII, Delhi: Light and Life Publisher, 1979, p. 13.

Gupta, N.S. and N.C. Prabhakar, *Socio-Economic Development of J&K*, Jammu: JayKay Book House, 1988.

India: Social Development Report, 2006, Council for Social Development.

Miller, David, *Social Justice*, London: OUP, 1976.

Rawls, John, *A Theory of Justice*, Cambridge,Mass.:Belknap Press of Harvard University, 1971.

Saxena, A., *Shifting Manifestations: Scheduled Castes in Jammu and Kashmir*, Jammu: Saksham Books International, 2009.

Sharma, K., *Socio-Political Aspiration of J&K People*, Jammu: Akshay Publisher, 1995.

Sharma, S.C., 'Socio-Religious Activities of the Arya Samaj in J&K State', *MD University Research Journal*, Vol-3 (2), October, 1985.

Singh, T.K. and Balouria, *Tarikh-i-Rajgan Jammu-Wa-Kashmir*, Lahore: Prakash Steam Press, 1929, p. 32.

Soodan, S.S., *Jammu under the Reign of Maharaja Hari Singh*, Jammu: Vinod Publication, 1997, p. 47.

Tilly, Frank, *History of Philosophy*, New Delhi: SBW Publication, 2000.

Wakhlu, S., *The Rich Heritage of J&K: Studies in Art, Architecture, History and Culture of the Region*, Delhi: Gyan Publishing House, 1998.

15

Social Justice in Economic Perspective

Displacement of People by Land Acquisition for Industrialization in India

Bhaskar Majumdar

We accept industrialization as an inescapable route through which mankind has to traverse for development. Even if the route is not singular, the fact remains that for decolonized countries of post-Second World War period it is the route shown by the industrial revolution in Britain. We also accept that this route inflicts injustice on people who get delinked from the means of production by being displaced from the assets like land. Any social action has unequal consequences, sometimes measured by social costs and benefits. The observed consequences put forward the question of justice – social and economic. We acknowledge that through industrialization the workers get united as a working class to come out from their earlier local economy based inertia and start realizing 'their own strength, with perseverance at work and with a spirit of enterprise' leading to an 'enduring improvement in their social position' (Plum, 1977: 68). In the economic history of India, modern industry was supposed to wipe out the hereditary divisions of labour based on the Indian castes and hence remove the 'decisive impediments to Indian progress and Indian power'. Industrialization is seen as not only inescapable but also a step forward in breaking the 'self-sufficient inertia of the villages' (Marx, 2006).

In a national economy, land shows its ultimate limitations by being perfectly inelastic unless a new territory is annexed by the state. Thus, the controllers of means of production gradually move away from dependence on land and move towards techniques of production that are land-saving and capital-cum-labour using. This shows a shift from agriculture to industry that carries with it not only relocation of capital but also labour. Industrialization shows the possibility of relocation of workers from rural (agricultural) to urban (industrial) sector. In Russia, planned industrialization after the 1917 Revolution led to millions of peasants being removed forcibly from land and shunted into urban industries, mining, hydroelectric projects, thousands of collective farms (kolkhozy), and state farms (sovkhozy) (Magill, 1997: 723–724). In UK around 1600 AD, 2.76 per cent of the total land was enclosed and 50,000 persons out of a total population of around 4 million were forcefully evicted. In China since the 1950s around 10 million people have been displaced due to hydraulic and hydroelectric projects alone (Sarkar, 2007: 1,436).

The paper addresses the question of social justice focusing on displacement of people following acquisition of land by the state for industrialization. The rest of the paper is structured as follows.

In Section I, the paper talks about late industrialization and delayed acquisition of agricultural land for industrialization in India. Section II presents the scenario on land acquisition and the living conditions of the land-dependent working population in India. In Section III, the paper presents land acquisition in praxis and displacement of people in India. Section IV talks about the new law on land acquisition in India in the context of state-led social justice. Finally, Section V discusses social justice in economic perspective.

Late Industrialization and Delayed Acquisition of Agricultural Land for Industrialization in India

In India, while the absolute number of population working on land increased, the percentage of population remained more or less unchanged during the post-Independence 60 years. Its agriculture is characterized by a monotonically declining land-man ratio, low labour productivity and declining share of agriculture in national income over time. This gets reflected in low purchasing power of the people dependent on agriculture. While accepting the need for protection of cultivable land as the major base for food security of one-sixth of world population settled in India, the question remains why as high as 70 per cent of India's population remained a benchmark for the last 60 years for agriculture to absorb.

Development became production-centred by transformation of natural resources. At the early stage of human civilization, nature did not show inadequacy but provided enough resources to satisfy the basic needs of life. Later, unequal physical power, desire for more private appropriation in the collective consumption basket and hence acquiring increasing control over nature led to discontinuation of collection as the dominant mode of fulfilling needs. Forest-based living opened the scope for cultivation of crops reversing the man-nature control mechanism. The forest mode of living did not resist the emerging agriculture mode of living, in spite of the fact that in the process, increasing area of the forests had to be cleaned by cutting of trees. Cultivation gave scope for processing of raw materials leading to the setting up of industries. Gradually, agriculture and industry became the two pillars of the economy. Since the scope for agriculture is limited by the size of land and its uses by type and frequency, the question arose about setting up of industries by location and time. As opposed to limited flexibility in locating agricultural practices, industrial set-up has higher flexibility by its location and change. Generally the factors for setting up of industries relate to the availability of raw materials, market size-cum-access, transport and communication, and availability of electricity and other physical infrastructure, own industry concentration or cluster of firms for externality advantages and inter-industry linkages (Bandyopadhyay, 2007: 4). Annihilation of agricultural land and agriculturists' displacement are natural corollaries.

Late industrializing countries like India face several economic problems due to the falling carrying capacity of land. The initial condition in India in 1951 showed a size of population more than that of any country in the world, excepting China, in time 60 years ahead. The land-man ratio in India is declining fast because of, apart from the natural increase in population, service sector-led urbanization and conversion of agricultural land for industrial purposes. Agriculture-industry linkages often work in favour of the latter during industrialization which is reflected by declining relative share of agriculture in national income and hence reducing per capita income for people by unchanged percentage of rising population settled in agriculture. People settled in the rural regions have a history of moving out because of various push and pull factors. For example, often the sale of land occurs under distress while deruralization by absence of local wage work drives people out. In a caste-ridden rural society, as in most regions in India, private land is often sold when the owner opts for anonymity-cum-liberty and hence moves to cities. This may seem surprising when he has stake in the land that he owns which makes him better off, relatively to an urban industrial proletariat even if the subsistence farming that he was practicing was technologically inferior to capitalist farming. Oppressive rural social identity for persons aspiring to move up the economic ladder relative to liberating urban economic identity perhaps shows the difference. Extension of urban boundary also often snatches the little land that the income-asset poor had. Apart from the natural shift of agricultural land to non-agricultural purposes, there is the state-sponsored shift empowered by the 1894 Land Acquisition Act formulated and implemented during the British colonial rule. This Act empowers the state government to acquire any land from private hands for public purposes decided implicitly by the state (GOI, The Land Acquisition Act, 1894). Though the 1894 Act was most comprehensive and guiding principle for the periods following, there were some other Regulations and Acts that empowered the British Government in India to acquire land for physical infrastructure and public works. These included Regulation 1, 1824 of Bengal Code and Act XLII of 1850 in British India (Khasnobis, 2009: 63). Development by land acquisition displaces the people at the bottom from the trajectory of development.

Acquisition of agricultural land for industrial purposes in India is not new. Since Independence, the state has been executing development following a top-down approach and setting up large industries and projects like mines, dams, ports, plants and expansion of road and rail network, each of which displaced people. Heavy industrialization was at the core of India's planned development and hence large areas had to be acquired. The state of Orissa used 40,000 hectares of land for industry between 1951 and 1995. The state of West Bengal used two million hectares of land between 1947 and 2000 for industry. The corporate sector has been targeting mining land in Orissa, Jharkhand and Chhattisgarh. Mostly the mineral-rich as well as government land-abundant backward states are being targeted for acquisition of land. Construction of dams to feed drought-prone areas, of which the

Narmada Dam Project is notoriously known for the disputes around the Narmada river that flows into the Arabian sea after passing through the states of MP, Gujarat and Maharashtra, led to displacement of people. The trade off was between the livelihood loss of the displaced on the one hand and the gain for others by irrigation-fed agriculture and supply of drinking water for the dry regions on the other. It is not only acquisition for public sector units, it is also for private players like Reliance, ESSAR, Jaypee for both power generation and mining that inescapably will displace people (Sharma and Singh, 2009: 62, 64–66). Displacement by declaration and payment of money compensation does not make it voluntary.

Land Acquisition and the Living Conditions of the Land-Dependent Working Population in India

Land was never thought to be a factor of production in industry, either because land was abundant in supply relative to what was required or because the required land area was insignificant relative to the available land area of any particular economy. The relatively less area required for setting up of industries was also because of the increasingly processed industrial output that moves far away from dependence on land by area. Land acquisition actually implies acquisition of a physical area that covers cultivable soil area, plus plantations, water bodies, residential buildings, animal sheds and many other assets that 'land by area and volume' carry. These are very significant for the livelihood of the people dependent on land. Land is not only a means of production but is also a base for the land-dependent people to exercise other opportunities like employment, locating animal shed and the like. Land is not only a commodity; it is a base of livelihood in rural India.

Large-scale displacement of settled people occurs when the large-scale industries enter into the land market. This is because these industries like to set up new plants or expand the initially set up plant near the commodity-cum-labour market and choose that location where physical infrastructure is already available. This also ensures cluster benefits by external economies and linkage effects. The proximity to market-cum-physical infrastructure simultaneously means settled population by housing. The injustice does not exhibit itself unless the locally settled people try to resist displacement. Obviously the landless people dependent mainly on Common Property Resources (CPRs) are outside the purview of compensation of any type. Assuring compensation for eviction of people from land is a pledge by the state in a post-feudal stage (Khasnobis, 2009: 52–53). This also establishes land acquisition as a legal process executed by the state through compensation 'voluntarily received' by the evicted. The justice by compensation conceals the injustice of eviction.

The first victims in the forward movement of technology are the people at the bottom of the socio-economic ladder. This is the section that is displaced by execution of any infrastructure development projects which are usually state-sponsored and capital-based. Development first excludes the vulnerable sections from the initial benefits of possessing productive assets like land and subsequently encompasses them in social safety nets. These sections lack the capacity to be a part of the decision-making processes of mega development projects planned by the state for various reasons, including multiple boundaries erected against them by literacy and education, elite language (English by colonial inheritance), caste, community, height-weight-colour of the person, gender, access to institutions, and holding powerful posts by which they are obstructed from entering into the domain of privileges. The additional factors that perpetuate vulnerability of these sections are their ignorance, immobility and living in tradition-custom-belief. As a corollary, these people at the bottom of the power structure fail to calculate the way they should withstand the pressure of change. In the same process often they symbolize anti-change. What they fail to communicate is that the impact of change planned by the state is unequal; it benefits those who are at the doorsteps to welcome change, that is, the already privileged by the power of the purse, education and free walk on the corridors of power; it goes against those who are rooted, tradition-bound, and localized. Injustice by initial exclusion from land and justice by inclusion in safety net go together.

Agriculture involves not only land and domestic animals, but also the plantations, the common grazing land, the common space for the local community, and the known environment. Unlike open agricultural space, often understood as CPR, industrial space is closed. Hence, 'abrupt' acquisition of agricultural land for industrial purposes will definitely cause twin shocks for the displaced people, one by forced exclusion from land and the other by natural exclusion from newly created industrial space.

Land Acquisition in Praxis and Displacement of People in India

The World Commission on Dams (WCD) estimated that between 40 and 80 million people had been displaced worldwide only because of large dams (WCD, 2000). Since Independence around 60 million persons have been victims of forced displacement in India (Fernandes, 2007). Because of the expansion of the core sectors like power, mining, irrigation and other heavy industries, between 30 and 50 million people had been displaced, as estimated by Action Aid. Displacement is seen as the side effect of capitalist development (Chakrabarti and Dhar, 2010: 3). What is seen as side effect may bring about disaster for the displaced.

The nature of displacement may be exogenous due to war, partition, and ethnic conflicts, or due to natural disasters like drought, flood, and earthquake. In India, development projects like dams and canals displaced 70.9 per cent of all the people displaced by state-led development projects up to 1989. For industrial set-up, it was 6.4 per cent. Overall 25.5 per cent of the displaced could be rehabilitated (Table 1).

Table 1

Displacement by Land Acquisition in India, 1947–89

Rank	*No. of Persons Displaced*	*% of Displaced*	*Purpose/Project*
1.	1,10,00,000	25.0	Dams and Canals
2.	17,00,000	26.5	Coal and Other Mines
3.	10,00,000	30.0	Industries
4.	6,00,000	25.0	Sanctuaries and Parks
5.	12,00,000	25.0	Others
	1,55,00,000	25.5	Total

Source: Fernandes and Rao, 1989.

Displacement of population, because of acquisition of land by the state, is directly proportional to the area of land acquired, given the region-specific density of population. The land area required, in turn, is directly proportional to the type of projects undertaken. We cite here two examples of the recent past of land acquisition in UP, one for NTPC representing the public sector and one for Reliance Energy Limited in the private sector, both for generation of electricity.

Example I:
Land Acquisition in Meja, District Allahabad, UP

In the power sector, the NTPC Ltd. and Uttar Pradesh Rajya Vidyut Nigam Ltd. (UPRVUNL) on the 22 November 2007 signed a Memorandum of Understanding (MoU) to set up a thermal power plant of 1,320 MW at Kohrarghat of Meja tehsil in Allahabad District of east UP. The UP government acquired a total land area of 2500 acres for setting up the plant covering seven villages, namely, Kohrar, Bhagdeva, Esauta, Mai Khurd, Salaia Kala, Salaiya Khurd, and Patai Dandi that reportedly affected the livelihood of 469 settled households. The acquired area being mainly stony and rocky, the displacement was minimal though it was to have an adverse impact on community support-cum-social integration. Because of loss of cultivable land, wells, common grazing land, fruit trees and timber trees, this adversely affected agricultural output and food security. Loss of CPR led to loss of fodder, fuel and materials like dry grass used for constructing roofs of rural houses. The worst hit were the landless stone quarry workers belonging to the lowest order of social hierarchy like the *Nishads, Mushahars, Kols, Chamars, Pasis, Dhaikars, Domars, Pals*, and Muslims, who had no entitlement for compensation and who lost their only source of livelihood.

The major reasons reported for pending or delayed payment of compensations were court cases, 'speed money' asked by the Lekhpal, disputes related to canal, outstanding bank loans of the displaced persons, errors in name written on the bank cheque book, objection to the rate of compensation, disputes between Treasury and SLRO, official apathy, family disputes, expiry of date shown on the bank cheque, etc. The loss of Common Property Resources (CPRs) remains unaddressed perhaps because it is owned by no single individual. Most of the displaced households await rehabilitation.

Example II:
Land Acquisition in Dadri, District Ghaziabad, UP

To set up the 3500 MW gas-based power plant with an estimated project cost of ₹ 25,000 cr. in Dadri region in Ghaziabad district, in western UP, the Government of Uttar Pradesh (UP) acquired about 1,011 hectare of land in 2004 in seven villages for Reliance Energy Generation Ltd. (REGL). The villages were Dehra, Jadopur, Bajhera Khurd, Kakrana, and Dhaulana. The other two affected villages, namely, Nandlalpur and Baharmandpur, were found to be un-inhabited. Most of the land acquired was earlier used for agricultural purposes. Pasture or common grazing land was not acquired. The major assets covered in land acquisition were canals, ponds and wells. On 13 July 2007, the Government of India gave environmental clearance to the project.

Land acquisition in Dadri could have displaced over 6,000 families. The rate of compensation was fixed at ₹ 150 per square yard that was more than the maximum market rate prevailing there prior to land acquisition. The market rate immediately after land acquisition was ₹ 300 at the minimum and ₹ 400 at the maximum. The loss to the cultivators for surrendering product value per year was enormous while revenue loss on account of land rent was marginal. Combined together, the loss because of land acquisition for the cultivators and government was significant (Majumdar, 2007).

The farmers alleged that the government did not do justice to the displaced. The unorganized farmers formed an association called Maharana Pratap Sangram Sangharsh Samiti and claimed a compensation of ₹ 500 per sq metre. The farmers staged a demonstration in front of the Collectorate in August 2004. On 3 January 2006, the farmers again expressed their dissent against the rate of compensation. On 30 December, Reliance Energy Ltd. decided to start the construction work by digging the fields of Sripal Singh in Jadopur village. The farmers protested against it. Following the protests by the project affected persons against the announced rate of compensation, and based on the impact of loss of fertile agricultural land, the Allahabad High Court's Division Bench on the 4 December 2009, quashed the urgency powers to acquire land exercised by the then government and cancelled the acquisition of land of 2,500 acres in Dadri. It passed order acting on writ petitions filed by the farmers and the former Prime Minister, late Mr V.P. Singh, claiming that the petitioners were forced to sign on documents and accept the meagre compensation offered by the Collector. The Court said that the farmers had the option to refund the compensation received.

New Law on Land Acquisition in India: State-Led Social Justice

Article 31 Section A of the Constitution of India (Compulsory Acquisition of Property) empowers the State to acquire land based on payment of compensation at a rate which shall not be less than the market value prevailing (The Constitution of India, p. 14). Nearly after a century, the first Land Acquisition Act, 1894 was comprehensively amended in 1984. The Conference of the revenue secretaries of states followed in July 1989 that endorsed the major provisions of the 1984 amendment. The principle that continued to govern land acquisition till then was that compensation alone was 'payable in lieu of deprivation'. The Draft National Policy for Rehabilitation of Persons (1996), displaced as a consequence of acquisition of land, of the Ministry of Rural Development, Government of India (GOI), however, acknowledged that cash compensation was not an acceptable proposition for most of the tribal people. The 1996 Draft observed at the same time that 'majority of our mineral resources, including coal, iron ore, and manganese reserves are located in the remote and backward regions mostly inhabited by tribals' (Report, 1996). The implication is that land acquisition for resources will displace first the tribals. After a decade, the Government of India approved the National Policy on Rehabilitation and Resettlement, 2007, replacing the earlier National Policy on Resettlement and Rehabilitation for Project Affected Families, 2003 (Chakrabarty and Dhar, 2010: 4).

The Government of India introduced The Land Acquisition (Amendment) Bill, 2007 in the Lok Sabha (Lower House of Indian Parliament) on 30 November 2007 duly signed by the Minister of Rural Development, Sri Raghuvansh Prasad Singh, that was a Bill 'further to amend the Land Acquisition Act, 1894' (Lok Sabha, 2007, website). Once passed, it will be called the Land Acquisition (Amendment) Act, 2007. The Bill 2007 acknowledges that 'acquisition of land leads to displacement of people, depriving them of their livelihood and shelter, restricting access to their traditional resource base, and uprooting them from their socio-cultural environment. These have traumatic, psychological and socio-cultural consequences for the affected population, which call for protecting their rights, including those of the weaker sections of society, particularly tribals, and tenants.

Rehabilitation and resettlement of the persons and families affected by involuntary acquisition of private land and immovable property is of paramount importance'. Following the Bill 2007, 'public purpose' restricts 'the scope of land acquisition under the Act to provision of land for strategic purposes vital to the state, and for infrastructure projects where the benefits accrue to the general public ...'. The expression 'person interested' in the principal Act

(1894) is proposed to be expanded in the new Act (2007) 'to include tribals and other traditional forest dwellers, who have lost any traditional rights recognized under the Scheduled Tribes and Other Traditional Forest Dwellers (Recognition of Forest Rights) Act, 2006 ...' and expanded to include 'persons having tenancy rights under the relevant State laws ...'.

Specifically, in Section 3 of the Principal Act (1894) clause (f) is proposed to be substituted for broader expression of 'public purpose' to include:

(i) the provision of land for strategic purposes relating to naval, military and air force works or any other work vital to the State;
(ii) the provision of land for infrastructure projects of the appropriate government, where the benefits accrue to the general public; and
(iii) the provision of land for any other purpose useful to the general public ... As proposed, the expression 'infrastructure project' shall include:
    (i) any project relating to generation, transmission or supply of electricity;
    (ii) construction of roads, highways, bridges, airports, ports, rail systems or mining activities;
    (iii) water supply project, irrigation project, sanitation and sewerage system; or
    (iv) any other public facility as may be notified in this regard by the Central Government in the Official Gazette.

In Section 3 of the Principal Act (1894), after clause (cc), the following clause shall be inserted, namely:

The determination of market value of land being acquired following Bill 2007 is pledged to include 'the market value of the buildings and other immovable property or assets attached to the land or building which are to be acquired', 'the value of trees and plants', 'the value of the standing crops damaged during the process of land acquisition proceedings'.

The 2007 Bill says that 'any person interested who has not accepted the award may, by written application to the Collector, require that the matter be referred by the Collector for the determination of the Court, whether his objection be to the measurement of the land, the amount of the compensation, the persons to whom it is payable, or the apportionment of the compensation among the persons interested'. The guidelines of judgment, as mentioned in the proposed 2007 Act, says that 'in determining the amount of compensation to be awarded for land acquired under this Act, the Court shall take into consideration, in addition to the market-value of the land at the date of the publication of the notification, awarding a sum of thirty per centum on such market-value, keeping in mind the compulsory nature of the acquisition'. The 2007 Bill also guarantees that the amount of compensation awarded by the Court shall not be less than the amount awarded by the Collector.

Following the proposed Act 2007, the State (of India) owns the responsibility of land acquisition for which the catalyst is the district Collector and the Disputes Settlement body is the Court. The role of the judiciary is limited by the guidelines provided by the proposed Act. By regulating market value of land for 'the compulsory nature of the acquisition', by guiding the judiciary in determining compensation, the state aims to 'rule' development with guaranteed social justice.

A Critique on 'Conventional State Justice'

The catalyst in land acquisition is the state in India. The 'person interested' in the context of land acquisition by the state de facto includes all those going to be affected by land acquisition. In particular, the 'person interested' is really the tribals, the original settlers on land who generally do not possess any land records (even many of them being not at all aware of any such needed records), the small and marginal farmers, the tenants and sharecroppers, the agricultural wage-workers (settled in the locality and migrants). These really interested persons generally do not express their interests. While the migrant agricultural workers living on the bottom-most plank by socio-economic measure is disempowered by the new Bill by not being allowed to ask the District Collector for payment of any compensation when his employer's plot of land is lost by acquisition for purposes other than agriculture, the employer by being a small farmer is disempowered by being in the queue to receive compensation, the time distance between acquisition and compensation being 60 days. It is beyond the capacity of tribals and the socio-economically downtrodden section in Indian society, unless politically mobilized, to raise voice for compensation equal to 30 per cent markup of prevailing market rate. The small and marginal farmers may feel shaky to move the Court and remain happy with whatever cash compensation they are offered. Judiciary by its cobweb nature may itself be a trap for them. Fear factor works for the holders of petty property lest it is also lost in the process of bargaining and negotiating with the administrative authority. 'Public purpose' interpreted by the state becomes irrelevant in absence of the participation of the underprivileged public. The trade-off between the interests of the light weight large public and heavyweight few elite gets natural expression in favour of the latter.

People solely dependent on land-based low-yield occupations often feel alienated from the political state. Other than participating in the political process of voting, most of the people at the bottom of the social ladder do not have much idea about what the state stands for. They are not part of the mainstream education system and hence have reasons not to understand the language of the judiciary as embedded in laws and acts that served the British colonial administration in India. Land acquisition by the state from the possession of these people thus becomes fait accompli. The disbelief between the 'village poor labourer' and the 'town rich non-labourer' has sharpened around land acquisition that benefits the latter at the cost of the former. In first appearance the landowner in villages is 'money compensated' by the state, but then he is deprived of future opportunities and uprooted from his culture. For launching projects in cities, the state aims for vertical measures like constructing flyovers for surface transport, tunnels underground for metro rail and tube rail so that buildings and other assets possessed by the urbane civil society, both public and private, are not affected; however, when it comes to the rural areas the same state targets horizontal expansion by acquisition of private and collective cultivable land and hence eviction of vulnerable people. It is arguable that the state followed similar measures for conversion of rural areas into urban areas in India in a time-neutral manner. But time of 21st century by reaction of people and civil society is sharply different from earlier centuries by size and density of population, democracy and voice of people. The question of 'prior informed consent' thus becomes relevant now that might not have been relevant earlier. The state takes pre-emptive measures by 'inclusion' in the safety net of social welfare measures of those against whom the state took initiatives to throw out of the development trajectory. Since high growth is urgent for operationalization of trickle down, the state first evicts people from land by its acquisition, makes them expendable and then catches them in the safety net. The objects caught in the net are never asked if they had the right to self-determination in the development map. The map is drawn and guarded by the state.

It takes more than a generation for people to find out a space to get settled by developing social relations. These inter-generational social relations are destroyed by one stroke of land acquisition. Such lands are often under multi-cropping. By acquiring such fertile land the development strategy of the state remains self-defeated by 'rural displacement-led urban slumization'. Extension of the urban boundary by such acquisition subsidizes the economically well off by assured supply of cheap labour from the 'newly displaced' villagers converted urban slum dwellers. Both land and necessary labour, thus, are curved out by land acquisition for the industry-cum-urban economy. Such displacements will have impact on social relations, will impose social Darwinism by the state, will empower industrial capitalists by enhancing their unhindered access to natural resources, convert marginal and small landowners into manual labour-based wage workers (supposedly unfit for industrial job), expanding labour size in informal sector, impose forced migration on urban areas, and consequent slumization. Fixing and paying cash as compensation to the displaced is a non-substitute of life-saving land for the land-dependents. Urban-type resettlement of the displaced does not help because the domestic animals that they have need common space (CPRs) for grazing. Since village space is horizontal while urban space is vertical, the former for low population density and the latter for high population density, hence urbanization does not help the people accustomed with village mode of living of the recent past. Unless similar village life is recreated elsewhere by rehabilitation of the displaced, the villagers feel robbed off their earlier livelihood. Nearby rehabilitation is constrained by further expansion of the industrial plant. The once displaced people remain vulnerable by 'future' unanticipated displacement.

The concern of the state and the concern of the society are not necessarily synonymous. State represents only the dominant political society and camouflages it by an all encompassing behaviour. The state-representing political society is propertied-cum-civil and settled as opposed to the vulgar one that is roaming-illegal-doubtful citizens. Civil society operates within the frame of colonially inherited institutions and corporate capital (Chatterjee, 2008: 12). When the ruling state elite dictates terms of development in a capitalist system in transition for accelerated forward movement, surrender of agricultural land for industrial purposes is a corollary. This is because the life-saving foodgrains cannot for long satisfy the non-satiety of the section that is well ahead of thinking about fulfillment of basic needs.

State is strengthened internally by imposition of laws it formulates for non-or-restricted access of the original settlers in forests and on land. State is strengthened in the name of protection of forests and land. On the other hand, state has a tendency to allow private capital to convert natural resources, including land, into consumable goods for those who were in the mainstream. The sections that are declared non-mainstream now were the original insiders. These insiders were the tribals and the Dalits who distanced themselves from private property understood by 'excludability'. The sections who protected these resources over time immemorial are now evicted. Their lifestyle is not backed by any state laws but as a natural practice in life because it was not only considered to be their life-support system but also their deity. By state reservation and acquisition of land, collective social ownership-cum-use is surrendered – what gets supreme is state authority.

In the post-feudal power structure, industrial capitalists are well ahead of agricultural landlords. The state considers agriculture as a source of surplus to feed the non-agriculture sector. Hence the state decides to acquire land for industrial purposes that show economic advancement. Areas declared as 'urban' are never acquired for agricultural purposes because the accepted trajectory is conversion of rural region into urban region, agriculture into industry, hiking the economy above subsistence level, and shift from nature dependence to man dependence.

Land carries dual meaning by its uses by the people. Land essentially has precautionary value as opposed to immediate exchange value to its holders. For the state, land is a resource for conversion into gross domestic product. In view of the state, it is encroachment by the people on the land/forests that the state thinks should remain reserved and protected. In view of the affected people, it is displacement and loss of livelihood. The ultimate decision-maker is the state that calculates the costs and benefits of land acquisition. State is the ultimate protector of the valid citizens. Hence, forced injustice is ruled out from the action-plan of the state.

For Social Justice in Economic Perspective

If industrialization is inescapable and hence land acquisition becomes a compulsion, displacement of people is a corollary. The measures that we suggest below in the context of land acquisition aim at minimizing social injustice in India:

- The 1894 Land Acquisition Act should be repealed because it was enacted in the interest of the colonial government.
- The farmers whose self-consumption is more than 50 per cent of self-production of the foodgrains should be exempted from giving up land under distress; otherwise such farmers will be forced to become net buyers of foodgrains at a subsequent price higher than the initial sale price.
- The target for land acquisition by the state has to be the absentee landlords, the land owners with 'distress free' double settlement and the big landowners. The land that remains idle as estate and 'benami' should be acquired.
- The target for acquisition of land has to be barren, fallow, and far from human settlement.
- The displaceable people have to be drawn as equal partners in the decision-making processes right from the time of proposal of land acquisition by the state, if it is in 'public interest'.
- Even if displaceable people give consent to give up land, it is to be examined by an autonomous body if the future of the nation will be endangered by deforestation, diminishing water table, emission of gas and other health hazards. It is also to be examined if the local people gave consent for fear and political pressure or for immediate urgency to get lump sum money as compensation.
- The real resource of a country is not the factory as such but the land, the rivers, the mines, the forests, the coastal belt, and above all the people. A national policy needs to be formulated to preserve these resources.
- Paying one-time money compensation is no solution for the people who live with land, domestic animals, water, hills and forests. The people settled in the rural economy should be economically accommodated in the same region through income-employment programmes.
- There has to be a Land Rights Commission to work as a vigilant over the activities of the government so far as land market is concerned.

- Price setting pre-acquisition has to be done by the government in consultation with the local Panchayat.
- In case a cluster of villages or a specified portion of a few villages are acquired for the setting up of an industry, the beneficiary industry has to shoulder corporate social responsibility through adoption of villages.
- The compensation has to cover land price post-acquisition plus the cost of surrendering domestic animals and other productive assets (including plantations, ponds, well etc.) plus the cost for surrendered opportunity to have access to common space (CPR) plus the cost for security loss (based on the assumption that village security in livelihood is preferred to that in cities and other difficult areas). While the prevailing price in the land market in the sub-urban areas may work as a proxy for post-acquisition of land, it becomes extremely difficult to suggest valuation for security loss.
- The state has to re-create similar CPR for the displaced. For the persons who are displaced by land acquisition, the government should declare a National Policy to:
    - ensure food security by provision of BPL cards as a component of India's general food security,
    - develop budding indigenous technology to assist the displaced for their skill upgradation,
    - ensure micro-credit to the displaced people with no property mortgage,
    - promote vocational education and training before acquisition of private land for industrial purposes,
    - provide low cost rural housing to the displaced,
    - promote local rural resources for repetitive, durable and multiple uses at the location of rehabilitation of the displaced, and
    - provide the displacement/rehabilitation card to the displaced person.

References

Bandyopadhyay, D., 'A Political Choice', *Mainstream*, March, 2007.

Chakrabarti, Anjan and Anup Dhar, *Dislocation and Resettlement in Development: From Third World to the World of the Third*, New York: Routledge Studies in Development and Society, 2010.

Chatterjee, Partha, 'Democracy and Economic Transformation in India', *Arthavijnana*, 2008, vol. L (1).

Constitution of India, (As Amended up to the Constitution [45th Amendment] Act), Allahabad: Central Law Agency, 1982.

Fernandes, Walter, J.C. Das and Sam Rao, 'Displacement and Rehabilitation: An Estimate of Extent and Prospects' in Walter Fernanades and Enakshi Thukral (eds.) *Development, Displacement and Rehabilitation: Issues for a National Debate*,New Delhi: Indian Social Institute, 1989.

Fernandes, Walter, 'Singur and the Displacement Scenario', *Economic and Political Weekly*, 20 January 2007.

GOI, The Land Acquisition Act, 1894 (As Amended up to 1985).

Khasnobis, Ratan, 'Land Acquisition Act and Social Justice: A Study on Development and Displacement' in Bose, P.K. and Das, S.K. (eds.) *State of Justice in India*, vol. 1, New Delhi: Sage, 2009.

Lok Sabha, The Land Acquisition (Amendment) Bill, 2007 (Bill No. 97 of 2007).

Magill, Frank N. (ed.), *International Encyclopedia of Economics*, Vols. I and II, London: Routledge, 1997.

Majumdar, Bhaskar, 'Development Hydra: Two Cases of Forced Industrialization in India', Report submitted to G.B. Pant Social Science Institute, Allahabad: Mimeo, 2007.

Marx, Karl, 'The Future Results of the British Rule in India', in James P. and Phillip, D. (ed.), *Globalization and Violence*, vol. 2, London: Sage, 2006.

Plum, Warner, 'Industrialization and Mass Poverty: Points from Two Centuries of Debate', tr. Lux Furtmuller, Friedrich-Ebert-Stiftung: Bonn, Germany, 1977.

Report, 1996, *Economic and Political Weekly*, 15 June.

Sarkar, Abhirup, 'Development and Displacement, Land Acquisition in West Bengal', *Economic and Political Weekly*, 21 April 2007.

Sharma, R.N. and Shashi R. Singh, 'Displacement in Singrauli Region: Entitlements and Rehabilitation', *Economic and Political Weekly*, 2009, vol. XLIV (51).

World Commission on Dams, 'Dams and Development: A New Framework for Decision-Making', London: Earthscan, 2000.

16

Free Legal Aid as a Fundamental Right in India

Reality or Still a Distant Dream?

Sanjay Gupta

Legal aid constitutes an important ingredient of the general notions of equal justice, equality before law and equal protection of law. These notions, though hallmarks of a modern society, remain dead letters for the poor who are unable to access the doors of justice and take benefit of the legal system that professes to work for one and all. For the deprived and disadvantaged people, principles of equal justice do not mean anything if they are unable to get the fruits of the legal and judicial systems upholding these basic values. Unless certain mechanisms are devised and established in the legal framework of a country, real justice cannot be secured to the disadvantaged people. The issue of access to justice has been a major problem confronting humanity from times immemorial prompting rulers and legal scholars to find ways to dispense justice for one and all, without any barriers. The need for affordable and cheap justice is felt much more in modern times, than at any other time, as people's lives have become full of tensions and problems. Anxieties and worries have gripped almost all walks of human life, including both personal and professional lives. There are increased cases of marriage break-ups, family disturbances, domestic violence, loss of jobs, cuts in wages or benefits or discrimination in public life and so on and so forth. All these problems have legal dimensions which need effective and prompt remedies. Scholars hold that 'legal problems are the problems of everyday life. They occur when people divorce, lose their jobs, migrate, die (inheritance), have an accident (personal injury), buy goods or services that do not work as expected, or see their business cooperation fail'.[1] With the establishment of modern liberal democracies in the beginning of the 20th century, the case for equal justice became all the more crucial, particularly in the developing and under-developed world. It was realized that unless nations include equal justice as their constitutional obligation and work towards its realization zealously, equal justice would remain a glorious myth for the poor and the illiterate people. It was because of this that the question of equal justice and its variants as legal aid, prompt justice, cheap justice, etc. became serious issues of discussion and deliberation and were ultimately given constitutional or legal status in many countries.

The term legal aid refers to the help provided to people, who on account of poverty or their weak social and economic status or other associated disadvantages, are unable to seek shelter of the court or legal system for protecting their interests and getting their problems resolved. Their vulnerable position in the society prevents them from accessing or affording legal services by themselves due to the disadvantages associated with them. This disadvantage is sought to be removed by providing him the services of a lawyer by the government or any organization that can fight his case and represent him in the court. Thus, legal aid is defined as 'a legal assistance provided, as by a specially established organization, for those unable to afford an attorney',[2] or 'it is a means-tested benefit in the form of financial assistance to persons to meet the cost of advice and representation in legal proceedings'.[3] The *Encyclopedia Britannica* defines legal aid as a 'phrase which is acquired by usage and court decisions, a specific meaning of giving to person of limited means grants or for nominal fees, advice or counsel to represent them in court in civil and criminal matters'.[4] According to *Collins English Dictionary*, legal aid is a means-tested benefit in the form of financial assistance for persons to meet the cost of advice and representation in legal proceedings.'[5] Similarly, the Webster's new *World Law Dictionary* defines it as 'the free or inexpensive services of an attorney, provided to individuals, typically criminal defendants, who are not otherwise able to afford an attorney.' All these definitions underlie the fact that it is a 'means' or a 'mechanism' provided to the poor and the weak, by the state or any other organization, who are unable to pay for themselves to seek legal remedy to get justice. It is an instrument which aims to undo their inability by providing them legal services in the form of free advice and representation by a legal counsel. This is done to make them equal before the law and to secure them justice.

While in criminal matters, the state makes provision for assigning a legal counsel to an accused to represent him, in civil matters, an individual, though does not have this right per se, is to be provided free legal assistance by a state if his case falls within the eligibility criterion devised by the state. In this way, efforts are made to provide legal equality so that they do not have to suffer on account of their weak social and economic status. Today, more emphasis is given to alternative dispute resolution mechanism which facilitates the resolution of disputes outside the court, with mutual settlement among the disputing parties. This lessens the burden on courts and saves their valuable time and energy at the same time. The state gives assistance to poor people to take advantage of the ADR mechanism through expert legal advice of the lawyers. In this way, legal aid contributes to the legal emancipation of the weaker classes and ensures legal equality and easy accessibility to the justice system. That's why legal aid has become part and parcel of most of the legal systems around the world. Lord Denning describes this development in the post Second World War as a matter of great importance. He observes: 'The greatest revolution in the law since the post-Second World War has been the evolution of the mechanism of the system for legal aid. It means that in many cases the lawyers' fees and expenses are paid for by the state: and not by the party concerned. It is a subject of such importance that I venture to look at the law about costs-as it was-as such it is-and as it should be'.[6]

Development of Legal Aid Movement in India

The concept of 'equal justice' or 'justice to all' is not something that originated in modern India rather its roots can be traced to ancient India where the kings were supposed to uphold the *dharma* (righteousness) and *nyaya* (justice) for the common people. The king was under a moral obligation to serve the people with selfless service and dedication, and an unjust king who failed in his duties forfeited his rights to rule and it was legitimate for the people to remove him by force. *Manusmriti* casts a duty on a king to administer justice and treat all his subjects as equal irrespective of their social status or beliefs. The king was bound by his duties towards *dharma* and *nyaya* by a set of religious code which constantly guided him in the administration of justice in social, economic and political aspects, whose sanctity has to be preserved and developed.[7] In the medieval era India, the king was guided by the Islamic law in resolving people's disputes notwithstanding the religion of the disputant parties to the case. But even then, Hindus were governed by Hindu Law if they were a party to the dispute. It was the Mughal Emperor, Jahangir, who was renowned for giving justice to one and all, without any discrimination on grounds of religion, birth or social status. Because of his even-handed approach of dispensing justice to one and all, he became very popular as a 'just king'.

However, the formal history of legal equality and legal justice in India starts with the adoption of the Constitution of India. Although initially there were no direct legal aid provisions in the Constitution, it was inherent in other provisions of the Constitution, mainly Article 14 which obligates the State to provide equality before law and equal protection to everyone without any discrimination on grounds of race, religion, caste, gender, age or place of birth. Owing to this obligation, there was sufficient realization in the government and the judiciary that the poor, which then constituted a big part of the Indian population, needed to be provided with legal assistance and legal education. Thus, since 1952, the Government of India started taking initiative to address the problem of legal aid for the poor and destitute through various Ministerial Law Conferences and Commissions. Schemes of legal aid were developed under the supervision of Justice H.N. Bhagwati, of Bombay High Court and Justice Trevore Harris of Calcutta High Court'.[8]

Justice Bhagwati's work subsequently led to the setting up of a Law Commission by the Central Government under the chairmanship of eminent jurist, M.C. Setalvad to make recommendations for making legal aid programme an effective instrument for rendering social justice. In its report, the Law Commission emphasized that free legal aid is a service which should be provided by the State to the poor. The State must, while accepting the obligation, make provision for funds to provide legal aid. The legal community must play a pivotal role in accepting the responsibility for the administration and working of the legal aid scheme. It owes a moral and social obligation and, therefore, the Bar Association should take a step forward in rendering legal aid voluntarily. These would include representation by lawyers at government expenses to accused persons in criminal proceedings, in jails, and appeals. 'The Commission also recommended the substitution in Order XXXIII, Civil Procedure Code of the word 'pauper' with 'poor persons'.[9]

Based on the recommendations of the Law Commission, a national scheme of legal aid was formulated by the Government of India in 1960 according to which legal aid was to be provided in all courts including tribunals. The scheme envisaged the establishment of committees at the state, district and tehsil levels. However, owing to the financial constraints, the state did not take much interest in the scheme and consequently the recommendations could not be implemented.

Besides the states' inability, the judicial attitude towards the legal aid too was not encouraging. This became clear in *Janardhan Reddy v. State of Hyderabad*[10] and *Tara Singh v State of Punjab*[11], in which the court took a narrow view of statutory provisions giving a person the right to lawyer. The judgment said that this was, '*a privilege given to accused and it is his duty to ask for a lawyer if he wants to engage one or get his relations to engage one for him. The only duty cast on the Magistrate is to afford him the necessary opportunity (to do so).*' Even with regard to cases pertaining to capital punishment, the early judgments of the Supreme Court seemed narrow when it declared that 'it cannot be laid down in every capital case where the accused is unrepresented the trial is vitiated.' These instances establish that perhaps the broader framework of legal aid in the newly independent India was not yet clear and more efforts were required to establish the system in the right perspective.

Taking another initiative in 1973, the government constituted a committee under the noted jurist, Justice Krishna Iyer to suggest measures for devising and elaborating the legal aid scheme. The committee gave valuable recommendations for setting up of legal aid committees in each district, at state level and at the Centre. It also suggested that an autonomous corporation be set up to effectively implement the legal aid scheme. The committee recommended encouraging the concept of legal aid camps and *nyayalayas* (courts) in rural areas. It also called for incorporating legal aid provision in the Constitution of India.

The government accepted the recommendations in 1976 and by the 42nd Constitutional Amendment Act, Article 39(A) was introduced in the Directive Principles of State Policy. In September 1980, the 'Committee for Implementing Legal Aid Schemes' (CILAS) was constituted under the chairmanship of then Chief Justice P.N. Bhagwati to monitor and implement legal aid programmes on a uniform basis in all the states and Union Territories. 'CILAS' evolved a model scheme for legal aid programmes applicable throughout the country by which several legal aid and advice boards were set up in the states and Union Territories.

Significant changes were witnessed in the late 1970s particularly with regard to the *Maneka Gandhi* case in 1978.[12] This case widened the scope and ambit of fundamental rights taking into account not only the fundamental rights enumerated in part III of the Constitution but also including all such rights that became associated or formed part of these rights. Following this, the courts widened their perspective with respect to the civil liberties. While disclosing shocking state of affairs and callousness of our legal and judicial system causing enormous misery and sufferings to the poor and illiterate citizens resulting into totally unjustified deprivation of personal liberty, Justice P.N. Bhagwati, made the following observations:

> This unfortunate situation cries aloud for introduction of an adequate and comprehensive legal service programmes, but so far, these cries do not seem to have evoked any response. We do not think it is possible to reach the benefits of the legal process to the poor to protect them against injustice and to secure to them their constitutional and statutory rights unless there is a nation-wide legal service programme to provide free legal services to them.

The negative judicial attitude towards the legal aid showed signs of change that was reflected in the Courts' recognizing legal aid as a fundamental right under Article 21 in the case *Sunil Batra v. Delhi Administration*.[13] This case defined the scope and ambit of the right to legal aid. The court declared that there can be two situations in which a prisoner would be entitled for legal aid to be given. First, to seek justice from the prison authorities and second, to challenge the decision of such authorities in the court. Thus, legal aid was to be introduced at two levels – in the judicial proceedings and before the prison authorities which were administrative in nature.

At the beginning of the 1980s, two important cases came to the Supreme Court which proved to be crucial in the development of free legal aid in India. In *Hussainara Khatoon* case[14], a writ of habeas corpus petition was brought on behalf of the large number of men, women, and children, who were detained in jail in the State of Bihar for years awaiting trial for minor offences, which, even if proven, would not have warranted punishment for more than a few months, or perhaps for a year or two. Despite this, they were deprived of their freedom for periods ranging from three to 10 years without even as much as a trial date. The Supreme Court issued a clarion call to the government:

> We may also take this opportunity of impressing upon the Government of India as also the State Governments, the urgent necessity of introducing a dynamic and comprehensive legal service programme with a view to reaching justice to the common man. Today, unfortunately, in our country the poor are priced out of the judicial system with the result that they are losing faith in the capacity of our legal system to bring about changes in their life conditions and to deliver justice to them. The poor in their contact with the legal system have always been on the wrong side of the law. They have always come across law for the poor rather than law of the poor. The law is regarded by them as something mysterious and forbidding – always taking something away from them and not as a positive and constructive social device for changing the socio-economic order and improving their life conditions by conferring rights and benefits on them. The result is that the legal system has lost its credibility for the weaker sections of the community. It is, therefore, necessary that we should inject equal justice into legality and that can be done only by dynamic and activist scheme of legal services.

The court further ruled: 'It is an essential ingredient of reasonable, fair and just procedure to a prisoner who is to seek his liberation through the court's process that he should have legal services available to him. Free legal service to the poor and the needy is an essential element of any reasonable, fair and just procedure.' The court invoked Article 39(A) which provides for free legal aid and has interpreted Article 21 in the light of Article 39(A).

It upheld the right to free legal aid to be provided to the poor accused persons 'not in the permissive sense of Article 22(1) and its wider amplitude' but in the peremptory sense of article 21 confined to prison situations.'

In *Khatri (II) v. State of Bihar*[15], two prisoners lost their eyesight as a result of police torture while in custody. The Court directed the Registrar of the Supreme Court to conduct an enquiry with respect to the torture. He determined that legal representation was not provided to the prisoners because neither requested counsel when they were brought before the magistrate initially or on remand. The Court directed that unless the accused is not willing to take advantage of free legal services provided by the state, he must be provided legal representation at the cost of state. Justice P.N. Bhagwati, referring to Supreme Court's mandate in Khatoon, wrote:

> It is unfortunate that though this Court declared the right to legal aid as a fundamental right of an accused person by a process of judicial construction of Article 21, most of the states in the country have not taken note of this decision and provided free legal services to a person accused of an offence. The state is under a constitutional mandate to provide free legal aid to an accused person who is unable to secure legal services on account of indigence, and whatever is necessary for this purpose has to be done by the state.

The court's commitment to legal aid were reemphasized in the 1986 case of *Sukhdas v. Union Territory of Arunachal Pradesh*[16] in which Justice P.N. Bhagwati, while referring to the decision of *Hussainara Khatun*'s case and some other cases, made the following observations in paragraph 6 of the said judgment:

> Now it is common knowledge that about 70 per cent of the people living in rural areas are illiterate and even more than that percentage of the people are not aware of the rights conferred upon them by law. Even literate people do not know what are their rights and entitlements under the law. It is this absence of legal awareness which is responsible for the deception, exploitation and deprivation of rights and benefits from which the poor suffer in this land. Their legal needs always stand to become crisis oriented because their ignorance prevents them from anticipating legal troubles and approaching a lawyer for consultation and

advice in time and their poverty magnifies the impact of the legal troubles and difficulties when they come. Moreover, of their ignorance and illiteracy, they cannot become self-reliant; they cannot even help themselves. The Law ceases to be their protector because they do not know that they are entitled to the protection of the law and they can avail of the legal service programmes for putting an end to their exploitation and winning their rights. The result is that poverty becomes with them a condition of total helplessness. This miserable condition in which the poor find themselves can be alleviated to some extent by creating legal awareness amongst the poor. That is why it has always been recognized as one of the principal items of the programmes of the legal aid movement in the country to promote legal literacy. It would be in these circumstances made a mockery of legal aid if it were to be left to a poor, ignorant and illiterate accused to ask for free legal service, legal aid would become merely a paper promise and it would fail of its purpose.

Constitutional Provisions and Legislative Enactments Enabling Legal Aid

These developments, basically judicial in nature, marked a turning point for the institutionalization of legal aid in India. As noted above, though there were no direct provisions on legal aid in the Constitution, the changing attitude of the judiciary had a significant impact in filling this vital gap in the Constitution which came by way of 42nd Amendment to the Constitution in 1976. This amendment inserted a new provision namely Article 39(A) in part 1V of the Constitution dealing with Directive Principles of State Policy. This provision sought to provide equal justice and free legal aid to the poor and downtrodden sections of the society for achieving social justice. It lays down:

> Equal justice and free legal aid: The State shall secure that the operation of the legal system promotes justice, on a basis of equal opportunity, and shall, in particular, provide free legal aid, by suitable legislation or schemes or in any other way, to ensure that opportunities for securing justice are not denied to any citizen by reason of economic or other disabilities.

Other provisions concerning legal aid are inherent in several other articles of the Constitution. For instance, Article 14 guarantees provides for equality before law and equal protection of law. This equality of law is meaningless unless poor litigants are provided adequate legal support free of cost to fight their cases in a court of law. To an economically weak or a socially vulnerable person, legal equality is a myth as he/she is simply unable to access the courts due to his inability to pay for the court's and the lawyer's fees to redress his problems. This want of means to obtain access to courts renders a person with unequal justice. Unfortunately, this inequality has grown massively over the years due to the enormous growth in state welfare legislation catering to the needs of the socially and economically vulnerable sections of people. The growth in the complexity and the sheer expanse of law, it appears, has confused people about their rights and legal entitlements as they fail to understand the cumbersome legislations and the remedies provided therein in case of infringement by the state. If at all he understands, he is unable to access the courts due to the costly bureaucratic procedures involved. Resultantly, he becomes a victim of unequal justice. Thus, Article 39(A), when read with Article 14, ensures equality before law to a person by enabling him to access a court of law irrespective of his weak economic or social status and thus ensure justice on the basis of equality of opportunity to all.

Next to Article 14, Article 21 guarantees the right to life and personal liberty of people. No one can be deprived of this right except by the *procedure established by law* which, in effect means a procedure which is just, fair and reasonable (*Maneka Gandhi Case*, 1978). Natural justice is a pre-condition to 'fair procedure' requirement and natural justice involves the right to be heard. The right to hearing in jurisprudence means the right to be heard through a counsel. Thus, if the right to counsel is mandatory for a just and fair trial, it involves *per se* that the accused has adequate means to defend himself. The Supreme Court, on a number of occasions, have observed that where a person who is accused of a crime punishable with imprisonment is entitled to free legal aid as a matter of fundamental right under Article 21 if he/she is unable to afford a counsel on account of his/her extreme poverty. Besides, the court has also declared that the counsel of the accused should also be afforded sufficient time and facility to prepare the defence. The contravention or the non-fulfillment of these legal safeguards would invalidate the trial and even his subsequent conviction irrespective of the fact that the undertrial did not ask for legal aid. Article 22 (1) mandates that a person who is arrested shall be informed about the grounds of his arrest as also he shall have the right to consult a lawyer of his choice and be represented in a court of law to defend himself. Further, Article 38 obligates the state to promote the welfare of the people by creating a social order where justice (social, economic and political) shall pervade all the institutions of national life. The above provisions thus make it amply clear that the State has been ordained to secure a legal system, which promotes justice on the basis of equal opportunity. Besides these constitutional provisions, legal aid clauses have also been incorporated in the civil and criminal codes of India.

Legal aid provisions are also contained in *Civil Procedure Code, 1908*. Order 33 provides for filing of suits by indigent persons. It enables persons who are too poor to pay court fees and allows them to institute suits without payment of requisite court fees. Likewise the *Criminal Procedure Code, 1973* also, through Section 304, provides that where in a trial before the Court of Session, the accused is not represented by a pleader and where it appears to the court that the accused has not sufficient means to engage a pleader, the Court shall assign a pleader for his defence at the expense of the state. This section further empowers the state government to extend the application of the above provision in relation to any class or trials before other courts in the State.

Legal aid movement in India since the 1950s has had a powerful influence on the government making it feel the acute necessity of enacting legislations to implement the constitutional provisions for realizing legal aid in India. Informed by its own sources, the government itself expressed dissatisfaction with the existing position of justice delivery system. It has acknowledged the fact the poor and underprivileged sections of society have suffered the worst under the present system. Justice Bhagwati gave a powerful fillip to the need of establishing legal machinery for the regulation and implementation of legal aid scheme through his noted judgement in the 1986 case of *Sukhdas v. Union Territory of Arunachal Pradesh*. In another case, the Supreme Court observed: 'We do not think it is possible to reach the benefits of the legal process to the poor, to protect them against injustice and secure them their constitutional and statutory rights unless there is a nation-wide legal service programme to provide free legal services to them.'[17]

These and other similar decisions led to the enactment of The Legal Services Authorities Act, 1987 to accomplish the vision of providing legal aid to the exploited masses of this country, and under this Act, bodies such as NALSA and SCLSC were created to ensure free legal aid to poor and under privileged.

Legal Services Authority Act, 1987

Legal Services Authorities Act was passed by the Parliament in 1987. It was enforced in November 1995 after certain amendments were introduced therein by the Amendment Act of 1994. Passed against the backdrop of the case noted above, the Act gave a statutory base to legal aid programmes throughout the country on a uniform pattern for providing quicker and cheaper means of 'access' for the poor. The Act envisaged establishing a nationwide uniform network for providing free and competent legal services and assistance to the weaker sections of the society on the basis of equal opportunity. The Act also ensured that opportunities for securing justice were not denied to any citizen by reason of economic or other disabilities. It provides for the constitution of a National Legal Services Authority and a Supreme Court Legal Services Committee for the Centre, State Legal Services Authority and a High Court Legal Services Committee for each state, District Legal Services Authority and a Taluk Legal Services Committee for every district.[18]

One of the important achievements of the Act was that it established *Lok Adalats* (People's Courts) whose aim was to make justice accessible to the most common man by resolving disputes by compromise and settlement. It ensured that the operation of legal system promoted justice on the basis of equal opportunity. Lok Adalats have its roots in the history and culture of India. The introduction of *Lok Adalats*, or public courts, gave a renewed strength to the justice delivery apparatus of India and gave a new platform to the underprivileged litigants to approach these courts and get their disputes settled.

National Legal Services Authority (NALSA), 1994

Set up in 1994 under the Legal Services Authority Act, 1987, NALSA monitors and evaluates implementation of legal services available under the Act. It is the apex body entrusted to formulate policies and principles to secure legal services to the needy. It lays down guidelines for the State Legal Services Authorities to implement the legal aid schemes and programmes throughout the country and grants funds for the same. The current Chief Justice of

India is the Patron-in-Chief and a senior judge of the Supreme Court of India is the Executive Chairman of NALSA.[19]

The Act provides that in every state, a State Legal Services Authority is to be constituted to give effect to the policies and directions of the Central Authority (NALSA) and to give legal services to the people and conduct *Lok Adalats* in the state. The head of the State Legal Services Authority is the Chief Justice of the state High Court who is its Patron-in-Chief. A serving or retired judge of the High Court is nominated as its Executive Chairman.

Each district under the Act shall have a District Legal Services Authority to implement Legal Aid Programmes and Schemes in the district. The District Judge of the District is its ex-officio Chairman. At the Taluk level, there is a *Taluk Legal Services Committee* which is set up for each *Taluk* or *Mandal* or for a group of Taluk or Mandals to harmonize the activities of legal services in the Taluk and to hold *Lok Adalats*. Every Taluk Legal Services Committee is headed by a senior Civil Judge operating within the jurisdiction of the Committee who is its ex-officio Chairman.[20]

The Central Authority shall constitute a Committee to be called the Supreme Court Legal Services Committee for the purpose of exercising such powers and performing such functions as may be determined by regulations made by the Central Authority. NALSA is laying great deal of emphasis on legal literacy and legal awareness campaign. Almost all the State Legal Services Authorities are identifying suitable and trustworthy NGOs through whom legal literacy campaign may be taken to tribal, backward and far-flung areas in the country. The effort is to publicize legal aid schemes so that the target group, for whom Legal Services Authorities Act has provided for free legal aid, may come to know about the same and approach the concerned legal services functionaries.[21]

NALSA has also directed the State Legal Services Authorities to constitute legal aid cells in jails so that the prisoners lodged therein are provided prompt and efficient legal aid to which they are entitled by virtue of Section 12 of Legal Services Authorities Act, 1987. The provisions of the Act obligates the central authority, the NALSA, to direct the State Legal Services Authorities to set up committees for evaluation of the actual benefit received by the beneficiaries under Section 12 of the Act in respect of each project and programme, and to send copy of such reports to NALSA. The Act also calls upon the national and state level legal bodies to take necessary steps for ensuring commitment to the provisions in Part-IV of the Constitution.

Eligibility for Legal Aid

Legal aid in criminal cases is a fundamental right under the Constitution, but in civil cases, it is means-tested and is to be provided by the Legal Aid Committees upon satisfying the eligibility conditions as mentioned under Legal Services Authorities Act, 1987. According to Section 2(1) (a) of the Act, legal aid can be provided to a person for a 'case' which includes a suit or any proceeding before a court. Section 2(1) (a) defines the 'court' as a civil, criminal or revenue court and includes any tribunal or any other authority constituted under any law for the time being in force, to exercise judicial or quasi-judicial functions. As per Section 2(1)(c) 'legal service' includes the rendering of any service in the conduct of any case or other legal proceeding before any court or other authority or tribunal and the giving of advice on any legal matter.

The procedure for obtaining legal aid in criminal and civil cases is little different. In criminal cases, application for free legal aid is directly sent by the accused from the jail to the High Court appealing against the order of a lower court. The judge then forwards it to the legal aid committee for arranging a lawyer for the accused. In civil cases, the litigant directly approaches the legal aid committee, which scrutinizes his application. The Committee then directs the litigant to submit a proof of his income on the basis of which it examines the eligibility criteria of the applicant and the existence of a prima facie case so as to determine whether a person is destitute enough to be given a state lawyer free of cost. The Committee bears all the expenditure including the Court Fee and all incidental expenses in connection with the case. The person to whom legal aid is provided is not called upon to spend anything on the litigation once it is supported by the Legal Services Authority.

Under The Legal Services Authorities Act, 1987 every citizen whose annual income does not exceed ₹ 25,000 is eligible for free legal aid in cases before subordinate courts and high courts. In cases before the Supreme Court, the limit is ₹ 50,000. This limit can be increased by the state governments. Limitation as to the income does not apply in the case of persons belonging to the Scheduled Castes, Scheduled Tribes, women, children, mentally ill, disabled person, a victim of trafficking in human beings, victim of atrocity, flood, drought, earthquake or industrial disaster, an industrial workman, in custody, including custody in a protective home or in a juvenile home or in a psychiatric hospital or psychiatric nursing home.

Besides provisions of free legal aid, the 1987 Act also provides for *Lok Adalats* (People's Courts) for dispensing legal aid to the poor litigants. *Lok Adalats* are bodies set up by the government as mechanisms to encourage consensual resolution of disputes in order to avoid unforeseeable delays, prohibitive costs and uncertain results of litigation in the courts. *Lok Adalats* have jurisdiction to determine compromise or settlement between the parties to a dispute in any pending case. In addition, they have jurisdiction over any matter not pending before the court for which the *Lok Adalat* is organized, but for which the court has jurisdiction. *Lok Adalats* do not have jurisdiction in respect of any case or matter relating to an offence not compoundable under any law. The court may refer a case to the *Lok Adalat* where the parties agree, or where one party makes an application to refer the case to the *Lok Adalat* for settlement. If the court is satisfied that there is a possibility of settlement and an appropriate matter for cognizance by the *Lok Adalat*, then the court shall refer the case to the *Lok Adalat*. In order to plug certain loopholes in the Legal Services Authorities Act, 1987, the Act was amended in 1994 that paved way for the establishment of permanent *Lok Adalats*.

Legal Aid and the Role of NALSA

Over the years, NALSA has played a significant role in institutionalizing legal aid in India for the poor and powerless people. It has formulated a number of schemes to bring the poor people in the mainstream of national life and provide them with easy access to justice. NALSA implemented a 'Legal Aid Counsel Scheme' to enable legal assistance to the under trial prisoners who, due to the want of resources or other disabilities, cannot engage a counsel to defend them. Under the Act, now an undertrial will have the right to be provided with a Legal Aid Counsel who will be attached to each Magisterial Court. Legal Counsels provide assistance and defend a person who is not able to engage a counsel from the very beginning of the case, that is, from the time he or she is produced in a court. With the amendment of the Legal Services Authorities Act, 1987, now permanent *Lok Adalats* have been established under Section 19 of the Act in all the districts of the country. Under this scheme, the Lok Adalat, are now organized regularly at designated venues, even away from court complexes and the cases which remain unsettled are taken up in the next Lok Adalat. Lok Adalats have, thus, acquired permanency and continuity and are no more occasional.

NALSA has enacted a Counselling and Conciliation Scheme to encourage the settlement of disputes by way of negotiations and conciliation. Under this scheme, Counselling and Conciliation Centres are being set up in all the districts of the country for guiding and motivating the migrants to resolve their disputes amicably. NALSA has devised a 'Legal Literacy Programme' to provide basic legal knowledge to the poor people to enable them to understand law so that they are able to claim their rights, fight for their rights and improve their social status, all of which will contribute to usher in social change.

From time to time, NALSA has been holding Legal Aid Camps through State and Taluka Legal Services Authorities in the rural and slum areas for educating the weaker sections as to their rights and for encouraging them to settle their disputes through alternative dispute resolution mechanism. The poor people are informed and educated about their rights, privileges, benefits which are available to them under various government schemes. It has also been organizing seminars, conferences, workshops and meetings with government officials and the academic institutions concerned with imparting legal services to the people in various parts of the country. It has developed audio-visual spots and publicity material to make the common man aware of the various aspects of the legal services programmes. Documentary films have also been prepared and are being screened in the different parts of the country through Directorate of Field Publicity, Government of India.

NALSA has drawn up a scheme for accreditation of Voluntary Social Service Institutions to establish a nation-wide network of voluntary agencies in order to spread legal literacy, legal awareness and publicity for legal services throughout the nook and corner of the country. All the State Legal Services Authorities have been urged to identify Social Service Institutions in all districts and give them accreditation. NALSA has also been involved in employment generation programmes for the vulnerable people. In partnership with the State Legal Services Authorities, it is working on a scheme, 'Supporting the Implementation on National Rural Employment Guarantee Scheme (NREGS) for generating awareness through Legal Literacy and Awareness Campaign and to establish a grievance redressal forum by organizing Lok Adalats to resolve the disputes/complaints or legal problems of any person in respect of implementation of the scheme and employment guaranteed under NREGA. Further, NALSA prepared a Plan of Action for the financial year 2009–10 to implement the Legal Aid Schemes and Legal Services Programmes of NALSA in accordance with the object of the Legal Services Authorities Act, 1987. Besides, NALSA has also introduced a *Para-Legal Volunteer Scheme.* This scheme aimed at creating a reservoir of volunteers from among the rural people to act as intermediates between the common people and legal services institutions at Central, state, district and Taluka levels.

In addition, NALSA also introduced the concept of *Legal Aid Clinics* under which these clinics are sought to be established in the rural areas and in the academic institutions. Among other things, the plan includes establishing Legal Aid Clinics in all Gram Panchayats (similar to primary health centres) by engaging competent lawyers as legal consultants in the clinics and give them wide publicity with the help of local self-government institutions. This plan also envisaged the setting-up of Legal Aid Clinics in all law colleges and law universities and to encourage students to adopt remote village areas as their area of operation. In urban areas, colonies and slums where economically and socially backward people reside were to be chosen for setting up Legal Aid Clinics. Law students were to be guided by a team of senior professors/lecturers, including part-time lecturers. Rapport between the students and the people of the adopted area should be maintained throughout the year. In appropriate cases, senior students and postgraduate students who have already enrolled as lawyers, may be entrusted with the filing and conducting of the litigation in the courts free of cost. The plan prohibited the collection of any fee from the beneficiaries of legal aid clinic.

Further, the NALSA initiated the *Legal Aid Scheme* which sought to bring in more competent, well-known and senior lawyers for rendering Legal Services and Legal Aid. To make legal aid a success, the scheme includes payment of better honorarium to the lawyers who provide legal aid; inclusion of all designated senior lawyers in the Legal Aid Schemes and requesting them to undertake at least two cases free of charge every year; annual evaluation of the progress of cases in which Legal Aid was given.

Like National Legal Aid Authority, the State Legal Services Authorities also formulated similar schemes in 2009–10 to realize the legal aid for the poor. Among other features, these schemes emphasized the importance of publicity of legal aid schemes. This comprised developing liaison with the Information and Broadcasting Ministry and Prasar Bharti for timely briefing about the projects and programmes to the press and media; using hoardings, producing short-films, skits in CD form and distributing copies to all TLSEc and DLSAs; and printing of publicity materials like posters, pamphlets, booklets and distributing the required quantity of such materials to all States Legal Services Authorities in requisite number, and advertisements in newspapers and television (both private and government owned), etc.

Action taken for the implementation of these plans has yielded favourable results. Data available reveals that during the plan period 2009–10, about 7.25 lakh Lok Adalats were held throughout the country in which more than 2.68 crore cases had been settled. More than ₹ 7,593 lakh had been awarded compensation to people in approximately 16.87 lakh motor accident cases. More than 3 crore people had been benefitted through legal aid and advice throughout the country in which about 75 lakh persons belonging to Scheduled Caste and 15 lakh people of Scheduled Tribe communities were the beneficiaries. More than 18 lakh people were women and about 12 lakh people in custody were also benefitted.[22]

As a result of these revolutionary legislation and the consequent policies and programmes formulated under them, there has been positive results. Legal aid in India is now institutionalized and has reached all parts of the country – cities, towns, districts and villages. Tens and thousands of poor people have been benefitted by legal aid services. This notable change in the scenario has come about basically due to the shift in the approach of the Supreme Court towards the concept of legal aid from a 'duty of the accused to ask for a lawyer' to a 'fundamental right of an accused to seek free legal aid'.

Realizing the magnitude of poverty and associated disadvantages, the Supreme Court, through its numerous decisions, made it amply clear that the gigantic problems of poverty, illiteracy and exploitation cannot be dealt through traditional judicial means of court and litigation, rather a distinct method has to be adopted to address the deeply entrenched socio-economic problem that has its roots in the deep past. Thus, in one of its judgements, the Supreme Court observed: 'We do not think it is possible to reach the benefits of the legal process to the poor, to protect them against injustice and secure them their constitutional and statutory rights unless there is a nation-wide legal service programme to provide free legal services to them. In such a state of affairs it is imperative for state to take steps to keep the confidence of masses in the justice system breathing'.[23]

The court, in particular, has played a major role in the institutionalization of legal aid and has ruled that free legal aid is a necessary adjunct of the rule of law.[24] Its strong rulings led to the creation of some very important committees by the government that recommended the enactment of Legal Services Authorities Act, 1987 through which the national legal aid body, NALSA, and *Lok Adalats* (People's courts) were established, whose goals were to accomplish the vision of providing legal aid to the exploited masses of this country.

These measures proved to be milestones in laying a firm foundation of legal aid in India. The national judiciary has constantly exhorted and reminded the government about the pressing need of delivering legal aid which alone can make the poor accessible to the complex and costly legal system. By popularizing the concept of legal aid, the Court has sought to bring legal justice nearer to the poverty-stricken people, establish legal equality and facilitate the easy accessibility of justice to vulnerable and poor people. In pursuance of this goal, the Court has cautioned the government, and pulled up the administration and the legal authorities for their callous attitude and negative approach in implementing the constitutional provisions on legal aid from time to time.

The Actual Scenario

However, despite the best efforts and intentions of the judiciary, and the government contributing by bringing in legislation and creating the national legal aid body, the NALSA, and regularizing the *Lok Adalats* (People's Courts) for easy dispensation of legal aid services to the poor people, the legal aid movement has not yet achieved its goal in a substantial way. There is still a wide gap between the goals aspired to and actual achievements. The actual scenario defies the optimism as portrayed by official records and statistics.

It is a matter of concern that the objective of legal aid that was spelt out by the Supreme Court in *Hussainara Khatoon case v Home Secretary, State of Bihar* (AIR 1979, SC 1369) as being to affect 'distributive justice, effective implementation of welfare benefits and elimination of social and structural discrimination against the poor' still remains a distant dream. Despite 23 years of the coming into force of the national legal aid act, speedy justice and free legal aid have not yet been achieved. Progress in implementing legal aid schemes and bringing cheap justice to the poor is still a distant goal due to the many shortcomings and gaps that prevails in the system notwithstanding having one of the best legal aid paraphernalia. The huge number of pre-trial detainees languishing in different jails of India for years together waiting for justice speaks volumes about the state of legal aid in criminal matters. The same is the situation in the civil area where numerous problems abound and poor people are unable to get timely and costless remedy. Although there are several laws and policies for the depressed people and well-established administrative machinery with ample resources, the same is not reaching the targeted sections, else the problem of back log cases would not have been so serious.

In India, as elsewhere, land is an important factor in one's life. It is an important economic, social and psychological capital. Particularly, for the rural masses, it is an important source of livelihood and an asset adding to the security and status to their life. But the deprivation of this important source due to various reasons has resulted in appalling poverty for them. To redress the problem, the government has enacted several provisions and formulated schemes to protect the right to land of the rural poor. Special courts, special laws and special procedures have been enacted, including the provision of legal aid, to resolve land disputes but they have not been effective in rendering justice and securing their lands.

The issue of land acquisition by the government affecting the poor has become a crucial one in recent years. Land laws are increasingly being framed and reframed to suit more the interests of the market forces than the interests of the poor rural peasants. The market forces represented by the MNCs and big business houses, in collusion with the government, have been involved, in the business of land grabbing belonging to the rural farmers. The government has been accused of selling agricultural lands at throw away prices to the private sector in spite of violent protests by the farmers. Overcome by neo-liberal exhortations, these public and private forces are setting up mega development projects, such as, Special Economic Zones (SEZs), Exclusive Economic Zones (EEZs), housing projects, manufacturing units, multiplexes, all across India in the name of development, which, though necessary for development, is happening at the cost of the rich agricultural lands belonging to poor farmers, and which defies all norms of sustainable development.[25]

With the increased acquisitions, land has become scarce, resulting in increase pressure on land. Consequently, land disputes have increased together with an increase in land litigation. While the better off farmers have made representations in the court, the poor farmers have suffered in the absence of the legal support and ignorance of legal aid laws thus making them more vulnerable and exploitable. Thousands of cases are pending in various civil and revenue courts, with no possibility of early solutions or remedies. In fact, in recent years, civil disputes have dominated over criminal matters in many states. For instance, out of the total legal aid applications received by the Maharashtra legal aid committee in 2009, a majority of these cases relate to land acquisition proceedings, appeals against orders passed by family courts, battles to get compensation from the state or disputes over ownership of land.[26]

Many of the poor litigants are unaware about the legal aid schemes and even if they do, they are unable to get things done in the complex legal system of India. The number of potential claims for many legal disputes – for example, missing land lease cases (called 'pattas'), for restoration of lands from which they have been ejected illegally, and for receipt of land they have been awarded in the land records but in fact have never possessed – have increased manifold in various courts. According to an estimate, about 2 per cent of lands in rural areas, 5 per cent in urban and 28 per cent in peri-urban areas are affected by land disputes. Land litigants and government authorities spend more than ₹ 750 crores per annum on settling land disputes.[27] These and many more social problems having legal dimensions in areas such as family disputes, property disputes, divorce, domestic violence, child exploitation, human trafficking etc. abound calling for immediate legal assistance to be provided to the poor and weak masses suffering at the hands of exploiters be it the government or private individuals. The Legal Services Authorities Act 1987, though a landmark enactment providing wide powers to the legal aid authorities, has not been able to make the desired impact in restoring justice to the poor people who are unable to afford legal services. The strengths of the Act has not yet been harnessed to its optimum giving rise to delay in justice and access to justice still remaining a distant dream for the depressed people.

Obstacles and Remedies

Many factors can be attributed to the unsatisfactory results achieved so far, i.e. since the inception of the Legal Services Authorities Act 1987. But the prime among them as observed by Justice Bhagwati, the principle architect of legal aid in India[28] is the 'lack of legal awareness' by the poor masses, the main victims, because of which the problem has got aggravated. People are still not aware of their basic rights due to which the legal aid movement has not achieved its goal yet. Ignorance of law has led to deprivation of rights and benefits to the poor. When people in urban areas are not sufficiently aware of their legal rights, one can realize the position at the lower levels, that is, at the village level. Poor farmers and rural labourers have suffered at the hands of the vested elements. They have been deprived of their land, animals and property because of the presence of vested elements who want to keep the rural masses ignorant and isolated from the legal, social and economic developments.[29]

The lack of legal awareness and knowledge among poor people, the prime sufferers, has perpetuated poverty and exploitation in underdeveloped regions of India. This, in turn, has led to the erosion of people's faith in the administration of justice, as more violence can be seen in places where, on the one hand, the legal aid is not effective and, on the other hand, the agricultural lands of poor have been acquired in the name of development without providing any proper legal succour or remuneration. There have been increased instances of clashes between the farmers and the State as their lands, the only source of their livelihood, have been taken away and their approach to the court has also proved too difficult owing to their lack of legal awareness, judicial complexity and the costly legal system. In the absence of effective legal aid machinery, people are resorting to settle their disputes and protect their basic rights out of the court and in the streets, with more faith in their muscle power than in the rule of law. In backward and underdeveloped states, where the condition of poor is still pathetic and the legal system is not effectively working for them, the fear of anarchy arises.

This glaring situation can be stemmed by imparting legal knowledge to the deprived rural masses about their basic legal rights as well as by providing them free legal aid and assistance. They should be educated about their basic rights. This can be done with the help of the NGOs who have a wider reach extending to the villages and greater appeal with the rural people and poor communities. The legal aid movement has to go to the grassroot level and help to discover, identify and solve the problems and difficulties of the poor. This process has to be supplemented by a systematic and sustained imparting of legal knowledge and information to the rural people, increasing their legal capacity and equipping them with free legal aid so as to take up their grievances with the state through legal means and channels.

Weak and ineffective implementation of legal aid provisions is another potential source of tension for the poor and suppressed people. As mentioned before, there is no dearth of good judgments and legislations on free legal aid. The only problem is with regard to their implementation. In many cases, these legal provisions have not been implemented at all, besides their weak implementation. As a result, they have proven to be 'glorious myths for the poor people'[30] Thus, the need of the hour is to focus and emphasize on the effective and meaningful implementation of the laws which have already been passed instead of bothering for enacting new laws. The role of legal aid in this direction is of immense significance, as it has the potential to restore the rule of law, people's faith in the legal administration and create an egalitarian society where the laws and its benefits are not known and exercised only by the rich and powerful but also by the disadvantaged people. The institution of legal aid can thus act as a bridging device between the 'haves' and 'have nots'.

Another important reason for the inefficient delivery of legal aid in India is the role of lawyers. Their less than enthusiastic role has, among other reasons, acted as barriers to justice for the poor. Their lack of motivation for delivering legal aid has resulted 'in a constant backlog of about 2.53 crore cases in civil and criminal courts. Although crores of cases are disposed off every year, there is an influx of at least 1.42 crore new cases.'[31]

As it is not a lucrative field for lawyers, there are not very many lawyers specializing in legal aid. Even lawyers serving on legal aid committees or placed in the lawyers' legal aid panel, do not take much interest in the case primarily due to the low fees paid to them. They do not have any motivation or the desire to work sincerely and diligently for the case and bring it to a successful end in a reasonable period of time. Rather, the norm has been that legal aid has become a field for the new, inexperienced and junior lawyers whereas it is a specialized field, requiring skills and experience to defend a disadvantaged and poor litigant against his powerful opponent which may be a state or an individual person.

Many a times, lawyers assigned to provide legal aid and paid out of public funds do not faithfully represent their clients, casting serious doubt on the credibility of the scheme of legal aid provided to weaker sections of society. Some lawyers engaged by legal aid committees hold their clients' cases for ransom by employing delay tactics. These lawyers compel their clients, many innocent, to pay additional amounts of money to them, even though they are supposed to obtain their fee from the legal aid committee. One of the reasons for this is that the remuneration paid to lawyers by the legal aid committee is very low and sometimes does not even meet the lawyer's incidental expenses. As a result, the quality of legal aid work gets compromised which defeats the whole concept of legal aid.

Thus, what is required, among other things as suggested above, is also to improve the remuneration of the lawyers doing legal aid cases. As is too well known, free service is incompatible with quality. To maintain quality, proper payment to lawyers dealing in legal aid cases must be paid and only this can ensure greater commitment of lawyers to legal aid delivery and preserve the quality of legal aid. Also, the eligibility of lawyers to be selected for legal aid committees should be enhanced to include only those lawyers who have developed expertise in the fields in which poor persons face problems. Experience and age qualifications should also be incorporated in the selection process. Besides, senior and experienced lawyers should be persuaded and promoted to deliver free legal aid. Further, the law ministry should ensure the senior lawyers do at least 10 cases a year free of charge.[32]

The role of the voluntary agencies too has been less than satisfactory. Their performance is marked by a lack of professionalism, absence of committed volunteers, legal experts and advisors. There is no systematic training for the volunteers, no incentive for them to work for the deprived classes and no real involvement of law students, researchers and the teaching faculty in legal aid work that is capable of changing the present scenario to the advantage of the hapless masses who wait endlessly for succour from the government or the voluntary organizations.

Concepts like legal aid clinics and legal aid hospitals, though sounding highly technical and sophisticated, have produced little social capital worthy of solving the pressing social and economic problems of the disadvantaged classes. In all, the legal aid scenario, though have advanced over the years, has yet to travel a great distance before a semblance of an egalitarian society could become visible to an observer or a researcher.

Conclusion

The demand for justice is as vital for the desperate and vulnerable masses as much as it is for the affluent but undoubtedly it is much more for the deprived people who need special assistance from the State to access justice to protect themselves against the misuse of State power or of an individual's power. Thus, if suitable measures can be taken to plug the many gaps, as discussed above, in the existing legal aid delivery system, the situation can be improved to a great extent. The change in the condition of the poor which is very much required and, which unfortunately is not much visible at the moment, can be affected if sincere and effective steps are taken in right earnest and unless this is done, perhaps the glorious legislation and neat plans for the hapless masses will prove futile in realizing the dreams of social justice through the legal aid mechanism.

Notes

1. A. Buck, N.J. Balmer and P. Pleasence, 'Social Exclusion and Civil Law, The Experience of Civil Justice Problems Among Vulnerable Groups', *Social Policy and Administration*, 2005, 39(3), pp. 302–322; A. Currie, 'The Legal Problems of Everyday Life' in A Rebecca L. Sandefur (ed.), *Access to Justice*, Bingley, UK: Emerald, 2009.
2. *The American Heritage Dictionary*, New York: Houghton Miffin, 2009.
3. *Collins Standard, sixth edition* (7 July 2003).
4. *Encyclopaedia Britannica*, 2008.
5. *Collins English Dictionary*, 10th edition, London: Harper Collins, 2009.
6. Lord Denning, *What Next in the Law*, London: Butterworths, 1982.
7. George Buhler (tr. and ed.), *The Laws of Manu*, Sacred Books of the East, vol. 25, Oxford: Clarendon, 1886.
8. Justice P.N. Bhagwati and Justice Trevore Harris of Calcutta 'Law as Struggle: Public Interest Litigation in India', Rajeev Dhawan (ed.), 36 JILI 325, 1994.
9. Roma Mukherjee, *Women, Law & Free Legal Aid*, New Delhi: Deep & Deep, 1998.
10. *Janardhan Reddy* v. *State of Hyderabad*, AIR (1951) SC 217.

11. *Tara Singh* v. *State of Punjab*, AIR (1951) SC 411.
12. *Maenka Gandhi* v. *UOI*, AIR (1978) SC 597.
13. *Sunil Batra* v. *Delhi Administration*, AIR (1978) 4 SCC 494.
14. *Hussainara Khatoon* case, AIR (1980) 1 SCC 98.
15. *Khatri(II)* v. *State of Bihar* (*Khatri(II)* v. *State of Bihar* (1981) AIR, 1 SCC 623 (Bhagalpur Blinded Prisoners' case).
16. *Sukhdas* v. *Union Territory of Arunachal Pradesh*, AIR (1986) S.C. 991.
17. *Hussainara* v. *Home Secretary, State of Bihar*, AIR (1979) SC 1377.
18. Website of 'The Legal Services Authority Act, 1987'. <http://lawmin.nic.in/la/subord/nalsa.htm>. Also see, <http://www.karmayog.org/centralgovtacts/centralgovtacts_6593.htm>.
19. Ibid.
20. Ibid.
21. Ibid.
22. *India Year Book 2010*: Justice and Law.
23. *Hussainara* v. *Home Secretary*, State of Bihar, AIR 1979 SC 1377.
24. *Khatri* v. *State of Bihar*, A.I.R. 1981 SC 928.
25. S.G. Vombatkere, Special Economic Zones – Neo-Zamindari Zones? in *Mainstream*, 9th December 2006, 9. In this issue, there is an appeal with a demand for 'a national moratorium on all acquisition and displacement till a national consensus is arrived at'. The appeal makes a demand for 'a national policy for overhauling the land acquisition, SEZ and related acts and for providing an effective blueprint to protect the interests and concerns of all the affected persons'. The appeal is signed by Justice V.R. Krishna Iyer, the former judge of the Supreme Court, and many academics, such as Rajni Kothari and other public persons (p. 5).

    Also see 'Political Economy of India? Special Economic Zones: a Conceptual Frame Work' 23 April 2011, *Times of India*, 'Farmers take RIL to court over SEZ land acquisition', 11 November 2006, p. 15; The Hitavada, Govt to go slow on IT SEZs, 9 November 2006, p. 13.).
26. Kartikeya, 'Begging for Legal Aid', TNN, 11 June 2009. <http://articles.timesofindia.indiatimes.com/2009-06-11/mumbai/28194188_1_legal-aid-anjali-waghmare-new-lawyer>.
27. 'On Legal Aid to Secure Land Rights to the Rural Poor: Role of Government, NGOs and Paralegals'; <http://www.legallyindia.com/Events-calendar-and-law-school-conferences/556-Legal-Aid-to-Secure-Land-Rights-to-the-Rural-Poor>.
28. Report of Committee for Implementing Legal Aid Schemes 1981. This Committee was constituted by the Government of India had, by a resolution dated 26 September 1980 under the chairmanship of Mr Justice P.N. Bhagwati to monitor and implement legal aid programmes on an uniform basis in all the States and Union Territories. CILAS evolved a model scheme for legal aid programmes applicable throughout the country by which

several legal aid and advice Boards were set up in the States and Union Territories.

29. Prachi P. Prabhu, Legal Aid : A Myth or Reality? <http://docs.google.com/viewer?a=v&q=cache:ORsFw6kAs2oJ:www.lawyrs.net/file/publications/367-LEGAL%2520AID-Article.doc+prachi+p.+prabhu-+LEGAL+AID%E2%80%94A+MYTH+OR+REALITY.+Published+in+the+journal&hl=en&gl=uk&pid=bl&srcid=ADGEESiMFRW_bhqCYmkahJ0-OFGzUKScUdxuJDCLIqcXEcoRb6PUKLOCEEwweWaA5WrvWsk8VbElfNLTOfOQ8-V4ZUtHQmmLvDz-TILGg-u2x6oLQFk86E0ILBoEbbchHQsICthHPyiv&sig=AHIEtbRrXKIyA2VOI3WvMC6kK6dKoDIgEw>.
30. Prachi P. Prabhu, Legal Aid – A Myth or Reality? ibid.
31. Rashmi Raman and Nisha Venkataraman, 'Grafting Faith: Legal Aid Services in India', Paper prepared for the 3rd International Conference on Therapeutic Jurisprudence, 7–9 June 2006, Perth, Western Australia.
32. Deepshikha, Role of Advocates in Implementation of Legal Aid Schemes. 22 November 2009. <http://www.legalserviceindia.com/article/l396-Role-Of-Advocates-In-Implementation-of-Legal-Aid-Schemes.html>.

Part III

Gender Perspectives of Social Justice

17

Gender and Development

Theoretical Perspectives

Mohit Bhattacharya

Although 'engendering development' is nowadays a much talked about topic, yet there seems to be a less than adequate understanding of the basic concepts and issues involved in this crucial development dialogue. The researchers, students, policy planners and administrators need, therefore, to have some clarity about the basic concepts, theories, and discourses that stimulate the gender development debate. This is necessary in the interest of better analysis and understanding of the gender-related development issues and to properly integrate gender interests and needs into policies and programmes.

It is now widely acknowledged that in India, despite many spectacular advances in different sectors, there remains an undeniable gap between women and men regarding their political, economic, and social conditions. Referring to the Indian situation, Dreze and Sen wrote[1]: 'Inequality between men and women is one of the most crucial disparities in many societies, and this is particularly so in India.' In this context, we can refer to Martha Nussbaum's classic[2] – *Women and Human Development: The Capabilities Approach* – which starts with the startling statement: 'Women in much of the world lack support for the fundamental functions of a human life'. Referring to India, Nussbaum observes: 'even when they (women) live in a constitutional democracy such as India, where they are equals in theory, they are second-class citizens in reality'.

In this connection, the following comment from the UNDP's landmark *Human Development Report*, 1997 is worth our quotation:

> A creative commitment to gender equality will strengthen every area of action to reduce poverty – because women can bring new energy, new insights, and a new basis for organization.

Gender-Blind Development

Discussions on 'development' have been going on for a pretty long time with considerable sophistication and heated debates since the emergence of the Third World in the post-World War II international scene. The specificity of 'gender' issue as a central theme in development discourse is, however, of recent origin. For the first time, the clarion call came from the *Human Development Report*, 1995 as it cautioned: 'Human Development, if not engendered, is endangered'. The Report sounded a timely warning that human welfare consists of the welfare of both women and men. Many field researchers have revealed glaring disparities among men and women in terms of 'rewards and deprivations'. As it has been pointed out[3]:

> Women and men share many aspects of living together, collaborate with each other in complex and ubiquitous ways, and yet end up – often enough – with very different rewards and deprivations. From looking at the state of advantages and deprivations that women and men respectively have, there is an important need to look at the contrast between (*i*) the efforts and sacrifices made by each, and (*ii*) the rewards and benefits respectively enjoyed. This contrast is important for a better understanding of gender injustice in the contemporary world. The exacting nature of women's efforts and contributions, without commensurate rewards, is a particularly important subject.

Our effort in this paper is to identify the contemporary theoretical feminist perspectives in terms of perceived problems for women, their ability to solve them, focus areas for improvement, and suggest strategies for reaching development aims.

Three Perspectives

To enable an understanding of the situation concerning women and gender in relation to development, an analytical framework consisting of three main theoretical feminist perspectives in international development policies has been quite popular. Applied as analytical tools, these consisted of:

- Ester Boserup's perspective of Women's role in economic development (WID)
- Women and Development (WAD)
- Gender and Development (GAD)

Ester Boserup's book[4] *Woman's Role in Economic Development* was first published in 1970 and became unique at the time of its publication due to her groundbreaking perspective, with findings and statistics showing how women were affected by economic development. Boserup challenged the trickle-down effect of development, but she was unable to free herself from the basic framework of the then reigning development theory – 'modernization theory'. At the time of Boserup's writing, the idea of modernization assumed that a trickle-down effect of economic development would benefit all. Boserup indicated that a possible trickle-down effect of development would not benefit men and women equally. She also described the division of labour between men and women in three different development stages, the rural stage, the urban stage and the transitional stage from rural to urban society. These different environments implied a variation of possibilities and hardships for women. Boserup criticized the modernization theory in the sense that development would not be equally beneficial. At the same time, she could not break away from the spell of modernization theory, which stated that a developing country's development goal was to become an industrial country. To be able to reach the industrial stage of development it had to undergo the same stages that had already been passed by the developed countries.

Women in Development (WID)

The first approach, commonly known as Women in Development (WID) approach, was based on theories of modernization and liberal feminism. These theories evolved into a perspective that aimed to integrate women in the development process. Following the empirical findings of Ester Boserup in the 1970s, the feministic theory embodied in the WID perspective became widespread. The WID theory continued to challenge the assumption that modernization alone would increase gender equality.

The WID perspective continued to exist within the modernization paradigm, with the intention to develop countries by adopting Western technologies, institution and values. The perspective emphasized on equal opportunities for women, which originated in a liberal perspective on feminism. The liberal conceptions agreed on the need of a defined line between the public sphere that was regulated by the government and the private sphere, which was untouchable by the government. Maintaining a clear line between the public and private sphere was according to liberal feminism necessary, in order to preserve liberty. Policies were proposing the removal of discriminatory practices in institutions or the creation of alternative institutions that supported women. The increase of female representation in elected and appointed positions in the government was also of concern for liberal feminists.

To enable the inclusion of women in the developing process, women-oriented policies were needed with the ambition to enhance women's efficiency and consequently advance the economic development. This required improvements in the access to education, training, property and credit to be able to improve and facilitate the possibility of employment. Women were supposed to be integrated, often in activities that were specific for women. In these projects they were usually viewed as passive recipients.

The WID approach increased women's income, improved their health and strengthened their resources in the short-term, but the sustainability faltered because it disregarded the unequal relationship between men and women. The focus on Women in Development thereby tended to be blind to the roles and responsibilities of men regarding women's position in society. This conformed to the liberal feminist position as it was less concerned about empowerment or bringing about radical change in the position of women in society.

Obviously, the WID approach has some shortcomings. It does not question the existing social structures or explore the nature and sources of women's oppression. Nor does it take into account the effects of colonialism, capitalism and imperialism on women's lives. WID sees women merely as a unit of analysis, and fails to consider the implications of race, class and gender having significant bearings on women's oppression.

Yet, the 'Women in Development approach' is still commonly used by international organizations including the World Bank, the United Nations, and others.

Women and Development (WAD)

The second approach called 'Women and Development' or WAD is primarily a neo-Marxist, feminist approach with a strong emphasis on the importance of social class and the exploitation of the 'Third World'. This approach emerged in the second half of the 1970s in response to the limitations of modernization approach.

WAD gets some of its theoretical base from 'dependency theory', whose main thesis is that, at the global level, 'developed' regions became developed through the penetration and exploitation of other 'underdeveloped' regions.

The WAD approach assumes that women have always been active participants in development. Advocates of this approach say that both the paid and unpaid labour of women is essential to development. In contrast to WID, the WAD approach believes that under global capitalism, which is essentially based on exploitation and iniquitous distribution of wealth, it is futile to expect the end of women's oppression and exploitation.

The major criticism of the WAD approach is that it fails to undertake a full-scale analysis of the relationship between patriarchy and women's subordination. It implicitly assumes that women's participation will improve if institutional structures change. Although work which women do inside and outside homes is central to development, WAD preoccupies itself with the productive aspect at the expense of the reproductive side of women's work and lives.

Gender and Development (GAD)

Gender And Development (GAD), the third approach, emerged from grassroot organizations and the feminists from developing countries. It partly emerged as a critique against WID, additionally focusing on areas of interest that was not included in the previous perspectives. This was thereby a reaction to the perceived absence of what was viewed as fundamental factors that structured and maintained gender inequalities. The process of developing a new paradigm began in the early 1980s with a socialist-feminist approach that emphasized the relationship between men and women. The GAD-focus on improving women's position in society thereby replaced the WID approach. Women's status in society was perceived to be deeply affected by material conditions and their position in the economy. A perspective on 'Gender and Development' recognized the effect of patriarchal power in the societies at national, community and household level. Both the material conditions of women and patriarchal authority were defined and maintained by the accepted norms and values of gender relations in a specific society. This 'social construction of gender' was viewed as socially (not biologically) constructed patterns of behaviour with the possibility of being transformed if desired.

The 'Gender and Development (GAD) approach' uses a much more holistic perspective and recognizes the importance of social, economic, and political factors in women's lives. GAD is concerned with the social construction of gender, and welcomes the potential contributions of men, particularly men who share their concern with gender equity and social justice. GAD acknowledges women as agents of change rather than as passive recipients of development services. The focus of GAD is also to strengthen women's legal rights. This approach evolved from the WID in the late 1980s with an aim for full equality of women within the framework of economic development.

The socialist anchoring of the GAD perspective was also influenced by the envisioned society where the different structures of subordination (of women) are imagined as abolished. The GAD approach thereby interconnected other forms of oppression and social constructions by involving the issues of race, class, colonial history, culture and position in the international economic order and under diverse societal conditions in the South. These were key points for the Blacks and developing world feminists, who argued that policies should be grounded in the actual context of people's lives. They advocated a participatory process that would include all women who were concerned, converging with the socialist feminists in the GAD perspective on development. The GAD interventions addressed the unequal gender relations, which prevented inequitable development that usually obstructed women from full participation.

The GAD approach has, no doubt, been useful to the conduct of deeper and extensive research in feminist economic and social conditions; but its applicability to the problems of everyday world of women's living and working has been suspect as it proposes a re-examination of the way in which social structures and institutions affect women's oppression. In addition, its incorporation of 'men' within the more capacious 'gender' category has given rise to a suspicion that GAD's effectiveness would depend largely on the goodwill of men.

The DAWN

The plea for going beyond both the WID and the WAD approaches has been triggered by the query that neither addresses the fundamental factors that structure and maintain gender inequalities. This was the reason for the emergence of the GAD approach – also referred to as the 'empowerment approach' or 'gender-aware planning'.

A complementary stream of thought and movement, much broader in scope and more radical in spirit, emerged in the 1980s known as the DAWN (Development Alternatives with Women for a New Era). DAWN (Development Alternatives with Women for a New Era) surfaced in the 1980s as the groundbreaking network of feminists from the global South. The idea for DAWN arose at a meeting in Bangalore in 1984, when a group of feminists from the South assembled and mounted a comprehensive critique of the development model for the 1985 UN Third World Conference on Women in Nairobi. The platform that emerged from this meeting, *Development, Crisis and Alternative Visions: Third World Women's Perspectives* became the little blue bible of the women's movement for years to come. It collected local and regional experiences of women in the global South into a new analytical framework that changed the terms of debate on women's issues and development. DAWN's analysis focused on the ways that growth-oriented macro-economics, neo-colonial international relations and militarism connect and perpetuate the marginalization of women in the developing world. This platform, supported by the active participation of its staunch advocates and originators, revealed the flaws in the underlying principles and structure of the development agenda, injected the women's movement with a macro-economic perspective and initiated the conceptual change from the 'Women in Development' to the 'Gender and Development' approach. As a network of activist feminist scholars and researchers, DAWN works for economic and gender justice and sustainable democratic development. It provides a forum for thematic feminist research, analyses and advocacy on global issues – economic, social and political – affecting the livelihoods, living standards, rights and development prospects of women especially the poor and the marginalized women in the regions of the South. DAWN has inverted the traditional question: What kind of human development can best promote economic competitiveness and growth? Gita Sen, on behalf of DAWN, has posed instead the question: What kind of economic development can best promote human development? Sen has argued that if this became the central question of development, different answers would be sought and different policies would be designed and implemented.[5]

Concerning the issues of nationalistic or economic wars, the emergence of competitive trading blocs, and the changing role of multilateral institutions, DAWN has put three critical questions on the research agenda of the Southern feminists:

- What role can and should we play in bringing about internal peace?
- How will trading blocs affect our employment and responsibilities for livelihoods?
- How can we improve consciousness about development in cooperation with Northern groups?

The feminists of North and South are coalescing and synthesizing their research concerns. Alternative Women in Development (AltWID), a network of Northern feminists, based in Washington, DC, published a study of the impacts of Reaganomics on women in the United States, *Reagonomics and Women: Structural Adjustment US Style – 1980–1992* (AltWID, 1992). The study showed that Reaganomics had the same impacts on women in the United States as structural-adjustment policies have in the South – the joining ideological thread being neoclassical economics.

In another publication entitled *Breaking Boundaries: Women, Free Trade and Economic Integration,* AltWID explained why free trade is a women's issue. In their view, market policies are not gender blind and 'the impact of supply side policies has altered family life; relations between women, men and children; women's and men's roles; and women's relative economic status.' AltWID has been collaborating with feminist networks in the North and South on projects, conferences, and political strategies.

Feminist researchers in the North recognized the need to contextualize the discourse on development to show its effect on women and development. This is an application of the analytical strategies they used in critiquing the metanarratives of social theory to show its gendered and exclusionary nature.

Since the late 1980s, the neo-liberal ideas emanated posing a state vs. market debate under which preference had been given to 'market' on the plea of oversized state as a drain on public resources. The 'welfare state' and the 'bureaucratic administration' were targeted as inflating the state budget to the detriment of market expansion. State restructuring meant, under the circumstances, cut back on social overheads like health care and education costs. With the state roll-back philosophy, the trend was toward deinstitutionalizing people through early hospital discharges and closures of nursing homes and facilities for the disabled. Money had to be saved by closing hospitals and cutting school programs leading to slimmer state administration. It bode ill for women's job prospect and income as women used to fill the majority of state-financed jobs in health, social services, and education. These state jobs provided women with wages and employment conditions better than those in the private sector. With state restructuring, wages were frozen and jobs disappeared. The situation affected both women and men in terms of loss of employment and income and forced them into lower paying jobs in the private sector or the fast-growing informal economy.

We will have occasion to discuss later some of the new and innovative projects that came to be designed to confront this gloomy economic spectacle. In this endeavour to cope with the adverse economic situation, feminist movements and many progressive NGOs in the South had shown considerable ingenuity, as discussed in a separate section below.

Women, Environment, and Sustainable Development (WED)

The WED approach was sparked by grassroots women's experiences in 'Third World' social movements such as the Chipko, Narmada Valley, and Greenbelt movements[6]. It was also influenced by the experiences of women working for peace movements. In the US, the WED approach stemmed from the eco-feminist movement. Eco-feminism makes connections between the struggle for the dignity of women and respect for the different processes of life. Eco-feminist action is aimed at the preservation of the life of present and future generations, both male and female, in a human perspective and in a wide biological and cosmic perspective.

The WED approach covers a variety of areas including forestry, agriculture, irrigation, and water systems. The WED includes women's relationship to the environment in the context of economic development as well as the many harmful effects that the degradation of environment has had on women's lives. Examples include increased work burden to provide household necessities such as water and fuel, as well as the effects of air and water pollution. Local circumstances vary considerably in respect to the ecological zone as well as class, race, ethnicity and age. The origin of the term 'sustainable development' is to be traced to the famous Brundtland Report – *Our Common Future* – a path-breaking report on the theme (Brundtland was the Chairperson of the World Commission on Environment and Development that produced the Report as a prelude to the Earth Conference held at Rio de Janeiro in 1992). As defined by the Brundtland Commission, 'sustainable development' is 'development that meets the needs of the present without compromising the ability of future generations to meet their own needs'.

Kamla Bhasin[7] has identified the following components of sustainable development:

1. It must be in harmony with nature (if nature is to sustain us, we must sustain nature).
2. It must be people-centred and oriented (people have to be seen as the subjects, not the objects, of development).
3. It must be women-centred (recognizing the responsibility that women have always assumed for catering to the basic needs of society).
4. It must cater to the needs of the majority (consumption levels of the rich and industrialized world must be reduced).
5. There must be decentralization of decision-making and control over resources within countries and internationally.
6. Democracy must become more participatory and direct, unleashing the latent energies of the people.
7. At every level, sustainable development must promote the politics of peace, non-violence, and respect for life.

In short, sustainable development for many feminists from the South and the North implies a new kind of political, economic, social, and cultural system and a new value orientation. Also, this approach signifies a longer term planning perspective (as against instant use and throw perspective) taking account of locally based resources including human resources and 'local knowledge', treating 'nature and natural resources' as durable assets to be carefully pressed into development with an eye to their steady replenishment and regeneration.

Critics of WED Approach

The major criticism of the WED approach is the focus on the woman/nature and man/nature connections, which obscures the dynamic aspects of environmental degradation and how it affects different groups, women as well as men, over time. The wider changes necessary to halt environmental destruction and the process of environmental recovery is as much women's task as it is men's. In other words, larger societal development issues like 'environmental degradation' or 'poverty' need not be viewed in narrow man/woman duality term. It needs total synergic strength from everyone's concerted effort across the board to face up to the big civilizational challenges.

Policy Planning

Gender concerns need to be integrated with the overall development policies of public authorities at all levels of governance. Attempts are now being made to reposition the entire governance system in each country to have a practical reflection of 'gender concerns' in the overall governing system of different nations.

Mainstreaming

Governments in particular and other organizations including major international organizations like the World Bank, UNDP, etc. are seeking to advance gender equality and equity through the mainstreaming of gender in development planning, budgeting, project planning and implementation. 'Gender mainstreaming requires that gender be brought into the centre of discussions about development, and not marginalized as a 'woman's issue'.[8] Thus gender mainstreaming makes gender central to all aspects of development planning and practices. Broadly, it refers to the application of gender perspectives to all legal and social norms and standards, to all policy development, research, planning, advocacy, development, implementation, and monitoring as mandatory for all participatory institutions and agencies. Women's empowerment through gender mainstreaming is expected to bring about overall societal development by addressing gender inequalities in all aspects of development, across all sectors and programmes, especially in the decision-making structures at all governmental levels. The Commonwealth Secretariat[9] has come out with a model for achieving this in the shape of a Gender Management System

(GMS) – an integrated system of structures, mechanisms and processes for advancing gender equality and equity.

The Secretariat Manual rightly cautions that gender planning should not be seen as a separate, parallel process to mainstream development planning but should transform mainstream planning to address the needs of women and poor people generally through an economically, socially and environmentally sustainable process.

These shifting stands have occasioned an increasing space for policy initiatives and interventions in favour of poor women in the Third World. There has been a gradual shift in orientation of these policy approaches towards women from 'welfare', to 'equity' to 'anti-poverty' to 'efficiency' and finally to 'empowerment'.

World Bank Report, 2001

We have earlier referred to the landmark document of the World Bank entitled *Engendering Development*. While releasing the Report (mentioned at the beginning of this discussion) on *Engendering Development Through Gender Equality in Rights, Resources and Voice* (2001), the then World Bank President, James D. Wolfensohn, in his 'Foreword' to the Report, expressed anxiety that despite considerable advances in gender equality in recent decades, gender discrimination remains a problem in most parts of the world. To quote his profound remark:

> The nature and extent of the (gender) discrimination vary considerably across countries and regions. In no region of the developing world are women equal to men in legal, social, and economic rights. Gender gaps are widespread in access to and control of resources, in economic opportunities, in power, and political voice. Women and girls bear the largest and most direct costs of these inequalities – but the costs cut more broadly across society, ultimately harming everyone. For these reasons, gender equality is a core developmental issue – a development objective in its own right. It strengthens countries' abilities to grow, to reduce poverty, and to govern effectively. Promoting gender equality is thus an important part of a development strategy that seeks to enable *all people* – women and men alike – to escape poverty and improve their standard of living. Economic development opens many avenues for increasing gender equality in the long run; but growth alone will not deliver the desired results.

What is urgently needed is an institutional environment that provides equal rights and opportunities for women and men and policy measures that address persistent inequalities.

The World Bank Report draws attention to the phenomenon of worldwide spread of gender discrimination in many dimensions of life, despite considerable advances in gender equality in recent decades.

Against this background, the World Bank Report argues for a three-part strategy for promoting gender equality:

- *Reform institutions to establish equal rights and opportunities for women and men.* Reforming legal and economic institutions is necessary to establish a foundation of equal rights and equal opportunities for women and men. Because the law in many countries continues to give unequal rights to women and men, legal reforms are needed, particularly in family law, protection against violence, land rights, employment, and political rights.
- *Foster economic development to strengthen incentives for more equal resources and participation.* Rising income and falling poverty levels tend to reduce gender disparities in education, health, and nutrition. Higher productivity and new job opportunities often reduce gender inequalities in employment. And investments in basic water, energy, and transportation infrastructure help reduce gender disparities in workloads.
- *Take active measures to redress persistent disparities in command over resources and political voice.* Because institutional reforms and economic development may not be sufficient – or forthcoming – active measures are needed to redress persistent gender disparities in the short to medium term.

In the light of what has been stated above it is now being impressed on country governments, especially in the developing nations, that the issue of women's development needs to be centrally situated in any worthwhile national, regional and local level planning exercise.

Concluding Observations

There is a gradual realization now dawning on most policy planners that more than anything else 'awareness raising' is of crucial importance in any attempt to empowering women. This sentiment has been well expressed in a recent discussion paper by a former lady parliamentarian:[10] 'That the development model has bypassed women is a generally accepted idea today; so the question of development is now rejected altogether so that 'empowerment' becomes a mere cultural matter, a question of advocacy and awareness raising. Even while all those 'fruitless' general welfare measures like public distribution system and education and health subsidies are taken away, we think we may succeed in raising self-confidence in women, in instilling into them an 'awareness' of empowerment. We think she can become, through her mere awareness, a participant in the process of social change.'

The prevailing mood in India has been well documented in a recently published anthology entitled *Empowerment of Women: Emerging Dimensions* at the end of a discourse initiated by the National Seminar at the University of Allahabad in 2005 on 'Women and Political Process in India: Need for Empowerment'. To quote the editor of the volume in this context[11]:

> Effective change cannot be brought about without a simultaneous movement to change the social and economic structures and the culture i.e. social values and attitudes. A social welfare approach has now given way to a gender centric paradigm of development which would be able to enhance the central human capabilities essential for human dignity. Power sharing will inevitably occur when women are able to command economic resources and when they are educated. As we enter the new millennium the state initiatives will continue to play an important role, but (this) must be backed by a broad based women's movement.

This sounds like an avid expectation and a call for definitive action. One can only hope and pray that there will be in coming years a conjoint effort by the assertive civil society activists and the responding public authorities.

Notes

1. Jean Dreze and Amartya Sen, *India: Economic Development and Social Opportunity*, Delhi: Oxford University Press, 1996.
2. Cambridge: Cambridge University Press, 2000.
3. S. Anand and A. Sen, 'Gender Inequity in Human Development: Theories and Measurement', Occasional Paper 19, *Paper Prepared for the Human Development Report 1995*, New York: UNDP, 1995.
4. Ester Boserup, *Woman's Role in Economic Development*, London: Earthscan, 1970.

5. Gita Sen and Caren Grown, *Development Crises and Alternative Visions: Third World Women's Perspectives*, London: Earthscan, 1988.
6. See, in this connection, Vandana Shiva, *Staying Alive: Women, Ecology and Development*. New Delhi: Kali for Women, 1988.
7. K. Bhasin, 'Some Thoughts on Development and Sustainable Development' *Women in Action*, 1993, 1, pp. 10–18.
8. Alan Greig, Michael Kimmel, and James Lang, 'Men, Masculinities and Development: Broadening our Work Towards Gender Equality', UNDP, *Gender in Development Series*, May 2000.
9. See in this context the imaginatively brought out practical user-friendly manual by the Commonwealth Secretariat: Viviene Taylor, *Gender Mainstreaming in Development Planning: A Reference Manual for Governments and Other Stakeholders*, London: Commonwealth Secretariat, June 1999.
10. Malini Bhattacharya, 'Paradigm Shifts in Women's Studies', in Arunabha Ghosh (ed.), *Women in India: Problems, Potentialities and Power*, Kolkata: Mitram, 2010.
11. Krishna Gupta, 'Women Empowerment in India – Emerging Dimensions', in Krishna Gupta (ed.), *Empowerment of Women: Emerging Dimensions*, New Delhi: S. Chand, 2010.

18

Women's Rights as Human Rights

Mahendra Prasad Singh

Men and women equally partake in humanity by birth, notwithstanding the biological difference between them in terms of anatomy. Hence it is axiomatic that women's rights are human rights, rights that are naturally enjoyed by every human being by virtue of being human. The supposed vulnerability of women arising in the anatomical difference and procreative function cannot be construed to deduce the proposition that anatomy is destiny. Differences and disparities between men and women are, in fact, based on differential upbringing and conditioning among the genders, and are therefore socially constructed.

Nevertheless, with the possible exception of matrilineal societies, patriarchy has been an oppressive fact of history in practically all civilizations the world over. Moreover, among the variety of disparities such as the ones based on race, ethnicity, class, etc. gender disparities have been the most persistent and pernicious. With the rise of liberalism and democracy in modern times, other disparities came to be questioned earlier than those based on gender. This was for the reason that the distinction between the private and the public spheres in liberalism as also religion-based family laws of marriage and property generally kept the state out of bounds in these matters. This is an irony and a paradox in view of glaringly iniquitous conditions of women both nationally and internationally. In the world today, women notionally form half of the population, but perform nearly two-third of its work hours, receive one-tenth of world's income, and own less than one-hundredth of world's property. They are also fewer than 5 per cent of the heads of governments and lower than 10 per cent of parliamentarians (popularly elected House). Their greater vulnerability to social, cultural, and economic discrimination, and to domestic and social violence and crime in normal as well as riotous and war situations are patent facts of life all over the world with variations only of degrees across countries and cultures and climes (Binion, 1995: 511).

Even in regard to political suffrage, women happened to be the last section of the population to be enfranchised. The problem of their social and economic empowerment has, in fact, proved to be much more complex and intractable. Even in terms of their political empowerment, they have still a long way to go. But what is notable is that the present is the most propitious time for the idea of gender equality. And no one can hold back an idea for too long whose time has come.

II

For reasons outlined above, when human rights are stated, all is not stated; it needs to be supplemented by women's rights as a special variant of human rights. Ideally, a time may come when the difference between human rights and women's rights may dissolve or become obsolescent. In that eventuality, feminism and humanism may become merged into one indistinguishable ideology or theory. That it has not happened in the past cannot be taken as an improbability in the future. For a basic lesson that philosophy of science teaches us is that the past cannot foreclose the future. There is a certain degree of fixity in the past, but the future is wide open. Indeed, entirely unanticipated developments in the future give us new ways of looking back at and reinterpreting the past.

Feminist theory made its appearance earlier at the level of individual social or political thinkers than at the level of collective political action by the peoples or nations. There have been at least three waves of feminism in the thought of individual political thinkers, in terms of my somewhat parsimonious version of a review of feminist writings by Rosemarie Tong (2003). Prominent voices in the first stage of feminist thought argued that the women must emulate the same traits and qualities as men in order to be their equal. Mary Wollstonecraft in the 18th century and John Stuart Mill in the 19th century illustrate this line of thinking.

Wollstonecraft in her monograph *A Vindication of the Rights of Women* (1792) observed that the society expected men to be educated in 'morals' whereas women were taught 'manners'. Men were supposed to be rational and abstract in their thinking, and strong, whereas women were thought to be sentimental, contingent, self-indulgent, and weak. The remedial equality with men could be attained, according to Wollstonecraft, if women cultivated the same virtues as men. John Stuart Mill, too, in his *On the Subjection of Women* (1869) lamented their subjugation and advocated that the society must provide the same rights and privileges as are enjoyed by men. This feminist perspective may be called the 'sameness' theorem of the feminist theory.

The second stage of the feminist thought may be called the 'difference' theorem of feminism as it stressed on the differences rather than the importance of being the same as men. This phase also came to be marked by some degree of cleavage between liberal feminists like Betty Friedan (1974) and radical feminists like Sulasmith Firestone (1970) and Mary Vetterling-Braggin (1982). In fact, liberal feminists largely continued the point of view of the British feminist thought of the 18th and 19th centuries mentioned above. As the first President of the National Organization for Women (NOW) in the USA, Friedan took the leading role in formulating a Bill of Rights for Women in 1967. Radical feminists asserted their sexuality androgynously and sought sexual pleasures of all types – heterosexual, lesbian, and autoerotic, celebrating the new developments in reproductive, contraceptive, and genetic technology as a factor reducing the vulnerability of women due to the biological difference with men (Firestone, 1970).

Some other radical feminists, on the other hand, refuted androgyny and masculinity and advocated the ideal of essential femaleness, predicated on 'gentleness, modesty, humility, supportiveness, empathy, compassionateness, nurturance, intuitiveness, sensitivity, unselfishness' (Vetterling-Braggin, 1982: 6).

Some yet other radical feminists emphasized the dangers of heterosexual sex as the prime cause of male domination, macho sadism and female masochism. Lesbianism to them appeared as a way to escape these dangers. Yet other feminists wished to discard artificial reproductive or unproductive techniques and rely on their natural capacity to procreate or refuse to procreate in order to enhance their utility and respect in male estimation (Corea, 1985).

The third stage of the feminist thought is marked by what may be called the 'diversity' theorem of feminism. According to this view, the women condition is not simply defined in terms of the female gender. It is significantly determined by the variables of race, religion, ethnicity, class, and age. Thus, the question of gender equality is confounded in a complex web of causation, almost a vicious circle. This diversity view of feminist thought finds its most acute expression in postmodern feminism that rejects any uniform foundational value of gender equality and allows a radical relativism of values contingent on variety of identities and subcultures. Thus gender emerges neither as a resultant of biology nor as an overarching social construction but as a conceptual grid through which radically different values can be interpreted or deconstructed and reconstructed (Lauretis, 1994).

III

At the level of collective political action by the peoples and nations, the earliest declaration of rights are human rights in general without any special or separate concern with the rights of women. The American Declaration of Independence made by the second Continental Congress attended by the delegates from the 13 rebellious English colonies on 4 July 1776, for example, simply stated: 'We hold these truths to be self-evident, that all men are created equal, that they are endowed by their creator with certain inalienable rights, that among these are Life, Liberty and the pursuit of Happiness.' The Declaration of the Rights of Man and Citizen made by the National Assembly of France in the wake of the French Revolution on 26 August 1789, 'resolved to set forth a solemn declaration of the natural, inalienable and sacred rights of man ...' The Declaration of the Rights of the People of Russia and of the Working and Exploited Peoples of the world made by the All Russian Congress of Soviets made in January 1918 set 'as its fundamental task the destruction of any exploitation of man by man, the complete abolition of the division of society into classes, the merciless suppression of the exploiters, the establishment of a socialist organization of society and the victory of socialism in all countries ...'

Among these early declarations of rights, the Karachi Resolution of the Indian National Congress (29–31 March 1931) was perhaps the first that proclaimed 'equal rights and obligations of all citizens, without any bar on account of sex.' This resolution presaged all the fundamental rights and directive principles of State policy that came to be guaranteed by the Constitution of independent India in 1950. However, the makers of the Indian Constitution stopped short of guaranteeing some special rights of women comparable to those provisionally guaranteed to the 'socially and educationally backward classes of citizens or for the Scheduled Castes and the Scheduled Tribes' (Article 15, clause 5; the latter added by the First Constitutional Amendment, 1951). Representational reservation for women to the tune of 33 per cent of the local government councils in rural and urban areas had to wait until the 73rd and 74th constitutional amendments in 1992/93 and the conforming laws enacted by the state legislatures subsequently. A proposed representational reservation for women in State Legislatures and Parliament has been debated for a decade but not yet enacted due to lack of consensus in the political class and political parties.

IV

Now, we come to some select international declarations of human rights and scan them from the feminist perspective. The Universal Declaration of Human Rights (UDHR) adopted by the General Assembly of the United Nations on 10 December 1948, provide a common standard of human rights worthy of 'achievement for all peoples and all nations' 'without distinction of any kind, such as race, colour, sex, language, religion political or other opinion, national or social origin, property, birth or other status' (Article 2). Here again we find a general prohibition against gender-related discrimination but no special rights or reverse discrimination in favour of women in view of their acute or abnormal backwardness.

The UDHR (1948) was subsequently supplemented by two additional declarations by the UN General Assembly: (a) the International Covenant on Civil and Political Rights (1966), and (b) the International Covenant on Economic, Social and Cultural Rights (1966). Both came into force in 1976 following ratification by the member-states. Both the covenants guarantee the human rights to every person, child or adult, regardless of any socio-economic-political differences, including those based on gender. The one and the only one age or gender-specific human rights promised under the civil and political rights covenant is that a death sentence shall not be imposed for crimes committed by a person below eighteen years of age and a pregnant woman (Article 5).

Feminists argue that given the grossly unequal status of women in the prevailing laws in most countries, a gender-blind law in reality works in favour of patriarchy. The ends of justice would not be served by anything less than an affirmative action or reverse discrimination.

From among the myriad of other international covenants and conventions, I intend to briefly refer to the three such documents: (a) Convention on the Elimination of All Forms of Discrimination Against Women adopted by the UN General Assembly in 1979 that came into force in 1981, (b) Declaration on the Right of Development adopted by the UN General Assembly in 1986, and (c) Convention on the Rights of the Child adopted by the UN General Assembly in 1989 and enforced in 1990. The convention on women's rights seeks to ensure complete equality with men before the law in all respects. It specifically also declares that the adoption by states of 'temporary special measures aimed at accelerating *de facto* equality between men and women shall not be considered discrimination as defined in the present convention' (Article 4, clause 1). This international sanction for affirmative action in favour of women is not evidently matched in the national laws, however.

The Declaration on the Right to Development declares development as 'an inalienable human right by virtue of which every human person and all peoples are entitled to participate in, contribute to and enjoy economic, social, cultural and political development, in which all human rights and fundamental freedoms can be fully realized' (Article 1, clause 1). The convention on the child rights in a very comprehensive charter ensuring protection against exploitation and conditions for proper development under parental care and material assistance and support by the state.

An analytical retrospective view on the evolution of human rights is suggestive of different stages through which they have developed. My teacher, political theorist Professor Christian Bay at the University of Alberta in Canada used to talk about the growth of three packages of rights, namely, the Blue Rights or the rights against the state engendered by the bourgeois revolutions in the UK, USA, and France; the Red Rights or the rights against hunger produced by the socialist revolutions in the Soviet Union, Eastern Europe, and the People's Republic of China; and the Green Rights or the rights to clean environment and healthy life created by the movements for ecological protection and sustainable development.

Similarly, others have talked about three generations of rights. The first generation rights are primarily concerned with civil and political rights born out of the liberal and democratic movements since the 19th century. These are the 'negative' rights against the arbitrary action by the State. The second generation rights are primarily related to social, economic, and cultural equality and social security typical of welfare and socialist states. The third generation rights include the more recent concern with environmental and developmental rights including special rights of women and children (Dev et. al., 1996: xi-xv).

The Vienna Declaration of Human Rights, proclaimed at a world conference to review the progress of UDHR (1948) and subsequently endorsed by the UN General Assembly, aptly remarks: 'All human rights are universal, indivisible and interdependent and interrelated' (Article 5). The Millennium Development Goals of the United Nations believe that we can end poverty by 2015. They reiterate: 'We are committed to making the right to development a reality for everyone and to freeing the entire human race from want' (paragraph 11). These goals need to be made part of the constitutions of the member-states for their entrenched and determined pursuit. For minorities and women, 'rights, equality, and development may not be achieved simply by putting them in the constitution and even in government policies. For them, the issue is not recognition of cultural distinctiveness. In fact, it may be recognition of different needs or meeting similar needs in appropriate ways' (Ghai and Cottrell, 2011: 147–148).

In addition to the foregoing universal or global human rights systems, there are three regional human rights systems in Europe, Americas, and Africa. The European human rights system comprises two major treaties: the European Convention of Human Rights and Fundamental Freedoms (1950) and the European Social Charter (1961). As monitoring and enforcement mechanisms the European Commission of Human Rights and the European Court of Human Rights were instituted. Now the former has become obsolete and replaced by the court itself, which accepts applications complaining violations from individuals as well as states. The Inter-American human rights system emerged with the adoption of the Americas' Declaration of Rights and Duties of Man in April 1948, being the first regional human rights instrument of a general nature, predating the UDHR (1948) by more than six months. Alongside were also set up the Inter-American Commission on Human Rights and the Inter-American Court of Human Rights. The third and most recent of the regional systems of human rights is the African Charter of Human and Peoples' Rights (1981). It was first adopted under the aegis of the Organization of African Unity, which was subsequently replaced by the African Union. It is monitored and interpreted by the African Commission on Human and Peoples' Rights set up in 1987. An African Court on Human and Peoples' Rights is also mooted under a protocol to the Charter adopted in 1998 under which the foregoing Commission is proposed to be incorporated into the Court. The operationalization is still in process at this writing.

V

In view of all-pervasive patriarchy and the diversity theorem of postmodern feminism discussed above, the full realization of women's human rights would not be a cakewalk. It will require a concerted strategy of action by the state, civil society, market, and national and international organizations to actualize the goals of gender equality and justice advocated in the feminist thought and national and international declarations of human rights surveyed above. To my mind, constitutional entrenchment of these rights, conforming laws and public policies, including affirmative action by way of special rights such as reservations on the part of nation-states, hold the key to the achievement of women's rights as human rights in India and the world at large.

The human rights texts that we have rapidly reviewed above are distinguishable into at least the following categories: political thought/theory, national declarations, national constitutional or legal bill of rights, regional human rights instruments, and UN-UDHR and other universal international declarations and conventions. If we assess these texts in terms of degrees of freedom as to their formulation, if not implementation, the free will and imagination enjoyed by a political thinker is unparalleled, followed by an empirical political theorist working under the double binds of rational imagination and normative justification, on the one hand, and the constraints of factual evidence, on the other. If formulation and implementation are jointly considered, a national human rights charter emerges as the most efficacious proposition for the simple reason that a sovereign nation-state that produces it is not dependent on any other power to beg for its implementation. The case of regional and universal declarations is different. Their formulation, declaration, ratification, and implementation are all in stages dependent on the sovereign will of the high contracting parties, mostly or all members of the United Nations.

Nevertheless, as we have argued above, women's rights even within the domain of domestic jurisdiction of nation-states still leave much to be desired, and they need instruments of special rights in the form of protective reservation or affirmative action. In the international domain, both globally and regionally, a lot still depends on the sovereign will of the state, though women's rights may be undertaken as a political mission animated by new ideas in national government, international relations, and organizations such as 'governance' and 'cosmopolitan democracy'. Governance goes beyond the structure of government and brings in administration in collaboration with the institutions of civil society like non-governmental organizations (NGOs) and the market (World Bank, 1991; Rosenau, 1999). Cosmopolitan democracy refers to new developments allowing civil and economic relations among communities across international boundaries in international law without negating state sovereignty, rather jointly facilitated by the neighbouring states in the supranational region (Held, 1994; Archibugi, 2008).

References

Agarwal, Bina, *A Field of One's Own: Gender and Land Rights in South Asia*, New Delhi: Cambridge University Press, 1996.

Archibugi, Daniele, *The Global Commonwealth of Citizens: Towards Cosmopolitan Democracy*, Princeton: Princeton University Press, 2008.

Bakshi, P.M., *The Constitution of India*, eleventh ed., Delhi: Universal Law Publishing, 2011.

Baxi, Upendra, *The Future of Human Rights*, New Delhi: Oxford University Press, 2008.

Binion, Gale, 'Human Rights: A Feminist Perspective', *Human Rights Quarterly*, 1995, Vol. 17(3).

Corea, Gena, *The Mother Machine: Reproductive Technologies from Artificial Insemination to Artificial Wombs*, New York: Harper and Row, 1985.

Dev, Arjun, Indira and Supta Das, *Human Rights: A Source Book*, New Delhi: Indian Council of Educational Research and Training, 1996.

Firestone, Sulasmith, *The Dialectic of Sex*, New York: Bantam Books, 1970.

Friedan, Betty, *The Feminine Mystique*, New York: Dell, 1974.

Ghai, Yash and Jill Cottrell, *The Millennium Declaration, Rights, and Constitutions*, New Delhi: Oxford University Press for UNDP, 2011.

Held, David, 'Democracy: From City-States to a Cosmopolitan Order?' in Wolfgang Momsen's *The Polity Reader in Social Theory,* Cambridge: Polity Press, 1994, Chapter 29.

Lauretis, Terrecy de, 'The Essence of the Triangle, or Taking the Risks of Essentialism Seriously', in N. Schor and E. Weed, (eds.), *The Essential Difference,* Bloomington: Indiana University Press, 1994.

Mill, John Stuart, *On the Subjection of Women*, New York: Fredrick A. Stokes Company, 1911, first published 1869.

Rosenau, James N., 'Towards an Ontology for Global Governance' in Martin Hewson and Thomas Sinclair (eds.) *Approaches to Global Governance Theory*, Albany: State University of New York Press, 1999.

Singh, Ujjwal Kumar (ed.), *Human Rights and Peace: Ideas, Laws, Institutions and Movements*, New Delhi: Sage Publications, 2009.

Tong, Rosemarie, 'Gender and Sexual Discrimination', in Hugh LaFollette (ed.), *The Oxford Handbook of Practical Ethics*, New York: Oxford University Press, 2003, pp. 219–244.

Vetterling-Braggin, Mary, *'Feminity', 'Masculinity' and 'Androgyny': A Modern Philosophical Discussion*, Totowa: Roman & Littlefield, 1982.

Wollstonecraft, Mary, *A Vindication of the Rights of Women*, London: Penguin, 1988, first published, 1792.

World Bank, *World Development Report, 1991: The Challenge of Development,* New York: Oxford University Press, 1991..

19

Women and Politics of Violence

An Essay on Attitudinal Fundamentalism

Chandrakala Padia

Women are everyday subject to violence throughout the globe. They are *aliens* within their families, societies, states and also within the international community. It is a tragedy that the myths that have long sustained woman's inferiority, continue to influence modern society. Most of the atrocities committed against her are justified in the name of tradition and culture. One of the prime reasons for treating women in this manner is the internalization of some of the discriminatory attitudes by the members of the society.

This can be termed as 'attitudinal fundamentalism', the disease which has spread like a virus in the blood of our system. The roots of this ailment lie in three major factors: predominance of male-centric attitudes in philosophy at all levels, be it methodology, epistemology or metaphysics; systemic and structural mechanism of patriarchal control of women; and economic, social and political predominance of man and subsequent dependency of woman. The solution lies in challenging modern literary canons and privileged traditions of cultural interpretations, creating world-wide awareness against such a degrading treatment of woman, and also in deconstructing false understandings of experience, subjectivity, identity and consciousness.

However, the sphere of the present paper is limited to the analysis of fundamentalism at the philosophical level. It tries to project how, since the dawn of civilization, most of the philosophers have adopted a viewpoint which totally overlooks the experiences of women and often supports such ideas which put them in a position of pure dominance and servility. I would like to begin my paper with a quotation by Catharine A. MacKinnon:

> We need to know the inequality of the sexes is lived out, threaded from one moment to the next through million of lifetimes of habit into individual identities and social relations. We need to know more about how women experience and respond to being second class, from unconsciousness and denial and collaboration in consciousness and resistance and confrontation. We need to know precisely how the benefits and burdens of this system are allocated – including the way showcase indulgences to be a few women in a rich liberal state purchase legitimacy for a system that functions nationally and internationally at the expense of all women. We need to know how this system gives each, woman a survival stake in the system that is killing her.[1]

Fundamentalism in Philosophy

Traditional philosophy, throughout, has been shaped by men who have evaluated the whole universe on the basis of their experiences, their values, and their views of the world. Even the academic feminist philosophers were educated in the philosophical traditions of these men only. The philosophical methods, employed by the traditional philosophers have specifically undermined women's values, and have made her experiences invisible. Their writings suffer from 'value hierarchy', and 'normative dualism'. The former is reflected in their attaching greater value to what they consider as higher – men, culture, minds, or reason, and lesser value to what they treat as lower-women, nature, bodies or emotions. The latter is reflected in their interpreting things always in terms of exclusive disjunctions – mind/bodies, reason/emotion, man/woman, and so on. Caren J. Warren calls it as the 'logic of domination' – an attempt to justify the subordination of the lower by the higher.[2]

Thus, the traditional mode of thinking have defined the methods and subject matter of philosophy in ways that undervalue women's experiences and refrain them to move from the position of objects to position of subjects, of lower, and of agent.

At the Methodological Level

Let me first explain this fundamentalism at the methodological level. If we look to the method recommended by history, we discover that in spite of difference of opinion among the philosopher, the method they choose is male oriented.[3] The reasons are manifold.

Male philosophers have generally been inclined towards abstract general thought and tend to find universals clearer and more comfortable than particulars. Women, however, think most readily in terms of particulars. Male philosophers seek objective truth and have often believed that *emotion and personal feeling are impediments to truth,* since they can seldom be generalized objectively; the women scholars consider *direct personal experience an important component of truth*, and pay particular attention to the emotional content of claims.[4] Feminists, however, believe that a neutral approach often fails to understand the particularity and emotionality of the truth it tries to discover.

One more flaw of the traditional method is its adherence to single discipline which comes in the way of establishing truth. A genuine collective cross disciplinary research is required for discovering the truth. A theory that does not contribute to political change is of only limited interest. To quote Janice Moulton:

> By making truth an all or nothing affair, and encouraging us to seek any hole in a colleague's argument by which her/his position might be demolished, we foster a rather frightening model of the pursuit of truth.[5]

In fact, what has been claimed to be objective and universal by the male philosophers, is in reality the male point of view. How can any statement be treated as objective and universal if it does not incorporate women's experiences also. Moreover, even women's experience cannot be treated as absolutely true because women experience within patriarchy. Hence they often suffer from a bias in their perspective.

The attempt should be to rid them off from the shackles of patriarchal society and then learn from their experiences. Then only, any perspective or thought can be treated as authentic.

At the Epistemological Level

There is all pervading fundamentalism at the epistemological level throughout Western epistemology. The question 'how do you know' is always answered as: 'through reason'. Here reason and rationality are treated as roads to objective knowledge. This reason is always defined in opposition to emotion. Emotion is rather viewed with suspicion and even hostility. It has been rightly commented by a scholar: 'Not only has reason been contrasted with emotion, but it has also been associated with the mental, the cultural, the universal, the public, and the male, whereas emotion has been associated with the irrational, the physical, the natural, the particular, the private, and of course, the female.'

This derogatory Western attitude towards emotion, like the earlier Western contempt for sensory observation, is staunchly criticized by the feminist philosophers. They argue that it is a blunder not to recognize the significance of emotion. It is, like sensory perception, necessary to human survival. It is only emotions which prompt us to act appropriately, to approach some people and situations and to avoid others, to caress or cuddle, fight or flee. Without emotion, human life would be unthinkable. Moreover, emotions have an intrinsic as well as an instrumental value. Although not all emotions are enjoyable or even justifiable, as we shall see, life without any emotion would be life without any meaning.[6]

All this has a very demeaning effect on our ways of thinking, and on the psyche of male members of the society. Within the context of Western culture, it has often been found that people have been encouraged to control or even suppress their emotions. Consequently, it is not unusual for people to be unaware of their emotional state or to deny it to themselves and other. This lack of awareness, especially combined with a neopositivist understanding of emotion that construes it just as a feeling of which one is aware, lends plausibility to the myth of dispassionate investigation. But lack of awar ness of emotions certainly does not mean that emotions are not present subconsciously or unconsciously, or that subterranean emotions do not exert a continuing influence on people's articulated values and observations, thoughts and actions. To quote Catharine A. MacKinnon:[7]

> Objectivity is the epistemological stance of which objectification is the social process, of which male dominance is the politics, the acted out social practice. That is, to look at the world objectively is to objectify it. The act of control, of which what I have described is the epistemological level, is itself eroticized under the male supremacy. To say women are sex objects is in this way redundant. Sexualized objectification is what defines women as sexual and as women under male supremacy.[8]

The associations between 'male' and 'rational' and between 'female' and 'non-rational' have, of course, a very long history. The idea that the rational is somehow specially associated with masculinity goes back to the Greek founding fathers of rationality as we know it. Aristotle thought that a woman was 'as it were an impotent male, for it is through a certain incapacity that the female is female'. This intrinsic[9] female incapacity was a lack in the 'principle of soul' and hence[10] associated with an incapacity in respect of rationality. 'The claim is not of course that women do not have rationality, but they have it in an inferior, fainter way. They have rationality, they are distinguished from the animals by being rational. Yet they are not equal to men. They are somehow lesser men, lesser in respect of the all-important thing rationality.'[11]

Later, Saint Augustine in *The Confessions* displays a similar reluctance to fully extend the privilege of male rationality to women:

> And finally we see man, made in your image and likeness ruling over all the irrational animals for the very reasons that he was made in your image and resembles you, that is because he has the power of reason and understanding. And just as in man's soul there are two forces; one which is dominant because it deliberates and one which obeys because it is subject to such guidance, in the same way in the physical sense, woman has been made for man. In her mind and her rational intelligence she has a nature the equal of man's, but in sex she is physically subject to him in the same way as our natural impulses need to be subjected to the reasoning power of the mind, in order that the actions to which they lead may be inspired by the principles of good conduct.[12]

> Then you took man's mind, which is subject to none but you and needs to imitate no human authority, and renewed it in your own image and likeness. *You made rational action subject to the rule of the intellect, as woman is subject to man.*[13]

What we discover both in Aristotle and Augustine is a hierarchical model of knowing, which is unacceptable to female scholars. For then *emotions are neither more basic than observation, reason, or action in building theory, nor secondary to them.* Each of these human faculties reflects an aspect of human knowing inseparable from the other aspects.[14] Women, therefore, seek a theory of knowledge that will focus on understanding rather on 'justification, verification, and control' and will find value in first person experiential stories.[15] It should be non-hierarchical and anti-foundationalist.

At the Ontological Level

It is a fact that all the traditional male metaphysicians have often sought to provide answers to broad questions such as, 'What are the fundamental categories and structures of reality?', 'What is the nature of things?', 'What is being as such?', and 'What is existence (or what does it mean to exist)?, only through the knowledge rooted in their own experiences.'

All such traditional metaphysics is male-centred. Its practitioners are men, usually men of privilege; they are the products of androcentric cultures who have had little reason to question the limitations their cultures imposed on their viewpoint. In their metaphysical theories, they examine the presuppositions of, try to account for, and attempt to systematize *their* gendered experience. The fact that it is male experience that is reflected on in metaphysics should not surprise us. For it is a customary part of the privilege of the dominant group to be in the position to define reality for themselves and for their subordinates. Naming and defining reality are among the ways in which the dominant group takes and keeps possession of its world. Several dichotomies – self-other, spirit-matter, mind-body, and active-passive – are the creations of this ontology only and reflect the fundamental opposition of male-female, dominant-subordinate, and valued-devalued beings.

All this has prompted fundamentalist to challenge all such philosophical concerns and address question that spring from women's experience, pertain to women's ways of being, and help us see the ways in which some women's very existence has simply been denied. Simone de Beauvoir believes that women have had the world mediated for them by men; she means that men have told women what the nature of things is. Women have not been expected to 'trouble out heads about' question, such as, 'what is reality' or 'of what is the world constituted?'

Caroline Whitbeck calls for the rejection of the model of dualistic opposition; she posits instead a model based on the relation of differentiation, not of opposition.[16] Carol Gould feels that this self-other opposition is at the heart of other dualistic oppositions, such as theory-practice, culture-nature, spirit-matter, mind-body, human-divine, political-personal, public-private (or productive-reproductive), knower-known, theory-practice, lover-beloved, that figure prominently in 'western thought.'[17]

It would be quite pertinent here to analyse in depth the philosophy of some of those thinkers whose writings suffer from this dualism. To begin with Aristotle's thought, dualism runs from his early thinking recorded in the *Physics* to his late work in *Generation of Animals.* Aristotle took the dualistic opposition between male and female as his *starting point,* and he used it as the model for the relation of form to matter, which is at the core of his entire ontology.[18] Form is rational and active; matter is irrational and passive. Thus, far from being a quaint aberration in Aristotle's thought, his construal of the relation between male and female as dualistic opposition is crucial to his ontology. According to Aristotle, only the free adult male (in fact only the Athenian citizen) qualifies as a full person, because only he has fully functioning and authoritative rational capacity (*Politics* Book 1). Aristotle says explicitly, and repeatedly, that to be born female is the most common kind of deformity.[19] Because only the free male adult (Athenian citizen) has full and authoritative rational powers, his relation to others, i.e. to female non-slaves, to slaves, and to children (presumed free and male), is largely determined by his obligation to reason for them.

In view of Aristotle's analogy between the relation of male to female and the relation of form to matter, it is not surprising that in the *Politics* he needs explicitly to disclaim the view that the relation of a man to a woman is necessarily that of a master to a slave. (This is a view that he attributes to the 'barbarians' in a handy bit of projection). Aristotle argues that wives, for example, are to be managed, whereas slaves and children are to be ruled as a monarch rules his subjects. According to Aristotle, the female is naturally attracted to the male (although not the reverse), and so the wife, unlike the slave or barbarian, willingly accepts management by the husband.

The same dualism underlies Hegel's version of patriarchy and the individualism of Sartre's *Being and Nothingness.* An illuminating account of the central place of sexual dualism in Sartre's discussion of the dualistic opposition between the for-itself and the in-itself. Indeed, these philosophical frameworks exhibit the features of dualism even more explicitly than do Hobbesian-Lockean individualism and Aristotelian patriarchy. For example, in Hegel's

Phenomenology of Spirit, the presupposition of an opposition between self and other is underscored by the statement that 'the relation of the two self-conscious individuals is such that they prove themselves and each other, through a life and death struggle'.[20]

According to individualism, the self is assumed to be a peer, that is, only the perspective of the peers is taken into account. Furthermore, only such peers are regarded as full persons, in the sense that the only decisions that are regarded as significant are the decisions of peers. The person is regarded as an atom, in the sense that individualism ignores both the interdependence of people and their historical character. The denial of interdependence is a consequence of confining attention to the peers of later to all men. Restriction of the concept of a person so that it extends only to peers – and ignores the women, children, and (for a period) enslaved men and labourers – ignores the agency of the latter groups and the dependency of the peers on them. In particular, the practices regarded as women's work are ignored.

The atomistic representation of persons is implicit not merely in the work of those thinkers from Hobbes and Locke through Nozick, who emphasize the individual's right to pursue self-interest, but also in the work of those from Rousseau through Rawls, who assume they can find the notion of a just society on an agreement among ideal individuals who are construed as existing apart from the history of their relationships and, therefore, apart from their own cultural and intellectual history.

Marilyn Frye refashions the traditional male way of dealing with the question: 'What is reality?' Frye shows us how women have been erased by the patriarchal concept or reality. Reality is what is seen to be, and what is not seen is not real. Women who are not seen (or not visible to men) are thereby not real; they do not exist. There are two kinds of erasure of women that have by now become 'often noted'. One is the conception of human history as a history of the acts and organizations of men, and the other is a long and sordid record in Western civilization of the murder and mutilation of women. Both of these erasures are extended into the future, the one in fiction and speculation, the other in the technological projects of sperm selection for increasing the proportion of male babies, of extra-uterine gestation, of cloning, of male to female transsexual reconstruction. Both sorts of erasure seem entwined in the pitched religious and political battle between males who want centralized male control of female reproductive functions, and males who want individualized male control of female reproductive functions.[21]

This all pervading fundamentalism proves that what Catharine MacKinnon claims is correct: 'Gender here is a matter of dominance, not difference. Feminists have noticed that women and men are equally different but not equally powerful ... [What] I mean simply that men are not socially supreme and women subordinate by nature; the fact that socially they are, constructs the sex difference as we know it. I mean to suggest that the social meaning of difference-in this I include difference-is gender-based.'[22]

Notes

1. Catharine A. MacKinnon, *Feminism Unmodified,* Cambridge: Harvard University Press, 1987, p. 2.
2. Caren J. Warren, 'Critical Thinking and Feminism', *Formal Logic,* 1988,10(1).
3. Even a philosopher like Descartes who claims to have invented a method which would be suitable 'even for women' is questionable. His generous claim that women were capable of truth, they have minds as well as bodies become redundant when he further claimed that pursuit for truth required a concentration that should be free from all practical demands.
4. Many psychologists have proved it that women tend to prefer social interactive process than men. Carol Gilligan has tried to prove it by clearly defining the differences between the two. Men are abstract and universalistic in their approach, whereas women are concrete and relativists in their approach. Men are more power sharing and rights enjoying, whereas women are more responsibility sharing and relation building. See Carol Gilligan, *In a Different Voice,* Cambridge, Mass.: Harvard University Press, 1982.
5. Janice Moulton, 'A Paradigm of Philosophy: The Adversary Method', in Sandra Harding and Merril B. Hintikka (eds.) *Discovering Reality,* Dordrecht: D. Reidel, 1983, pp. 149–64.
6. See Alison M. Jaggar, and Susan R. Bordo, (eds.), *Gender/Body/Knowledge: Feminist Reconstruction of Being and Knowing.* New Brunswick, N.J.: Rutgers University Press, 1989.
7. Ibid., p. 139.
8. Catharine A. MacKinnon, *Feminism Unmodified,* Cambridge, Mass.: Harvard University Press, 1987, p. 50.
9. Aristotle, *Generation of Animals,* Book 1, Chapter 20, 727a15.
10. Ibid., Book II, Chapter 3, 737a25.
11. Genevieve Lloyd, 'The Man of Reason', *Metaphilosophy,* 1979, 10, pp. 18–37.

12. Augustine, *The Confessions,* tr. R.S. Pine., Baltimore: Penguin Classics, 1961, p. 344.
13. Ibid., p. 345, Emphasis mine.
14. It is interesting to note that acknowledging the importance of emotion for knowledge is not an entirely novel suggestion within the Western epistemological tradition. The archrationalist, Plato himself, came to accept in the end that knowledge required (a very purified form of) love. It may be no accident that in the Symposium Socrates learns this lesson from Diotima, the wise woman.
15. See Lorraine Code, 'Experience, Knowledge and Responsibility', in Morwenna Griffiths and Margaret Whitford (eds.) *Feminist Perspective in Philosophy,* Bloomington, I.N.: Indiana University Press, 1988, pp. 187–204.
16. See, Caroline Whitbeck, 'A Different Reality: Feminist Ontology' in Ann Garry and Marilyn Pearsall (eds.), *Women, Knowledge, and Reality,* New York: Routledge, 1992, pp. 51–67.
17. Carol Gould (ed.), *Beyond Domination: New Perspectives on Women and Philosophy,* Totowa, N.J.: Rowman & Allanheld, 1984, pp. 64–68.
18. Aristotle, *Physics:* Book Alpha, 192a.
19. Aristotle, *Generation of Animals* 728a, 18 and 766b, 20.
20. See Hegel, *The Phenomenology of Spirit,* tr. A.V. Miller, Oxford: Oxford University Press, 1977, pp. 113–14.
21. Marilyn Frye 'To See and be Seen: The Politics of Reality' in Ann Garry and Marilyn Pearsall, (eds.), *Women, Knowledge, and Reality,* London: Routledge, 1989, pp. 77–92.
22. Catharine MacKinnon, *Feminism Unmodified,* Cambridge, Mass.: Harvard University Press, 1987, p. 51.

20

Trajectories of Women's Fiction in India

Sumita Parmar

The phrases 'once upon a time' and 'what happened then' constitute the essence of what the novel does, i.e. tell a story. The hunger for listening to stories and the corresponding desire to tell stories is as old as language itself though, ironically, as a genre, the novel is younger than poetry, drama and prose. Curling up with a book that can hold your attention, transport you into a different world, make you a stake-holder in the life of fictional characters – these are some of the expectations that one has of a novel – expectations that are so satisfactorily met.

But at no other time has the novel had to extend itself as much as today in order to accommodate the creations which emerge out of the intersections of the races, of gender, of the politics of region, location and nation, of majorities and minorities, of the subaltern and the powerful, the heterosexual and the homosexual and so on in ever changing permutations and alignments. Thus it engenders debates regarding its nature, development and points of discourse vis-à-vis its form and content. However, about theory, the brilliant novelist and story teller par excellence, Toni Morrison, makes a succinct comment. '... the less the better' she says. And in keeping with the spirit of this statement, while the discussions go on and new theories emerge in the rarefied atmosphere of academia, while theorists scramble and strive to contain the novel within definitions, unmindful of it all, it keeps on with its journey down the paths of reinvention and transfiguration, as it endeavours to negotiate the terrain of the modern world.

Women have had a rather symbiotic relationship with the novel. When it first appeared, in the 17th century, it was considered somewhat of an upstart form by blue blooded academics and perceived in a way similar to the way the elite and the aristocracy perceive the nouveau riche or the arrivistes. For women it was considered to be particularly undesirable, carrying within it the potential to corrupt their relatively untutored and 'innocent' minds and therefore, because it was a bad influence on them, it merited condemnation. However, from such a position, the novel moved to a point when the majority of its creators and its consumers became women. But it was only when the novel began to acquire respectability, slowly gaining admittance to the (predominantly male) world of academia that it established its cultural centrality in literature.

More than any other literary form, the novel mirrors the events that happen in society. It imbibes the changes that take place, reflects how they transform social structures, how mindsets evolve, how history impacts people and how in a dynamic process the novel is itself created and transformed by the very processes it reflects. It has been frequently said about great novels that they are more accurate in their depiction and rendering of the social realities of their times than historical, economic, or sociological books/archives. Thus, novels are and become socio-cultural documents fulfilling more roles than just literary.

The Indian Context

The writing of novels in English by Indian women began only from the middle of the 19th century and is fundamental to the spread of the English language and education. In the words of Uma Chakravarti, 'The decisive moment for the emergence of new genres of writing and corollary developments that provided an impetus to women's writing as well as the fallout from this occurred in the middle of the nineteenth century. Processes of class formation and the creation of a middle-class constituency that tied up with a new instrumental basis for the introduction and expansion of English education accounted for a 'bhadralok' culture, not just in Bengal but also in the other Presidencies, particularly Bombay and later, Madras'[1]

It is also important to bear in mind that till the 18 century 'literacy amongst women was abominably low'[2] and by and large, women in India were not educated, except in the affairs of the house, in order and most of all, to become good wives and mothers. Education in English came even later. In fact, the actual reason for women being taught English was to make them worthy mates of their Western educated husbands, '... thus while bhadralok men constituted the salariat – revenue officers, magistrates, and other officials – and the professional middle-class – such as journalists, lawyers, teachers, and so on – their womenfolk had no job-oriented purpose which required them to be educated. Why then should they be educated? Because they were required to produce a new bhadralok male at home ...'[3] In fact, the initial moves to teach women English were met with much hostility and resistance and it was only when some leading families in Bengal – like the Tagore family – took the lead and set an example by bringing English education into their homes that a reluctant social acceptance began to take place. Thus, it was only in the mid-19th century when 'women in well-to-do homes started having tutors at home that we find Indian women writing again'.[4] Even so, the spread of English in India really began only after the use of English became official, particularly in those schools which were funded or supported by the State. Maharashtra and Bengal were the two states that were pioneers in this matter and the very first novel in English by a woman in India was written by a Maharashtrian and published in the year 1853. The novel was called *Saguna: A Story of a Native Christian Life* – and the writer was Krupabai Sattianadhan an outstanding woman who dedicated her short life to educating girls. She wrote a second novel as well, entitled *Kamala: A Study of Hindu Life*. During the same period, Rajalakshmi Devi wrote *The Hindu Wife* (1876) which was followed by Toru Dutt's *Bianca* (1878). Thus, Krupaben Sattianadhan, Rajalakshmi Devi and Toru Dutt are the foremothers of the novel written in India in English by women. Even at that time, the novels were critical of the conditions of women in society and they advocated social reform and the education of women.

Several factors were at play in the writing of novels in English by Indian women in the initial stages in the mid and late 19th century. These were, first of all, the relatively small number of women who were equipped to write in English and a proportionately small number who could read what was written. The native readership was miniscule even taking into account the number of men readers. In fact, the larger readership comprised either Britishers or Europeans residing in India or outside it. Second, the women who wrote were members of a very privileged section of society, well-to-do, educated and relatively liberated – since it would have been impossible to write without the support of a father, husband or brother – hence their exposure to the world was somewhat confined. Therefore, third, it seems inevitable that the choice of the subjects must also have been influenced by these factors (In fact it is ironic that this is a refrain often heard in our own times as well, when it is alleged that writers who write in English, do so with a keen eye on the markets abroad, and woo the non-native readership). As the fight for Independence, gained momentum, a nationalist discourse evolved which privileged the achievement of Independence over all other issues including those regarding women. However, after Independence, several women writers emerged who articulated the fundamental concerns regarding the position of women in the newly formed nation. They were reinforced by the Constitution of the country:

> Although, in India, colonial rule and the freedom struggle marked the beginning of an awakening among women, different streams within the anti-imperialist anti-feudal struggle posited different, even contentious, images of identities for women. But the nationalist consensus symbolized in the Fundamental Rights Resolution of the Indian National Congress, 1931, postulated freedom, justice, dignity and equality for women as essential for nation building. The constitution assured these rights.[5]

M.K. Naik in his *A History of Indian English Literature,* referring to the time makes a comment to the same effect. He says the period saw 'the emergence of an entire school of women novelists'[6] Joel Kuortti, on the other hand, disagrees with Naik but concedes that, 'In my opinion these writers do not form any kind of school; nevertheless one cannot dismiss the fact that since the 1970s, more and more women writers have emerged.[7] From the year 1853, with Sattianadhan's publication, to contemporary times, in the hands of Indian women writers, the novel has traversed a long and eventful distance. The past 50 years particularly have witnessed an enormous increase in the volume of novels written by women in India. When we look at the fiction written by women in India today we find that there is not just a wide variety of thematic concerns and narrative styles, but a confidence of tone and the presence of feminist concerns clearly stated. The writings are nuanced and address issues about which earlier there had been relative silence such as the questions of autonomy and selfhood and the importance of acknowledging the role and contribution of women to society. The thematic concerns are frequently introspective as the focus has shifted from husband, children and family to the self. In fact, the stories of women are only now beginning to be told and the voices of those who have been traditionally marginalized and sans voice find representation in it. In the sphere of Dalit writing, Bama, well-known contemporary Dalit woman writer has played a vital role in putting Dalit writings in the limelight. Two of her novels have been translated into English – *Vanmam* or *Vendetta* and *Karukku*. She says:

> Wealth, power, social standing, status bestowed by having been born into a particular caste – all these weaken human relationships. When people are denied humane treatment, when their self-respect as human beings is destroyed, they raise protesting voices. But these voices are interpreted as threatening howls by those intent on vendetta and violence, and they are mercilessly crushed. Wealth, power, upper-caste status and the might of the government itself are used against those who possess none of these, and this violence is sought to be justified. This is the situation everywhere.[8]

The words are both poignant and quietly powerful and they speak for the marginalized everywhere. Her work addresses the intersection of gender, caste and class as well as the connivance of women in the suppression of other women. She quotes Ambedkar and Srinivasan:

> Ambedkar's words to Gandhi were, 'I have no country'. In the same way, when Rettaimalai Srinivasan refused to shake hands with King Goerge V, saying, 'I am an untouchable in India. You are not supposed to touch my hand' … that is very important for us Dalits. Those are the images that give us power. Today I speak to you as 'Bama', with the impact made on me with these events and writings. Without these things we would not be sitting here and talking. Before 1993 I was unknown. Today when I say, 'I', it includes people like me. All these things together form our collective identity and help us all to act together. I cannot claim for myself the identity of an individual, a Dalit woman, I am part of a collective awareness. I carry their voices.[9]

Thus, changing conditions at different periods in the recent history of our country impacted on the concerns and themes of the novels that women wrote, but certainly from the 19th century onwards, their voices grew from muted and mild expressions of feminist concerns to assertive and confident expressions and critiques. Women writers focused on the spaces of home and family. They dealt with issues which impinged on the lives of women and constrained their growth due to culturally prescribed roles. They wrote about and against 'the positing of images which emphasize women's productive role as the only natural historical one'[10] These writings were concurrent with a growing awareness among women regarding their rights. There was a clear movement from the mere description and the rendering of women's reality to the fact of agency. This was reflected in the nature and aspirations of the female characters that began to appear in the fiction being written from the 1960s onwards. In that sense the novel has negotiated an uneven terrain in the past century and traversed into subjects so far unrepresented in fiction.

Indian Women Novelists

The beginnings of the tradition of Indian women's writing of fiction in English, as mentioned earlier, can be traced back to Sattianadhan, Dutt and Rajalakshmi Devi. Even in the initial stages, the writings of these women were political in the sense that the themes touched on the conditions of women, their status in society, and the need for transformative change and education. After them, in the early part of the 20th century, in 1905 Begum Rokeya, Sakhawat Hussain (1880–1932) published *Sultana's Dream*. Hussain was both a pioneer and crusader and given the social milieu and the prevailing social norms of the time, it is incredible to see how radical her novel was. Passionately involved in the education of women, she exploded in her writings the myth that the intention of confining and secluding women from active social life, both in Hindu and Muslim society, was to actually accord them honour. A clear feminist consciousness in her novel looks objectively at the world and perceives the skewed gender roles prevailing in it. *Sultana's Dream* is a feminist utopia that antedates by a decade the much better known feminist novel *Herland* by Charlotte Perkins Gilman.'[11] First published in a Calcutta magazine in 1905, it is a skillfully crafted story of 'reverse *purdah*' and somewhat in the style of Swift's *Gulliver's Travels* describes a land where the men are confined to the homes and responsible for looking after the children while the women run the world. 'By bringing this perceptive feminist foremother to the attention of a wider readership now, we hope to remedy a long period of neglect and make it clear that feminist sentiments grow from indigenous roots, without depending on foreign influence'[12], says Hanna Papanek, while introducing Rokeya Sakhawat Hossain.

Four years before the publication of *Sultana's Dream*, Cornelia Sorabji, in 1901, had written *Love and Life Behind the Purdah* also called *Purdanasheen*. The book depicted the life women led behind *purdah* and the constraints and hindrances it caused in their full development as human beings. Her training as a lawyer and advisor to various wealthy Hindu and high caste women gave her access to the lives that they led behind the *purdah* and she wrote with authenticity about their confined lives. Sorabji published other novels as well. *Shohola: Child Mother* (1920) addresses the issue of child marriage. Swaran Kumari Ghoshal was another pioneering author who published in the second decade of the century. She wrote three novels and her *An Unfinished Song* (1913) is in the nature of a bildungsroman of a young eight-years-old girl and her journey into youth and womanhood. As time passed, the numbers and the volume of the writings by women grew steadily and subtle and gradual changes in the themes and subjects that the novelists chose to write about became noticeable.

There were Santha Rama Rau (*Remember the House*, 1956), Shakuntala Sriganesh (*The Little Black Box*, 1955) and Attia Hosain (*Sunlight on a Broken Column*, 1961) – all three wrote only a single novel each. The novels cannot be called feminist novels. They were primarily about the perceptions of women about the enclosed spaces they occupied. Nonetheless, though the writings were not always overtly feminist in content, a latent feminist consciousness underlay much of them. Other writers were more prolific and I mention just some of the works. Kamala Markandaya (*Nectar in a Sieve*, 1954; *Some Inner Fury*, 1957; *Silence of Desire*, 1961; *Possession*, 1963) who frequently chose to write stories with economic or political frameworks and Nayantara Saghal who wrote with the volatile political developments as the backdrops of her plots (*A Time to be Happy*, 1957 and *This Time of Morning*, 1965) come into this category. There were also writers like Ruth Prawar Jhabvala (*To Whom She Will*, 1955; *Heat and Dust*, 1975; which was awarded the Booker Prize, and *Two Virgins*, 1973) and Anita Desai (*Cry the Peacock*, 1963; *Voices in the City*, 1965; *Bye Bye Blackbird*, 1971; *Fasting and Feasting*, 1999). Jhabvala is a German Jew married to a Parsi and

Desai has a German mother. Both the women have made India their home. Their novels too, while addressing cultural interactions and issues pertinent to the Indian context, explored and critiqued the woman question – the objectification of women, the perception that they were economic liabilities because of the custom of dowry and the analyses of the dynamics between men and women both within and outside marriage.

In the 1950s and 1960s, the impact of the freedom struggle was reflected substantially in the novels that were written by women. The writing was largely hermeneutic in nature – it was a time of historical reconstitution. However, the discourse of nation which developed during the period was largely a male one and women felt the 'othering' inherent in it acutely. Thus within the ideological framework of nationalism, a strong sense of social injustice and the pervasiveness of the patriarchal paradigms run in the thematic concerns of the writers. This is clearly evident in the novels of Markandaya, Sahgal, and Hosain. Interestingly, while Marakandya wrote about the rural poor and the conflicts between the urban and the rural, the West and the East, Saghal located her plots within the upper and middle-classes. She exposed as myth the belief that education and professional training granted privileges to women vis-à-vis men. During this period, 'The nexus between modernity and nationalism led to the concept of a 'new woman', one who was permitted to step out in ways that had not been possible before, but equally one who was often contradictorily circumscribed by arbitrarily defined notions of Indianness'[13] Also, for the writer of novels, as eminent critic Meenakshi Mukherjee, put it, 'The problem was to reconcile two sets of values – one obtained by reading an alien literature and the other available in life'[14]

In 1979, Rama Mehta was awarded the Sahitya Akademi Award for her novel *Inside the Haveli*, a portrayal of traditional Rajput aristocracy and the story of a modern Bombay girl's marriage to a member of this class. A trained sociologist and, incidentally, the first woman to be selected for the prestigious Indian Foreign Services, Rama Mehta was able to reproduce the minutiae of the lives of the wealthy as she saw in real life. However, though the novel does address the debate on the issue of *purdah*, and there was no convincing resolution that it offered essentially sustaining the feudal system that it described, it was an important novel.

In 1980, Sashi Deshpande published her first novel, *The Dark Holds No Terror*, in which she addressed the subject of violence within a marriage. She has written nine novels so far accompanied by short stories and several essays. Winner of the prestigious Sahitya Akademi Award for her novel *That Long Silence*, Deshpande is a highly respected writer whose oeuvre consists of stories of the urban middle-class woman juggling between the worlds of home and profession, trying to locate identity and redefine the parameters of family. In her quiet style, she has done much to portray the angst and ambivalence that women in this class face. Four years earlier, in 1976, Kamala Das published *My Story* where she candidly discussed her unsatisfactory sexual life in her marriage, laying the responsibility on her husband. The book was path-breaking in the sense that it ushered in a more direct and open treatment of sex in the works of Indian women writers. Hitherto sex was implied in the novels, but not explicitly shown. Namita Gokhale's *Paro* (1984) paved the way for more sexually explicit writings and Shobha De wrote with even less inhibitions. Her *Socialite Evenings* (1989) described graphically, the exotic sex lives of high society in Mumbai.

A number of Indian women novelists made their debut in the 1990s using a variety of narrative techniques, magical realism, and fantasy to render the complex story of the Indian woman and producing novels which revealed the true state of Indian society and its treatment of women. Githa Hariharan won for the Best First Novel in 1992, the Commonwealth Writers prize for her *A Thousand Faces of Night*. Meena Alexander's *Nampally House* (1991), Nisha Da Cunha's *Old Cypress* (1991) Anjana Appachana's *Incantations and Other Stories* (1991) Kusum Ansal's *Sheltering Shadows: A Novel* (1992), Mrinal Pande's *Daughter's Daughter* (1993), Sunetra Gupta's *Memories of Rain* (1996) a Sahitya Akademi award winner, Rani Dharker' *The Virgin Syndrome* (1997), Chitra Banerjee Divakaruni's *The Mistress of Spices* (1997), Gauri Deshpande's *The Lackadaisical Sweeper* (1997) Manju Kapur's *Difficult Daughters* (1998) Sarla Barnabas' *The Khan Trilogy* (1998) are among the other better known novels of the decade.

However, the one event that catapulted Indian women writers to the centre of the international world of fiction and focused attention on them was the winning of the Man Booker Prize by Arundhati Roy for *The God of Small Things* in 1997. The book got rave reviews and drew attention also for the phenomenal amount of half a million pounds it got as an advance. In the meantime, Roy has continued to write essays and non-fiction on contemporary issues, often being drawn into controversy. She announced that she has begun work on another work of fiction in 2007. Other prestigious Literary Awards followed. Jhumpa Lahiri won the 2000 Pulitzer for her *Interpreter of Maladies*. She published *Unaccustomed Earth* in 2008 which, like her earlier collection of short stories, is based on intercultural relations and interactions. Kiran Desai was awarded The Man Booker in 2006 for her *Inheritance of Loss*. Earlier she had won the Betty Trask Award for her first novel *Hullabaloo in the Guava Orchard*. Bharti Mukherjee who lives in the States and calls herself an American has been writing since 1971 when she published *The Tiger's Daughter*. Several other novels followed, some of them being *Wife* (1975) *Desirable Daughters* (2002) and *The Tree Bride* (2004). Continuing the flow, more writers joined the group in the first decade of the 21st century, Manju Padmanabhan published *Escape* (2008) and *Mrinal Pande Devi* (2000), Malathi Rao's *Disorderly Women* (2007) was a Sahitya Akademi Award winner as was Rupa Bajwa's *The Sari Shop* (2006).

Conclusion

What is found today when we look at the fiction written by women in India is not just a wide variety of thematic concerns and narrative styles, but a confidence of tone and the presence of feminist concerns clearly stated. In the words of Antonia Navarro-Tejero:

> The image of women in fiction has undergone a change during the last four decades. Women writers have moved away from traditional portrayals of enduring, self-sacrificing women toward conflicted female characters searching for identity, no longer characterized and defined simply in terms of their victim status. In contrast to earlier novels, female characters from the 1980s onwards assert themselves and defy marriage and motherhood … . Recent writers depict both the diversity of women and the diversity within each woman, rather than limiting the lives of women to one ideal. The novels emerging in the 21st century furnish examples of a whole range of attitudes towards the imposition of tradition, some offering an analysis of the family structure and the caste system as the key elements of patriarchal social organization. They also re-interpret mythology by using new symbols and subverting the canonic versions. In conclusion, the work of Indian women writers is significant in making society aware of women's demands, and in providing a medium for self-expression and, thus, re-writing the History of India.[15]

Agency, articulation, autonomy, explorations and acknowledgements of the needs of the body, sexuality, strategies of survival and of surviving whole – these are the features that mark contemporary Indian women's fiction and short stories. Raji Narsinhan's collection of short stories entitled *The Illusion of Home* is representative of the tone of the writings that are being done today. The stories are about tough women who have survived the most desperate of situations and who resist erasure. A dispassionate critique of culture, tradition and religion and the role they have played in the reinforcement of patriarchal hegemony frequently constitutes the subtext of the novels. Consequently a new Indian woman is becoming visible in the pages of the fiction written by these women – complex, conflicted but also determined and confident. No longer a victim but her own agent.

Notes

1. Nabanita Deba Sena et al., *Five Novellas by Women Writers*, New Delhi: OUP, 2008, p. xii.
2. Geeta Dharmarajan, *Separate Journeys*, New Delhi: Katha, 1998.
3. *Five Novellas*, p. xiii
4. Dharamrajan, Introduction
5. Maya Khullar (ed.), *Writing the Women's Movement: A Reader*, New Delhi: Zubaan, 2005. p. 49
6. M.K. Naik, *A History of Indian English Literature*, New Delhi: Sahitya Akademi, 1982, p. 213
7. Joel Kuortti, *Tense Past, Tense Present*, Kolkata: Stree, 2003, p. 2
8. Bama, *Vanmam: Vendetta*, tr. Malini Seshadri, New Delhi: OUP, 2008. p. vii.
9. Ibid., p. 151
10. Khullar, p. 50
11. Jahan Roushan (ed.), *Sultana's Dream*, New York: The Feminist Press, 1988, p. vii
12. Ibid., p. vii
13. Geetanjali Singh Chanda, *Indian Women in the House of Fiction*, New Delhi: Zubaan, 2008, p. 1
14. Ibid., p. 4
15. Antonia, Navarro-Tejero, Modern Indian Women Writers in English, <www.literature-study-online.com/essays/indian women-book.html>.

Index